INTELLIGENCE ANALYSIS

FIFTH EDITION

SAGE was founded in 1965 by Sara Miller McCune to support the dissemination of usable knowledge by publishing innovative and high-quality research and teaching content. Today, we publish over 900 journals, including those of more than 400 learned societies, more than 800 new books per year, and a growing range of library products including archives, data, case studies, reports, and video. SAGE remains majority-owned by our founder, and after Sara's lifetime will become owned by a charitable trust that secures our continued independence.

Los Angeles | London | New Delhi | Singapore | Washington DC | Melbourne

INTELLIGENCE ANALYSIS

A TARGET-CENTRIC APPROACH

ROBERT M. CLARK

FIFTH EDITION

FOR INFORMATION:

CQ Press

An imprint of SAGE Publications, Inc.

2455 Teller Road

Thousand Oaks, California 91320

E-mail: order@sagepub.com

SAGE Publications Ltd.

1 Oliver's Yard

55 City Road

London, EC1Y 1SP

United Kingdom

SAGE Publications India Pvt. Ltd.

B 1/I 1 Mohan Cooperative Industrial Area

Mathura Road, New Delhi 110 044

India

SAGE Publications Asia-Pacific Pte. Ltd.

3 Church Street

#10-04 Samsung Hub

Singapore 049483

Acquisitions Editors: Carrie Brandon, Michael Kerns

Editorial Assistant: Zachary Hoskins

Production Editor: David C. Felts

Copy Editor: Amy Marks

Typesetter: C&M Digitals (P) Ltd.

Proofreader: Lawrence W. Baker

Indexer: Wendy Allex

Cover Designer: Candice Harman

Marketing Manager: Jennifer Jones

Printed in the United States of America.

Library of Congress Cataloging-in-Publication Data

Names: Clark, Robert M.

Title: Intelligence analysis : a target-centric approach / Robert M. Clark.

Description: Fifth edition. | Los Angeles : CQ Press, 2016. | Includes bibliographical references and index.

Identifiers: LCCN 2015049722 | ISBN 978-1-5063-1681-9 (pbk. : alk. paper)

Subjects: LCSH: Intelligence service—Methodology.

Classification: LCC JF1525.I6 C548 2016 | DDC 327.12—dc23 LC record available at http://lccn.loc.gov/2015049722

This book is printed on acid-free paper.

Certified Chain of Custody
SUSTAINABLE Promoting Sustainable Forestry
FORESTRY www.sfiprogram.org
INITIATIVE SFI-01268

SFI label applies to text stock

16 17 18 19 20 10 9 8 7 6 5 4 3 2 1

Contents

Tables, Figures, and Boxes

7   Creating the Model

8   Denial, Deception, and Signaling

9   Systems Modeling and Analysis

10   Network Modeling and Analysis

Part II   The Estimative Process

Preface

The first edition of this book was published in 2003, soon after the terrorist attack on U.S. soil of September 11, 2001, and the U.S.-led invasion into Iraq, more commonly called the Iraq War, on March 20, 2003. Those two events focused the world's attention on apparent failures of the U.S. intelligence community.

But as Professor Stephen Marrin has pointed out, in the case of the 9/11 attack, more important are the strategic policy failures that preceded the intelligence failures.[1] And as former national intelligence officer Paul Pillar has pointed out, the 9/11 Commission report (published in September 2004) appears to have been shaped to fit political purposes rather than to conduct an objective inquiry.[2] Arguably, *both* the 9/11 attack and the weapons of mass destruction (WMD) debacle resulted primarily from failures in U.S. strategic policy, abetted by intelligence failures. The intelligence failures in both cases were collaborative rather than causative.

Nevertheless, the two events caused enough consternation within the United States to spawn bipartisan commissions of inquiry, resulting in the aforementioned 9/11 Commission report and the Iraqi WMD Commission report (published in March 2005). These two documents have provided us with perhaps the most detailed assessments of intelligence failures ever written at the unclassified level. The reports have led directly to dramatic and controversial changes in the structure of the U.S. intelligence community.

If an intelligence community is interested in real improvement, it should begin with a focus on *function* and *process,* not on structure. An effective intelligence function and process then will lead to an effective structure. A major contribution of the 9/11 Commission and the Iraqi WMD Commission was their focus on a failed process, specifically on that part of the process where intelligence analysts interact with their policy customers.

Thus, this book has two objectives:

- The first objective is to redefine the intelligence process to help make all parts of what is commonly referred to as the "intelligence cycle" run smoothly and effectively, with special emphasis on both the analyst-collector and the analyst-customer relationships.
- The second goal is to describe some methodologies that make for better predictive analysis.

The book discusses a better intelligence analysis process (one that appears to be emerging within the U.S. and other intelligence communities), and puts specific analysis techniques in context, showing how they interrelate within that process.

An intelligence process should accomplish three basic tasks. First, it should make it easy for customers to ask questions. Second, it should use the existing base of intelligence information to provide immediate responses to the customer. Third, it should manage the expeditious creation of new information to answer remaining questions. To do these things, intelligence must be collaborative and predictive: collaborative to engage *all* participants while making it easy for customers to get answers; predictive because intelligence customers above all else want to know what will happen next.

What I call a *target-centric* intelligence process helps analysts and customers accomplish these three tasks by bringing together all participants in the production of sound intelligence. Though intelligence communities are organized hierarchically, the target-centric process outlines a collaborative approach for intelligence collectors, analysts, and customers to operate cohesively against increasingly complex opponents. We cannot simply provide more intelligence to customers; they already have more information than they can process, and information overload encourages intelligence failures. The community must provide what is called "actionable intelligence"—intelligence that is relevant to customer needs, is accepted, and is used in forming policy and in conducting operations. Collaboration enables such intelligence. The convergence of computers and multimedia communications allows analysts, collectors, and their customers to interact more closely as they move from traditional hierarchies to networks—a process that had already begun to emerge before the restructuring of the U.S. intelligence community.

The second objective is to clarify and refine the analysis process by drawing on existing prediction methodologies. These include the analytic tools used in organizational planning and problem solving, science and engineering, law, and economics. In many cases, these are tools and techniques that have endured despite dramatic changes in information technology over the past fifty years. All can be useful in making intelligence predictions, even in seemingly unrelated fields. In fact, a number of unifying concepts can be drawn from these disciplines and applied when creating scenarios of the future, assessing forces, and monitoring indicators. The book highlights these concepts in boxes called "Analysis Principles" and treats them as fundamental principles of intelligence analysis. These boxes should make the book a valuable reference even as the world continues to change.

This book's primary audiences are practicing intelligence analysts and university students who are interested in entering the profession. However, it is also intended to be of interest to all intelligence professionals and customers of intelligence, in governments and private sectors. Intelligence practitioners can spend their entire careers on highly specialized topics, and many books are devoted to topics covered only briefly here. This book, rather, is a general guide, with references to lead the reader to more in-depth studies and reports on specific topics or techniques. The book offers insights that intelligence customers and analysts alike need in order to become more proactive in the changing world of intelligence and to extract more useful intelligence.

Many examples of intelligence failures are discussed in the book, possibly leading a reader to get the impression that we experience more failures than successes. Quite the opposite is true. Most major intelligence services probably have more analytic successes than failures. But there are reasons that successes cannot be published, leaving the failures, real and perceived, more visible. This book focuses a lens on the missteps for two reasons. First, sharing our intelligence failures openly ensures that there will be fewer of them in the future. Second, as in any field of endeavor, we probably learn more from our failures than from our successes.

This fifth edition has been prepared primarily in response to suggestions made by readers. The previous editions' wide use in academia and by government agencies and contractors has resulted in a number of excellent recommendations, and I have attempted to incorporate those ideas throughout. The book has several new chapters and extensive new material on analytic methodologies. The remainder of the book also has been extensively revised and updated.

All statements of fact, opinion, or analysis expressed are those of the author and do not reflect the official positions or view of the CIA or any other U.S. government agency. Nothing in the contents should be construed as asserting or implying U.S. government authentication of information or agency endorsement of the author's views. This material has been reviewed by the CIA to prevent the disclosure of classified information.

Notes

1. Stephen Marrin, "The 9/11 Terrorist Attacks: A Failure of Policy Not Strategic Intelligence Analysis," *Intelligence and National Security*, 26, no. 2–3 (May 2011): 182–202.
2. Paul R. Pillar, *Intelligence and U.S. Foreign Policy: Iraq, 9/11, and Misguided Reform* (New York: Columbia University Press, 2011).

Acknowledgments

M any people throughout the U.S. and British intelligence communities, academia, and the business intelligence world have provided wisdom that I have incorporated; I cannot name them all, but I appreciate their help. I am especially grateful to reviewers within and outside the U.S. intelligence community who have contributed their time to improving the text. Above all, I'm thankful for the efforts of my wife and partner in this effort, Abigail, whose extensive revisions made this a better book.

In addition to several anonymous reviewers, I wish to thank Michael Collier (Eastern Kentucky University), Ronald Vardy (University of Houston), and Tony Wege (College of Coastal Georgia). I also want to thank the acquisitions editor at CQ Press, Michael Kerns; CQ Press production editor David Felts; and CQ Press copy editor Amy Marks for shaping the finished product.

Robert M. Clark
Wilmington, North Carolina

1

Introduction

The greatest derangement of the mind is to believe in something because one wishes it to be so.

Louis Pasteur

We learn more from our failures than from our successes. As noted in the preface to this book, there is much to be learned from what have been called the two major U.S. intelligence failures of this century—the September 11, 2001, attack on U.S. soil and the miscall on Iraqi weapons of mass destruction. So this book begins with an overview of why we sometimes fail.

Why Intelligence Fails

As a reminder that intelligence failures are not uniquely a U.S. problem, it is worth recalling some failures of other intelligence services in the past century:

- *Operation Barbarossa, 1941.* Josef Stalin acted as his own intelligence analyst, and he proved to be a very poor one. He was unprepared for a war with Nazi Germany, so he ignored the mounting body of incoming intelligence indicating that the Germans were preparing a surprise attack. German deserters who told the Russians about the impending attack were considered provocateurs and shot on Stalin's orders. When the attack, named Operation Barbarossa, came on June 22, 1941, Stalin's generals were surprised, their forward divisions trapped and destroyed.[1]
- *Singapore, 1942.* In one of the greatest military defeats that Britain ever suffered, 130,000 well-equipped British, Australian, and Indian troops surrendered to 35,000 weary and ill-equipped Japanese soldiers. On the way to the debacle, British intelligence failed in a series of poor analyses of their Japanese opponent, such as underestimating the capabilities of the Japanese Zero fighter aircraft and concluding that the Japanese would not use tanks in the jungle. The Japanese tanks proved highly effective in driving the British out of Malaya and back to Singapore.[2]

- *Yom Kippur, 1973.* Israel is regarded as having one of the world's best intelligence services. But in 1973 the intelligence leadership was closely tied to the Israeli cabinet and often served as both policy advocate and information assessor. Furthermore, Israel's past military successes had led to a certain amount of hubris and belief in inherent Israeli superiority. Israel's leaders considered their overwhelming military advantage a deterrent to attack. They assumed that Egypt needed to rebuild its air force and forge an alliance with Syria before attacking. In this atmosphere, Israeli intelligence was vulnerable to what became a successful Egyptian deception operation. The chief intelligence officer of the Israeli Southern Command suppressed an Israeli intelligence officer's report that correctly predicted the impending attack. The Israeli Defense Force was caught by surprise when, *without* a rebuilt air force and having kept their agreement with Syria secret, the Egyptians launched an attack on Yom Kippur, the most important of the Jewish holidays, on October 6, 1973. The attack was ultimately repulsed, but only at a high cost in Israeli casualties.[3]
- *Falkland Islands, 1982.* Argentina wanted Great Britain to hand over the Falkland Islands, which Britain had occupied and colonized in 1837. Britain's tactic was to conduct prolonged diplomatic negotiations without giving up the islands. There was abundant evidence of Argentine intent to invade, including a report of an Argentine naval task force headed for the Falklands with a marine amphibious force. But the British Foreign and Commonwealth Office did not want to face the possibility of an Argentine attack because it would be costly to deter or repulse. Britain's Latin America Current Intelligence Group (dominated at the time by the Foreign and Commonwealth Office) concluded accordingly, on March 30, 1982, that an invasion was not imminent. Three days later, Argentine marines landed and occupied the Falklands, provoking the British to assemble a naval task force and retake the islands.[4]
- *Afghanistan, 1979–1989.* The Soviet Union invaded Afghanistan in 1979 to support the existing Afghan government, which was dealing with an open rebellion. The Soviet decision to intervene was based largely on flawed intelligence provided by KGB chairman Yuri V. Andropov. Andropov controlled the flow of information to General Secretary Leonid Brezhnev, who was partially incapacitated and ill for most of 1979. KGB reports from Afghanistan created a picture of urgency and strongly emphasized the possibility that Prime Minister Hafizullah Amin had links to the Central Intelligence Agency (CIA) and U.S. subversive activities in the region.[5]

  The conflict developed into a pattern in which the Soviets occupied the cities while the opposing forces, called the mujahedeen, conducted a guerrilla war and controlled about 80 percent of the country. The mujahedeen were assisted by the United States, Pakistan, Saudi

Arabia, the United Kingdom, Egypt, and the People's Republic of China. As the war dragged on, it saw an influx of foreign fighters from Arab countries, eager to wage jihad against the Soviet infidels. Among these fighters was a young Saudi named Osama bin Laden, who later would gain notoriety in another conflict. Faced with increasing casualties and costs of the war, the Soviets began withdrawing in 1987 and were completely out of the country by 1989, in what has been called the "Soviet Union's Vietnam War."

The common theme of these and many other intelligence failures discussed in this book is *not* the failure to collect intelligence. In each of these cases, the intelligence had been collected. Three themes are common in intelligence failures: failure to share information, failure to analyze collected material objectively, and failure of the customer to act on intelligence.

Failure to Share Information

From Pearl Harbor to 9/11 to the erroneous estimate on Iraq's possession of weapons of mass destruction (WMD), the inability or unwillingness of collectors and analysts to share intelligence has been a recurring cause of failure.

Intelligence has to be a team sport. Effective teams require cohesion, formal and informal communication, cooperation, shared mental models, and similar knowledge structures—all of which contribute to sharing of information. Without such a common process, any team—especially the interdisciplinary teams that are necessary to deal with complex problems of today—will quickly fall apart.[6]

Nevertheless, the Iraqi WMD Commission (the Commission on the Intelligence Capabilities of the United States Regarding Weapons of Mass Destruction, which issued its formal report to President George W. Bush in March 2005) found that collectors and analysts failed to work as a team.[7] They did not effectively share information. And though progress has been made in the past decade, the root causes for the failure to share remain, in the U.S. intelligence community as well as in almost all intelligence services worldwide:

- Sharing requires openness. But any organization that requires secrecy to perform its duties will struggle with and often reject openness.[8] Most governmental intelligence organizations, including the U.S. intelligence community, place more emphasis on secrecy than on effectiveness.[9] The penalty for producing poor intelligence usually is modest. The penalty for improperly handling classified information can be career-ending.[10] There are legitimate reasons not to share; the U.S. intelligence community has lost many collection assets because details about them were too widely shared. So it comes down to a balancing act between protecting assets and acting effectively in the world. Commercial organizations are more effective at intelligence sharing because they tend to place more emphasis on effectiveness than on secrecy; but they also have less risk of losing critical sources from compromises.

- Experts on any subject have an information advantage, and they tend to use that advantage to serve their own agendas.[11] Collectors and analysts are no different. At lower levels in the organization, hoarding information may have job security benefits. At senior levels, unique knowledge may help protect the organizational budget. So the natural tendency is to share the minimum necessary to avoid criticism and to protect the most valuable material. Any bureaucracy has a wealth of tools for hoarding information, and this book discusses the most common of them.

- Finally, both collectors of intelligence and analysts find it easy to be insular. They are disinclined to draw on resources outside their own organizations.[12] Communication takes time and effort. It has long-term payoffs in access to intelligence from other sources, but few short-term benefits.

In summary, collectors, analysts, and intelligence organizations have a number of incentives to conceal information and not enough benefits to share it. Despite the pressures of U.S. intelligence community leaders to be more collaborative, the problem is likely to persist until the incentives to share outweigh the benefits of concealment.

Failure to Analyze Collected Material Objectively

In each of the cases cited at the beginning of this introduction, intelligence analysts or national leaders were locked into a *mindset*—a consistent thread in analytic failures. Falling into the trap that Louis Pasteur warned about in the observation that begins this chapter, they believed because, consciously or unconsciously, they wished it to be so. Mindset can manifest itself in the form of many biases and preconceptions, a short list of which would include the following:

- *Ethnocentric bias* involves projecting one's own cultural beliefs and expectations on others. It leads to the creation of a "mirror-image" model, which looks at others as one looks at oneself, and to the assumption that others will act "rationally" as rationality is defined in one's own culture. The Yom Kippur attack was not predicted because, from Israel's point of view, it was irrational for Egypt to attack without extensive preparation. Afghanistan did not fit into the ideological constructs of the Soviet leadership. Their analysis of social processes in Afghanistan was done through the bias of Marxist-Leninist doctrine, which blinded the leadership to the realities of traditional tribal society.[13]

- *Wishful thinking* involves excessive optimism or avoiding unpleasant choices in analysis. The British Foreign Office did not predict an Argentine invasion of the Falklands because, in spite of intelligence evidence that an invasion was imminent, they did not want to deal with it. Josef Stalin made an identical mistake for the same reason prior to Operation Barbarossa. In Afghanistan, Soviet political and military leaders expected to be perceived as a progressive anti-imperialist force and were surprised to discover that the Afghans regarded the Soviets as foreign invaders and infidels.[14]
- *Parochial interests* cause organizational loyalties or personal agendas to affect the analysis process.
- *Status quo biases* cause analysts to assume that events will proceed along a straight line. The safest weather prediction, after all, is that tomorrow's weather will be like today's. An extreme case is the story of the British intelligence officer who, on retiring in 1950 after forty-seven years' service, reminisced: "Year after year the worriers and fretters would come to me with awful predictions of the outbreak of war. I denied it each time. I was only wrong twice."[15] The status quo bias causes analysts to fail to catch a change in the pattern.
- *Premature closure* results when analysts make early judgments about the answer to a question and then, often because of ego, defend the initial judgments tenaciously. This can lead the analyst to select (usually without conscious awareness) subsequent evidence that supports the favored answer and to reject (or dismiss as unimportant) evidence that conflicts with it.

All of these mindsets can lead to poor assumptions and bad intelligence if not challenged. And as the Iraqi WMD Commission report notes, analysts often allow unchallenged assumptions to drive their analysis.[16]

Failure of the Customer to Act on Intelligence

In some cases, as in Operation Barbarossa and the Falkland Islands affair, the intelligence customer failed to understand or make use of the available intelligence.

A senior State Department official once remarked, half in jest, "There are no policy failures; there are only policy successes and intelligence failures."[17] The remark rankles intelligence officers, but it should be read as a call to action. Intelligence analysts shoulder partial responsibility when their customers fail to make use of the intelligence provided. Analysts have to meet the challenge of engaging the customer during the analysis process and help ensure that the resulting intelligence is accepted and taken into account when the customer must act.

In this book I devote considerable discussion to the vital importance of analysts' being able objectively to assess and understand their customers and their customers' business or field. The first part of the book describes the collaborative, "target-centric" approach to intelligence analysis that demands a close working relationship among all stakeholders, including the customer, as the means to gain the clearest conception of needs and the most effective results or products. Some chapters also discuss ways to ensure that the customer takes into account the best available intelligence when making decisions.

Intelligence analysts have often been reluctant to closely engage one class of customer—the policymakers. In its early years, the CIA attempted to remain aloof from its policy customers to avoid losing objectivity in the national intelligence estimates process.[18] The disadvantages of that separation became apparent, as analysis was not addressing the customer's current interests, and intelligence was becoming less useful to policymaking. During the 1970s, CIA senior analysts began to expand contacts with policymakers. As both the Falklands and Yom Kippur examples illustrate, such closeness has its risks. But in many cases analysts have been able to work closely with policymakers and to make intelligence analyses relevant without losing objectivity.

What the Book Is About

This book develops a process for successful intelligence analysis—including avoiding the three themes of failure we've just covered.

Studies have found that no baseline standard analytic method exists in the U.S. intelligence community. Any large intelligence community is made up of a variety of disciplines, each with its own analytic methodology.[19] Furthermore, intelligence analysts routinely generate ad hoc methods to solve specific analytic problems. This individualistic approach to analysis has resulted in a great variety of analytic methods, more than 160 of which have been identified as available to U.S. intelligence analysts.[20]

There are good reasons for this proliferation of methods. Methodologies are developed to handle very specific problems, and they are often unique to a discipline, such as economic or scientific and technical (S&T) analysis (which probably has the largest collection of problem-solving methodologies). As an example of how methodologies proliferate, after the Soviet Union collapsed, economists who had spent their entire professional lives analyzing a command economy were suddenly confronted with free market prices and privatization. No model existed anywhere for such an economic transition, and analysts had to devise from scratch methods to, for example, gauge the size of Russia's private sector.[21]

But all intelligence analysis methods derive from a fundamental process. This book is about that process. It develops the idea of creating a model of the intelligence target and extracting useful information from that model. These two steps—the first called "synthesis" and the second called "analysis"—make up what is known as intelligence analysis. All analysts naturally do this. The key to avoiding failures is to *share* the model with collectors of information and customers of intelligence. There are no universal methods that work for all problems, but a basic process does exist.

Also, analysis has to have a conceptual framework for crafting the analytic product. This text defines a general conceptual framework for all types of intelligence problems. In addition to being an organizing construct, it has been argued that conceptual frameworks sensitize analysts to the underlying assumptions in their analysis and enable them to better think through complex problems.[22]

There also are standard, widely used analytic techniques. An analyst must have a repertoire of them to apply in solving complex problems. They might include pattern analysis, trend prediction, literature assessment, and statistical analysis. A number of these techniques are presented throughout the book in the form of analysis principles. Together, they form a problem-solving process that can prevent the types of intelligence blunders discussed earlier.

A few methodologies, though, are used across all the analytic subdisciplines. They are called structured analytic techniques, or SATs. SATs are taught in most courses on intelligence analysis. But their use has resulted in some criticism. For instance, one author notes that

> The problem is that many SATs stunt broad thinking and the kind of analysis that busy policymakers want. At the same time, single-minded attention to technique runs the risk of reducing analyses to mechanical processes that require only crunching of the "right" data to address policymaker needs.[23]

Despite the criticisms, SATs can have value in analysis if used at the right point in the process. The challenge is that novices can become overwhelmed by the number of SATs and uncertain where to apply them in the process. In this book, the focus is on the most useful SATs and they are introduced at the point where they should be applied. SATs are not discussed in great detail herein, as they are well covered in other texts.[24]

Sherman Kent noted that an analyst has three wishes: "To know everything. To be believed. And to exercise a positive influence on policy."[25] This book will not result in an analyst's being able to know everything—that is why we will continue to have estimates. But chapters 1–15 should help analysts to learn or refine their tradecraft of analysis, and chapters 16–19 are intended to help them toward the second and third wishes.

Summary

Intelligence failures have three common themes that have a long history:

- Failure of collectors and analysts to share information. Good intelligence requires teamwork and sharing, but most of the incentives in large intelligence organizations promote concealment rather than sharing of information.

- Failure of analysts to objectively assess the material collected. The consistent thread in these failures is a mindset, primarily biases and preconceptions that hamper objectivity.
- Failure of customers to accept or act on intelligence. This lack of response is not solely the customer's fault. Analysts have an obligation to ensure that customers not only receive the intelligence but also fully understand it.

This book is about an intelligence process that can reduce such failures. A large intelligence community develops many analytic methods to deal with the variety of issues that it confronts. But the methods all work within a fundamental process: creating a model of the intelligence target (synthesis) and extracting useful information from that model (analysis). Success comes from sharing the target model with all stakeholders.

Notes

1. John Hughes-Wilson, *Military Intelligence Blunders* (New York: Carroll and Graf, 1999), 38.
2. Ibid., 102.
3. Ibid., 218.
4. Ibid., 260.
5. Svetlana Savranskaya, ed., *The Soviet Experience in Afghanistan: Russian Documents and Memoirs*, National Security Archive, October 9, 2001, https://www2.gwu.edu/~nsarchiv/NSAEBB/NSA EBB57/soviet.html.
6. Rob Johnson, *Analytic Culture in the US Intelligence Community* (Washington, D.C.: Center for the Study of Intelligence, CIA, 2005), 70.
7. *Report of the Commission on the Intelligence Capabilities of the United States Regarding Weapons of Mass Destruction*, March 31, 2005, www.wmd.gov/report/wmd_report.pdf, overview.
8. Johnson, *Analytic Culture*, xvi.
9. Ibid., 11.
10. There exists some justification for the harsh penalty placed on improper use of classified information; it can compromise and end a billion-dollar collection program or get people killed.
11. Steven D. Leavitt and Stephen J. Dubner, *Freakonomics* (New York: HarperCollins, 2005), 13.
12. Johnson, *Analytic Culture*, 29.
13. National Security Archive, "The Soviet Experience in Afghanistan."
14. Ibid.
15. Amory Lovins and L. Hunter Lovins, "The Fragility of Domestic Energy," *Atlantic Monthly*, November 1983, p. 118.
16. *Report of the Commission*, March 31, 2005.
17. William Prillaman and Michael Dempsey, "Mything the Point: What's Wrong with the Conventional Wisdom about the C.I.A." *Intelligence and National Security*, 19, no. 1 (March 2004): 1–28.
18. Harold P. Ford, *Estimative Intelligence* (Lanham, Md.: University Press of America, 1993), 107.
19. Johnson, *Analytic Culture*, xvii.
20. Ibid., 72.
21. CIA Center for the Study of Intelligence, "Watching the Bear: Essays on CIA's Analysis of the Soviet Union," Conference, Princeton University, March 2001, http://www.cia.gov/cis/books/watchingthebear/article08.html, 8.

22. Jason U. Manosevitz, "Needed: More Thinking about Conceptual Frameworks for Analysis—The Case of Influence." *Studies in Intelligence*, 57, no. 4 (December 2013), 22, https://www.cia.gov/library/center-for-the-study-of-intelligence/csi-publications/csi-studies/studies/vol-57-no-4/pdfs/Manosevitz-FocusingConceptual%20Frameworks-Dec2013.pdf.

23. Ibid.

24. For two very good examples, see CIA, *A Tradecraft Primer: Structured Analytic Techniques for Improving Intelligence Analysis* (Washington, D.C.: Author, March 2009), and Richards J. Heuer Jr. and Randolph H. Pherson, *Structured Analytic Techniques for Intelligence Analysis* (Washington, D.C.: CQ Press, 2011).

25. George J. Tenet, "Dedication of the Sherman Kent School," *CIA News & Information*, May 4, 2000, https://www.cia.gov/news-information/speeches-testimony/2000/dci_speech_05052000.html.

2

Intelligence in Twenty-First-Century Conflict

The supreme art of war is to subdue the enemy without fighting.

Sun Tzu, *The Art of War*

Our idea of what constitutes conflict has changed substantially in the past two decades. The conflicts that have erupted around the globe bear little resemblance to the interstate wars of the previous millennium. These new types of conflicts have been referred to by terms such as *shadow wars* or *hybrid wars*.[1] One writer on the subject has described them as follows:

> The state on state conflicts of the 20th century are being replaced by Hybrid Wars and asymmetric contests in which there is no clear-cut distinction between soldiers and civilians and between organised violence, terror, crime, and war.[2]

Chinese People's Liberation Army colonels Qiao Liang and Wang Xiangsui in 1999 published a book entitled *Unrestricted Warfare*. In it they described their vision of a new form of conflict. Their book may have gotten more attention in Washington than it ever did it in Beijing, but it was prophetic about what was to come in this century. Its main points were as follows:

> (I)f in the days to come mankind has no choice but to engage in war, it can no longer be carried out in the ways with which we are familiar.

> . . . the degree of destruction is by no means second to that of a war, represent(ing) semi-warfare, quasi-warfare, and sub-warfare, that is, the embryonic form of another kind of warfare.

> War which has undergone the changes of modern technology and the market system will be launched even more in atypical forms. In other words, while we are seeing a relative reduction in military violence, at the same time we definitely are seeing an increase in political, economic, and technological[3] violence.

If we acknowledge that, the new principles of war are no longer "using armed force to compel the enemy to submit to one's will," but rather are "using all means, including armed force or non-armed force, military and non-military, and lethal and non-lethal means to compel the enemy to accept one's interests."[4]

Conventional wars that involve large-scale engagements (such as the first and second Persian Gulf Wars) undoubtedly will continue. But much of intelligence today is about what are being called shadow wars, hybrid wars, or unrestricted conflict, which are not conventional and which extensively involve nonstate actors. The conflict in Syria/Iraq, the Afghan insurgency, the Ukraine crisis, and Boko Haram's activities in Africa all exemplify this type of conflict. Law enforcement must deal with another type of unconventional conflict with transnational criminal enterprises. Transnational corporations must also deal with types of competition that business leaders thirty years ago would not recognize—including conflicts with customers and suppliers.

The types of conflicts themselves aren't new. Guerrilla warfare dates back to ancient history; when faced with superior military force, an opponent inevitably moves to what has been called asymmetric warfare (a form of conflict that exploits dissimilarities in capability between two opponents). Guerrilla warfare was common in ancient China. Nomadic and migratory tribes such as the Scythians, Goths, and Huns used forms of it to fight the Persian Empire, the Roman Empire, and Alexander the Great. Similar tactics were used with success during the American Revolution and the Civil War. Niccolò Machiavelli in his book *The Prince* described all of the types of conflicts that are prevalent today, along with advice on how a national leader should deal with them.

Nature of Twenty-First-Century Conflict

The unique features of twenty-first-century conflicts—the ones that distinguish them from conflicts of past eras—have been shaped by globalization and the Internet. The two dominant characteristics involve the increased roles of networks and of nonstate actors in conflicts.

Networks

John Arquilla and David Ronfeldt of RAND Corporation described the idea of conflict between networks in their discussion of the impact of new communications and information technologies on military structures, doctrines, and strategies. They coined the term *netwar* and defined it as a form of information-related conflict, in which opponents form networks—also known as network-centric conflict. Specifically, Arquilla and Ronfeldt use the term to describe the "societal struggles" that make use of new technologies.[5] The technologies they discuss were (and are) available and usable anywhere, as demonstrated by the Zapatista netwar back in January 1994: A guerrilla-like insurgency had developed in Chiapas, Mexico, led by the Zapatista National

Liberation Army. The Mexican government's repressive response caused a collection of activists associated with human-rights, indigenous-rights, and other types of nongovernmental organizations (NGOs) elsewhere to link electronically with similar groups in Mexico to press for nonviolent change. What began as a violent insurgency in an isolated region mutated into a nonviolent but disruptive social netwar that engaged the attention of activists around the world and had both nationwide and foreign repercussions for Mexico. The Zapatista insurgents skillfully used a global media campaign to create a supporting network of NGOs and embarrass the Mexican government in a form of asymmetric attack.[6]

Two decades later, in 2015, netwars were active in many regions of the world involving states, commercial entities, and other nonstate actors. In the Middle East, two major protagonists headed major networks in conflicts across the region:

- Iran was providing financial and military support to Hezbollah in Lebanon, to the regime of President Bashar Al-Assad in Syria, to the Zaydi Houthis in Yemen, and to Shiite militias in Iraq. Under the banner of Shiite solidarity, Iran also provided nonmilitary aid for industrial projects, madrasas, mosques, and hospitals in Shiite regions.
- Saudi Arabia, for its part, provided weaponry and funding to Sunni combatants in Syria, Iraq, and Yemen. Riyadh also deployed its military forces to support the Sunni cause in some cases. In 2011, it sent armored units into Bahrain to quell the pro-democracy rallies of the country's Shiite majority. During 2015, it led aerial attacks against the Zaydi Houthis.[7]

Criminal, insurgent, and terrorist groups have their own networks that conduct economic, political, and military activities on a global scale. Their ability to access financing, advanced weaponry, and recruits extralegally makes them powerful players in international affairs—more powerful than many states, in fact. Their skill in adapting to changing environments and to threats also exceeds that of most governments.

Networks, of course, have been used in conflicts for centuries. The American Revolution, after all, was a kind of netwar: Thirteen colonies were supported by France on one side; and Great Britain was supported by loyalists and some American Indian tribes on the other. Both world wars involved conflicting networks of states. But the importance of networks in conflicts has increased because of the new tools discussed later in this chapter and the enhanced role of nonstate actors, discussed next.

Nonstate Actors

Participants in twenty-first-century conflicts are not just governments. Many networks, as the preceding section indicates, are comprised of nonstate actors. They include criminal groups, commercial enterprises, and many other types of NGOs. The Zapatista netwar described earlier indicates the importance of nonstate actors. Some commercial enterprises, for example, engage in illicit arms traffic, support the narcotics trade, and facilitate funds laundering. While states continue to be the principal brokers of power, increasingly there exists a profusion of nonstate centers of power that include unconventional and transnational organizations. These groups operate with their own rules and norms that differ markedly from the traditional rules observed by governments.[8]

Intelligence is concerned with the following major nonstate actors:

- *Insurgents*. A few recent conflicts illustrate the direction of twenty-first-century conflicts where insurgency is involved: the conflict between Israel and Hezbollah in Lebanon, 2006; the emergence and expansion of Daesh (referred to in the United States as the Islamic State of Iraq and the Levant [ISIL] or Islamic State of Iraq and Syria [ISIS]) beginning in 2011; and the Ukrainian separatist conflict that began when Russia seized the Crimea in 2014. These conflicts had several features in common. The insurgents made use of sophisticated weaponry such as armor and antiarmor weapons and surface-to-air missiles. They had support from states not directly involved in the conflict—with Iran supporting Hezbollah, some Gulf states supporting Daesh, and Russia supporting Ukrainian separatists.
- *Transnational criminal enterprises*. These Mafia-like groups engage in narcotics and human trafficking, piracy, illegal trafficking in natural resources and wildlife, cybercrime, and funds laundering—in the process destabilizing regions, subverting governments, and operating in failed states. The largest such group, Japan's Yamaguchi-gumi, engages in drug trafficking, gambling, and extortion. Yamaguchi-gumi has an annual revenue of about $80 billion, more than the gross domestic product of countries such as Libya and Cuba.
- *Individuals*. Networks must communicate to plan and execute operations, giving intelligence an opportunity to discover their plans. The "lone wolf" poses a different problem. When a single person rather than a unit or an organization is the key player, the intent to commit a terrorist act is far more difficult to identify. Most lone-wolf attacks are by followers of radical movements—often, but not exclusively, radicalized Islamists. For example, in July 2011, Norwegian right-wing extremist Anders Breivik killed 77 people in a bomb attack in Oslo followed by a shooting spree on a nearby island.

These nonstate actors use strategies and tactics designed to outmaneuver their conventional opponents. They use creative techniques that don't involve direct encounters with superior force and increasingly make use of advanced technologies and tools of conflict. What's new is the nature of the tools, lethal and nonlethal, that can be used and the strategies that accompany them. These are different enough from past methods that they change the nature of the game. Let's take a closer look at some of them.

Tools of Conflict

In the 1960s the U.S. military defined four top-level levers through which a state exercises its power to influence events or deal with opponents. The military called these levers *instruments of national power*: political, military, economic, and psychosocial. Over the years, there have been several iterations of this breakdown. Some authors divided "psychosocial" into psychological and informational.[9] In the business world, the levers are almost the same: political, economic, environmental, and social. The argument has been made that technology is a fifth major instrument of national power, or of business power, on the same level as the other four. Technology certainly is a factor (and often the critical factor) in intelligence assessments.

Four such instruments are used widely today: diplomatic (or political), information, military, and economic, usually referred to by the acronym DIME. We'll use the DIME construct in this book, though the name is misleading; these are also instruments of power for organized groups other than states.

Diplomatic

The diplomatic or political instrument has a long history. While the diplomatic instrument is an old one, it remains a powerful tool for mustering the others—information, military, and economic. The most effective instrument wielded by the United States against the Soviet Union during the Cold War arguably was diplomatic: the organization of military and economic alliances aimed at thwarting Soviet expansion and limiting Soviet influence worldwide. This was the execution of the U.S. "containment" policy.

The use of diplomacy to form networks and alliances against opponents still can be highly effective. In 2014 the United States led in the formation of a coalition with European Union and international partners to impose stiff sanctions on Russia for its actions in Ukraine. For their part, opposing nonstate actors can use political tools to covertly infiltrate and subvert uncooperative or hostile governments. For the conflicts described in this chapter, each group has some level of backing by a nation-state.

Information

The information instrument has been the game-changer in twenty-first-century conflicts, enabling more effective use of the other tools as well as being a tool for mobilizing supporters, recruiting fighters, and obtaining funding.

Worldwide, both the participants in conflicts and the events they create receive extensive media attention. The international press covers all such conflicts in detail, often taking a sensational view. And the participants leverage this coverage to promote their views and rally international support.

The Internet has become the most prominent vehicle for applying the information instrument. Most visible is the surface web, which is used for obtaining information and for communication. But nonstate actors make extensive use of the *deep web*—the part not indexed (and, therefore, not searchable) by search engines. Terrorists and transnational criminal groups especially use *darknets*[10] within the deep web to communicate clandestinely.

Cyber operations are used extensively by nonstate actors who rely on both the deep web and social media in the surface web to conduct such operations. These operations are useful for raising funds, distributing propaganda, discrediting opponents, recruiting followers, and targeting critical infrastructure or opposing leadership for the application of other instruments. Daesh has become a leading example of how to use cyber operations effectively in conflicts. It has used social media to recruit jihadists in the United States and Europe and to encourage lone-wolf attacks on military and law enforcement personnel.[11]

Cyber operations often are used to attack; to shape social and political views, to attack infrastructure or economies, or to conduct hacking attacks on web sites. In that role, they arguably could be considered as a type of military tool (the application of a different type of force). But because they are linked so closely to other information tools, offensive cyber operations are treated in this book as an information instrument.

Military

We've seen many advances in the capabilities of military units, thanks to the application of technology. Two classes of weaponry have been developed and improved over the past few decades and now have changed the nature of the military instrument.

One class is precision weaponry, which until recently was a tool used only by advanced powers. Its value derives from its use in precisely attacking high-value targets and minimizing collateral damage. Highly accurate air-to-ground missiles, guided by laser designators, Global Positioning System (GPS), or both, have been the tools of choice in counterterrorism operations. Increasingly, precision weapons that include surface-to-air missiles have been acquired by less advanced countries and non-state actors.

The opposite class involves indiscriminate weapons, often used as instruments of terror or in a form of asymmetric warfare used against advanced military powers or hostile populations. This weapons class includes improvised explosive devices (IEDs); suicide bombers; rockets launched against urban areas; and chemical, biological, nuclear, and radiation weapons.

Economic

International organizations and coalitions rely on sanctions and embargoes as economic instruments against states that defy international norms, using the political instrument to enforce them. Nonstate actors rely on the military instrument to acquire economic benefits—piracy, kidnappings, and hostage-taking being examples. And both state and nonstate actors rely on economic tools to conduct financial transactions that subvert the international rule of law.

The economic instrument uses the Internet extensively, both for traditional financial transactions and for the informal transactions that characterize an undercover economy. Currency manipulation and international trade in illegal goods are examples:

- The Hawala informal system for transferring money long has existed in the Middle East, North Africa, and India. It comprises a large network of funds brokers that functions on mutual trust. Hawala operates in parallel to but separate from international banking and financial channels. It now relies heavily on the Internet for communicating the details of funds transfers.
- Since its invention in 2008, the bitcoin has become an important online payment mechanism. This virtual currency relies on peer-to-peer transactions. While it is widely used in legitimate financial transactions, the bitcoin also serves those who want to avoid having their transactions tracked.
- The dark web is a primary vehicle for online payments of all types that participants wish to conceal. Darknet markets sell drugs, software exploits, and assassination and fraud services, among others. The Silk Road case, described below, illustrates how the practice works.

Between 2011 and 2013, Ross Ulbricht led a team that created and managed the largest online black market for illegal drugs in the world. Called "Silk Road," the website operated as a darknet, concealing itself and its users by relying on the Tor browser. (Tor protects the identity, location, and transactions of a user by bouncing communications through a distributed network of relays run by volunteers across the globe.) Silk Road sold illegal goods, mostly drugs such as heroin, methamphetamine, MDMA, and LSD, using only bitcoins for transactions. During its nearly three years in operation, the Silk Road team collected 614,305 bitcoins in commissions—worth approximately $80 million at the time of Ulbricht's arrest in October 2013.[12] In May 2015, Ulbricht was sentenced to life in prison for his role in Silk Road.

Synergy of the Tools

The examples in this chapter mostly involve military actions, where *military* is defined in a broad sense to mean "use of armed force." But many conflicts of intelligence interest today are not military. And both military and nonmilitary conflicts make use of diplomatic, economic, and information dimensions, usually applied in a synergistic fashion. The negotiations between Western powers and Iran on constraining Iran's nuclear weapons program in 2014–2015 are an example of nonmilitary conflict that encompassed all of these factors. Both sides developed political coalitions for support—with the United States, European powers, several Middle Eastern countries, and some NGOs on one side; and the Iranians, Russians, and some NGOs on the other. Economic levers included trade embargoes against Iran. Iran in turn used its economic and political connections to evade sanctions to some extent. Both sides used the information instrument to rally political and social support: The Western powers played to fears of a nuclear-armed Iran, and the Iranian government for its part stoked anger at the United States and appealed to Iranian pride about independence from foreign pressure. Information conflict within the Middle East also targeted social divisions, with Iran rallying Shiite Muslims to its cause, and Saudi Arabia leading the Sunni Muslims in opposition. The military element was there, of course, in the hint that if negotiations didn't succeed, then a physical attack on Iran's nuclear material production facilities might be in the cards.

The Conflict Spectrum

Military organizations commonly define three levels of conflict: strategic, operational, and tactical.[13] Policymakers, law enforcement, and businesses experience similar levels of conflict. The types of intelligence are often defined to mirror these three levels, though like the conflict levels themselves, the lines between types of intelligence are often blurred. Sometimes, it is difficult for the customers of intelligence to tell where they are in the spectrum; the activities indicated in Figure 2-1 occasionally are all going on at the same time. Conflict, here, does not necessarily mean physical conflict. It can refer to business competition, negotiations, or the normal process of law enforcement.

Against any opponent in a conflict, three successive levels of action can be taken. One can attempt to *prevent*, *deter*, or *prevail*. Figure 2-1 shows a spectrum that includes these levels of action. Preventive operations tend to be strategic and to focus on planning. Actions intended to deter or prevail are mostly tactical; they transition from planning to managing the developing crisis and executing the plans. *This is not a clean division.* It illustrates the type of activity often conducted at a specific level. But deterrence, for example, could occur at the strategic, operational, or tactical level.

Prevent

Executives, policymakers, and operations organizations first try to prevent a disadvantageous situation from developing. Examples include preventing

- The opponent from organizing and acquiring momentum
- The opponent from acquiring or developing a capability, a strategy, or a new weapons system
- The opponent from making an unfavorable decision
- The opposing negotiations team from taking a certain position
- A country from acquiring a nuclear weapon
- Juveniles from forming or joining gangs

Prevention can also include making an existing situation more advantageous, for example, by encouraging an opponent to reverse an unfavorable decision that has been made; rolling back an opponent's existing capability; or inducing the opponent to abandon a favorable position or pull out of a contested area.

Deter

Deterrence is used when it is too late for prevention. Examples include the following:

- Deterring an attack
- Deterring the use of a capability or weapons system
- Deterring the opponent from escalating or aggravating a crisis
- Creating uncertainty that induces the opponent to be cautious
- Deterring gang members from criminal activity

Prevention keeps a situation from becoming unfavorable; deterrence focuses on an opponent's potential actions to resolve an already unfavorable situation in its favor.

Prevail

When all else fails, the goal is to resolve the conflict on favorable terms. Examples include the following:

- Defeating the opponent in armed combat
- Creating a perception that an insurgent opponent is losing, in order to deny recruiting and popular support
- Destroying the opponent's weapons of mass destruction or sources of revenue
- Taking market share away from the opponent in commerce
- Arresting and incarcerating criminals
- Dismantling international criminal networks
- Imposing trade embargoes

Figure 2-1   The Conflict Spectrum

Level of action:	Prevent	Deter	Prevail
Level of conflict:	Strategic	Operational	Tactical
Activities called for:	Planning	Plan execution	Crisis management
Time frame:	Long	Short	Immediate

Until September 11, 2001, when terrorists attacked the World Trade Center and the Pentagon, the U.S. Department of Defense's Central Command (CENTCOM) was focused primarily on prevention and deterrence regarding the Taliban and Al Qaeda in Afghanistan. After 9/11, CENTCOM moved quickly into operational planning and then into tactics for defeating its opponents. In 2015, France could not prevent Islamic terrorists from targeting the humor magazine *Charlie Hebdo*, but it could deter them with police guarding the magazine's headquarters. And when deterrence failed in the January 7, 2015, attack on *Charlie Hebdo* that killed twelve people, the French were able to move to the prevail stage, subsequently killing the two terrorists who were responsible.

The Function of Intelligence

Twenty-first-century conflicts call for a different pattern of intelligence thinking, if we in the intelligence business are to provide the support that our customers need. The next few chapters detail how to provide such support. As an introduction, though, we'll spend the rest of this chapter focusing on the role that intelligence has always played and still must play in dealing with these types of conflicts. Then we'll look at how the methodology works.

The Nature of Intelligence

Intelligence is about *reducing uncertainty in conflict*. Because conflict can consist of any competitive or opposing action resulting from the divergence of two or more parties' ideas or interests, it is not necessarily physical combat. If competition or negotiation exists, then two or more groups are in conflict. There can be many different levels, ranging from friendly competition to armed combat. Context determines whether another party is an opponent or an ally. Parties can be allies in one situation, opponents in another.[14] For example, France and the United States are usually military allies, but they sometimes are opponents in commercial affairs.

Reducing uncertainty requires that intelligence obtain information that the opponent in a conflict prefers to conceal. This definition does not exclude the use of openly available sources, such as newspapers or the Internet, because competent analysis of such open sources frequently reveals information that an opponent wishes to hide. Indeed, intelligence in general can be thought of as the complex process of understanding meaning in available information. A typical goal of intelligence is to establish facts and then to develop precise, reliable, and valid inferences (hypotheses, estimations, conclusions, or predictions) for use in strategic decision making or operational planning.

How, then, is intelligence any different from the market research that many companies conduct or from traditional research as it is carried out in laboratories, think tanks, and academia? After all, those types of research are also intended to reduce uncertainty. The answer is that most of the methods of intelligence research are identical to those pursued in other fields, with one important distinction: In intelligence, when accurate information is not available through traditional (and less-expensive) means, then a wide range of specialized techniques and methods unique to the intelligence field are called into play. Academics are unlikely to have intercepted telephone communications at their disposal as a means for collection and analysis. Nor must a lab scientist deal routinely with concealment, denial, or deception.

Because intelligence is about conflict, it supports *operations* such as military planning and combat, diplomatic negotiations, trade negotiations and commerce policy, and law enforcement. The primary customer of intelligence is the person who will act on the information—the executive, the decision maker, the combat commander, or the law enforcement officer. Writers therefore describe intelligence as being *actionable* information. Not all actionable information is intelligence, however. A weather report is actionable, but it is not intelligence.

What distinguishes intelligence from plain news is the support for operations. The customer does (or should do) something in response to intelligence, whereas television viewers typically do not do anything in response to the news—though they may do something about the weather report. The same information can be both intelligence and news, of course: Food riots in Somalia can be both if the customer takes action on the information.

We said earlier that intelligence supports decision making across the spectrum of conflict. Intelligence, like operations, can be broadly defined at the top level as being *strategic, operational,* or *tactical*—so long as it is recognized that the divisions among them are blurred, and all three types can occur at the same time.

Strategic Intelligence

Strategic intelligence deals with long-range issues. For the military customer, strategic intelligence is produced for the senior leadership. It is used to prepare contingency plans, determine what weapons systems to build, and define force structures.[15] For national customers generally, strategic intelligence is used to create national policy, monitor the international situation, and support such diverse actions as trade policymaking or national industrial policymaking. For corporations, it typically supports strategic planning, market development plans, and investment.

Whether building a target model from scratch or updating an existing one, an analyst must spend much time because there are lots of options. One can consider many possible scenarios, and the situation can evolve many different ways because strategic intelligence takes a long-term analytic view.

Strategic intelligence involves much the same process in government and business. Both look at the political structure and alliances of opponents, both create biographical or leadership profiles, and both assess the opponent's technology.

Strategic intelligence is tougher than tactical intelligence, which we'll discuss later. The analyst has to command more sophisticated analytic techniques. The process is similar or identical to that used for tactical intelligence but usually is more complex because of the longer predictive time frame. One problem is that the intelligence analyst is seldom able to put aside short-term tactical support to customers while developing a clientele having the long-term view.[16] The analyst needs a champion in the customer suite to support him or her in strategic intelligence because tactical intelligence, dealing with immediate issues, usually consumes all available resources.

The essence of strategic intelligence is best understood in terms of the methodology used in strategic planning, known as SWOT:

Strengths

Weaknesses

Opportunities

Threats

The SWOT methodology is the basis of all strategic planning, though it is not always made explicit. New techniques for strategic planning pop up from time to time, but SWOT always underlies them.

Operational Intelligence

Operational intelligence focuses on the capabilities and intentions of adversaries and potential adversaries. It is defined as the intelligence required for planning and execution of specific operations. Operational intelligence therefore has to be predictive also.

At the national level, once policy has been established, the intelligence customers have to develop operational plans to execute the policy or to carry out the strategic plan. A few examples of the many possible ones are included here:

- It could involve planning for diplomatic negotiations. Intelligence then has to determine what the opposing negotiators want and what they will agree to.
- It could involve planning for a trade embargo. Here, intelligence must determine what sanctions are likely to be effective and what the target country can do to defeat sanctions.
- It could involve support to research and development (R&D) that will result in new weapons systems. R&D support has to be predictive, because it can take years for a development program to produce a new weapons system, and the system must be effective in that future environment.

Operational intelligence in diplomatic efforts could support, for example, planning the negotiation of an arms reduction treaty. In law enforcement, operational intelligence is defined as intelligence that supports long-term investigations into multiple, similar targets. In this definition, operational intelligence is concerned primarily with identifying, targeting, detecting, and intervening in criminal activity.[17] It might, for example, support planning for the takedown of an organized crime syndicate. In business intelligence, it might support a campaign to gain market share in a specific product line.

The SWOT method that we examined for strategic planning is useful also for operational planning, though the emphasis is different. When you're making plans, you are more focused on opportunities that derive from opponent weaknesses. A key point to remember is that the opponent's strengths translate directly to your threats, and the opponent's weaknesses provide your side with opportunities. Intelligence has the job of identifying those strengths and weaknesses.

For the military, operational intelligence has a specific name. The Army and Air Force call it *intelligence preparation of the battlefield*. The Navy likes to use the term *intelligence preparation of the battlespace*. Whatever the name, the process involves the detailed analysis of the enemy, surface conditions (terrain or sea conditions), and weather within a specific geographic area. It starts before the next operation and continues throughout combat operations. Its goals include understanding the adversary's forces, doctrine, tactics, and probable courses of action, together with the physical and environmental characteristics of the target area.

Intelligence preparation of the battlefield is a recent name for a very old technique. At the battle of Marathon in 490 B.C.E., the Greeks determined the only feasible route for a Persian attack (think of geospatial intelligence here), and stationed their forces in a narrow valley along that route that maximized the advantages of the Greek phalanx formation taking the Persian cavalry out of the battle.

The military coined the term *operational intelligence* to describe intelligence that is primarily used by combatant and subordinate joint force commanders and their component commanders. It keeps them abreast of events within their areas of responsibility and estimates when, where, and in what strength an opponent will stage and conduct campaigns and major operations.[18] But operational intelligence also is used by national-level, law enforcement, and business entities to support operational planning, as we'll discuss in this chapter.

The best operational intelligence is predictive. Analysts have to visualize the enemy's tactical formations, the effect of terrain and weather, and how the enemy might alter his formations to adapt to specific terrain and weather. But predicting an opponent's future actions is difficult. Analysts lack complete information because of gaps in collection capability or because of the opponent's denial and deception. The job of intelligence is, again, *to reduce uncertainty* by assessing capabilities and likely courses of action.

To continue with the SWOT concept, the opportunities assessment typically supports targeting. During the targeting process, intelligence selects targets in accordance with the military commander's guidance, objectives, and the results of the intelligence preparation of the battlespace. Targets may be either physical targets, such as bridges and command centers, or functional targets, such as enemy command and control capability. Two historical examples of how the process works are the 1990–1991 coalition operations called Desert Shield/Desert Storm, and the 2006 conflict between Hezbollah and Israel in Lebanon. These two examples illustrate the challenges of operational intelligence in more recent decades as compared with earlier conventional conflicts.

Operation Desert Shield/Desert Storm. During Operation Desert Shield and throughout the air operations of Desert Storm, U.S. Navy and Army special operations personnel and force reconnaissance Marines established a series of observation sites along the border between Kuwait and Saudi Arabia. These sites were used for continuous visual and signals intelligence (SIGINT) surveillance of Iraqi forces across the border. Information from these ground sites was combined with imagery and SIGINT collected by coalition aircraft in the theater. The process provided an intelligence picture of the locations, combat capability, and intentions of Iraqi units in Kuwait, as well as indications of the vulnerability of Iraqi forces along the Iraq/Saudi Arabian border west of Kuwait. This thorough intelligence preparation of the battlespace contributed significantly to the subsequent successful ground offensive to liberate Kuwait.[19]

Operation Desert Shield/Desert Storm was a coalition operation, so allied forces were also customers of the intelligence that supports operational planning. The trend is to such joint actions. These present a number of challenges that are associated with intelligence sharing, discussed later in this book.

Lebanon War, 2006. On July 12, 2006, Hezbollah militants in Lebanon fired rockets at Israel, as a diversion for an ambush on an Israeli patrol. During the ambush, Hezbollah fighters killed three Israeli soldiers and captured two. Hezbollah then demanded the release of Lebanese prisoners in Israel in exchange for the captives. Israel responded by attacking Hezbollah and Lebanese civilian targets, followed by imposing an air and naval blockade and conducting a ground invasion of Lebanon. Hezbollah in turn launched more rockets into Israel and began a campaign of guerrilla warfare in southern Lebanon.

The Israelis' operational intelligence preparation for the conflict was strikingly different from the coalition preparation for Desert Shield/Desert Storm. Hezbollah fighters were well equipped with combat and communications gear, were well trained, and used tactics designed to maximize their advantages— fighting from well-fortified positions in urban areas with advanced weaponry that included anti-tank guided missiles. They focused on inflicting casualties on the Israeli Defense Forces (IDF) because of a perceived unwillingness of the Israelis to accept casualties. Both made use of the media and NGOs such as Human Rights Watch and Amnesty International to garner international support—with Hezbollah pointing to Israeli attacks on civilians and the civilian infrastructure, and Israel arguing that Hezbollah was using civilians as human shields. After the conflict ended with a cease-fire on August 14, 2006, both sides claimed victory. Though Israel appeared to have won in terms of relative casualties, Hezbollah emerged relatively intact with an enhanced reputation from having stood up to the much more powerful IDF.

Israeli intelligence support failed in several areas. They targeted bunkers that Hezbollah had deliberately set up as decoys, missing most of the 600 concealed ammunition and weapons bunkers in the region. Their targeting of Hezbollah leaders in Beirut and their communications infrastructure also failed. Hezbollah, for its part, demonstrated a SIGINT capability that allowed it to anticipate Israeli moves and succeeded in "turning" Israeli human intelligence (HUMINT) assets in southern Lebanon to feed back misleading information to Israeli intelligence.[20]

To conclude the SWOT concept, operational intelligence has to assess threats. For example, intelligence must give an accurate picture of the opponent's missile threat by calculating where the missiles might go, how quickly the opponent can fire them, and which of your own forces are in the threat envelope.

Operational intelligence to support law enforcement has its own name, and it very much resembles intelligence preparation of the battlespace in a civil environment. It is called *intelligence-led policing.*

The term *intelligence-led policing* originated in Great Britain. The Kent Constabulary developed the concept after experiencing substantial increases in property-related offenses during a time when it was dealing with budget cuts. The constabulary believed that only a few people were responsible for a large percentage of burglaries and automobile theft. Its hypothesis—which subsequent events proved to be valid—was that police would have the best effect on crime by focusing on these most common offenses.[21]

Operational intelligence to support intelligence-led policing can take several forms. Analysts can anticipate crime trends so that law enforcement can take preventive measures to intervene or mitigate the impact of those crimes. Intelligence that supports, for example, planning to shut down a gang operation or a narcotics ring would be operational. As an example, to help fight terrorism and domestic extremism, the California Department of Justice examines criminal group characteristics and intervention consequences to determine which groups pose the greatest threat to the state.

Operational planning in business can take many forms, as can the nature of the intelligence to support such planning. Planning a campaign to reduce the market share of a competitor requires good knowledge of the competitor's weaknesses. Negotiations with suppliers or large customers require much the same sort of knowledge that is needed to support international treaty negotiations: what the other side has to have, and what it is willing to give up.

Tactical Intelligence

The military uses the term *tactical intelligence* to refer to quick-reaction intelligence that supports ongoing operations. As was true at the operational level, intelligence has a well-established role at tactical levels that is spelled out in military doctrine. This form of intelligence is associated with a concept that the U.S. military calls *battlespace awareness*. Tactical intelligence is used at the front line of any conflict. It is used by field commanders for planning and conducting battles and engagements. Tactical intelligence locates and identifies the opponent's forces and weaponry, enhancing a tactical commander's ability to gain a combat advantage with maneuver, weaponry on target, and obstacles. It allows tactical units to achieve positional advantage over their adversaries.[22]

Tactical intelligence to support the military became much more important during the 1990s because of weapons technology trends. The trend toward employing highly precise weaponry and operations placed a premium on highly accurate data. Intelligence systems that can geolocate enemy units to within a few meters became more important than before. The rapidly expanding field of geospatial analysis supports such surgical operations with mapping, charting, and geodesy data that can be used for the guidance of "smart" weapons.[23]

Add to that a new field of combat—cyber operations—that is still in development and may be poorly understood by some commanders. Surgical operations in the cyber world are at least as important as surgical operations in the physical world.

The result, as one author has noted, is that

> Many of the new C4ISR systems (including national systems), and much of the effort and funds expended by the Intelligence Community since the Gulf War, have focused on providing direct, real-time support to forces engaged in combat by closing the "sensor-to-shooter" loop and to meeting the information needs of the senior-level commanders directing those operations. When there are American forces deployed in active military operations, as there have been on a near-continual basis since the end of the Cold War, the highest priority is now accorded to providing intelligence to support them.[24]

The dominance of U.S. capabilities for battlespace awareness has resulted in an added task for tactical intelligence. Targets on the battlefield typically exceed the number of available sensors and weapons that can be used against them. Thus it is important to find and attack the most important targets. So, tactical intelligence has the job of identifying the enemy forces, systems, and activities that will yield the highest payoff in terms of disrupting enemy operations and reducing his combat effectiveness. Again, cyber operations have added a whole new dimension in disrupting enemy combat effectiveness.

Battle damage assessment (or combat damage assessment) could be considered the final stage of battlespace awareness. It includes not only physical damage assessment, but also functional damage assessment. Physical damage assessment quantifies the extent of damage to a material target. An example would be imagery indicating the center span of a bridge has been destroyed, thus severing an enemy resupply line. Functional damage assessment determines the disruption of operational targets by "nonkinetic" attack. For example, it would assess the effectiveness of electronic jamming on enemy command and control capabilities. Battle damage assessment relies heavily on quick-reaction intelligence, because the commander has to decide quickly what targets need to be attacked again.

Much of law enforcement intelligence also tends to be tactical in orientation. In the law enforcement world, tactical intelligence is defined as that which contributes to the success of specific investigations.[25] But tactical intelligence is used every day in situations well removed from military actions and law enforcement, as the following example illustrates:

> A satellite photo of the Earth spins slowly on a large plasma screen, with markers indicating the sources of online threats. At rows of computer workstations, analysts monitor firewalls and other online defenses. The displays, the layout, and the security guards all evoke the image of a war room—which it is, but for a new type of war.
>
> This is Symantec's war room. Here, a different type of intelligence analyst deals with junk e-mailers who are trying to stay one step ahead of filters and blacklists that block spam; of the hackers that constantly work to bypass bank firewalls; and of the viruses that can flow into thousands of computers worldwide in a few seconds.
>
> Symantec maintains the war room to defend banks and Fortune 500 firms against cyber threats. This room was the front line of the battle against SQL Slammer as it surged through the Internet, knocking out police and fire dispatch centers and halting freight trains; against MSBlaster, as it clogged corporate networks and forced web sites offline; and against the graffiti viruses with such innocuous names as Melissa and ILoveYou.[26]

The analysts in Symantec's war room succeed in their tactical combat because they have *shared models* of viruses, worms, and Trojans instantly available. They model the operational patterns of East European organized crime groups that use viruses such as SoBig to track a user's keystrokes and to lift passwords and credit card numbers. They have models of the computers that are used to spread viruses. The great plasma screen itself displays a massive model of the Internet battlefront, where the beginning of new threats can be seen. Using these models and creating new ones on the fly, these tactical intelligence analysts can analyze and defeat a new virus in minutes.

Tactical intelligence is driven by the need for fast response in the military and law enforcement communities. For the national customers, it's a classified form of the news; it's called current intelligence.

Summary

Twenty-first-century conflicts have distinguishing features that are important for intelligence. They take a network form, the key players being nonstate actors that operate transnationally with the support or tolerance of governments. These actors may be criminal, insurgent, terrorist, commercial, or other nongovernmental organizations—or some combination. The resulting conflicts among such networks have been called netwars or network-centric conflicts.

As a result, much of intelligence today is about what are being called shadow wars, hybrid wars, or unrestricted conflict. Although these are not new types of conflicts, they present challenges because globalization and the ubiquitous Internet provide new tools for engaging in and prevailing in conflict.

The new tools of conflict can be thought of as dividing into four categories, known as the instruments of national (or organizational) power. These instruments are summarized in the acronym DIME: diplomatic (or political), information, military, and economic.

In these new conflicts, the primary job of all intelligence continues to be *reducing uncertainty* for the customers of intelligence. Intelligence analysis must support policy, planning, and operations across the spectrum of these new conflicts. The type of analysis and the speed with which it must be prepared and delivered to the customer vary accordingly. Analysis to support strategic intelligence tends to be in-depth research focused on capabilities and plans and to consider many possible scenarios.

Operational intelligence is more near-term, involving support to planning for specific operations. In military usage, it has a specific name: *intelligence preparation of the battlefield* (or *battlespace*). But operational intelligence also supports planning for economic and political activities such as trade embargoes and treaty negotiations.

Tactical intelligence support tends to be rapid response, or current intelligence, to support crisis management and plan execution; it is focused on the current situation and on indications and warnings. Again, the military gives it a specific name: *battlespace awareness*. Battle damage assessment is one phase of battlespace awareness. Much of the intelligence support to law enforcement and to countering cyber threats is tactical in nature.

Notes

1. Frank G. Hoffman, "Conflict in the 21st Century: The Rise of Hybrid Wars," http://www
   .potomacinstitute.org/images/stories/publications/potomac_hybridwar_0108.pdf.
2. Alan Dupont, "Transformation or Stagnation? Rethinking Australia's Defence," *Australian
   Journal of International Affairs*, 57, no. 1 (2003): 55–76.
3. In this context, *technological* refers to the use of information technology.
4. Qiao Liang and Wang Xiangsui, *Unrestricted Warfare* (Beijing: PLA Literature and Arts
   Publishing House, 1999), 5.
5. John Arquilla and David Ronfeldt, "Cyberwar Is Coming," in *Athena's Camp: Preparing for
   Conflict in the Information Age*, ed. John Arquilla and David Ronfeldt (Washington, D.C.: RAND
   Corporation, 1997).
6. David Ronfeldt and Armando Martinez, "A Comment on the Zapatista "Netwar," in *Athena's
   Camp*, 369.
7. David Motadel, "'Defending the Faith' in the Middle East," *New York Times*, May 23, 2015,
   http://www.nytimes.com/2015/05/24/opinion/sunday/defending-the-faith-in-the-middle-
   east.html?WT.mc_id=2015-MAY-OUTBRAIN-SHARED_AUD_DEV-0501-0531&WT.mc_
   ev=click&ad-keywords=MAYAUDDEV&_r=0.
8. U.S. Joint Forces Command, *Commander's Handbook for Attack the Network* (Suffolk, Va.: Joint
   Warfighting Center, 2011), http://www.dtic.mil/doctrine/doctrine/jwfc/atn_hbk.pdf.
9. David Jablonsky, "National Power," *Parameters* (Spring 1997): 34–54.
10. A darknet is a private network overlaid on the web that relies on connections between trusted
    peers.
11. "US Security Chief Warns of 'New Phase' in Terror Threat," *MSN News*, May 10, 2015, http://
    www.msn.com/en-us/news/us/us-security-chief-warns-of-new-phase-in-terror-threat/
    ar-BBjy1fG.
12. Patrick Howell O'Neill, "Silk Road Founder Ross Ulbricht Sentenced to Life in Prison," *The
    Daily Dot*, May 29, 2015, http://www.dailydot.com/crime/ross-ulbricht-sentencing-silk-road/.
13. JCS Joint Pub 2-0, "Joint Doctrine for Intelligence Support to Operations," Chapter III.
14. Walter D. Barndt Jr., *User-Directed Competitive Intelligence* (Westport, Conn.: Quorum Books,
    1994), 21–22.
15. Ibid.
16. Bill Fiora, "Moving from Tactical to Strategic Intelligence," *Competitive Intelligence Magazine*,
    4 (November–December 2001): 44.
17. Marilyn Peterson, "Intelligence-Led Policing: The New Intelligence Architecture," U.S. Department
    of Justice Publication No. NCJ 210681 (September 2005), 3.
18. JCS Joint Pub 2-0, Chapter III.
19. U.S. Navy, *Naval Doctrine Publication 2: Naval Intelligence*, http://www.dtic.mil/doctrine/jel/
    service_pubs/ndp2.pdf.
20. LTCOL Scott C. Farquhar, "Back to Basics: A Study of the Second Lebanon War and
    Operation CAST LEAD," May 2009, http://usacac.army.mil/cac2/cgsc/CARL/download/csipubs/
    farquhar.pdf.
21. Peterson, "Intelligence-Led Policing," 8.
22. Ibid.
23. Geodesy is concerned with the size, shape, and gravitational field of the Earth, its coordinate
    systems, and reference frames.
24. Jeffrey R. Cooper, *Curing Analytic Pathologies* [monograph], Center for the Study of
    Intelligence (December 2005), 32.
25. Peterson, "Intelligence-Led Policing," 3.
26. Andy Sullivan, "Attack of the Killer Bugs: Your Computer Could Be Hijacked by Scam Artists
    to Send Out Spam and Steal Your Bank Account," *Reuters Magazine* (January/February 2004).

Part I

The Analysis Process

P art I of this book is about the analysis process: how to do analysis. After an overview of the target-centric approach (chapter 3), it describes how to define and decompose the intelligence issue (chapter 4). Chapter 5 introduces two conceptual frameworks for performing analysis—the PMESII perspective and the idea of modeling the intelligence target. Chapters 6 through 11 go into more depth on modeling the target.

3

The Intelligence Process

The power of accurate observation is commonly called cynicism by those who have not got it.

George Bernard Shaw

George Lucas's original *Star Wars* movie describes the final stages of a human intelligence operation. The heroine, Princess Leia, places the plans for the evil Galactic Empire's ultimate battle machine, the Death Star, into the robot R2-D2, which is functioning as a mobile dead drop.[1] R2-D2 gets the plans to the rebel forces, whose scientific intelligence analyst briefs the rebel command on the plans, pinpoints the weak spot on the Death Star, and presents a brilliant analysis of the enemy defenses. Rebel fighter jockeys deliver proton torpedoes to the weak spot and destroy the Death Star. End of movie.

This *Star Wars* vignette accurately summarizes the intelligence process as it is popularly viewed. The people who collect intelligence information and execute the operations get the glory, the press, and the money. The intelligence analyst, working behind the scenes, gets the interesting problems to solve to make it all work.

Although the popular focus is on collection, most of the major failures in intelligence are due to inadequate or nonexistent analysis, and most of the rest are due to failure to act on the analysis, as noted in chapter 1. The information is usually there, at least in hindsight. So, unfortunately, is a large volume of misleading or irrelevant material that has to be examined and discarded. All intelligence organizations today are saturated with incoming information. Furthermore, in large intelligence communities, critical information about an intelligence matter may not be shared effectively because the intelligence activity is organized around the flawed concept of an "intelligence cycle."

To begin with, intelligence is always concerned with a *target*—the focus of the problem about which the customers want answers. The analyst's primary job is to develop a level of *understanding* of the target and communicate that understanding to the customer. In the *Star Wars* example, the target was the Death Star. The rebel intelligence effort supported operations by identifying its weak point and communicating that level of understanding to the customer.

Logic dictates that the intelligence process should revolve around how best to approach the target. That is exactly what the remainder of this book is concerned with: the steps to solving an intelligence problem, using a target-centric approach, and communicating *understanding* to the customer so that the customer can act based on that understanding. This process is different from that depicted in most introductory texts and courses, but it is the direction that intelligence is taking in practice. A brief review of the traditional intelligence cycle will illustrate why.

The Traditional Intelligence Cycle

Intelligence has traditionally been described as following a series of steps called the *intelligence cycle*. Figure 3-1 illustrates the cycle in elementary form.

The cycle typically begins with a *requirements* or *needs* step, which amounts to a definition of the intelligence problem. Usually it takes the form of a rather general question from an intelligence customer, such as, "How stable is the government of Ethiopia?"

Then comes *planning*, or *direction*—determining how the other components of the cycle will address the problem. Collectors have to be tasked to gather missing bits of information. Analysts have to be assigned to do research and write a report on Ethiopian government stability.

The cycle then proceeds to *collection*, or gathering information. Ethiopian newspapers have to be acquired. Communications intelligence (COMINT) has to be focused on Ethiopian government communications. Human intelligence (HUMINT) operatives have to ask questions of sources with knowledge of Ethiopian internal affairs.

From there, the information has to be *processed*. Foreign language material must be translated. Encrypted signals must be decrypted. Film or digital signals must be translated into visible imagery. Responses from HUMINT sources must be validated and organized into a report format.

Figure 3-1   The Traditional Intelligence Cycle

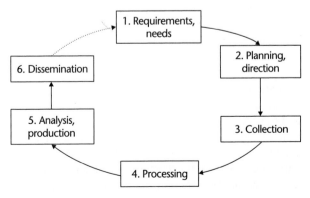

The newly collected and processed material must be brought together with relevant historical material to create intelligence in an *analysis* phase. An analyst must create outcome scenarios based on the current Ethiopian situation, generate profiles of Ethiopian leaders, and assess their likely responses to possible events. The analysis phase also typically includes a peer and supervisory review of the finished product, except in fast-moving, combat intelligence situations, in which simple fusion (discussed in chapter 18) is done.

The finished intelligence must be *disseminated* to the customer in a written report (usually sent electronically) or a briefing. Then comes a transition to new requirements or needs, and a new cycle begins.

Over the years the intelligence cycle has become almost a theological concept: No one questions its validity. Yet when pressed, many intelligence officers admit that the intelligence process "really doesn't work like that." In other words, effective intelligence efforts are not cycles. Here are some reasons why.

The cycle defines an *antisocial* series of steps that constrains the flow of information. It separates collectors from processors from analysts and too often results in "throwing information over the wall" to become the next person's responsibility. Everyone neatly avoids responsibility for the quality of the final product. Because such a compartmentalized process results in formalized and relatively inflexible requirements at each stage, it is more predictable and therefore more vulnerable to an opponent's countermeasures. In intelligence, as in most forms of conflict, if you can predict what your opponents will do, you can defeat them.

The cycle-defined view, when it considers the customer at all, tends to treat the customer in the abstract as a monolithic entity. The feedback loop inherent in a true cycle is absent; in practice, a gap exists between dissemination and needs. Customers, being outside the loop, cannot make their changing needs known. Why does this gap exist?

In government, intelligence officers and policymakers often are almost totally ignorant of one another's business.[2] In the military the gap may be less severe—the importance of intelligence has been ingrained in military culture over a long time. But as in the civilian side of government, an organizational demarcation usually exists. Most commanders and their staffs have not had intelligence assignments, and intelligence officers usually have not had operations assignments. They tend to speak different jargons, and their definitions of what is important in an operation differ. Military intelligence officers often know more about an opponent's capability than they do about their own unit's capability, and the commander often has the inverse problem.

In large intelligence organizations, such as those of the U.S. government, the collection element (see Figure 3-1) typically is well organized, well funded, and automated to handle high volumes of traffic. In contrast, the step wherein one moves from disseminated intelligence to new requirements is almost completely unfunded and requires extensive feedback from intelligence consumers. The system depends on the customers voicing their needs. Military organizations have a formal system for that to occur. Policymakers, with one important exception that is discussed in chapter 19, do not. The policymaker's input is largely informal, is dependent on feedback to the analyst, and often passes through several intermediaries. And for the newest class of customers of U.S. intelligence—law enforcement—the feedback is rudimentary. No entity has the clear responsibility to close the loop. Analysts and their managers, who typically have the closest ties to intelligence customers, usually determine customer needs. But it is too often a hit-or-miss proposition because it depends on the inclination of analysts who are dealing with other pressing problems.

The traditional conception of the intelligence cycle also prevails because it fits a conventional paradigm for problem solving. It flows logically from the precept that the best way to work on an intelligence problem is to follow a sequential, orderly, and linear process, working from the question (the problem) to the answer (the solution). One begins by understanding the question; the next step is to gather and analyze data. Analysis techniques are then applied to answer the question. This pattern of thinking is taught in the simplest problem-solving texts, and we use it almost instinctively. In fact, conventional wisdom says that the more complex the problem, the more important it is to follow this orderly flow. The flaw of this linear problem-solving approach is that it obscures the real, underlying cognitive process: The mind does not work linearly; it jumps around to different parts of the problem in the process of reaching a solution. In practice, intelligence officers might jump from analysis back to collection, then to requirements, to collection again, then back to analysis, in what seems a very untidy process, and which in no way resembles a cycle.

Despite its irrelevance to the real world of intelligence, the concept of an intelligence cycle persists. Some of the foremost experts in U.S. and British intelligence, such as former director of national intelligence Mike McConnell and noted British author Michael Herman, have questioned its relevance. Both McConnell[3] and Herman[4] noted that the so-called cycle is actually a collection of feedback loops. But old habits tend to fade very slowly, and so the intelligence cycle continues to be taught in introductory intelligence courses.

U.S. intelligence analysis guru Sherman Kent noted that the problems with the intelligence cycle—the compartmentation of participants, the gap between dissemination and needs, and the attempt to make linear a nonlinear process—are worse in large organizations and in situations far removed from the heat of conflict.[5] As Keith Hall, former director of the National Reconnaissance Office, observed, "During crisis the seams go away and all the various players pull together to create end-to-end solutions . . . but we don't do that well in a noncrisis situation."[6]

In summary, the traditional cycle may adequately describe the structure and function of an intelligence community, but it does not describe the intelligence process. In the evolving world of information technology, the traditional cycle may be even less relevant. Informal networks (communities of interest) increasingly are forming to address the problems that Kent identified and to enable a nonlinear intelligence process using secure web technology.

The cycle is still with us, however, because it embodies a convenient way to organize and manage intelligence communities like those in large governments and large military organizations. And it is in some respects a defensive measure; it makes it difficult to pinpoint responsibility for intelligence failures.

The cycle traces its lineage back to an automaker named Henry Ford. Over a century ago, Ford divided the labor by breaking the assembly of the Model T into eighty-four distinct steps. Each worker was trained to do just one of these steps. So you had interchangeable parts, division of labor, and a continuous flow of a standard product.

And it worked. The Model T had a remarkable run; first produced in 1908, it kept the same design until the last one, number 15,000,000, rolled off the line in 1927—something that hasn't happened since. Industry adopted the assembly line concept. Many governments did also. The Soviets built their entire system (industrial and consumer goods) on the Ford model. If you're producing one thing and demand is stable, it's efficient and easy to manage.

Fifty years ago, the automobile production "cycle" looked a lot like the traditional intelligence cycle. Marketing staff would come up with requirements for new cars. Designers would create a design and feed it to production. Production would retool the factory and produce the cars in a long assembly line. The cars came out at the end and went to a sales force that sold the cars to customers. And then marketing started on a new requirements set, beginning the cycle anew. No one had responsibility for the final result. Today automobile production is a team effort—with marketing, sales, design, and production staff sitting in the same room with consumer representatives, working together on a common target: the new automobile. This complex, interactive, collaborative, and social process results in the faster production of higher quality, more market-oriented products.

Finally, the "cycle" was designed to deal with the flow of reporting in cable or paper form. It provided an orderly, one-way flow. We set up intelligence organizations based entirely on slow flow of intelligence around the cycle. We kept that system even when first secure telephones, then secure computer communications, made it possible to speed things along. We even kept the name "production" as though we were building automobiles.

This book defines an alternative, interactive approach that is gaining currency in intelligence communities, for a world where intelligence problems will always be increasingly complex.

Intelligence as a Target-Centric Process

An alternative to the traditional intelligence cycle is to make all stakeholders, *including customers*, part of the intelligence process. Stakeholders in the intelligence community include collectors, processors, analysts, and the people who plan for and build systems to support them. U.S. customers on a given issue could include, for example, the president, the National Security Council staff, military command headquarters, diplomats, the Department of Homeland Security, state or local law enforcement, and the commanders of U.S. naval vessels. To include them in the intelligence process, the cycle must be redefined, not for convenience of implementation in a traditional organizational hierarchy, but so that the process can take full advantage of evolving information technology and handle complex problems.

Figure 3-2 defines this *target-centric*, or objective-oriented, view of the intelligence process. Here the goal is to construct a shared picture of the target, from which all participants can extract the elements they need to do their jobs and to which all can contribute from their resources or knowledge, so as to create the most accurate target picture. It is not a linear sequence, nor is it a cycle (though it contains many feedback loops, or cycles); it is a *network process*, a social process, with all participants focused on the objective. It has been accurately described within the U.S. intelligence community as a "network-centric collaboration process."[7]

Letitia Long, while director of the National Geospatial-Intelligence Agency, endorsed the idea of a fresh approach that replaces the cycle. She termed it "sequence neutrality," observing that

> It turns the traditional TCPED (tasking, collection, processing, exploitation, and dissemination) process focused on a suite of fixed targets inside out. It allows the analyst to form a hypothesis first and then search the data and even drive new collection to test the hypothesis. It also allows the analyst to integrate data before exploitation to focus an analyst's investigation on anomalies in the data that have been correlated. Our ability to know the unknown depends on this new approach to collection and processing data.[8]

Subsequently, the U.S. intelligence community has implemented a concept very similar to the target-centric approach. Called "object-based production," or OBP, it involves organizing intelligence efforts around "objects" (targets) of intelligence interest. It features cloud-based sharing of the state of knowledge of the intelligence target. The sharing includes customers as well—policymakers, warfighters, and foreign partners.[9]

Figure 3-2   A Target-Centered View of the Process

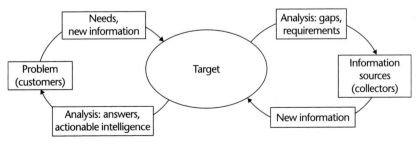

Figure 3-2 focuses on the role that all-source analysts must take in this new environment: pulling in customers. The analyst's job is to take inputs from many sources and provide support to many customers who have different timeline requirements and need different levels of analysis. The major characteristics of intelligence in today's environment are as follows:

- Analysis can take many forms and draw on many sources. It's common to draw on several sources to get a more complete picture. Extrinsic sources include specialized expertise from academia, social media, or industry.
- Analysis on any subject is a continuous process. Customers require intelligence support every day, some on shared issues, some on issues unique to them.
- Consequently, each of the steps in the intelligence process (collection, processing, exploitation, analysis, dissemination) is happening all the time on any given subject.

The traditional cycle wasn't designed to handle that environment. The target-centric approach is.

In the process depicted in Figure 3-2, customers who have operational problems look at the current state of knowledge about the target (the current target picture) and identify the information they need. Intelligence analysts, working with collectors who share the same target model, translate the needs into "knowledge gaps" or "information requirements" for the collectors to address. As collectors obtain the needed information, it is incorporated into the shared target model. From this picture, analysts extract actionable intelligence, which they provide to the customers, who may in turn add their own insights. They may also add new information needs.

Let us bring some meaning to the process shown in Figure 3-2: The date is December 2, 1993. Colombian police lieutenant Hugo Martinez watches the signal display on his computer screen and listens to his headphones as his police surveillance van moves through the streets of Medellin, Colombia. Electronic intelligence has traced the cell phone calls of drug kingpin Pablo Escobar to this neighborhood. Martinez is trying to find the exact house where a desperate Escobar is talking to his son about getting the family out of Colombia.

The signal on the computer screen and in the headphones strengthens and peaks. The van stops next to a house, and Martinez looks up to see a fat man standing at a window, holding a cell phone. The man turns away, and the cell phone conversation ends abruptly. Martinez reports to his commander: "I've got him located. He's in this house." The commander snaps out orders for all units to converge and surround the building. Five police officers force their way in the front door and exchange gunshots with the occupants. Ten minutes later, the gunfire stops. On the building rooftop, Pablo Escobar lies dead.[10]

This example, a true story, was the end of an intense cooperative effort between U.S. and Colombian intelligence officers that had endured for over a year. In this case, the intelligence effort had several customers—an operations team comprising the Colombian police, the U.S. Army support team in Colombia, and the Colombian and U.S. governments, each with different intelligence needs. The information sources included COMINT focused on Escobar's cell phones and those of his associates, HUMINT from Escobar's associates, and financial information from other sources. The operations team focused on finding Escobar; the intelligence analysts who supported them had a more extensive target that included Escobar's family, his business associates, his bankers, and his agents in the Colombian government. Escobar would not have been caught if the intelligence search had focused solely on him and had ignored his network.

In the Escobar case, as in other, less time-critical operations, intelligence analysis is implicit and pervasive. But it is not all done by analysts. The customers and the providers of information also participate and will do so whether the analyst welcomes it or not. Both customers and providers possess valuable insights about the target, and both want their insights included in the final analytic product. However, someone must make the process work: creating and maintaining the model of the target, eliciting customer needs and changing them into requirements for new information, accepting new information and incorporating it into the target model, and then extracting actionable intelligence and ensuring that it gets to the customer. All of these are functions that analysts have always performed. In the target-centric process, analysts still perform these functions, but collectors and customers cannot only see into the process but have more opportunity to contribute to it. The analyst's job becomes more like that of a process manager.

The team-generated model of the target is intended to facilitate and encourage interaction among collectors, analysts, and customers, who may be geographically remote from one another, via an electronic web. Because the team view is more interactive, or social, than the intelligence cycle view, it is a better way to handle complex problems. Because all participants share knowledge of the target, they are better able to identify gaps in knowledge and understand the important issues surrounding it. The team-generated view brings the full resources of the team to bear on the target. During U.S. operations in Afghanistan in 2002, intelligence officers used screens similar to Internet chat rooms to share data in an interactive process that in no way resembled the traditional intelligence cycle,[11] and they continued that successful pattern during Operation Iraqi Freedom. It now is an established method of producing tactical intelligence that is likely to be used in all future U.S. and coalition operations. But the method that has worked at the tactical level remains a work in progress at the national intelligence level.[12]

The target-centric approach is resilient. Because the participants collaborate, there is no single point of failure; another member of the network could step in to act as facilitator; and the whole team shares responsibility for the product.

The process is also able to satisfy a wide range of customers from a single knowledge base. There are usually many customers for intelligence about a given problem, and each customer has different needs. For example, military, foreign relations, financial, and foreign trade organizations all may need information about a specific country. Because there is a common target, their needs will overlap, but each organization also will have unique needs.

The target-centric approach has proven to work well for today's complex problems and issues. Though depicted as a cycle, the traditional process is in practice linear and sequential, whereas the target-centric process is collaborative by design. Its nonlinear analytic method allows for participation by all stakeholders, so that real insights into a problem can come from any knowledgeable source. Involving customers increases the likelihood that the resulting intelligence will be used. It also reminds the customers of (or introduces them to) the value of an analytic approach to complex problems. It has been asserted that in the United States, government has detached itself from the analytic process and relied too much on the intelligence community to do its analytic thinking.[13] Increasing policymakers' exposure to the analytic process could help reverse that trend.

The collaborative team concept also has the potential to address two important pressures that intelligence analysts face today:

- *The information glut.* Analysts are overloaded with incoming material from collectors. The team approach expands the team of analysts to include knowledgeable people from the collector, processor, and customer groups, each of whom can take a chunk of the information glut and filter out the irrelevant material. Business organizations have been doing this for years, and they now rely heavily on web-based private networks.
- *The customer demand for more detail.* All intelligence customers are demanding increasingly greater detail about targets. This should not be surprising given that targets are more networked and the range of the customer's options to deal with opponents using the DIME instruments has become richer. If the operations target is a building (such as an embassy or a command-and-control center), for example, intelligence may need to include the floor plan; the number of levels; whether it has a basement; the type of construction; roof characteristics; what type of heating, ventilation, and air conditioning it uses; when the building is empty; and so forth. Such details become critical when the objective is to place a smart bomb on the building or to take out the building's electric power.

For collaboration to work—for the extended team to share the data overload and provide the needed target detail—intelligence organizations have to provide incentives to share that outweigh the disincentives discussed in chapter 1. Team members have to have a wealth of mutual trust and understanding; both require team building and extended social interaction. Some companies have been highly successful at collaboration; the U.S. government is still working at it.

It is important to note also what the collaborative process is not. As Mark Lowenthal has stated, it is not a substitute for competitive analysis—the process by which different analysts present alternative views of the target.[14] Collaboration, properly handled, is intended to augment competitive analysis by ensuring that the competing views share as much information about the target as possible.

The Target

In Norfolk, Virginia, a young intelligence officer controls a Predator unmanned aerial vehicle (UAV) on patrol over Afghanistan. The Predator's video display shows a vehicle racing along a mountain road. Moving the Predator closer for a better view, the officer identifies the vehicle as a BMP, a type of armored personnel carrier. He calls in an AC-130 Spectre gunship on patrol nearby. As the AC-130 appears on the scene, the BMP lurches to a stop. The rear doors open, and the BMP disgorges Taliban soldiers running for cover. The Spectre's guns open up. In the Predator's video, the soldiers crumple one by one as the stream of gunship fire finds them.

The intelligence officer was able to order the attack by the AC-130 Spectre gunship because he had a mental picture of potential Taliban targets, and the BMP fit the picture in its location and characteristics. The BMP in Afghanistan was a specific operations target; the intelligence view of the target was much larger. It included details of the road network in Afghanistan that could support the BMP and maps delineating areas of Taliban control. A good mental model is essential when intelligence provides such close support to operations. The intelligence officer is under intense pressure to distinguish quickly between a troop carrier and a bus full of villagers, and the consequences of an error are severe.

The Target as a Complex System

As the BMP example suggests, the typical intelligence target is a *system*, not a single vehicle or building. Intelligence analysis therefore starts by thinking about the target in that fashion. A system comprises structure, function, and process, and the analyst has to deal with each of the three in systems thinking.[15] The *structure* is defined by a system's components and the relationships among them. *Function* involves the effects or results produced, that is, the outputs. *Process* refers to the sequence of events or activities that produce results. Chapter 9 discusses systems analysis in more detail.

The Escobar drug cartel is (or was) an example of a system. Figure 3-3 is a macro-level model of a cocaine cartel's structure, showing the major components and the relationships among them. Each of the components has a structure of its own, comprising subcomponents and their relationships. The coca supply component, for example, has subcomponents such as the farmers, land, seed, and farm equipment. A cocaine cartel also has several major functions, such as surviving in the face of state opposition, making a profit, and providing cocaine to its customers. Each component also has additional functions that it performs. The transportation and distribution infrastructure has the functions of getting cocaine from the processor to the customer, selling the drugs, and obtaining payment for them. As this example illustrates, most intelligence targets are systems that have subordinate systems, also called *subsystems*. The Escobar leadership comprised a subsystem whose structure included components such as security and finance; it had a function (managing the cocaine network) and a process for carrying it out.

As a counterexample, a geographic entity is not a system. A country, for example, is much too abstract a concept to be treated as a system. It does not have structure, function, or process, though it contains within it many systems that have all three. Consequently, a geographic entity could not be considered an intelligence target. The government of a region is a system—it has structure, function, and process.

Most intelligence targets are systems. Furthermore, most are *complex systems* because

- They are dynamic and evolving.
- They are nonlinear, in that they are not described adequately by a simple structure such as a tree diagram or the linear structure depicted in Figure 3-1 to illustrate the traditional intelligence cycle.

A cocaine supply network is a complex system. It is constantly evolving, and its intricate web of relationships does not yield easily to a hierarchical breakout. It can, however, usually be described as a network. Most complex systems of intelligence interest are, in fact, networks—the subject of the next section.

The Target as a Network

Though intelligence has always targeted opposing systems, it has often tended to see them as individual, rather than connected, entities. Such a narrow focus downplays the connections among organizations and individuals— connections that can be the real strength or weakness of an opposing system taken as a whole. That is why we focus on networks, which are treated in detail in chapter 10.

Networks, by definition, comprise *nodes* with *links* between them. Several types of networks have been defined, and they vary in the nature of their nodes and links. In communications networks, the nodes are points, usually

Figure 3-3   **Example Target: Cocaine Network**

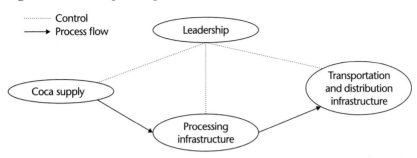

geographically separated, between which the communications are transmitted. A communications satellite and its ground terminals are communications nodes. The links are the communications means—for example, fiber optics, satellite communications, and wireless (cellular) telephones. In social networks, the nodes are people. The links show the relationships between people and usually the nature of those relationships. A social network exists, for example, at a cocktail party or in an investment club.

In this book, unless otherwise specified, *network* means a *target network* in which the nodes can be almost any kind of entity—people, places, things, concepts. A cocaine supply system is a target network. The links define relationships among the nodes. Sometimes the links quantify the relationship. Whereas communications networks and social networks are useful concepts in intelligence, the more powerful target network is a better concept for intelligence analysis and is widely used.

In intelligence, the opposing target network typically is some combination of governments; individuals; NGOs such as environmental, human rights, and religious groups; commercial firms; or illicit organizations, all tied together by some purpose, as suggested by the diagram in Figure 3-4. In conflicts, the goal of intelligence is to develop an understanding of the opposing network, so as to make the analyst's own network as effective as possible and render the opponent's network ineffective.

Analysts responsible for assessing the capabilities of an air defense network, a competing commercial firm or alliance, or a narcotics production and distribution network must take a network view. As an example, an analyst concerned with the balance of power in the Middle East might be tempted to look at Syria, Saudi Arabia, Iran, and Iraq separately. Yet no assessment of the future of the Middle East should ignore the continuing tensions among them—the constraining effects of past hostilities on any country's likely future actions and the opportunities that they provide for opponents. These individual countries are part of a larger target network bound by ties of mutual mistrust and suspicion.

Figure 3-4   Netwar Competition: Network versus Network

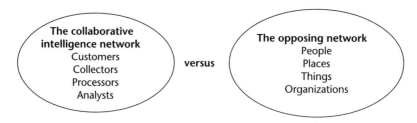

It is also important to look at both sides as networks. It may be easier, especially in a bureaucracy, to see the opponent's side as a network than to see that one's own intelligence and operational assets form a network and to fully exploit its strengths. General Stanley McChrystal, reflecting on his experiences in trying to make networks function effectively in Afghanistan, wrote that

> It takes a network to defeat a network. But fashioning ourselves to counter our enemy's network was easier said than done, especially because it took time to learn what, exactly, made a network different. As we studied, experimented, and adjusted, it became apparent that an effective network involves much more than relaying data. A true network starts with robust communications connectivity, but also leverages physical and cultural proximity, shared purpose, established decision-making processes, personal relationships, and trust. Ultimately, a network is defined by how well it allows its members to see, decide, and effectively act. But transforming a traditional military structure into a truly flexible, empowered network is a difficult process.[16]

The collaborative, collector-analyst-customer, target-centric approach creates an effective network to deal with the opposing network. Figure 3-5 shows the example of a cocaine supply target network and some components of the opposing (that is, U.S. and Colombian) intelligence customer network. As the figure indicates, it makes sense that U.S. law enforcement would target the transportation and distribution infrastructure, because much of that infrastructure is located within U.S. borders. U.S. law enforcement would not normally be able to target the cartel leadership in Colombia. Colombian law enforcement, by contrast, could target both the cartel leadership and its processing infrastructure, but it would probably find the leadership a more profitable target. The customer network shown in the figure is far from complete, of course; it might include political leadership in the United States and Colombia, for example, or regional and European government entities concerned about the cocaine trade.

Figure 3-5   Netwar Example against a Cocaine Network

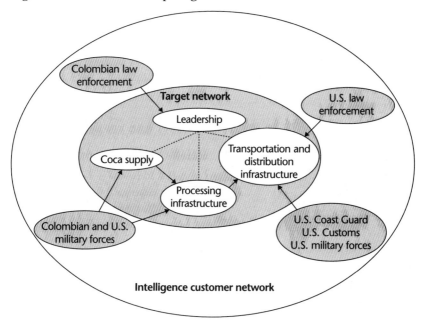

Chapter 2 introduced the concepts of netwar and the network target. Within the U.S. Department of Defense netwar has been referred to as *network-centric warfare*.[17] Defense planners have identified three themes:

- A shift in perspective from the single-node target to the network target
- A shift from viewing actors as independent to viewing them as part of a continuously adapting system
- A focus on making strategic choices to adapt—or merely to survive—in the changing system

Network-centric warfare is not a new concept in the business world.[18] Companies such as Royal Dutch Shell were creating networks of this kind, including allied outsiders, three decades ago. Participants in that network found it a powerful mechanism for bringing a wide range of expertise to bear on problems.[19] The World Wide Web has speeded the formation of such networks, and the network-centric approach has been adopted widely in the commercial world. Companies such as Cisco Systems and Wal-Mart have made the collaborative network a key part of their business strategies. In Wal-Mart's network-centric retailing approach, the company shares sales information with suppliers in near-real time so that they can better control production and distribution, as well as manage their own supply chains for Wal-Mart products.[20] Another example is the network-centric securities trading system Autobahn, created by Deutsche Morgan Grenfell.[21] Autobahn replaces the traditional, trader-centered (hierarchical) system of securities trading with a network system in which participants have equal access to securities pricing information. The advantage that the network-centric approach gives companies such as Wal-Mart and Deutsche Morgan Grenfell is that it forces their competitors to adopt similar approaches or lose out in competition.

Business intelligence is ahead of government intelligence in applying the netwar strategy. Even military organizations, with their traditions of hierarchical structure, seem to be adopting the advantages of the network structure, as General McChrystal's earlier quote illustrates. In cases when national intelligence efforts must deal with commercial entities, as they do in economic matters, weapons proliferation, and funds-laundering cases, intelligence analysts increasingly understand network-centric conflict. Furthermore, NGOs are becoming more involved in military, economic, political, and social issues worldwide, and NGO involvement usually makes any conflict network-centric, as it did with the Zapatistas in Mexico.

Any discussion of the network target should touch on *the* intelligence target of the past decade: Osama bin Laden. In person, he was a hard target to miss, being 6'5" tall and possessing a physical description that was well known throughout the world. But from 2001 to 2011, bin Laden proved to be an elusive target, almost impossible to find if considered alone. However, like Pablo Escobar, he had to run a large network and, of course, have some form of communication with it. Despite bin Laden's very good security system, intelligence analysts and collectors focused on the network as a target and were able to pinpoint his location in Abbottabad, Pakistan, in 2010–2011. The result was the SEAL Team 6 raid on May 2, 2011, that resulted in bin Laden's death.

It was a telling example of netwar in action. Even so, that it took nearly ten years for the allied intelligence services to track down bin Laden illustrates the importance of making the intelligence network as inclusive as possible. The opposing network, unfortunately, included significant elements of the Pakistani government that supported bin Laden, making allied intelligence operations in Pakistan more difficult.

Spatial and Temporal Attributes of the Target

In addition to being a system and a network, targets of intelligence interest typically have spatial and temporal attributes, and analysis must take these into account. Chapter 11 goes into detail on analyzing these attributes.

Many targets of intelligence interest are fixed geographically. These are mostly elements of a region's infrastructure. Cities and towns, lines of communication (roadways and railways), and installations all have fixed locations. The intelligence interest here is in determining their location (usually in coordinates for smaller targets) or their position on a map for lines of communication.

Many targets of interest, though, are mobile. People, ships, vehicles in general, and satellites all move in space. They may be in one place for a while, but they generally have to be characterized in both space and time.

And even fixed targets such as factories have events occurring around them, or change physically in some way. A missile silo or an airfield, for example, is fixed. But patterns of activity around the silo or airfield may indicate that something of intelligence interest is occurring. So we have to analyze even the fixed targets spatially and temporally.

Summary

Intelligence, when supporting policy or operations, is always concerned with a target. Traditionally, intelligence has been described as a cycle: a process starting from requirements, to planning or direction, collection, processing, analysis and production, dissemination, and then back to requirements. That traditional view has several shortcomings. It separates the customer from the process and intelligence professionals from one another. A gap exists in practice between dissemination and requirements. The traditional cycle is useful for describing structure and function and serves as a convenient framework for organizing and managing a large intelligence community. But it does not describe how the process works or should work.

Intelligence is in practice a nonlinear and target-centric process, operated by a collaborative team of analysts, collectors, and customers collectively focused on the intelligence target. The rapid advances in information technology have enabled this transition.

All significant intelligence targets of this target-centric process are complex systems in that they are nonlinear, dynamic, and evolving. As such, they can almost always be represented structurally as dynamic networks—opposing networks that constantly change with time. In dealing with opposing networks, the intelligence network must be highly collaborative. Historically, however, large intelligence organizations, such as those in the United States, provide disincentives to collaboration. If those disincentives can be removed, U.S. intelligence will increasingly resemble the most advanced business intelligence organizations in being both target-centric and network-centric.

Targets of intelligence interest have spatial attributes: They exist somewhere in space at a given instant. They also have temporal attributes: They move around or change as time passes. Identifying the target's location and monitoring its movements or other changes are important elements of the target-centric approach to intelligence.

Having defined the target, the first question to address is, What do we need to learn about the target that our customers do not already know? This is the intelligence problem, and for complex targets, the associated intelligence issues are also complex. The next chapter discusses how to define the intelligence issue.

Notes

1. A *dead drop* is a temporary concealment place for material that is in transit between two clandestine intelligence operatives who cannot risk a face-to-face meeting. A tin can next to a park bench or the interior of a personable robot are classic examples of dead drops.

2. David Kennedy and Leslie Brunetta, "Lebanon and the Intelligence Community," Case Study C15-88-859.0 (Cambridge, Mass.: Kennedy School of Government, Harvard University, 1988).

3. William J. Lahneman, *The Future of Intelligence Analysis*, Center for International and Security Studies at Maryland, Final Report, Vol. I (March 10, 2006), E-8.

4. Michael Herman, *Intelligence Power in Peace and War* (Cambridge, U.K.: Cambridge University Press, 1996), 100.

5. Quoted in Sherman Kent, "Producers and Consumers of Intelligence," in *Strategic Intelligence: Theory and Application*, 2nd ed., ed. Douglas H. Dearth and R. Thomas Goodden (Washington, D.C.: U.S. Army War College and Defense Intelligence Agency, 1995), 129.

6. Stew Magnuson, "Satellite Data Distribution Lagged, Improved in Afghanistan," *Space News*, September 2, 2002.

7. V. Joseph Broadwater, "I Would Make the T-PED Pain Go Away," memorandum for the record (U.S. National Reconnaissance Office, Washington, D.C., August 3, 2000, photocopy).

8. Letitia A. Long, "Activity-Based Intelligence: Understanding the Unknown," *Intelligencer: Journal of U.S. Intelligence Studies* (Fall/Winter 2013): 9.

9. Defense Intelligence Agency, "Modernizing Defense Intelligence: Object Based Production and Activity Based Intelligence" (briefing graphic), June 27, 2013, http://www.slideshare.net/RDSWEB/dia-activity-basedintelligence.

10. Mark Bowden, "A 15-Month Manhunt Ends in a Hail of Bullets," *Philadelphia Inquirer*, December 17, 2000.

11. Magnuson, "Satellite Data Distribution."

12. *Report of the Commission on the Intelligence Capabilities of the United States Regarding Weapons of Mass Destruction*, March 31, 2005, http://www.wmd.gov/report/wmd_report.pdf, 14.

13. Robert D. Steele, "The New Craft of Intelligence," February 1, 2002, http://www.strategicstudiesinstitute.army.mil/pubs/display.cfm?pubID=217.

14. Mark M. Lowenthal, "Intelligence Analysis," address to the Intelligence Community Officers' Course at CIA University, July 19, 2002.

15. Jamshid Gharajedaghi, *Systems Thinking: Managing Chaos and Complexity* (Boston: Butterworth-Heinemann, 1999), 110.

16. General (Retired) Stanley McChrystal, "It Takes a Network," *Foreign Policy*, February 21, 2011.

17. Arthur K. Cebrowski and John J. Garstka, "Network-Centric Warfare: Its Origin and Future," *Proceedings of the Naval Institute*, 124, no. 1 (1998): 28–35.

18. Liam Fahey, *Competitors* (New York: Wiley, 1999), 206.

19. Peter Schwartz, *The Art of the Long View* (New York: Doubleday, 1991), 90.

20. James F. Moore, *The Death of Competition: Leadership and Strategy in the Age of Business Ecosystems* (New York: HarperBusiness, 1996).

21. Cebrowski and Garstka, "Network-Centric Warfare."

4

Defining the Intelligence Issue

A problem well stated is a problem half solved.

Inventor Charles Franklin Kettering

The preceding chapter focused on the intelligence target—in most cases, a complex network. For such targets, there are typically several people who are interested in receiving intelligence. And these customers typically have different interests or different intelligence problems to which they want answers. The U.S. Department of Energy might be interested in Iraqi oil well activity to estimate current production; a field military commander might be interested in the same oil well activity to prevent the wellheads from being sabotaged. Therefore, all intelligence analysis efforts start with some form of problem definition.

The initial guidance that customers give analysts about an issue, however, almost always is incomplete, and it may even be unintentionally misleading. Thomas Fingar, drawing on his experience as chairman of the National Intelligence Council, cites a number of examples of flawed issue statements:

- In one case, intelligence customers were monitoring the progress of a program to protect Iraqi oil pipelines. They were pleased to note that no attacks had occurred on one pipeline segment—until an intelligence analyst posed the question that should have been part of the problem statement: Was that segment operational during the period in question? It turned out that the segment had been out of commission.[1]
- In another case, Fingar received a request from the National Security Council staff for an update on political reconciliation, economic reconstruction, and public safety in Iraq. Probing for details about this seemingly straightforward request, Fingar found that the staff director really wanted to know whether an NSC assumption—that progress on political reconciliation would facilitate progress in other areas—was supported by the evidence. (It was not.)[2]

Therefore, the first and most important step an analyst can take is to understand the issue in detail. He or she must determine why the intelligence analysis is being requested and what decisions the results will support. The success of analysis depends on an accurate issue definition. As one senior policy customer noted in commenting on intelligence failures, "Sometimes, what they [the intelligence officers] think is important is not, and what they think is not important, is."[3]

The poorly defined issue is so common that it has a name: the *framing effect*. It has been described as "the tendency to accept problems as they are presented, even when a logically equivalent reformulation would lead to diverse lines of inquiry not prompted by the original formulation."[4] We encounter it in many disciplines where the problem must be defined properly before it can be solved effectively. The classic example of framing was a 1982 study in which U.S. doctors were presented with two different formulations for the outcome of an operation. One set of doctors was informed that the operation had a 93 percent survival rate; the other set was told that the operation had a 7 percent mortality rate. Rationally, there should have been no difference in the doctors' decisions, since both statistics have the same meaning. But the doctors showed a definite preference not to operate when they were quoted a mortality rate instead of a survival rate.[5] Intelligence analysts often run afoul of the framing effect—one of the best-known examples being the National Intelligence Council's estimate on the Iraqi weapons of mass destruction program discussed in Appendix I.

For these reasons, veteran analysts go about the analysis process quite differently than do novices. At the beginning of a task, novices tend to attempt to solve the perceived customer problem immediately. Veteran analysts spend more time thinking about it to avoid the framing effect. They use their knowledge of previous cases as context for creating mental models to give them a head start in addressing the problem. Veterans also are better able to recognize when they lack the necessary information to solve a problem,[6] in part because they spend enough time at the beginning, in the problem definition phase. In the case of the complex problems discussed in this chapter, issue definition should be a large part of an analyst's work.

Issue definition is the first step in a process known as *structured argumentation*. We'll get into the details of structured argumentation in chapter 7. For now, the important thing to understand is that structured argumentation always starts by breaking down a problem into parts so that each part can be examined systematically.[7]

Statement of the Issue

In the world of scientific research, the guidelines for problem definition are that the problem should have "a reasonable expectation of results, believing that someone will care about your results and that others will be able to build upon them, and ensuring that the problem is indeed open and underexplored."[8]

Intelligence analysts should have similar goals in their profession. But this list represents just a starting point. Defining an intelligence analysis issue begins with answering five questions:

- *When is the result needed?* Determine when the product must be delivered. (Usually, the customer wants the report yesterday.) In the traditional intelligence process, many reports are delivered too late—long after the decisions have been made that generated the need—in part because the customer is isolated from the intelligence process. Also, tight deadlines are increasingly a challenge in all areas of intelligence; the customer values having precise and detailed intelligence in real time. The target-centric approach can dramatically cut the time required to get actionable intelligence to the customer because the customer is part of the process.
- *Who is the customer?* Identify the intelligence customers and try to understand their needs. The traditional process of communicating needs typically involves several intermediaries, and the needs inevitably become distorted as they move through the communications channels. Also, even if the intelligence effort is done for a single customer, the results often go to many other recipients. It helps to keep in mind these second-order customers and their needs, as well.
- *What is the purpose?* Intelligence efforts usually have one main purpose. This purpose should be clear to all participants when the effort begins and also should be clear to the customer in the result. The main purpose, for instance, might be to provide intelligence to support trade negotiations between the United States and the European Union. A number of more specific intelligence purposes support this main purpose—such as identifying likely negotiating tactics and pinpointing issues that might split the opposing negotiators. Again, customer involvement helps to make the purpose clear to the analyst.
- *What form of output, or product, does the customer want?* Written reports (now in electronic form) are standard in the intelligence business because they endure and can be distributed widely. When the result goes to a single customer or is extremely sensitive, a verbal briefing may be the form of output. Briefings have the advantage of customer interaction and feedback, along with a certainty that the intended recipient gets the message. Studies have shown that customers never read most written intelligence.[9] Subordinates may read and interpret the report, but the message tends to be distorted as a result. So briefings or (ideally) constant customer interaction with the intelligence team during the target-centric process helps to get the message through.
- *What are the real questions?* Obtain as much background knowledge as possible about the problem behind the questions the customer asks, and understand how the answers will affect organizational decisions.

The purpose of this step is to narrow the problem definition. A vaguely worded request for information is usually misleading, and the result will almost never be what the requester wanted.

Be particularly wary of a request that has come through several "nodes" in the organization. The layers of an organization, especially those of an intelligence bureaucracy, will sometimes "load" a request as it passes through with additional guidance that may have no relevance to the original customer's interests. A question that travels through several such layers often becomes cumbersome by the time it reaches the analyst. A question about the current Israeli balance of payments, for example, could wind up on the analyst's desk as instructions to prepare a complete assessment of the Israeli economy. In such situations, the analyst must go back to the originator of the request and close the loop. The problem of the corrupted communications channel is so pervasive in intelligence that it is covered in detail in chapter 7.

The request should be specific and stripped of unwanted excess. This entails focused (and perhaps repeated) interaction with the customer responsible for the original request—the executive, the policymaker, or the operations officer. Ask the customer if the request is correctly framed. The time spent focusing the request saves time later during collection and analysis. It also makes clear what questions the customer does *not* want answered—and that should set off alarm bells, as the next example illustrates.

When the United States was involved in Lebanon in 1983, U.S. policymakers did not want to hear from U.S. intelligence that there was no reasonable way to force Syrian president Hafez Al-Assad to withdraw from Lebanon.[10] The result of this disconnect between intelligence and the customer was a foreign policy debacle for the United States. On October 23, 1983, terrorists blew up the Marine barracks at Beirut International Airport with a truck bomb that killed 241 Marines. The United States subsequently withdrew from Lebanon.

Policymakers can sometimes choose not to be informed by intelligence on selected issues, as they did in Lebanon. If the issue is important enough, though, the analyst has to find a way to deal with that choice. Chapter 19 discusses how to respond when the customer is antipathetic to intelligence.

After answering these five questions, the analyst will have some form of problem statement. On large (multiweek) intelligence projects, this statement will itself be a formal product. The issue definition product helps explain the real questions and related issues. Once it is done, the analyst will be able to focus more easily on answering the questions that the customer wants answered.

The Issue Definition Product

When the final intelligence product is to be a written report, the issue definition product is usually in précis (summary, abstract, or terms of reference) form.

The précis should include the problem definition or question, notional results or conclusions, and assumptions. For large projects, many intelligence organizations require the creation of a concept paper or outline that provides the stakeholders with agreed terms of reference in précis form.

If the intelligence product is to be a briefing, a set of graphics will become the final briefing slides. If possible, the slides should be turned into a notional briefing (that is, a briefing with assumptions, notional results, and conclusions) and shown to the customer; this approach will improve the chances that the final report will address the issues in the customer's mind.

Either exercise will help all participants (customers, collectors, and analysts) understand their assignments or roles in the process. Think of it as a going-in position; no one is tied to the précis or notional presentation if the analysis later uncovers alternative approaches—as it often does.

Whether the précis approach or the notional briefing is used, the issue definition should conclude with an issue decomposition view.

Issue Decomposition

The basic technique for defining a problem in detail has had many names. Nobel laureate Enrico Fermi championed the technique of taking a seemingly intractable problem and breaking it into a series of manageable subproblems. The classic problem that Fermi posed for his students was, "How many piano tuners are there in Chicago?" The answer could be reached by using the sort of indirect approach that is common in the intelligence business: by estimating how many families were in the city, how many families in the city per piano, and how many pianos a tuner can tune a year.[11] Glenn Kent of RAND Corporation uses the name *strategies-to-task* for a similar breakout of U.S. Defense Department problems.[12] Within the U.S. intelligence community, it is sometimes referred to as *problem decomposition* or "decomposition and visualization."

Whatever the name, the process is simple: Deconstruct the highest level abstraction of the issue into its lower-level constituent functions until you arrive at the lowest level of tasks that are to be performed or subissues to be dealt with. In intelligence, the deconstruction typically details issues to be addressed or questions to be answered. Start from the problem definition statement and provide more specific details about the problem. The process defines intelligence needs from the top level to the specific task level via *taxonomy*—a classification system in which objects are arranged into natural or related groups based on some factor common to each object in the group. At the top level, the taxonomy reflects the policymaker's or decision maker's view and reflects the priorities of that customer. At the task level, the taxonomy reflects the view of the collection and analysis team. These subtasks are sometimes called key intelligence questions (KIQs) or essential elements of information (EEIs).

The issue decomposition approach has an instinctive appeal. We naturally tend to form hierarchical social arrangements and to think about issues hierarchically. Issue decomposition follows the classic method for problem solving.

It results in a requirements, or needs, hierarchy that is widely used in intelligence organizations. A few examples from different national policy problem sets will help to illustrate the technique.

Figure 4-1 shows part of an issue decomposition for political intelligence on a given country or region of the world. For simplicity, only one part of the decomposition is shown down to the lowest level.

Figure 4-1 illustrates the importance of taking the decomposition to the lowest appropriate level. The top-level question, "What is the political situation in Region *X*?" is difficult to answer without first answering the more specific questions lower down in the hierarchy, such as "What progress is being made toward reform of electoral systems?"

Another advantage of the hierarchical decomposition is that it can be used to evaluate how well intelligence has performed against specific issues or how future collection systems might perform. Again referring to Figure 4-1, it is difficult to evaluate how well an intelligence organization is answering the question, "What is the political situation in Region *X*?" It is much easier to evaluate the intelligence unit's performance in researching the transparency, honesty, and legitimacy of elections, because these are very specific issues.

Obviously there can be several different issues associated with a given intelligence target or several different targets associated with a given issue. If the request is for an overall assessment of a country's economy, rather than its political situation, then the decomposition might look very much like that shown in Figure 4-2. Because of space limitations, the bottom of the figure shows only four of thirteen question sets. At the bottom level, issues

Figure 4-1   Political Situation Issue Decomposition

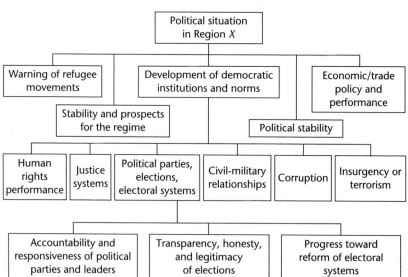

Figure 4-2 Country *X* Economic Issue Decomposition

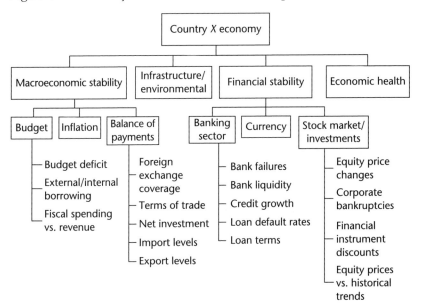

such as terms of trade and corporate bankruptcies can be addressed with relative ease, compared with high-level questions such as "What is country *X*'s financial stability?"

These two issue decompositions are examples of the sorts of issues that intelligence analysts typically encounter about a target, and both are oriented to broad information needs (here, political and economic). But the decomposition can be much more specific and more oriented to the customer's options for attacking the problem. Figure 4-3 illustrates an example—intelligence support to the design of economic sanctions against a country, the type that might have been used to design sanctions against Iraq during the 1990s. An intelligence analyst might have difficulty in directly answering this question from a policymaker: "Tell me what I need to know to develop economic sanctions against country *X*." So the analyst would create a decomposition of the issue and answer more specific questions such as, "What impact will sanctions have on the economy?" and integrate the answers to provide an answer to the top-level question.

No matter how narrow the top-level intelligence task, it can likely be broken out into an array of specific questions. If the job is to assess the capabilities of an opponent's main battle tank, then an analyst would consider the tank's speed, range, armor, and firepower. Maintenance requirements, quality of crew training, logistics, and command and control supporting the tank should also be examined. Without these less obvious components, the tank is simply an expensive piece of metal and a threat to no one.

Figure 4-3   Economic Sanctions Issue Decomposition

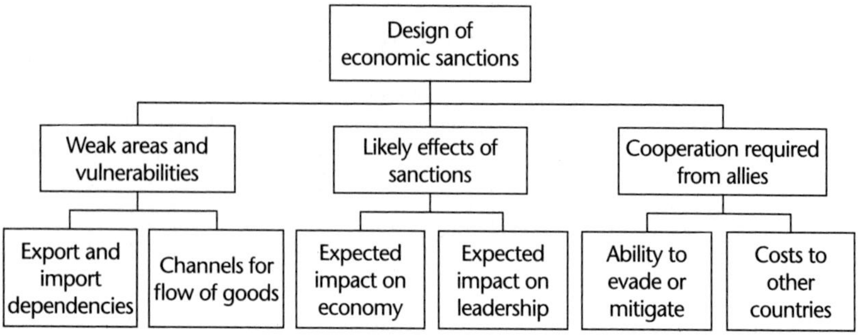

Design of economic sanctions
- Weak areas and vulnerabilities
  - Export and import dependencies
  - Channels for flow of goods
- Likely effects of sanctions
  - Expected impact on economy
  - Expected impact on leadership
- Cooperation required from allies
  - Ability to evade or mitigate
  - Costs to other countries

Complex Issue Decomposition

We have learned that the most important step in the intelligence process is to understand the issue accurately and in detail. Equally true, however, is that intelligence problems today are increasingly complex—often described as nonlinear, or "wicked." They are dynamic and evolving, and thus their solutions are, too. This makes them difficult to deal with—and almost impossible to address within the traditional intelligence cycle framework. A typical example of a wicked issue is that of a drug cartel—the cartel itself is dynamic and evolving and so are the questions being posed by intelligence consumers who have an interest in it.

A typical real-world customer's issue today presents an intelligence officer with the following challenges:[13]

- *It represents an evolving set of interlocking issues and constraints.* Only by working through the problem to get answers can one understand the ramifications. Often even when the project is complete, an analyst finds out from the customer that he or she didn't fully appreciate the issues involved. The narcotics example has an evolving set of interlocking issues and constraints. Take the constraints on possible solutions: Selectively introducing poison into the narcotics supply to frighten consumers and kill demand might reduce drug use, but it is not an acceptable option for the United States.
- *There are many stakeholders—people who care about or have something at stake in how the issue is resolved.* (Again, this makes the problem-solving process a fundamentally social one, in contrast to the antisocial traditional intelligence cycle.) The contraband narcotics problem has many stakeholders on both sides of the problem. Among the stakeholders trying to eliminate contraband narcotics are the Drug Enforcement Agency, law enforcement, U.S. customs, the military, U.S. banks, and governments in drug-producing countries. The opposing side's

stakeholders include the cartel, its supporters in the foreign government, the financial institutions that it uses for funds laundering, farmers, processors, intermediaries, street forces, and drug users. And the stakeholders each have different perspectives. Consider the Pablo Escobar example from chapter 3. From the U.S. point of view, the problem was to stem the flow of narcotics into the United States. From the Colombian government point of view, the problem was stopping the assassinations and bombings that Escobar ordered.

- *The constraints on the solution, such as limited resources and political ramifications, change over time.* The target is constantly changing, as the Escobar example illustrates, and the customers (stakeholders) change their minds, fail to communicate, or otherwise change the rules of the game. Colombians didn't want high-visibility "gringos" involved in the hunt for Escobar, though they relaxed this constraint as they gained confidence in the U.S. operatives.[14] The U.S. government didn't want to be associated with killings of Escobar's relatives, business associates, and lawyers. The result is that the issue definition is dynamic; it cannot be created once and left unchanged.

- *Because there is no final issue definition, there is no definitive solution.* The intelligence process often ends when time runs out, and the customer must act on the most currently available information. Killing Escobar did not solve the narcotics problems of the United States or Colombia. Instead the rival Cali cartel became the dominant narcotics supplier in Colombia—an example of an unintended consequence.

Harvard professor David S. Landes summarized these challenges nicely when he wrote, "The determinants of complex processes are invariably plural and interrelated."[15] Because of this—because complex or wicked problems are an evolving set of interlocking issues and constraints, and because the introduction of new constraints cannot be prevented—the decomposition of a complex problem must be dynamic; it will change with time and circumstances. As intelligence customers learn more about the targets, their needs and interests will shift.

Ideally, a complex issue decomposition should be created as a network because of the interrelationship among the elements. In Figure 4-1 the "political stability" block is related to all three of the lowest blocks under "political parties, elections, and electoral systems," though they all appear in different parts of the hierarchy; political stability being enhanced, for example, when elections are transparent, honest, and legitimate. In Figure 4-3, "Ability to evade or mitigate" sanctions is clearly related to "Expected impact on economy" or "Expected impact on leadership," though they also are in different parts of the hierarchy. Iraq's ability to evade or mitigate sanctions during the 1990s was sufficient to minimize the impact on its leadership but insufficient to keep the Iraqi economy healthy. If lines connected all of the relationships that properly exist within these figures, they would show very elaborate networks. The resulting dynamic network becomes quite intricate and difficult to manage at our present stage of information technology development.

Although the hierarchical decomposition approach may be less than ideal for complex problems, it works well enough if it is constantly reviewed and revised during the analysis process. It allows analysts to define the issue in sufficient detail and with sufficient accuracy so that the rest of the process remains relevant. There may be redundancy in a linear hierarchy, but the human mind can usually recognize and deal with the redundancy. To keep the decomposition manageable, analysts should continue to use the hierarchy, recognizing the need for frequent revisions, until information technology comes up with a better way.

Structured Analytic Methodologies for Issue Definition

Throughout the book we discuss a class of analytic methodologies that are collectively referred to as *structured analytic methodologies* or SATs. This book does not attempt to cover all of the many techniques that have been described. Issue decomposition, discussed earlier, is the most relied upon such technique for defining an intelligence issue. But two other SATs are valuable in this process as well: brainstorming and a key assumptions check.

Brainstorming

Brainstorming is commonly used in problem solving to stimulate fresh thinking. In intelligence, it can be applied in any part of the analysis process as an aid to thinking. But it is most useful in the issue definition stage at the start of an analysis project to help generate a range of hypotheses.[16] A variant of brainstorming, called *starbursting*, is derived from the idea of a six-pointed star with each point labeled with one of the words *who, what, when, where, why,* and *how.* The technique is to brainstorm by asking questions about the intelligence problem—questions that start with one of these six words.[17]

One caution about brainstorming, though. Texts on the subject usually warn not to allow criticism during the exercise. A flawed premise of brainstorming, which has been popular for over sixty years, is that criticism inhibits original thinking. Studies have shown that the opposite is true: More original ideas and fresh approaches come from team efforts when criticism is encouraged rather than suppressed.[18] So it may be more effective to allow critiques during the session. The key is to create a climate up front in which participants understand they are on the same team and that all ideas, including debate, no matter how seemingly far out, contribute to a better final product.

Brainstorming is supposed to be a group activity. But there should be no lower limit to the number of people in a brainstorming group. If it's difficult to pull together a group, brainstorming still can be an effective tactic with two people. Many a successful enterprise has begun when two people with a cocktail napkin start drawing models while they exchange ideas. And star-bursting—asking the six questions—can be done by one person, if necessary.

The goal is to stimulate new thinking, especially about hypotheses. Getting that result is more important than following a defined set of rules.

Key Assumptions Check

As noted earlier in this chapter, assumptions form a part of the issue definition. So it is important to conduct a key assumptions check during this process. A key assumption is a hypothesis that (a) has been accepted as true and (b) will be a part of the problem definition or the final assessment product. A pitfall occurs when those assumptions are not questioned or doubted at the beginning of an analysis effort, and become simply accepted as fact thereafter.

The purpose of this check then is to identify any key assumptions, question their validity and relevance, and state them explicitly only after they have been accepted. The process begins with the statement of each assumption. Then, an analyst must ask why the assumption is valid and whether it remains valid in all circumstances.

Finally, a relevancy check needs to be done. To be "key," an assumption must be essential to the analytic reasoning that follows it. That is, if the assumption turns out to be invalid, then the conclusions also probably are invalid. CIA's *Tradecraft Primer* identifies several questions that need to be asked about key assumptions:

- How much confidence exists that this assumption is correct?
- What explains the degree of confidence in the assumption?
- What circumstances or information might undermine this assumption?
- Is a key assumption more likely a key uncertainty or key factor?
- Could the assumption have been true in the past but less so now?
- If the assumption proves to be wrong, would it significantly alter the analytic line? How?
- Has this process identified new factors that need further analysis?[19]

Example: Defining the Counterintelligence Issue

To illustrate, let's take an example of an issue that has all of the challenges listed in this chapter: that of counterintelligence.

Remember: It is easy to begin with a wrong definition of the issue. If that happens, and if the definition is not revised as discussed herein, then the best analysis in the world will not avert a bad outcome. In fact, the counterintelligence issue has been poorly addressed in many countries for many years because the effort to do so began from a wrong issue definition that was never reconsidered.

Counterintelligence (CI) in government usually is thought of as having two subordinate problems: security (protecting sources and methods) and catching spies (counterespionage). CI posters, literature, and briefings inevitably focus on the spies caught—probably because their primary purpose is to discourage treason. In doing so, they're also catering to the popular media perception of counterintelligence.

If the issue is defined this way—security and counterespionage—the response in both policy and operations is defensive. Personnel background security investigations are conducted. Annual financial statements are required of all employees. Profiling is used to detect unusual patterns of computer use that might indicate computer espionage. Cipher-protected doors, badges, personal identification numbers, and passwords are used to ensure that only authorized persons have access to sensitive intelligence. The focus of communications security is on denial, typically by encryption. Leaks of intelligence are investigated to identify their source.

But whereas the focus on security and counterespionage is basically defensive, the first rule of strategic conflict is that *the offense always wins*. So, for intelligence purposes, you're starting out on the wrong path if the issue decomposition starts with managing security and catching spies. The Iraqi WMD Commission recognized this flawed approach when it observed that U.S. counterintelligence has been criticized as being focused almost exclusively on counter-HUMINT, that is, on catching spies.[20]

A better issue definition approach starts by considering the real target of counterintelligence: the opponent's intelligence organization. Good counterintelligence requires good analysis of the hostile intelligence services. As we will see in several examples later in this book, if you can model an opponent's intelligence system, you can defeat it. So we start with the target as the core of the problem and begin an issue decomposition. Figure 4-4 illustrates the result: a simple first-level issue decomposition.

If the counterintelligence issue is defined in this fashion, then the counterintelligence response will be forward-leaning and will focus on managing foreign intelligence perceptions through a combination of covert action, denial, and deception. The best way to win the CI conflict is to go on the offensive (model the target, anticipate the opponent's actions, and defeat him or her). Instead of denying information to the opposing side's intelligence

Figure 4-4   Counterintelligence Issue Decomposition

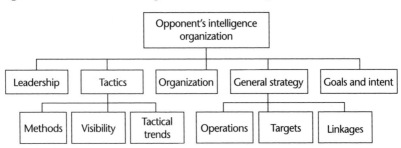

machine, for example, you feed it false information that eventually degrades the leadership's confidence in its intelligence services.

To do this, one needs a model of the opponent's intelligence system that can be subjected to target-centric analysis, including its communications channels and nodes, its requirements and targets, and its preferred sources of intelligence. How one uses such a model is discussed in the next chapter.

Summary

Before beginning intelligence analysis, the analyst must understand the customer's issue. This usually involves close interaction with the customer until the important issues are identified. The problem then has to be deconstructed in an issue decomposition process so that collection, synthesis, and analysis can be effective.

All significant intelligence issues, however, are complex and nonlinear. The complex problem is a dynamic set of interlocking issues and constraints with many stakeholders and no definitive solution. Although the linear issue decomposition process is not an optimal way to approach such problems, it can work if it is reviewed and updated frequently during the analysis process.

Along with decomposition, two other structured analytic methodologies are useful for issue definition. Brainstorming stimulates fresh thinking about the issue. Its variant, starbursting, has participants ask questions that start with *who, what, when, where, why,* and *how.*

Issue definition is the first step in a process known as structured argumentation. As an analyst works through this process, he or she collects and evaluates relevant information, fitting it into a target model (which may or may not look like the issue decomposition); this part of the process is discussed in chapters 5–7. The analyst identifies information gaps in the target model and plans strategies to fill them—the subject of chapter 20. The analysis of the target model then provides answers to the questions posed in the issue definition process. The next chapter discusses the concept of a model and how it is analyzed.

Notes

1. Thomas Fingar, "Analysis in the U.S. Intelligence Community: Missions, Masters, and Methods," in *Intelligence Analysis: Behavioral and Social Scientific Foundations,* ed. Baruch Fischoff and Cherie Chauvin (Washington, D.C.: National Academies Press, 2011), 10.
2. Ibid.
3. Stew Magnuson, "Satellite Data Distribution Lagged, Improved in Afghanistan," *Space News,* September 2, 2002, 6.
4. Matthew Herbert, "The Intelligence Analyst as Epistemologist," *International Journal of Intelligence and CounterIntelligence,* 19, no. 4 (December 2006): 666–684.
5. Barbara J. McNeill, Stephen G. Paulker, and Amos Tversky, "On the Framing of Medical Decisions," in *Decision Making: Descriptive, Normative, and Prescriptive Interactions,* ed. David E. Bell, Howard Raiffa, and Amos Tversky (Cambridge, U.K.: Cambridge University Press, 1988), 562–568.

6. Rob Johnson, *Analytic Culture in the US Intelligence Community* (Washington, D.C.: Center for the Study of Intelligence, CIA, 2005), 64.

7. Jill Jermano, *Introduction to Structured Argumentation*, DARPA Project Genoa Technical Report, May 2002.

8. Robert W. Lucky, "In Research, the Problem is the Problem," *IEEE Spectrum* (July 2011): 30.

9. Jack Davis, *Intelligence Changes in Analytic Tradecraft in CIA's Directorate of Intelligence* (Washington, D.C.: CIA Directorate of Intelligence, April 1995), 2.

10. David Kennedy and Leslie Brunetta, "Lebanon and the Intelligence Community," Case Study C15-88-859.0 (Cambridge, Mass.: Kennedy School of Government, Harvard University, 1988), 15.

11. Hans Christian von Baeyer, *The Fermi Solution* (Portland, Ore.: Random House, 1993).

12. Glenn Kent and William Simon, *New Challenges for Defense Planning: Rethinking How Much Is Enough* (Santa Monica, Calif.: RAND, 1994).

13. E. Jeffrey Conklin, "Wicked Problems and Fragmentation," CogNexus Institute, March 24, 2003, www.cognexus org/wpf/wickedproblems.pdf.

14. Mark Bowden, "Martinez Pushes Ahead with the Hunt," *Philadelphia Inquirer*, December 3, 2000.

15. David S. Landes, *The Wealth and Poverty of Nations* (New York: Norton, 1998), 577.

16. CIA, *A Tradecraft Primer: Structured Analytic Techniques for Improving Intelligence Analysis* (Washington, D.C.: Author, March 2009), 27.

17. Richards J. Heuer Jr. and Randolph H. Pherson, *Structured Analytic Techniques for Intelligence Analysis* (Washington, D.C.: CQ Press, 2011), 102.

18. Jonah Lehrer, "Groupthink," *New Yorker*, January 30, 2012, 22–27.

19. CIA, *A Tradecraft Primer*, 7.

20. *Report of the Commission on the Intelligence Capabilities of the United States Regarding Weapons of Mass Destruction*, March 31, 2005, chapter 11.

5

Conceptual Frameworks
for Intelligence Analysis

*If we are to think seriously about the world, and act effectively in
it, some sort of simplified map of reality . . . is necessary.*

Samuel P. Huntington, *The Clash of
Civilizations and the Remaking of World Order*

The introduction in chapter 1 stressed that analysis must have a conceptual framework for crafting the analytic product. "Balance of power," for example, was an important conceptual framework used by policymakers during the Cold War. A different conceptual framework has been proposed for assessing the influence that one country can exercise over another.[1] This chapter describes a two-step general conceptual framework for applying the target-centric approach. The first step is to view the target from specific analytic perspectives. The second is to create a model of the target. Let's start with the perspectives.

Analytic Perspectives—PMESII

In chapter 2, we discussed the instruments of national power—an *actions* view that defines the diplomatic, information, military, and economic (DIME) actions that executives, policymakers, and military or law enforcement officers can take to deal with a situation.

The customer of intelligence may have those four "levers" that can be pulled, but intelligence must be concerned with the *effects* of pulling those levers. Viewed from an effects perspective, there are usually six factors to consider: political, military, economic, social, infrastructure, and information, abbreviated *PMESII*. "Social" and "infrastructure" are not considered actions that can be taken but are in the category of *effects* of actions.[2] So which construct you use depends on whether you're thinking about

Figure 5-1   The PMESII Perspective

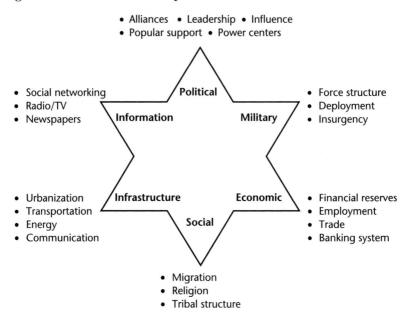

actions (DIME) or effects (PMESII). Policymakers and military command-ers naturally tend to think about actions. Intelligence analysts have to think about both the opponent's actions and the effects of customer actions. So in intelligence, and in this book, we'll take the view of PMESII as factors to address.

Figure 5-1 illustrates the PMESII perspective as a six-pointed star, with some examples of factors that might be of intelligence interest within each point of the star for a given national government. The examples in Figure 5-1 are far from exhaustive for a government, and they would look somewhat different if our focus were on an insurgent group or a transnational crimi-nal organization. Following is a more detailed explanation of what each point encompasses, with some typical questions that might be asked of the analyst:

- *Political.* Describes the distribution of responsibility and power at all levels of governance—formally constituted authorities, as well as infor-mal or covert political powers. (Who are the tribal leaders in the village? Which political leaders have popular support? Who exercises decision-making or veto power in a government, insurgent group, commercial entity, or criminal enterprise?)

- *Military.* Explores the military and/or paramilitary capabilities or other ability to exercise force of all relevant actors (enemy, friendly, and neutral) in a given region or for a given issue. (What is the force structure of the opponent? What weaponry does the insurgent group possess? What is the accuracy of the rockets that Hamas intends to use against Israel? What enforcement mechanisms are drug cartels using to protect their territories?)
- *Economic.* Encompasses individual and group behaviors related to producing, distributing, and consuming resources. (What is the unemployment rate? Which banks are supporting funds laundering? What are Egypt's financial reserves? What are the profit margins in the heroin trade?)
- *Social.* Describes the cultural, religious, and ethnic makeup within an area and the beliefs, values, customs, and behaviors of society members. (What is the ethnic composition of Nigeria? What religious factions exist there? What key issues unite or divide the population?)
- *Infrastructure.* Details the composition of the basic facilities, services, and installations needed for the functioning of a community, business enterprise, or society in an area. (What are the key modes of transportation? Where are the electric power substations? Which roads are critical for food supplies?)[3]
- *Information.* Explains the nature, scope, characteristics, and effects of individuals, organizations, and systems that collect, process, disseminate, or act on information. (How much access does the local population have to news media or the Internet? What are the cyber attack and defense capabilities of the Saudi government? How effective would attack ads be in Japanese elections?)

The typical intelligence problem seldom must deal with only one of these factors or systems. Complex issues are likely to involve them all. The events of the Arab Spring in 2011, the Syrian uprising that began that year, and the Ukrainian crisis of 2014 involved all of the PMESII factors. But PMESII is also relevant in issues that are not necessarily international. Law enforcement must deal with them all (in this case, "military" refers to the use of violence or armed force by criminal elements).

The target-centric model becomes critical here. But issue definition becomes tougher, and you need a systematic approach. The PMESII perspective results in the creation of several distinct models, as the example later in this chapter shows.

Modeling the Intelligence Target

The previous section discussed the PMESII conceptual framework for looking at an intelligence target from different perspectives. Now let's turn to the concept of *modeling* the target.

The target-centric approach and the issue definition process described in chapter 4 naturally lead to the creation of a model of the target, if the model does not already exist. Models are used so extensively in intelligence that analysts seldom give them much thought, even as they use them. Consider the following examples:

- Imagery analysts can recognize a nuclear fuel reprocessing facility because they have a mental model of typical facility details, such as the use of heavy reinforced concrete to shield against intense gamma radiation.
- In SIGINT, a communications or radar signal has standard parameters—it can be recognized because it fits an existing model in its radio frequency, its modulation parameters, and its modes of operation.
- Clandestine or covert radio communications signals can be recognized because they fit a specific model: They are designed to avoid interception, such as by using very short (burst) transmissions or jumping rapidly from one radio frequency to another.
- Economic analysts recognize a deteriorating economy because they have a checklist (a simple form of model) of indicators, such as budget deficit, balance of payments, and inflation. The economic issue decomposition shown in Figure 4-2 provides such a checklist.

The model paradigm is a powerful tool in many disciplines. As political scientist Samuel P. Huntington noted in the quote that begins this chapter, "if we are to think seriously about the world, and act effectively in it, some sort of simplified map of reality, some theory, concept, model, paradigm, is necessary."[4] Former national intelligence officer Paul Pillar described them as "guiding images" that policymakers rely on in making decisions.[5] We've discussed one guiding image—that of the PMESII concept. The second guiding image—that of a map, theory, concept, or paradigm—in this book is merged into a single entity called a *model*.

Or, as the CIA's *Tradecraft Primer* puts it succinctly:

all individuals assimilate and evaluate information through the medium of "mental models. . . ."[6]

Modeling is usually thought of as being quantitative and using computers. However, all models start in the human mind. Modeling does not always require a computer, and many useful models exist only on paper. Models are used widely in fields such as operations research and systems analysis. With modeling, one can analyze, design, and operate complex systems. One can use simulation models to evaluate real-world processes that are too complex to analyze with spreadsheets or flowcharts (which are themselves models, of course) to test hypotheses at a fraction of the cost of undertaking the actual activities. Models are an efficient communication tool for showing how the target functions and stimulating creative thinking about how to deal with an opponent.

Models are essential when dealing with complex targets (Analysis Principle 5-1). Without a device to capture the full range of thinking and creativity that occurs in the target-centric approach to intelligence, an analyst would have to keep in mind far too many details. Furthermore, in the target-centric approach, the customer of intelligence is part of the collaborative process. Presented with a model as an organizing construct for thinking about the target, customers can contribute pieces to the model from their own knowledge—pieces that the analyst might be unaware of. The primary suppliers of information (the collectors) can do likewise.

Analysis Principle 5-1 ●————————————————————————

The Essence of Intelligence

All intelligence involves creating a *model* of the target and extracting knowledge therefrom. (So does all problem solving.)

Because the model concept is fundamental to everything that follows, it is important to define it.

The Concept of a Model

A model, as used in intelligence, is an organizing constraint. It is a combination of facts, hypotheses, and assumptions about a target, developed in a form that is useful for analyzing the target and for customer decision making (producing actionable intelligence). The type of model used in intelligence typically comprises facts, hypotheses, and assumptions, so it's important to distinguish them here:

- *Fact.* Something that is indisputably the case.
- *Hypothesis.* A proposition that is set forth to explain developments or observed phenomena. It can be posed as conjecture to guide research (a *working hypothesis*) or accepted as a highly probable conclusion from established facts.
- *Assumption.* A thing that is accepted as true or as certain to happen, without proof.

These are the things that go into a model. *But,* it is important to distinguish them when you present the model. Customers should never wonder whether they are hearing facts, hypotheses, or assumptions.

Figure 5-2   The Model Hierarchy

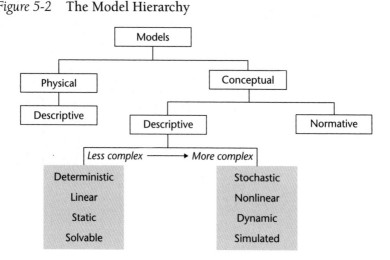

A model is a replica or representation of an idea, an object, or an actual system. It often describes how a system behaves. Instead of interacting with the real system, an analyst can create a model that corresponds to the actual one in certain ways. For example, results of a political poll are a model of how a population feels about a topic; today's weather map is a model of how the weather is expected to behave.

Figure 5-2 shows a hierarchy of models and forms the basis for the discussion that follows. As the figure indicates, models can be classified as physical or conceptual (abstract).

A *physical model* is a tangible representation of something. A map, a globe, a calendar, and a clock are all physical models. The first two represent the Earth or parts of it, and the latter two represent time. Physical models are always descriptive.

Conceptual models—inventions of the mind—are essential to the analytic process. They allow the analyst to describe things or situations in abstract terms both for estimating current situations and for predicting future ones. A conceptual model is not a tangible item, although it may be represented in tangible form. Mathematical models are conceptual; they can be created entirely in the mind. But they can be represented in tangible from by writing the equations on a sheet of paper. A conceptual model may be either descriptive, describing what it represents, or normative. A normative model may contain some descriptive segments, but its purpose is to describe a best, or preferable, course of action. A decision-support model—that is, a model used to choose among competing alternatives—is normative.

In intelligence analysis, the models of most interest are conceptual and descriptive rather than normative. Some common traits of these conceptual models follow.

- *Descriptive models can be deterministic or stochastic.*

  In a deterministic model the relationships are known and specified explicitly. A model that has any uncertainty incorporated into it is a stochastic model (meaning that probabilities are involved), even though it may have deterministic properties.[7] Consider the anecdote about drug kingpin Pablo Escobar described in chapter 3. A model of the home in which Escobar was located, and the surrounding buildings, would have been deterministic—the details were known and specified exactly. A model of the people expected to be in the house at the time of the attack would have been stochastic, because the presence or absence of Escobar and his family could not be known in advance; it could only be estimated as a probability.

- *Descriptive models can be linear or nonlinear.*

  Linear models use only linear equations (for example, $x = Ay + B$) to describe relationships. It is not necessary that the situation itself be linear, only that it be capable of description by linear equations. The number of automobiles produced in an assembly line, for example, is a linear function of time. In contrast, nonlinear models use any type of mathematical function. Because nonlinear models are more difficult to work with and are not always capable of being analyzed, the usual practice is to make some compromises so that a linear model can be used. It is important to be able to justify doing so, because most real-world intelligence targets are complex, or nonlinear. A combat simulation model is nonlinear because the interactions among the elements are complex and do not change in ways that can be described by linear equations. Attrition rates in combat, for example, vary nonlinearly with time and the status of remaining military forces. A model of an economy is inherently nonlinear, but the econometric models used to describe an economy are simplified to a set of linear equations to facilitate a solution.

- *Descriptive models can be static or dynamic.*

  A static model assumes that a specific time period is being analyzed and the state of nature is fixed for that time period. Static models ignore time-based variances. For example, one cannot use them to determine the impact of an event's timing in relation to other events. Returning to the example of a combat model, a snapshot of the combat that shows where opposing forces are located and their directions of movement at that instant is static. Static models do not take into account the synergy of the components of a system, where the actions of separate elements can have a different effect on the system than the sum of their individual effects would indicate. Spreadsheets and most relationship models are static.

A dynamic model, by contrast, considers several time periods and does not ignore the impact of an action in time period 1 on time period 2. A combat simulation model is dynamic; the loss of a combat unit in time period 1 affects all succeeding time periods. Dynamic modeling (also known as simulation) is a software representation of the time-based behavior of a system. Where a static model involves a single computation of an equation, a dynamic model is iterative; it constantly recomputes its equations as time changes. It can predict the outcomes of possible courses of action and can account for the effects of variances or randomness. One cannot control the occurrence of random events. One can, however, use dynamic modeling to predict the likelihood and the consequences of their occurring. Process models usually are dynamic because they envision flows of material, the passage of time, and feedback. Structural and functional models are usually static, though they can be dynamic.

- *Descriptive models can be solvable or simulated.*
  A solvable model is one in which there is an analytic way of finding the answer. The performance model of a radar, a missile, or a warhead is a solvable problem. But other problems require such a complicated set of equations to describe them that there is no way to solve them. Worse still, complex problems typically cannot be described in a manageable set of equations. In complex cases—such as the performance of an economy or a person—one can turn to simulation.

  Simulation involves designing a model of a system and performing experiments on it. The purpose of these "what if" experiments is to determine how the real system performs and to predict the effect of changes to the system as time progresses. For example, an analyst can use simulation to answer questions such as these: What is the expected balance of trade worldwide next year? What are the likely areas of deployment for mobile surface-to-air missiles in country *X*? What is the expected yield of the nuclear warheads on country *Y*'s new medium-range ballistic missiles?

Using Target Models for Analysis

Often, particularly in military combat or law enforcement operations, the creation and analysis of a target model is a quick and intuitive process. Let's begin with a simple example, one that is relevant to military combat operations.

Consider the BMP personnel carrier racing along an Afghan mountain road that was described in chapter 3. The problem definition in that example was very simple: locate Taliban forces in the region so that the Spectre gunship can neutralize them. This time, however, the intelligence officer has an additional problem: He must determine when the BMP will reach a nearby village, where a Doctors Without Borders team is currently providing medical assistance.

The officer has a mental model of the BMP's performance; he knows its maximum speed on typical mountain roads. He has the Predator's information giving the present position of the BMP. And he has a map—a geographic model—that allows him to determine the distance between the BMP's present position and the village. Combining these models and performing a simple computation (analysis), he produces a predictive *scenario* (a combination of several models into a more comprehensive target model), concluding that the BMP will arrive in the village in twenty-five minutes and the Doctors Without Borders team will be toast unless the Spectre gunship arrives first.

Where the intelligence customer is a national leader, policymaker, law enforcement, or business executive, the analysis process is typically more deliberate than in this example. Consider the intelligence problems defined in the issue decompositions of Figures 4-1 and 4-2. The issue decomposition in both cases, when populated with specific intelligence, is also a type of target model that can serve many purposes. It can be used as a basis for requesting intelligence collection on specific topics shown in the boxes at the bottom level of the diagrams—a subject explored in detail in chapter 20. And it can be a framework in which to incorporate incoming intelligence—a subject discussed in chapter 7.

To illustrate, let's use the issue decomposition of a country's economy shown in Figure 4-2 and focus on one part of the overall economy: the country's financial stability, specifically the stability of the banking sector. You have five components that contribute to an assessment of the banking sector: bank failures, bank liquidity, credit growth, loan default rates, and loan terms. Most of these components can be described effectively by a simple type of model that is discussed in chapter 6: a temporal graphic. Using the available raw intelligence information, you draw curves showing the following:

- Bank failures over the past few years (a flat curve)
- Bank liquidity over the same time period (decreasing steadily)
- Credit growth (rising sharply)
- Loan default rates (stable until last year, and then started increasing)

You can also prepare another type of model, a comparative graphic that shows how loan terms compare to those offered by other countries (terms are much more favorable to lenders in the target country).

Combining all of these models into an overall picture of the banking sector, you can observe that although bank failures have been stable so far, the future does not look good. All of the other components of the model are showing unfavorable trends. On the basis of past experience, you can analyze the models to create a predictive model—another scenario—which indicates bank failures will rise dramatically in the near future, and the banking sector of the economy is headed for serious trouble.

This example illustrates how the issue decomposition is closely related to the target model, and can also be used to structure or organize the target model. Part II of this book explores the target model in more detail and illustrates the types of models that are used in analysis. Part III is devoted to analysis methodologies that use models—especially predictive methodologies.

Modeling Using PMESII

The preceding sections introduced the PMESII analytic perspective and the concept of modeling the intelligence target. Before going into how we analyze models, let's examine how these two concepts work together. We can create many models of a typical intelligence target such as a government, depending on the intelligence issue (chapter 3). Let's pick the state of Azerbaijan and look at a few of the possible models that we might need to use to address a specific issue: What are the possible "levers" that could be used to influence actions by the Azerbaijani government? Following the PMESII perspective, some possible models that might be constructed are described in the sections that follow—the set of models is far from complete, of course.

Political Model

The Azeri government, which eliminated presidential term limits in a 2009 referendum, has been accused of authoritarianism. President Ilham Aliyev appears to be firmly in charge. One could develop models of the political support that Aliyev has, his control over the judiciary and legislature, or government links with criminal elements, for example. One example model that is useful for assessing points of influence is a display of Azerbaijan's diplomatic ties with other countries, shown in Figure 5-3. The figure might be used as a starting point for analyzing the nature of Azerbaijan's diplomatic relationships for possible relationships that could be used to exert influence. It shows a few points of analytic interest: Azerbaijan does not have diplomatic relations with Armenia or the Republic of Somaliland, for example. That isn't greatly surprising; Azerbaijan has an unresolved conflict with Armenia, and Somaliland is generally considered to be part of Somalia, not a separate country. More surprising is that Azerbaijan is one of the few majority Muslim countries to have bilateral strategic and economic relations with Israel—a topic we revisit in the military model, next. The map shows that Azerbaijan has diplomatic relations with Tehran, but the relationships are strained because of Iran's support for the Armenians and Azerbaijan's connections to Israel.

Figure 5-3   Countries Having Diplomatic Relations with Azerbaijan

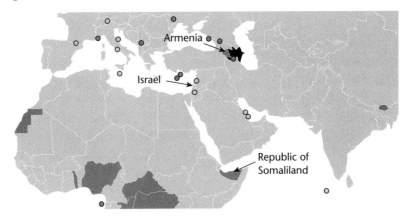

Military Model

Military models could describe deployments, mix of weaponry, or performance of weapons (aircraft, naval vessels, armored vehicles, artillery, air defense systems), for example. In the case of Azerbaijan, its military model is shaped by an unresolved conflict with Armenia over Nagorno-Karabakh, a primarily Armenian-populated region currently controlled by Armenia. Armenia and Azerbaijan began fighting over the area in 1988, and a tenuous cease-fire has existed since 1994. Figure 5-4 shows a model of key cooperative relationships between the Azerbaijani military and other countries that specifically addresses the question of levers of influence. In the figure, the thickness of the connection indicates the strength of the relationship:

- Russia is Azerbaijan's main arms supplier. Military and technical cooperation between the two is estimated to be about $4 billion.
- Turkey has provided Azerbaijan with a mix of light weaponry and other military equipment along with professional training for the Azerbaijani military. Turkey has agreed to provide troops if necessary in the event of a resumption of hostilities between Azerbaijan and Armenia over Nagorno-Karabakh.
- Azerbaijan and Israel cooperate in several areas of the defense industry, with Azerbaijan acquiring Israeli technology such as a capability to produce military UAVs.

- The North Atlantic Treaty Organization (NATO) assists Azerbaijan in defense organizational reforms.
- The United States has agreements providing for military cooperation with Azerbaijan, including special forces assistance.

Figure 5-4   Cooperative Relationships of the Azerbaijani Armed Forces

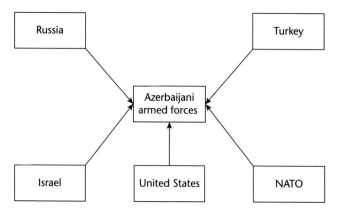

Economic Model

Azerbaijan has experienced high economic growth thanks to large and growing oil and gas exports. The model in Figure 5-5 illustrates this point and, in conjunction with the infrastructure model of Figure 5-7, suggests possible points of economic influence. One could model several of the nonexport sectors that have also experienced double-digit growth, including construction, banking, and real estate. Other economic models might track changes in gross domestic product (GDP), unemployment, inflation rate, or public debt to identify areas in which economic influence might be applied.

Social Model

Azerbaijan is a nation with a majority-Turkic and majority-Shiite Muslim population. Corruption and criminal activity are natural subjects for modeling as both are common throughout the country. Several ethnic groups exist, as illustrated in the ethnic model of Figure 5-6. This particular model could be useful in assessing influence actions involving the Armenians, a persecuted group, or restive groups such as the Talysh and Lezgins. A different model might take into account religious entities that support or oppose the government.

Figure 5-5   Petroleum Production and Consumption in Azerbaijan, 2003–2013

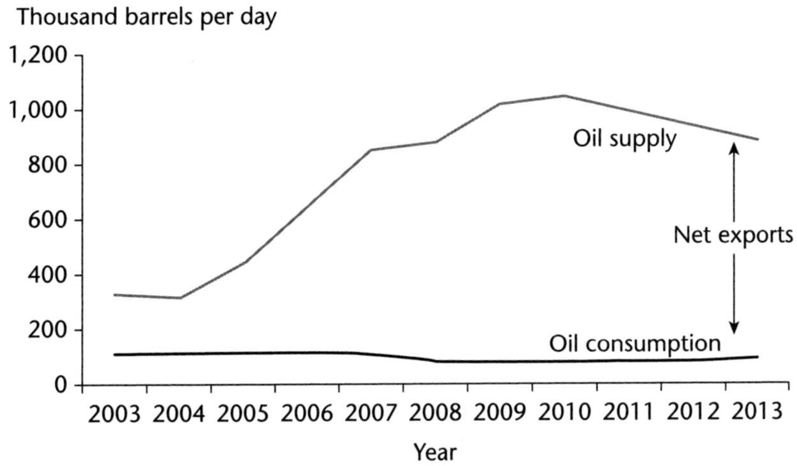

Thousand barrels per day

Source: "Azerbaijan International Energy Data and Analysis," U.S. Energy Information Administration, August 2014, https://www.eia.gov/beta/international/analysis_includes/countries_long/Azerbaijan/azerbaijan.pdf.

Note: 2013 data are preliminary estimates.

Infrastructure Model

Figure 5-5 illustrated the economic benefits of oil exports to Azerbaijan and their contributions to GDP. Oil exports through the Baku-Tbilisi-Ceyhan, Baku-Novorossiysk, and Baku-Supsa pipelines remain the main economic driver; these networks are illustrated in the infrastructure model of Figure 5-7.

Information Model

Figure 5-8 is an example of an information model. It shows the trend in Internet access for Azerbaijan. As the figure shows, access is growing steadily, partly as a result of the country's national strategy: creating an information and communications technology hub for the Caucasus region. Consequently, the Internet is mostly free from systematic government filtering or blocking. The government does not, however, tolerate political opposition postings online. The graphic is relevant in assessing the possible use of information operations as an information "lever" of influence.

These are fairly straightforward examples of a few models that illustrate the use of modeling across all of the PMESII perspectives. Again, many more such models would be needed to provide a detailed picture that addresses the question of levers of influence.

Figure 5-6   Ethnic Model of Azerbaijan

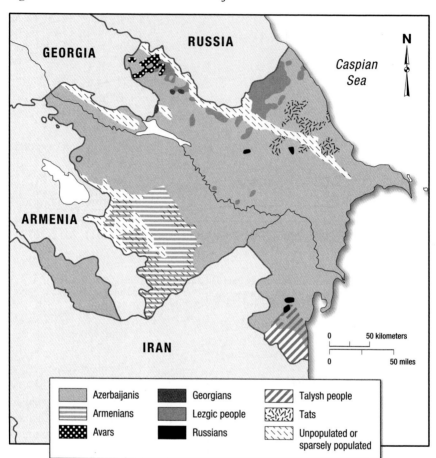

As another example of how a target model can be analyzed and used in
policymaking and policy execution, let's revisit the counterintelligence analysis
problem.

Using Models in Analysis

In chapter 4, we examined a simple counterintelligence (CI) issue decomposition model that has as its target a foreign intelligence service. We begin from
the block in Figure 4-4 labeled "General strategy" of the organization, which

Figure 5-7   Oil and Natural Gas Structure in Azerbaijan

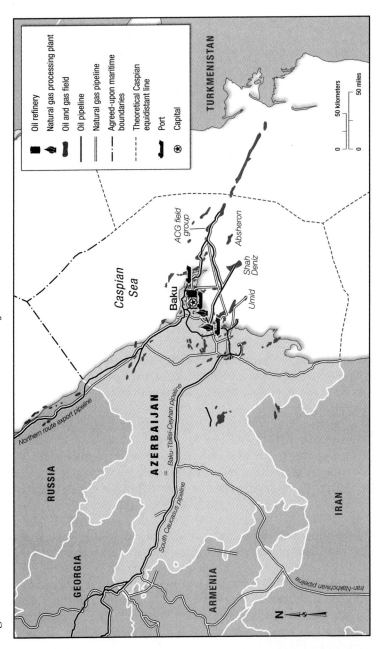

Source: "Azerbaijan International Energy Data and Analysis," U.S. Energy Information Administration, August 2014, https://www.eia.gov/beta/international/analysis_includes/countries_long/Azerbaijan/azerbaijan.pdf; U.S. Geological Survey, IHS EDIN.

Figure 5-8   Percentage of Internet Users in Azerbaijan by Year

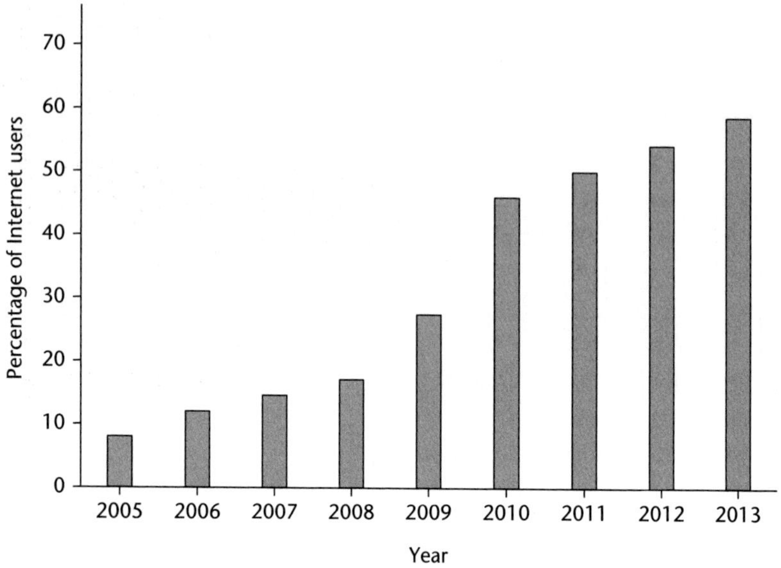

Source: Created by the author from United Nations statistical reporting, http://data.un.org/Data
.aspx?d=WDI&f=Indicator_Code%3AIT.NET.USER.P2.

has three subcategories—targets, operations, and linkages (to other intelligence services). The following section illustrates some example analyses of these subcategories taken from the target model, followed by two examples of the possible responses that analysis supports.

Note that this would be classified as an information model; it deals with how some governments obtain intelligence, or information. The model is exemplary and fairly basic; a complete analysis of the CI model would be far more detailed.

Targets

Most intelligence services have preferred strategic targets that closely align with their national interests. As examples, consider four countries with sizeable intelligence services having different targets: Russia, China, France, and Germany.

- Countries such as France and Germany are concerned with combating terrorism and promoting their economies through exports. So they focus on terrorism and economic intelligence.[8]
- China is particularly concerned with regional military threats, causing Chinese intelligence to target Taiwan. China also has a national interest in acquiring technology to develop both military and commercial strength.[9] So a major part of Chinese intelligence efforts focuses on acquiring advanced technology, especially from the United States.[10]

- Russia's priorities center on internal security (particularly against terrorist threats), and political, economic, and military events in neighboring countries, especially former Soviet republics. The Russian intelligence services divide these targets, with the SVU (successor to the KGB) going after political and economic targets, and the Main Intelligence Directorate (Glavnoye Razvedovatel'noye Upravlenie, or GRU) going after military targets.

Operations

Intelligence services prefer specific sources of intelligence, shaped in part by what has worked for them in the past; by their strategic targets; and by the size of their pocketbooks. The poorer intelligence services rely heavily on open source (including the web) and HUMINT, because both are relatively inexpensive. COMINT also can be cheap, unless it is collected by satellites. The wealthier services also make use of satellite-collected imagery intelligence (IMINT) and COMINT, and other types of technical collection.

- France and Germany make use of technical collection, including COMINT and computer intrusion techniques.[11] They are well equipped to do COMINT, because two of the premier COMINT hardware developers are located in France (Thales) and Germany (Rohde & Schwartz).
- China relies heavily on HUMINT, working through commercial organizations, particularly trading firms, students, and university professors far more than most other major intelligence powers do.[12]

In addition to being acquainted with opponents' collection habits, CI also needs to understand a foreign intelligence service's analytic capabilities. Many services have analytic biases, are ethnocentric, or handle anomalies poorly. It is important to understand their intelligence communications channels and how well they share intelligence within the government. In many countries, the senior policymaker or military commander is the analyst. That provides a prime opportunity for "perception management," especially if a narcissistic leader like Hitler, Stalin, or Saddam Hussein is in charge and doing his own analysis. Leaders and policymakers find it difficult to be objective; they are people of action, and they always have an agenda. They have lots of biases and are prone to wishful thinking.

Linkages

Almost all intelligence services have liaison relationships with foreign intelligence or security services. It is important to model these relationships because they can dramatically extend the capabilities of an intelligence service.

- During the Cold War, the Soviet Union had extensive liaison relationships with the intelligence services of its East European satellites. The Soviet intelligence services, however, were always the dominant players in the relationships. Since the breakup of the Soviet Union, Russia has been slowly developing new liaison relationships with some of the former Soviet republics.

- France and Germany share intelligence both directly and through NATO, and they have intelligence liaison arrangements with selected other countries.
- In the area of law enforcement, many countries share intelligence via Interpol, the international organization created to facilitate cross-border police cooperation.

Summary

Two conceptual frameworks are invaluable for doing intelligence analysis. One deals with the instruments of national or organizational power and the effects of their use. The second involves the use of target models to produce analysis.

The intelligence customer has four instruments of national or organizational power, as discussed in chapter 2. Intelligence is concerned with how opponents will use those instruments and the effects that result when customers use them. Viewed from both the opponent's actions and the effects perspectives, there are usually six factors to consider: political, military, economic, social, infrastructure, and information, abbreviated PMESII:

- *Political*. The distribution of power and control at all levels of governance.
- *Military*. The ability of all relevant actors (enemy, friendly, and neutral) to exercise force.
- *Economic*. Behavior relating to producing, distributing, and consuming resources.
- *Social*. The cultural, religious, and ethnic composition of a region and the beliefs, values, customs, and behaviors of people.
- *Infrastructure*. The basic facilities, services, and installations needed for the functioning of a community or society.
- *Information*. The nature, scope, characteristics, and effects of individuals, organizations, and systems that collect, process, disseminate, or act on information.

All intelligence involves extracting knowledge from a model of the target. Models in intelligence are typically conceptual and descriptive. The easiest ones to work with are deterministic, linear, static, solvable, or some combination. Unfortunately, in the intelligence business the target models tend to be stochastic, nonlinear, dynamic, and simulated.

From an existing knowledge base, a model of the target is developed. Next, the model is analyzed to extract information for customers or for additional collection. The "model" of complex targets will typically be a collection of associated models that can serve the purposes of intelligence customers and collectors. The models can be created relying on any of the PMESII factors or can be a composite of several factors.

Notes

1. Jason U. Manosevitz, "Needed: More Thinking about Conceptual Frameworks for Analysis—The Case of Influence," *Studies in Intelligence*, 57, no. 4 (December 2013), https://www.cia.gov/library/center-for-the-study-of-intelligence/csi-publications/csi-studies/studies/vol-57-no-4/pdfs/Manosevitz-FocusingConceptual%20Frameworks-Dec2013.pdf.

2. R. Hillson, "The DIME/PMESII Model Suite Requirements Project," *NRL Review* (2009): 235–239, www.dtic.mil/cgi-bin/GetTRDoc?AD=ADA525056.

3. Expansion of a list contained in the U.S. Army Training and Doctrine Command, "Operation Environments to 2028: The Strategic Environment for Unified Land Operations," August 2012, http://defenseinnovationmarketplace.mil/resources/TRADOC2028_Strategic_Assessment.pdf.

4. Samuel P. Huntington, *The Clash of Civilizations and the Remaking of World Order* (New York: Simon & Schuster, 1996), 29.

5. Paul R. Pillar, *Intelligence and U.S. Foreign Policy: Iraq, 9/11, and Misguided Reform* (New York: Columbia University Press, 2011).

6. CIA, *A Tradecraft Primer: Structured Analytic Techniques for Improving Intelligence Analysis* (Washington, D.C.: Author, March 2009).

7. A stochastic process is one in which the events of the process are determined by chance. Such processes are therefore analyzed using probability theory.

8. "Telecommunications, Satellites Said to Be Targeted for Espionage by France," *Common Carrier Week*, May 17, 1993.

9. Nicholas Eftimiades, *Chinese Intelligence Operations* (Annapolis, MD: Naval Institute Press, 1994), 22.

10. Office of the National Counterintelligence Executive, "Foreign Spies Stealing US Economic Secrets in Cyberspace: Report to Congress on Foreign Economic Collection and Industrial Espionage, 2009–2011" (Washington, D.C.: Author, October 2011), 4–5.

11. Samuel D. Porteous, "Economic Espionage: Issues Arising from Increased Government Involvement with the Private Sector," *Intelligence and National Security*, 9, no. 4 (October 1994): 735–752; Wayne Madsen, "Intelligence Agency Threats to Computer Security," *International Journal of Intelligence and Counterintelligence*, 6, no. 4 (Winter 1993): 413–488.

12. Eftimiades, *Chinese Intelligence Operations*, 22.

6

Overview of Models in Intelligence

One picture is worth more than ten thousand words.

Chinese proverb

The preceding chapters have introduced the concept of models and provided some examples of how analysts use them. The process of populating the appropriate model is known as synthesis, a term borrowed from the engineering disciplines. *Synthesis* is defined as putting together parts or elements to form a whole—in this case, a model of the target. It is what intelligence analysts do, and their skill at it is a primary measure of their professional competence. In this chapter we review the types of models commonly used to describe intelligence targets.

The most important models that find wide use in intelligence are only touched on in this chapter. Later chapters go into more detail, discussing how these models are created and used and some strengths and weaknesses of each type.

Creating a Conceptual Model

The first step in creating a model is to define the *system* that encompasses the intelligence issues of interest, so that the resulting model answers any problem that has been defined by using the issue definition process described in chapter 4. The system could be something as simple as a new fighter aircraft, a data processing center, an opium poppy field, or a new oil pipeline. Many questions in the current or tactical intelligence area can be so narrowly focused. The example given in chapter 3 of the BMP in Afghanistan was narrowly focused on the vehicle, its occupants, and the surrounding terrain. Problems coming into the Symantec war room are usually narrowly focused on an immediate virus, hacker, or Trojan horse of concern, its source, and its victims. However, few questions in strategic intelligence or in-depth research can be answered by using a narrowly defined target.

For the complex targets that are typical of in-depth research, an analyst usually will deal with a complete system, such as an air defense system that will use the new fighter aircraft; a narcotics growing, harvesting, processing, and distribution network, of which the opium poppy field is but a part; or an energy production system that goes from oil exploration through drilling, pumping, transportation (including the oil pipeline), refining, distribution, and retailing. In law enforcement, analysis of an organized crime syndicate involves consideration of people, funds, communications, operational practices, movement of goods, political relationships, and victims. Many intelligence problems will require consideration of related systems as well. The energy production system, for example, will give rise to intelligence questions about related companies, governments, suppliers and customers, and nongovernmental organizations (such as environmental advocacy groups). The questions that customers pose should be answerable by reference only to the target model, without the need to reach beyond it.

A major challenge in defining the relevant system is to use restraint. The definition must include *essential* subsystems or collateral systems, but nothing more. Part of an analyst's skill lies in being able to include in a definition the relevant components, and only the relevant components, that will address the issue.

A system, as explained in chapter 3, can be examined structurally, functionally, or as a process. The systems model can therefore be structural, functional, process oriented, or any combination thereof. Structural models include actors, objects, and the organization of their relationships to each other. Process models focus on interactions and their dynamics. Functional models concentrate on the results achieved, for example, a model that simulates the financial consequences of a proposed trade agreement.

After an analyst has defined the relevant system, the next step is to select the generic models, or model templates, to be used. These model templates then will be made specific, or "populated," using evidence (discussed in chapter 7). Several types of generic models are used in intelligence. The three most basic types are textual, mathematical, and visual. Many models of intelligence use are combinations of these three basic types.

Textual Models

Almost any model can be described using written text. The CIA's *World Factbook* is an example of a set of textual models—actually a series of models (political, military, economic, social, infrastructure, and information)—of a country. Some common examples of textual models that are used in intelligence analysis are lists, comparative models, profiles, and matrix models.

Lists

Lists and outlines are the simplest examples of a model. Benjamin Franklin favored a "parallel list" as a model for problem solving. He would list the arguments pro and con on a topic side-by-side, crossing off arguments on each side that held equal weight, to arrive at a decision. The list continues to be used by analysts today for much the same purpose—to reach a yes-or-no decision. The parallel list works well on a wide range of topics and remains very effective for conveying information to the customer. It also is often used in intelligence for comparative analysis—for example, comparing the performance of a Russian naval vessel with its U.S. counterpart or contrasting two cultures.

Comparative Models

Comparative techniques, like lists, are a simple but useful form of modeling that typically does not require a computer simulation. Comparative techniques are used in government, mostly for weapons systems and technology analyses. Both governments and businesses use comparative models to evaluate a competitor's operational practices, products, and technologies. This is called *benchmarking*.

A powerful tool for analyzing a competitor's developments is to compare them with your own organization's developments. Your own systems or technologies can provide a benchmark for comparison. One pitfall of comparative modeling is that you may be inclined to rely on models that you are familiar with, such as your country's organizational or industrial process models, instead of those of the target country. Such so-called *mirror imaging* leads to erroneous estimates. This and other pitfalls of comparative techniques are discussed in chapter 9.

Comparative models have to be culture specific to help avoid mirror imaging. A classic example of a culture-specific organizational model is the *keiretsu*, which is unique to Japan, though similar organizational models exist elsewhere in Asia. A keiretsu is a network of businesses, usually in related industries, that own stakes in one another and have board members in common as a means of mutual security. A network of essentially captive (because they are dependent on the keiretsu) suppliers provides the raw material for the keiretsu manufacturers, and the keiretsu trading companies and banks provide marketing services. Keiretsu have their roots in prewar Japan, which was dominated by four large conglomerates called *zaibatsu*: Mitsubishi, Mitsui, Sumitomo, and Yasuda. The zaibatsu were involved in areas such as steel, international trading, and banking and were controlled by a holding company.

Six keiretsu—Sumitomo, Mitsubishi, Mitsui, Dai-Ichi Kangyo, Sanwa, and Fuyo—dominate Japan's economy. Most of the hundred largest Japanese corporations are members of one or another of these "big six" keiretsu.[1]

An intelligence analyst who mirror images Western business practices in assessing the keiretsu would underestimate the close keiretsu cooperation between supplier and manufacturer and the advantages it gives in continual product development, quality improvements, and reductions in cost. But the analyst also would miss the weaknesses inherent in a dependency relationship that shields the partners from competitive pressures, which slows innovation and eventually erodes the market position of all the keiretsu parties.

To avoid the problem of mirror imaging, analysts sometimes create parallel models, side-by-side, for comparative modeling. This exercise helps to highlight the differences between one's own company or country model and that of the target and helps to catch potential areas of mirror imaging.

Profiles

Profiles are models of individuals—in national intelligence, of leaders of foreign governments; in business intelligence, of top executives in a competing organization; in law enforcement, of mob leaders and serial criminals. The purpose of creating profiles usually is to help predict what the profiled person will do in a given set of circumstances[2] or to aid the customer in negotiating with the profiled person. Chapter 15 discusses the use of profiles for predictive simulation.

Profiles depend heavily on understanding the pattern of mental and behavioral traits that are shared by adult members of a society—referred to as the society's *modal personality*. Several modal personality types may exist in a society, and their common elements are often referred to as *national character*. A recurring quip that reflects widely held—though tongue-in-cheek—views of national character goes:

Paradise is where:

the cooks are French

the mechanics are German

the police are British

the lovers are Italian

and it is all organized by the Swiss.

Hell is where:

the cooks are British

the mechanics are French

the police are German

the lovers are Swiss

and it is all organized by the Italians.

U.S. readers, after enjoying a laugh at this, might stop to reflect that, in many countries, common stereotypes of U.S. national character include obese people who are gorging on fast food with one hand, carrying a gun in the other, and arrogantly using up as many resources as possible as fast as possible in their materialistic quest for more and newer versions of everything.

Defining the modal personality type is beyond the capabilities of the journeyman intelligence analyst, and one must turn to experts. I offer here only a brief overview of the topic of behavioral profiles to indicate the importance of the concept in the overall decision-modeling problem, which is discussed in chapter 15. The modal personality model usually includes at least the following elements:

- *Concept of self*—the conscious ideas of what a person thinks he or she is, along with the frequently unconscious motives and defenses against ego-threatening experiences such as withdrawal of love, public shaming, guilt, or isolation
- *Relation to authority*—how an individual adapts to authority figures
- *Modes of impulse control and expressing emotion*
- *Processes of forming and manipulating ideas*

Three model types are often used for studying modal personalities and creating behavioral profiles:

- *Cultural pattern models* are relatively straightforward to analyze (see chapter 15) and are useful in assessing group behavior. They have less value in the assessment of an individual. Cultural patterns are derived from political behavior, religious idea systems, art forms, mass media, folklore, and similar collective activities.
- *Child-rearing systems* can be studied to allow the projection of adult personality patterns and behavior. They may allow more accurate assessments of an individual than a simple study of cultural patterns, but they cannot account for the wide range of possible pattern variations occurring after childhood.
- *Individual assessments* are probably the most accurate starting points for creating a behavioral model, but they depend on detailed data about the specific individual. Such data are usually gathered from testing techniques; the Rorschach (or "Inkblot") test—a projective personality assessment based on the subject's reactions to a series of ten inkblot pictures—is an example. However, test data are seldom available on individuals of interest to the intelligence business. In the mid-twentieth century, it was common to rely on the writings and speeches of individuals (*Mein Kampf, The Thoughts of Chairman Mao*) to construct a modal personality picture. More recently, videos of leaders such as Saddam Hussein, Kim Jong-Il, and Osama bin Laden are likely to be used. Sometimes, one is reduced to fragmented bits of information such as anecdotal evidence or handwriting analysis (graphology).

Another model template for individual personality assessments is the Myers-Briggs Type Indicator, which assigns people to one of sixteen different categories or types. There are four different subscales of Myers-Briggs that purport to measure different personality tendencies. As with other test-based assessments, the trick is to get test results on the target individual.

Interaction Matrices

A textual variant of the spreadsheet (discussed later) is the interaction matrix, a valuable analytic tool for certain types of synthesis. It appears in various disciplines and under different names and is also called a parametric matrix or a traceability matrix.[3] An interaction matrix is shown in Table 6-1. In 2005, four proposals were under consideration to be part of a South Asian gas pipeline project.[4] The interaction matrix summarizes in simple form the costs and risks of each proposal. So it is also a form of comparative model. The matrix is a concise and effective way to present the results of analysis. Table 6-1 permits a view of the four proposals that facilitates comparison.

An interaction matrix can be qualitative or quantitative, as Table 6-1 illustrates. A quantitative interaction matrix naturally fits into many of the commercially available decision-support software packages. It is typically used to ensure that all possible alternatives are considered in problem solving.

In economic intelligence and scientific and technical intelligence, it is often important to assess the impact of an industrial firm's efforts to acquire other companies. One model for assessing the likely outcome of a merger or an acquisition uses the five criteria that Cisco Systems uses to look at possible acquisitions. The criteria are listed in the first column of Table 6-2. In this interaction matrix model, the three candidates for acquisition are ranked on how well they meet each criterion; the darker the shading, the higher the ranking. This merger and acquisition model has potential applications outside the commercial world. In 1958 it would have been a useful tool, for example, to assess the prospects for success of the "merger" that year between Syria and Egypt that created the United Arab Republic. The proposed "merger" would

Table 6-1 Interaction Matrix—Gas Pipeline Proposals

Pipeline Proposals	Cost	Supporters	Risks
From South Pars field, Iran, to Karachi	$3 billion	Iran, Pakistan	Technical
From Iran to northern India	$4–5 billion	Iran, India	Political, security, cost
From Turkmenistan's Dauletabad field to Pakistan	$3.2 billion	Turkmenistan, Pakistan	Security
Underwater pipeline from Qatar to Pakistan	$3 billion	Qatar, Pakistan	Political, technical

Table 6-2   Matrix for Merger and Acquisition Analysis

Merger and acquisition criteria	Company A	Company B	Company C
Shared vision of where the industry is heading and complementary roles each company wants to play in it			
Similar cultures and chemistry			
A winning proposition for acquired employees, at least over the short term			
A winning proposition for shareholders, employees, customers, and business partners over the long term			
Geographic proximity, particularly for large acquisitions			

Source: Michelle Cook and Curtis Cook, "Anticipating Unconventional M&As: The Case of DaimlerChrysler," *Competitive Intelligence Magazine* (January–February 2001).

not have fared well against any of the criteria in Table 6-2, even the one on similar cultures, and in fact, the merger subsequently failed.

Mathematical Models

The most common modeling problem involves solving an equation. Most problems in engineering or technical intelligence are single equations of the form

$$f(x, y, z, t, \ldots, a, b, c, \ldots) = 0$$

or they are systems of equations of this form. Systems of equations are particularly prevalent in econometric synthesis/analysis; single equations are common in radar, communications, and ballistic missile performance analysis.

Most analysis involves fixing all of the variables and constants in such an equation or system of equations, except for two variables. The equation is then solved repetitively to obtain a graphical picture of one variable as a function of another. A number of software packages perform this type of solution very efficiently. For example, as a part of radar performance analysis, the radar range equation is solved for signal-to-noise ratio as a function of range, and a two-dimensional curve is plotted. Then, perhaps, signal-to-noise ratio is fixed and a new curve plotted for radar cross-section as a function of range.

Often the requirement is to solve an equation, get a set of ordered pairs, and plug those into another equation to get a graphical picture rather than solving simultaneous equations.

Spreadsheets

The computer is a powerful tool for handling the equation-solution type of problem. Spreadsheet software has made it easy to create equation-based models. The rich set of mathematical functions that can be incorporated in it, and its flexibility, make the spreadsheet a widely used model in intelligence.

Spreadsheets have many uses in intelligence, most commonly for looking at numerical data. Their value for numerical data is that the software can be used for data visualization, discussed later. Spreadsheets show relationships at a basic level.

Simulation Models

A simulation model is a mathematical model of a real object, a system, or an actual situation. It is useful for estimating the performance of its real-world analogue under different conditions. We often wish to determine how something will behave without actually testing it in real life. So simulation models are useful for helping decision makers choose among alternative actions by determining the likely outcomes of those actions. Simulation models have been used to simulate events such as the detonation of nuclear devices and their effects; to assess the outcome of armed conflicts; and to identify the environmental consequences of human activities. In intelligence, simulation models also are used to assess the performance of opposing weapons systems, the consequences of trade embargoes, and the success of insurgencies.

Simulation models can be challenging to build. The main challenge usually is validation: determining that the model accurately represents what it is supposed to represent, under different input conditions. Simulation models are discussed in detail in chapter 15.

Visual Models

Models can be described in written text, as noted earlier. But the models that have the most impact for both analysts and customers in facilitating understanding take a visual form.

Visualization involves transforming raw intelligence into graphical, pictorial, or multimedia forms so that our brains can process and understand large amounts of data more readily than is possible from simply reading text. Visualization lets us deal with massive quantities of data and identify meaningful patterns and structures that otherwise would be incomprehensible.[5]

Charts and Graphs

Graphical displays, often in the form of curves, are a simple type of model that can be synthesized both for analysis and for presenting the results of

Figure 6-1   The Exponential (or Disaster) Curve

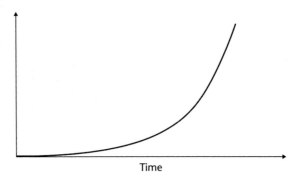

Population, pollution, child abuse, number of prisoners, or whatever phenomenon about which one wants to predict a disaster

Time

analysis. More curves are introduced and used in later chapters, but here let's look at one of the most common: a type of curve that projects changes over time. When experts extrapolate into the future, they often concentrate on one (or a few) forces that affect an entity, such as the economy or the environment. That can lead them to posit some kind of disaster based on models that use the variables, leading to the *exponential curve* or *disaster curve* shown in Figure 6-1. The creators of the disaster curve tend to ignore or discount the ability of other variables, especially responsive or limiting factors such as human adaptivity and technology, to change at the same rate or faster. A classic example is the exponential extrapolation of growth in telephones, made about 1900, which predicted that by 1920 the entire U.S. population would be working as telephone operators.[6]

Of course, the disaster curve doesn't usually hold up. An opposing reaction, feedback, contamination, or some other countervailing force steps in and retards the exponential growth curve so that an *S curve* results (see Figure 6-2). S curves are fairly common in predictive models.

Figure 6-2   The S Curve

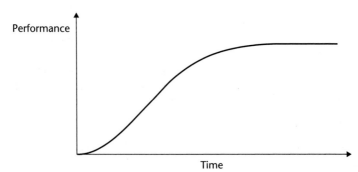

Performance

Time

Figure 6-3 The Normal Curve

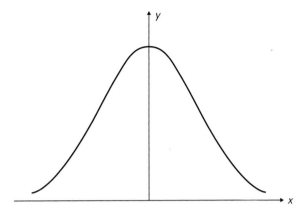

Many phenomena can be modeled by the *Gaussian curve,* or *normal curve,* shown in Figure 6-3. The intelligence of a population, variation in imagery quality, atmospheric dispersion of a chemical release, variation in securities pricing—all these and more can be represented by the normal curve. To illustrate, take the quality of a photograph. The quality of a photograph has an average value, indicated by the point where the curve in Figure 6-3 peaks. But if many (say, two hundred) photographs of a scene are taken with the same camera and their quality plotted, a curve of image quality like that of Figure 6-3 results; a few photographs will be exceptional (falling on the far right side of the curve), and a few will be poor (falling on the far left side of the curve).

Pattern Models

Many types of models fall under the broad category of *pattern models.* Pattern recognition is a critical element of all intelligence.[7] Most criminals and terrorists have a modus operandi, or standard operational pattern. Most governmental and industrial organizations (and intelligence services) also prefer to stick with techniques that have been successful in the past. An important aspect of intelligence synthesis, therefore, is recognizing patterns of activities and then determining in the analysis phase whether (a) the patterns represent a departure from what is known or expected and (b) the changes in patterns are significant enough to merit attention. The computer is a valuable ally here; it can display trends and allow the analyst to identify them. This capability is particularly useful when trends would be difficult or impossible to find by sorting through and mentally processing a large volume of data. Pattern analysis is one way to effectively handle complex issues.

One danger in creating a pattern model is that you may be tempted to find a pattern too quickly. Once a pattern has been settled on, it is easy to emphasize

Figure 6-4   Opium Production in Afghanistan, 1994–2014

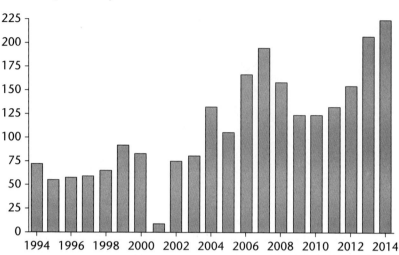

Hectares (thousands)

Source: United Nations Office on Drugs and Crime, "Afghanistan Opium Survey 2014," November 2014, http://www.unodc.org/documents/crop-monitoring/Afghanistan/Afghan-opium-survey-2014.pdf.

evidence that seems to support the pattern and to overlook, extenuate, or explain away evidence that might undermine it.

One type of pattern model used by intelligence analysts relies on statistics. In fact, a great deal of pattern modeling is statistical. Intelligence deals with a wide variety of statistical modeling techniques. Some of the most useful techniques are easy to learn and require no previous statistical training.

Almost all statistical analysis now depends on computers. The statistical software used should provide both a broad range of statistical routines and a flexible data definition and management capability. The software should have basic graphics capabilities to display such data visually as trend lines.

Histograms, which are bar charts that show a frequency distribution, are one example of a simple statistical pattern. An example that might be used in intelligence analysis is shown in Figure 6-4; it permits an analyst to examine patterns of opium production over time in Afghanistan and to correlate the changes with other events in the region (such as Taliban and government forces activities).

Advanced Target Models

The example models introduced so far are frequently used in intelligence. They're fairly straightforward and relatively easy to create. Intelligence also makes use of four model types that are more difficult to create and to analyze, but that give more in-depth analysis. We'll briefly introduce them here, and cover them in detail later, in chapters 9, 10, 11, and 14.

Systems Models

Systems models are well known in intelligence for their use in assessing the performance of weapons systems. But we deal with systems in all of the PMESII perspectives described in chapter 5. Systems models have been created for all of the following examples:

- A republic, a dictatorship, or an oligarchy can be modeled as a *political* system.
- Air defense systems, carrier strike groups, special operations teams, and ballistic missile systems all are modeled as *military* systems.
- *Economic* systems models describe the functioning of capitalist or socialist economies, international trade, and informal economies.
- *Social* systems include welfare or antipoverty programs, health care systems, religious networks, urban gangs, and tribal groups.
- *Infrastructure* systems could include electrical power, automobile manufacturing, railroads, and seaports.
- A news gathering, production, and distribution system is an example of an *information* system.

Creating a systems model requires an understanding of the system, developed by examining the linkages and interactions between the elements that compose the system as a whole. As stressed throughout this book,

- A system has *structure*. It is comprised of parts that are related (directly or indirectly). It has a defined boundary physically, temporally, and spatially, though it can overlap with or be a part of a larger system.
- A system has a *function*. It receives inputs from, and sends outputs into, an outside environment. It is autonomous in fulfilling its function. A main battle tank standing alone is *not* a system. A tank with a crew, fuel, ammunition, and a communications subsystem *is* a system.
- A system has a *process* that performs its function by transforming inputs into outputs.

Chapter 9 goes into more detail on systems models.

Relationship Models

Relationships among entities—people, places, things, and events—are perhaps the most common subject of intelligence modeling. There are four levels of such relationship models, each using increasingly sophisticated analytic approaches: hierarchy, matrix, link, and network models. The four are closely related, representing the same fundamental idea at increasing levels of complexity.

Relationship models require a considerable amount of time to create, and maintaining the model (known to those who do it as "feeding the beast") demands much effort. But such models are highly effective in analyzing complex problems, and the associated graphical displays are powerful in persuading customers to accept the results.

Hierarchy Models. The hierarchy model is a simple tree structure. Organizational modeling naturally lends itself to the creation of a hierarchy, as anyone who ever drew an organizational chart is aware. A natural extension of such a hierarchy is to use a weighting scheme to indicate the importance of individuals or suborganizations in it.

Matrix Models. The interaction matrix was introduced earlier. The relationship matrix model is different. It portrays the existence of an association, known or suspected, between individuals. It usually portrays direct connections such as face-to-face meetings and telephone conversations. Analysts can use association matrices to identify those personalities and associations needing a more in-depth analysis to determine the degree of relationships, contacts, or knowledge between individuals.[8]

Link Models. A link model allows the view of relationships in more complex tree structures. Though it physically resembles a hierarchy model (both are trees), a link model differs in that it shows different kinds of relationships but does not indicate subordination.

Network Models. A network model can be thought of as a flexible interrelationship of multiple tree structures at multiple levels. The key limitation of the matrix model discussed earlier is that although it can deal with the interaction of two hierarchies at a given level, because it is a two-dimensional representation, it cannot deal with interactions at multiple levels or with more than two hierarchies. Network synthesis is an extension of the link or matrix synthesis concept that can handle such complex problems. There are several types of network models. Two are widely used in intelligence:

- *Social network models* show patterns of human relationships. The nodes are people, and the links show that some type of relationship exists.
- *Target network models* are most useful in intelligence. The nodes can be any type of entity—people, places, things, concepts—and the links show that some type of relationship exists between entities.

Link and network models are discussed in chapter 10.

Spatial and Temporal Models

Another way to examine data and to search for patterns is to use spatial modeling—depicting locations of objects in space. Spatial modeling can be used effectively on a small scale. For example, within a building, computer-aided design/computer-aided modeling, known as CAD/CAM, can be a powerful tool for intelligence synthesis. Layouts of buildings and floor plans are valuable in physical security analysis and in assessing production capacity, for example. CAD/CAM models are useful both in collection and in counterintelligence analysis of a facility. CAD/CAM can be used to create a physical security profile of a facility, allowing an analyst to identify vulnerabilities by examining floor plans, construction details, and electronic and electrical connections.

Spatial models of local areas, such as city blocks, facilitate a number of analytic inferences. For example, two buildings located within a common security fence can be presumed to have related functions, whereas no such presumption would follow if the two buildings were protected by separate security fences. Spatial modeling on larger scales is usually called *geospatial modeling* and is discussed in more detail in chapter 11.

Patterns of activity over time are important for showing trends. Pattern changes are often used to compare how things are going now with how they went last year (or last decade). Estimative analysis (chapter 12) often relies on chronological models.

Scenarios

Arguably the most important model for estimative intelligence purposes is the scenario, a very sophisticated model, which is discussed in chapter 14. Alternative scenarios are used to model future situations. These scenarios increasingly are produced as virtual reality models because they are powerful ways to convey intelligence and are very persuasive. (Here, think of virtual worlds such as Second Life or massive multiplayer online roleplaying games such as World of Warcraft.) As a real-world example, virtual reality video tours of North Korea's Yongbyon Nuclear Research Center have been produced and posted online.

Target Model Combinations

Almost all target models are actually combinations of many models. In fact, most of the models described in the previous sections can be merged into combination models. One simple example is a relationship-time display. This is a dynamic model where link or network nodes and links (relationships) change, appear, and disappear over time. Another dynamic model is a space-time model such as used in activity-based intelligence (explained in chapter 11).

We also typically want to have several distinct but interrelated models of the target in order to be able to answer different customer questions. Let's illustrate with an example of organizing available intelligence about a biological weapons threat. Our issue is to assess the ability of country X to produce, deploy, and use biological weapons as a terror or combat weapon. You might start by synthesizing a generic model, or model template, based

Figure 6-5   Generic Biological Weapons (BW) System Process
Model

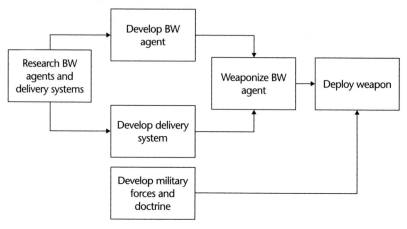

on nothing more than general knowledge of what it takes to build and use
biological weaponry. Such a generic process model would probably look like
Figure 6-5.[9]

But this generic model is only a starting point. From here, the model has
to be expanded and made specific to the target, the program in country *X*, in
an iterative modeling process that involves the creation of more detailed models called *submodels* or *collateral models*.

Submodels

One type of component model is a submodel, a more detailed breakout
of the top-level model. It is typical, for complex targets, to have many such
submodels of a target that provide different levels of detail. Participants in the
target-centric process then can reach into the model set to pull out the information they need. The collectors of information can drill down into more
detail to refine collection targeting and to fill specific gaps. The intelligence
customer can drill down to answer questions, gain confidence in the analyst's
picture of the target, and understand the limits of the analyst's work. The target
model is a powerful collaborative tool.

Figure 6-6 illustrates a submodel of one part of the process shown in
Figure 6-5.[10] In this scenario, as part of the development of the biological
weapons agent and delivery system, a test area has to be established and the
agent must be tested on animals.

Collateral Models

In contrast to the submodel, a collateral model may show particular
aspects of the overall target model, but it is not simply a detailed breakout of

Figure 6-6   Biological Weapons (BW) System Test Process Submodel

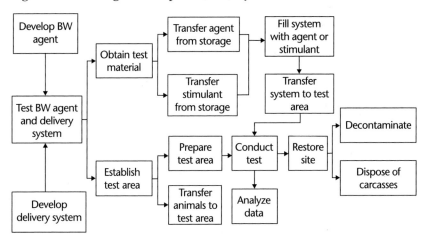

Figure 6-7   Biological Weapons (BW) Development Organizational Model

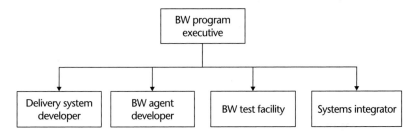

a top-level model. A collateral model typically presents a different way of thinking about the target for a specific intelligence purpose. For example, suppose that the customer needs to know how the biological weapons organization is managed, where the operations are located, and when the country might deploy biological weapons.

Figure 6-7 is a collateral model intended to answer the first question: How is the organization managed? The figure is a model of the biological weapons development organization and, like most organizational models, it is structural.

Figure 6-8 illustrates a spatial, or geographic, collateral model of the biological weapons target, answering the second question of where the biological weapons operations are located. This type of model is useful in intelligence collection planning, as discussed in chapter 20.

Another type of collateral model of the biological weapons target is shown in Figure 6-9—a temporal (chronological) model of biological weapons development designed to answer the question of when the country will deploy

Figure 6-8   A Collateral Model of Biological Weapons (BW) Facilities

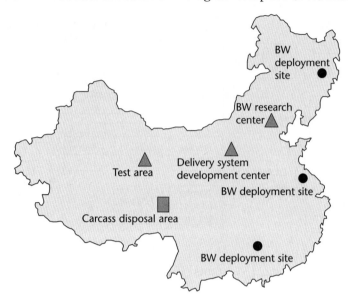

Figure 6-9   Chronological Model of Biological Weapons (BW)
Development

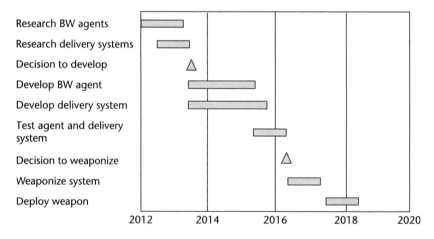

biological weapons. This model also is of value to an intelligence collector for timing collection efforts.

The collateral models in Figures 6-7 to 6-9 are examples of the three general types—structural, functional, and process—used in systems analysis. Figures 6-7 and 6-8 are structural models. Figure 6-9 is both a process model and a functional model. In analyzing complex intelligence targets, all three types are likely to be used.

These models, taken together, allow an analyst to answer a wide range of customer questions. A model like Figure 6-8 can help determine the likely use and targets of the deployed biological weapons system. The model shown in Figure 6-9 can help determine what stage the program is in and can help the intelligence customer with timing political, economic, or military action to halt the program or roll it back.

In practice, these models would be used together in an iterative analysis process. As an example of how the iterative approach works, begin with the generic model of Figure 6-5. From this starting point, the analyst might create the test process submodel shown in Figure 6-6. Prompted by the recognition that a biological weapons testing program must have a test site, the analyst would ask collectors to search for test areas having associated animal pens and certain patterns of biological sensor deployment nearby. The analyst also would request that the collectors search for a carcass disposal area. Assuming the collectors are successful, the analyst can create a collateral model—a map display like that shown in Figure 6-8. Based on observation of activity at the test site and disposal area, the analyst can refine the chronological model shown in Figure 6-9.

Consider again the hunt for Pablo Escobar from chapter 3. That was an example of an iterative process. The Colombian and U.S. intelligence teams created models of Escobar's cell phone communication patterns, his network of associates, and his financial structure. From analysis of these, collectors could be aimed at specific targets—a process that will be discussed in detail in chapter 20. As new intelligence was gathered on Escobar's cartel members, cell phone numbers, bank accounts, and pattern of operations, all of these models could be updated almost daily in a continuing, iterative process.

More complex intelligence targets can require a combination of several model types. They may have system characteristics, take a network form, *and* have spatial and temporal characteristics. These three commonly encountered model types are dealt with in chapters 9–11. And we often need to do more than describe the target from either the PMESII or systems/network perspectives in space and time. We also need to estimate future states of the target— the subject of chapters 12–14. Finally, one target model of any given type may not be enough. We may need to create multiple models, as discussed next.

Alternative and Competitive Target Models

Alternative and competitive models are somewhat different things, though they are frequently confused with each other. Let's look at them in turn.

Alternative Models

Alternative models are an essential part of the synthesis process. It is important to keep more than one possible target model in mind, especially as conflicting or contradictory intelligence information is collected. The Iraqi WMD Commission noted, "The disciplined use of alternative hypotheses could have helped counter the natural cognitive tendency to force new information into existing paradigms."[11] As law professor David Schum has noted, "the generation of new ideas in fact investigation usually rests upon arranging or juxtaposing our thoughts and evidence in different ways."[12] To do that we need multiple alternative models.

And, the more inclusive you can be when defining alternative models, the better—a point we'll return to in several chapters.

In studies listing the analytic pitfalls that hampered past assessments, one of the most prevalent is failure to consider alternative scenarios, hypotheses, or models.[13] Analysts have to guard against allowing three things to interfere with their need to develop alternative models:

- *Ego.* Former director of national intelligence Mike McConnell once observed that analysts inherently dislike alternative, dissenting, or competitive views.[14] But, the opposite becomes true of analysts who operate within the target-centric approach—the focus is not on each other anymore, but instead on contributing to a shared target model.
- *Time.* Analysts are usually facing tight deadlines. They must resist the temptation to go with the model that best fits the evidence without considering alternatives. Otherwise, the result is premature closure that can cost dearly in the end result.
- *The customer.* Customers can view a change in judgment as evidence that the original judgment was wrong, not that new evidence forced the change. Furthermore, when presented with two or more target models, customers will tend to pick the one that they like best, which may or may not be the most likely model. Analysts know this.

It is the analyst's responsibility to establish a tone of setting egos aside and of conveying to all participants in the process, including the customer, that time spent up front developing alternative models is time saved at the end if it keeps them from committing to the wrong model in haste.

A number of formal alternative analysis methodologies have been defined and given names such as "analysis of competing hypotheses," "argument mapping," "signpost analysis," and "challenge analysis." These are discussed in detail in the book *Structured Analytic Techniques for Intelligence Analysis*, by Heuer and Pherson.[15]

Alternative analysis applies structured techniques that challenge underlying assumptions and broaden the range of possible outcomes considered. Its purpose is to deal with the natural human tendencies to perceive information selectively through the lens of preconceptions, to search for facts that would confirm rather than discredit existing hypotheses, and to be unduly influenced by premature consensus within a group dynamic. Formal alternative analysis involves a fairly intensive and usually time-limited effort to challenge assumptions or to identify alternative outcomes.[16]

Some organizations, in an effort to force alternative analysis, will set up separate teams to do "alternative analysis"—though, technically, this is simply competitive analysis (discussed next) done within the same organization.

Competitive Models

It is well established in intelligence that, if you can afford the resources, you should have independent groups providing competing analyses. This is because we're dealing with uncertainty. Different analysts, given the same set of facts, are likely to come to different conclusions. The U.S. intelligence community, as a result of its size and the presence of analysis groups in most of its sixteen members, has done competitive analysis for years.

Sometimes the policymakers provide a competing target model. For example, in 1982 the United States committed Marines to Lebanon in an ambitious attempt to end a civil war, force occupying Israeli and Syrian armies out of Lebanon, and establish a stable government. The U.S. administration withdrew from Lebanon eighteen months later, its policy discredited and its reputation damaged, with more than 250 Americans dead, most of them Marines killed in a terrorist bombing. The U.S. intelligence community had one assessment of the Lebanon situation; the Washington policymaking community had a strikingly different assessment that envisioned Lebanon as a potential role model for future Middle East governments.[17] Table 6-3 shows a parallel list comparing these two alternative models of the Lebanon situation.

Table 6-3   Competitive Models of the Lebanon Situation in 1982

Policymakers	Analysts
We can negotiate speedy Israeli and Syrian withdrawals from Lebanon.	President Assad won't pull Syrian troops out unless convinced that he will be attacked militarily.
Lebanon can be unified under a stable government.	Lebanon in effect has no borders, and you can't say what a citizen is.
President Gamayel can influence events in Lebanon.	Gamayel doesn't control most of Beirut, and even the Christians aren't all behind him.
We have five military factions to deal with: Christian Phalange, Muslim militia, Syrian, Palestinian Liberation Organization, and Israeli forces.	There are forty militias operating in West Beirut alone.
The Marines are peacekeepers.	The Marines are targets.

Note that this is far from a complete picture of Lebanon, which today, as in 1982, has all the elements of a complex problem. The table also is more than a target model; it contains a number of analytic judgments or hypotheses that were drawn from two competing target models.

It is important to be inclusive when defining alternative or competitive models—a point we'll return to in several chapters. The model of a situation that isn't included may be the correct model. For instance, appendix I ("A Tale of Two NIEs") contains some alternative models that were not considered in the October 2002 national intelligence estimate on Iraq's WMD. The most important one, though, was based on an assumption: that because Saddam Hussein was stonewalling on inspections and concealing evidence of WMD, he must have WMD somewhere. The opposite possibility—that he *didn't* have WMD and didn't want his opponents in the region to know that fact—simply wasn't considered.

Summary

Creating a target model starts with defining the relevant system. The system model can be a structural, functional, or process model, or any combination. The next step is to select the generic models or model templates.

Lists and curves are the simplest form of model. In intelligence, comparative models or benchmarks are often used; almost any type of model can be made comparative, typically by creating models of one's own system side by side with the target system model.

Pattern models are widely used in the intelligence business. Chronological models allow intelligence customers to examine the timing of related events and plan a way to change the course of these events. Geospatial models are popular in military intelligence for weapons targeting and to assess the location and movement of opposing forces.

Relationship models are used to analyze the relationships among elements of the target—organizations, people, places, and physical objects—over time. Four general types of relationship models are commonly used: hierarchy, matrix, link, and network models. The most powerful of these, network models, are increasingly used to describe complex intelligence targets.

Many models are combinations of these generic model types. Predictive analysis, in particular, makes use of scenarios, and we will return to those.

Process models, which describe a sequence of events or activities that produce results, are often used to assess the progress of a development project.

Profiles of leaders and key executives are used to predict decisions. Such profiles rely on the ability of the analyst to define the modal personality type.

Competitive and alternative target models are an essential part of the process. Properly used, they help the analyst deal with denial and deception and avoid being trapped by analytic biases. But they take time to create, analysts find it difficult to change or challenge existing judgments, and alternative models give policymakers the option to select the conclusion they prefer—which may or may not be the best choice.

The next chapter discusses how to populate the model templates defined in this chapter.

Notes

1. "Facts from the Corporate Planet: Ecology and Politics in the Age of Globalization," *Wired*, October 23, 2002, http://www.wired.com/news/business/0,1367,8918,00.html.

2. Carolyn M. Vella and John J. McGonagle, "Profiling in Competitive Analysis," *Competitive Intelligence Review*, 11, no. 2 (2000): 20.

3. Theodore J. Gordon and M. J. Raffensperger, "The Relevance Tree Method for Planning Basic Research," in *A Guide to Practical Technological Forecasting*, ed. J. R. Bright and M. E. F. Schoeman (Englewood Cliffs, N.J.: Prentice Hall, 1980), 134.

4. Ian Gill, "Gas Pipeline Race," *ADB Review* (October 2005), Asian Development Bank, Manila, http://www.adb.org/Documents/Periodicals/ADB_Review/2005/vol37-5/gas-pipeline.asp.

5. Peter Buxbaum, "Showing to Tell," *Geospatial Intelligence Forum Magazine* (October 2013).

6. In one sense, this eventually turned out to be an accurate prediction. By the 1970s almost all telephones were either dial or push-button operated. As a result, almost all Americans over the age of ten are part-time telephone "operators" in the sense of the original extrapolation.

7. M. S. Loescher, C. Schroeder, and C. W. Thomas, *Proteus: Insights from 2020* (Utrecht, Netherlands: Copernicus Institute Press, 2000), 25.

8. U.S. Joint Forces Command, *Commander's Handbook for Attack the Network* (Suffolk, Va.: Joint Warfighting Center, 2011), http://www.dtic.mil/doctrine/doctrine/jwfc/atn_hbk.pdf.

9. Michael G. Archuleta, Michael S. Bland, Tsu-Pin Duann, and Alan B. Tucker, "Proliferation Profile Assessment of Emerging Biological Weapons Threats," Research Paper, Directorate of Research, Air Command and Staff College, April 1996.

10. Ibid.

11. *Report of the Commission on the Intelligence Capabilities of the United States Regarding Weapons of Mass Destruction*, March 31, 2005, chapter 1.

12. David A. Schum, "On the Properties, Uses, Discovery, and Marshaling of Evidence in Intelligence Analysis," Lecture to the SRS Intelligence Analysis Seminar, Tucson, Ariz., February 15, 2001.

13. Willis C. Armstrong, William Leonhart, William J. McCaffrey, and Herbert C. Rothenberg, "The Hazards of Single-Outcome Forecasting," in *Inside CIA's Private World*, ed. H. Bradford Westerfield (New Haven, Conn.: Yale University Press, 1995), 241–242.

14. William J. Lahneman, *The Future of Intelligence Analysis*, Center for International and Security Studies at Maryland, Final Report, Vol. 1 (March 10, 2006), E-6.

15. Richards J. Heuer Jr. and Randolph H. Pherson, *Structured Analytic Techniques for Intelligence Analysis* (Washington, D.C.: CQ Press, 2011).

16. "Rethinking Alternative Analysis to Address Transnational Threats," Kent School Occasional Papers, 3, no. 2 (October 2004).

17. David Kennedy and Leslie Brunetta, "Lebanon and the Intelligence Community," Case Study C15-88-859.0 (Cambridge, Mass.: Kennedy School of Government, Harvard University, 1988).

7

Creating the Model

Believe nothing you hear, and only one half that you see.

Edgar Allan Poe

This chapter describes the steps that analysts go through in populating the target model. Here, we focus on the synthesis part of the target-centric approach, often called *collation* in the intelligence business. We discuss the importance of existing pieces of intelligence, both finished and raw, and how best to think about sources of new raw data. We talk about how credentials of evidence must be established, introduce widely used informal methods of combining evidence, and touch on structured argumentation as a formal methodology for combining evidence. Analysts need to be familiar with all of these concepts in order to handle the collation process in populating the model.

In intelligence, collation is the organizing of relevant information in a coherent way, looking at source and context. It involves evaluating the information for relevance, credibility, and inferential force; and incorporating it into the target model.

The collation concept introduced here is developed further in succeeding chapters. It typically starts with a model template, or template set, of the sort described in chapter 6. Next, the job is to fit the relevant information into the templates. We talk about templates in the plural because we wind up with several of them when dealing with complex problems—both collateral and alternative models, as discussed in chapter 6.

Analysts generally go through the actions described here in service to collation. They may not think about them as separate steps and in any event aren't likely to do them in the order presented. They nevertheless almost always do the following:

- Review existing finished intelligence about the target and examine existing raw intelligence
- Acquire new raw intelligence

- Evaluate the new raw intelligence
- Combine the intelligence from all sources into the target model

Let's go through each of these actions in turn.

Existing Intelligence

Existing *finished* intelligence reports typically define the current target model. So information gathering to create or revise a model begins with the existing knowledge base. Before starting an intelligence collection effort, analysts should ensure that they are aware of what has already been found on a subject. Finished studies or reports on file at an analyst's organization are the best place to start any research effort. There are few truly new issues. The databases of intelligence organizations include finished intelligence reports as well as many specialized data files on specific topics. Large commercial firms typically have comparable facilities in-house, or they depend on commercially available databases.

So a literature search should be the first step an analyst takes on a new project. The purpose is to both define the current state of knowledge—that is, to understand the existing model(s) of the intelligence target—and to identify the major controversies and disagreements surrounding the target model. This is an essential step, yet it can be a dangerous one. The existing intelligence should not be accepted automatically as fact. Few experienced analysts would blithely accept the results of earlier studies on a topic, though they would know exactly what the studies found. The danger is that, in conducting the search, an analyst naturally tends to adopt a preexisting target model.[1] In this case, premature closure, or a bias toward the status quo, leads the analyst to keep the existing model even when evidence indicates that a different model is more appropriate.

To counter this tendency, it's important to do a *key assumptions check* on the existing model(s). In chapter 4, we discussed assumptions and the need for a key assumptions check in defining the intelligence issue. In looking at target models derived from existing finished intelligence, you should do a second check—this time, focusing on somewhat different topics. Do the existing analytic conclusions appear to be valid? What are the premises on which these conclusions rest, and do they appear to be valid as well? Has the underlying situation changed so that the premises may no longer apply?

Once the finished reports are in hand, the analyst should review all of the relevant *raw* intelligence data that already exist. Few things can ruin an analyst's career faster than sending collectors after information that is already in the organization's files.

Sources of New Raw Intelligence

Raw intelligence comes from a number of sources, but they typically are categorized as part of the five major "INTs" shown in this section. A more in-depth and detailed discussion is contained in two companion books: *Intelligence Collection* (Clark, 2014) and *The Five Disciplines of Intelligence Collection* (Lowenthal and Clark, 2015).

For bureaucratic reasons or because of historical precedent, most texts on intelligence sources are organized around some version of the U.S. perspective depicted in Figure 7-1. The U.S. intelligence community has divided the collection methods using the "INT" (short for *intelligence*) disciplines to define the areas of responsibility of large collection organizations such as the National Geospatial-Intelligence Agency (NGA) and the National Security Agency (NSA). As a result, "INT" names in the U.S. intelligence community are the result of bureaucratic initiatives, which means there are varying opinions and quibbles about whether sources are properly named and, indeed, whether one source or another should be even termed an INT. Nevertheless, it's important to at least understand the concept before we turn to an alternative view that has more relevance for intelligence analysts.

The definitions of each INT follow:

- *Open source (OSINT).* Information of potential intelligence value that is available to the general public
- *Human intelligence (HUMINT).* Intelligence derived from information collected and provided by human sources
- *Measurements and signatures intelligence (MASINT).* Scientific and technical intelligence obtained by quantitative and qualitative analysis of data (metric, angle, spatial, wavelength, time dependence, modulation, plasma, and hydromagnetic) derived from specific technical sensors
- *Signals intelligence (SIGINT).* Intelligence comprising either individually or in combination all communications intelligence, electronics intelligence, and foreign instrumentation signals intelligence
- *Imagery intelligence (IMINT).* Intelligence derived from the exploitation of collection by visual photography, infrared sensors, lasers, electro-optics, and radar sensors such as synthetic aperture radar wherein images of objects are reproduced optically or electronically on film, electronic display devices, or other media

Figure 7-1   The U.S. Collection Taxonomy

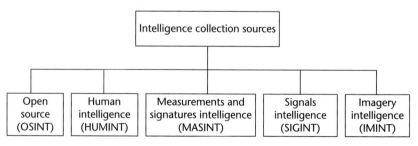

Some taxonomies replace IMINT (in Figure 7-1) with geospatial intelligence, or GEOINT. The United States has renamed the National Imagery and Mapping Agency as NGA, and a number of European nations regularly conduct Defence Geospatial Intelligence conferences, thus giving credence to the term. But as discussed in chapter 11, geospatial intelligence originated as and remains an all-source technique for synthesizing and analyzing a target model.

Although not shown in the taxonomy of Figure 7-1, signals intelligence (SIGINT) is divided into three distinct "INTs": communications intelligence (COMINT), electronic intelligence (ELINT), and telemetry interception; the latter is typically called *foreign instrumentation signals intelligence*, or FISINT. The lumping of COMINT, ELINT, and FISINT together as SIGINT is usually defended as being logical because they have in common the interception of some kind of signal transmitted by the target. But some MASINT sensors rely on a signal transmitted by the target, as well. Some observers would argue that "SIGINT" is in fact too general a term to use, when in most cases it means COMINT.

The taxonomy approach in this book is quite different. It strives for a breakout that focuses on the *nature of the material collected and processed*, rather than on the *collection means*. Figure 7-2 illustrates this view of collection sources. It divides intelligence collection into two major source types: literal and nonliteral (including a new form of literal intelligence that has recently come into prominence: cyber collection).

Traditional COMINT, HUMINT, and open-source collection are concerned mainly with *literal* information, that is, information in a form that humans use for communication. The basic product and the general methods for collecting and analyzing literal information are usually well understood by intelligence analysts and the customers of intelligence. It requires no special exploitation after the processing step (which includes translation) to be understood. It literally speaks for itself.

Nonliteral information, in contrast, usually requires special processing and exploitation in order for analysts to make use of it. It is important to understand the nature and limitations of such processing and exploitation.

One rationale for this division is that all-source analysts can challenge the interpretation of COMINT, HUMINT, cyber collection, or open source, given access to the original raw material (and with language and cultural expertise). But if the processor/exploiter of nonliteral material makes a judgment, it's difficult to contradict unless you are also an expert in the field. Interpreting a hyperspectral image or an ELINT recording takes special expertise that few of us possess.

The logic of this division has been noted by other writers in the intelligence business. British author Michael Herman observed that there are two basic types of collection: One produces evidence in the form of observations and measurements of things (nonliteral), and one produces access to human thought processes (literal).[2]

Figure 7-2   An Analyst's View of the Collection Taxonomy

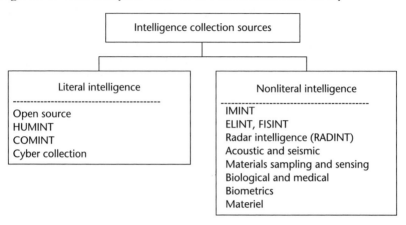

This is not a completely satisfactory, or "clean," separation. An important part of COMINT—traffic analysis—is not literal information; it depends on processing and interpretation. HUMINT sources are used in materials and materiel collection, which provide nonliteral intelligence. Overlaps will occur no matter what taxonomy is selected. But because of the way an analyst must treat the material, Figure 7-2 provides a more useful division than the one shown in Figure 7-1.

Analytic success requires understanding where to acquire data and the limits and pitfalls of the information available from the sources outlined in this chapter. A single data source seldom provides everything an analyst needs to populate a model of a complex target. Rather, a wide range of sources must be called on—in part to reduce the chances of being misled by a single source.

The automation of data handling has been a major boon to intelligence analysts. Information collected from around the globe arrives at the analyst's desk through the Internet or in electronic message form, ready for review and often presorted on the basis of keyword searches. A downside of this automation, however, is the tendency to treat all information in the same way. In some cases the analyst does not even know what collection source provided the information; after all, everything looks alike on the display screen. However, information must be treated differently depending on its source. And, no matter the source, all information must be evaluated before it is synthesized into the model—the subject to which we now turn.

Evaluating Evidence

The fundamental problem in weighing evidence is determining its credibility—its completeness and soundness. In the end, weighing evidence involves subjective judgments that the analyst alone must make. (Some helpful insights on reliability are contained in the two texts on intelligence collection cited earlier.)

The CIA's *Tradecraft Primer* describes a methodology for evaluating information validity, called the *quality of information check*. Its purpose is described as follows:

> Weighing the validity of sources is a key feature of any critical thinking. Moreover, establishing how much confidence one puts in analytic judgments should ultimately rest on how accurate and reliable the information base is. Hence, checking the quality of information used in intelligence analysis is an ongoing, continuous process. Having multiple sources on an issue is not a substitute for having good information that has been thoroughly examined. Analysts should perform periodic checks of the information base for their analytic judgments. Otherwise, important analytic judgments can become anchored to weak information, and any "caveats" attached to those judgments in the past can be forgotten or ignored over time.[3]

The quality of information check is described in more detail in the *Tradecraft Primer* and in other publications. This section discusses an alternative methodology for weighing evidence that entails three steps: evaluating the source, evaluating the communications channel through which the information arrives, and evaluating the evidence itself. The communications channel is often ignored, but it is a critical piece of the reliability puzzle, as we shall see.

At the heart of the evaluation process is one of the oldest analytic principles, Occam's razor. The name comes from William of Occam, who said, "It is vain to do with more what can be done with fewer."[4] In modern-day English, we know this as the KISS principle: Keep it simple, stupid! Possibly the most common example of Occam's razor is the advice given as the first action when a piece of electronic equipment doesn't work: Check to see if it is plugged in. Occam's razor is not an infallible principle; occasionally the correct explanation for a given set of facts is very complex or convoluted. Conventional wisdom is often wrong. And counterintelligence, especially denial and deception, is a possibility that the sciences do not have to contend with. However, a poor analyst can make data fit almost any desired conclusion, especially if he selectively discards inconvenient facts. So the razor is a valuable part of the analyst's toolkit (Analysis Principle 7-1).

Analysis Principle 7-1 ●────────────────────────

Occam's Razor

Explain your observations with the fewest possible hypotheses. In other words, choose the simplest explanation that fits the facts at hand.

Evaluating the Source

Accept nothing at face value. Evaluate the source of evidence carefully and beware of the source's motives for providing the information. Evaluating the source involves answering three questions:

- Is the source competent (knowledgeable about the information being given)?
- Did the source have the access needed to get the information?
- Does the source have a vested interest or bias?

In the HUMINT business, this is called determining *bona fides* for human sources. Even when not dealing with HUMINT, one must ask these three questions.

Competence

The Anglo-American judicial system deals effectively with competence: It allows people to describe what they observed with their senses because, absent disability, we are presumed competent to sense things. The judicial system does not allow the average person to interpret what he or she sensed unless the person is qualified as an expert in such interpretation.

Intelligence source evaluators must apply the same criteria. It is easy, in a raw intelligence report, to accept not only the observations of a source but also the inferences that the source has drawn. Always ask: What was the basis for this conclusion? If no satisfactory answer is forthcoming, use the source's conclusions with caution or not at all.

A radar expert talking about an airborne intercept radar performance is credible. If he goes on to describe the aircraft performance, he is considerably less credible. An economist assessing inflation prospects in a country might have credibility; if she goes on to assess the likely political impact of the inflation, the analyst should be skeptical.

Access

The issue of source access typically does not arise because it is assumed that the source had access. When there is reason to be suspicious about the source, however, check whether the source might not have had the claimed access.

In the legal world, checks on source access come up regularly in witness cross-examinations. One of the most famous examples was the "Almanac Trial" of 1858, where Abraham Lincoln conducted the cross-examination. It was the dying wish of an old friend that Lincoln represent his friend's son, Duff Armstrong, who was on trial for murder. Lincoln gave his client a tough, artful, and ultimately successful defense; in the trial's highlight, Lincoln consulted an almanac to discredit a prosecution witness who claimed that he saw the murder clearly because the moon was high in the sky. The almanac showed that the moon was lower on the horizon, and the witness's access—that is, his ability to see the murder—was called into question.[5]

Access can be a critical issue in evaluating the source. When CIA analysts prepared the national intelligence estimate concerning possible Iraqi WMD programs, they believed that the now-infamous source Curveball was reliable because his knowledge was detailed, technically accurate, and corroborated by another source's reporting. But, as a CIA group chief pointed out, the corroborating information simply established that Curveball had been to a given location, not that he had any knowledge of biological warfare activities being conducted there.[6]

Vested Interest or Bias

In HUMINT, analysts occasionally encounter the "professional source" who sells information to as many bidders as possible and has an incentive to make the information as interesting as possible. Even the densest sources quickly realize that more interesting information gets them more money.

Official reports from government organizations have a similar vested interest problem. Instead of giving it automatic credibility, be skeptical of this information. One seldom finds outright lies in such reports, but government officials may occasionally distort or conceal facts to support their policy positions or to protect their personal interests. U.S. researchers have occasionally provided U.S. government intelligence organizations with distorted information about their foreign contacts. The usual approach is to exaggerate the importance of their foreign counterparts' work as a ploy to encourage more funding for their own work. A report does not necessarily have more validity simply because it came from a citizen of one's own country rather than from a foreigner. Vested interest and bias are also common problems for analysts who are dealing with experts in the comparative modeling and benchmarking techniques discussed next.

Where comparison of systems or technologies is used, the usual approach is to compare systems or technology performance, as measured in one's own test and evaluation programs, with the estimates or data on the performance of the target's system. In assessing systems that use advanced technologies, test and evaluation results are especially important because many techniques work in theory but not in practice.

However, an intelligence organization faces a problem in using its own parent organization's (or country's) test and evaluation results: Many have been contaminated. Some of the test results are fabricated; some contain distortions or omit key points. An honestly conducted, objective test may be a rarity. Several reasons for this problem exist. Tests are sometimes conducted to prove or disprove a preconceived notion and thus unconsciously are slanted. Some results are fabricated because they would show the vulnerability or the ineffectiveness of a system and because procurement decisions often depend on the test outcomes.

Although the majority of contaminated cases probably are never discovered, history provides many examples of this issue. Chapter 13 discusses the story of Sims's continuous aim naval gunnery system, wherein the U.S. Navy tested a proposed new technique for naval gunnery. The test was designed to confirm the preconceived notion that the technique would not work, rather than to test a concept. During World War II both the British and the Germans conducted tests that were rigged to prove a point.[7] A more current example occurred a few years ago at one of the U.S. military test ranges. An airborne jammer was not performing as expected against a particular target-tracking radar. Investigation revealed that the radar had in fact been jammed, but the radar site personnel had tracked the jammer aircraft by using a second radar that was not supposed to be part of the test.

In addition to recognizing that your own organization's (or country's) test results may be contaminated, you also must deal with the parallel problem: The target organization may have distorted or fabricated its tests for similar reasons. In examining any test or evaluation results, begin by asking two questions:

- Did the testing organization have a major stake in the outcome (such as the threat that a program would be canceled due to negative test results or the possibility that it would profit from positive results)?
- Did the *reported* outcome support the organization's position or interests?

If the answer to both questions is yes, be wary of accepting the validity of the test. In the pharmaceutical testing industry, for example, tests have been fraudulently conducted or the results skewed to support the regulatory approval of the pharmaceutical.[8] The results can be similarly distorted in other industries. The lesson here is that it is unwise to rely on test reports alone.

A very different type of bias can occur when collection is focused on a particular issue. This bias comes from the fact that, when you look for something in the intelligence business, you may find what you are looking for, whether or not it's there. In looking at suspected Iraqi chemical facilities prior to 2003, analysts concluded from imagery reporting that the level of activity had increased at the facilities. But the appearance of an increase in activity may simply have been a result of an increase in imagery collection.[9]

This section presents a top-level view of source credibility. David Schum and Jon Morris have published a detailed treatise on human sources of intelligence analysis.[10] They pose a set of twenty-five questions divided into four categories: source competence, veracity, objectivity, and observational sensitivity. Their questions cover in more explicit detail the three questions posed in this section about competence, access, and vested interest.

Evaluating the Communications Channel

A second basic rule of weighing evidence is to look at the communications channel through which the evidence arrives. In a large intelligence system, collection requirements must move through a bureaucracy to a requirements officer, from there to a country desk, a field requirements officer, a SIGINT collector or a HUMINT case officer (for instance), then to an agent in the case of HUMINT; and the response then goes back through the reports chain. The message seldom gets through undistorted. This distortion of the message is expressed in physics as the second law of thermodynamics (Analysis Principle 7-2). The law has been modified for the intelligence field: The accuracy of a message through *any* communications system decreases with the length of the link or the number of intermediate nodes.

Analysis Principle 7-2 ●───────────────────────────

The Second Law of Thermodynamics

The second law of thermodynamics can be stated in several ways. Two of the simplest ways (they are equivalent) are

- No physical process is perfectly reversible. There is no such thing as perpetual motion.
- Entropy always increases with time. This could also be stated as "the degree of randomness always increases in a physical system."

This same principle occurs in communications engineering; Claude Shannon described it in his communications theory exposition.[11] Just as heat always flows so that entropy (chaos, randomness) increases, on a digital communications line the originally crisp pulses will gradually lose their shape over distance and disappear into the noise, as illustrated in Figure 7-3.

As is the case with an electronic communications channel that is being analyzed by applying Shannon's communications theory, some nodes in the intelligence communications channel contribute more "noise" than others. A communications pulse traveling down a noisy or distorted channel loses its shape and finally disappears in noise. The signal disappears completely or emerges as the wrong signal.

The same communications problem occurs in an organization. Large and complex systems tend to have more entropy. The result is often cited as "poor communication" problems in large organizations, and the effects can be observed in the large project curve discussed in chapter 9. Over a long chain of human communication, the equivalent of Figure 7-3 is that the received message bears little resemblance to what was originally sent.

In the business intelligence world, analysts recognize the importance of the communications channel by using the differentiating terms *primary sources* for firsthand information, acquired through discussions or other interaction directly with a human source, and *secondary sources* for information learned through an intermediary, a publication, or online. This division does

Figure 7-3   The Effect of Entropy on the Communications Channel

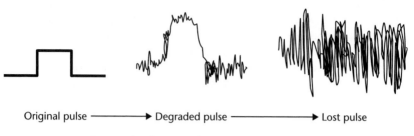

Original pulse ─────────► Degraded pulse ─────────────► Lost pulse

Entropy (randomness, chaos) always increases.

not consider the many gradations of reliability, and national intelligence organizations commonly do not use the primary/secondary source division. Some national intelligence collection organizations use the term *collateral* to refer to intelligence gained from other collectors, but it does not have the same meaning as the terms *primary* and *secondary* as used in business intelligence.

Rather than the primary-versus-secondary distinction or the collateral-evidence distinction, it is more important to look at the communications channel itself. Ask about the channel: What was it? Is this information being provided intentionally? If so, what part of it is true? Could it be deception or the sending of a message or signal to the opponent? If it is a message or signal, what is the message, and what is the reason for it?

Part of the communications channel is the processing, exploitation, and analysis chain that raw intelligence goes through before reaching the all-source analyst. It's not unheard of (though fortunately not common) for the raw intelligence to be misinterpreted or misanalyzed as it passes through the chain. Organizational or personal biases can shape the interpretation and analysis, especially of literal intelligence. It's also possible for such biases to shape the analysis of nonliteral intelligence, but that is a more difficult product for all-source analysts to challenge, as noted earlier.

The hearsay rule as applied in judicial proceedings is a recognition of the application of Shannon's theory and of entropy in human affairs. Under the hearsay rule, a witness cannot testify about what a person said to prove the truth of what was said; in the court's view, the message has traveled through too many intermediate nodes to be credible. Entropy has an effect on the credibility of some intelligence, and the credibility degrades in direct proportion to the number of nodes traversed.

Entropy has another effect in intelligence. An intelligence assertion that "X is a possibility" very often, over time and through diverse communications channels, can become "X may be true," then "X probably is the case," and eventually "X is a fact," without a shred of new evidence to support the assertion. In intelligence, we refer to this as the "creeping validity" problem. The Iraqi WMD Commission noted this as a major analytic failing; the premise that

Iraq had hidden WMD became, over time, a presumption and eventually an unrebuttable conclusion.[12]

Earlier, we discussed bias in the source. Bias can also be a problem in the communications channel. Years back, one U.S. intelligence organization had the good fortune to obtain an audio tap into a highly classified foreign installation. The problem with the tap was that the audio was very weak and not in English. One could barely discern that it was speech. One translator with very sharp ears was able to produce transcripts, however, and the product was some exciting and very disturbing intelligence; several reports went to top levels of the U.S. government.

The transcribed material was very good—too good, in fact, and technically inconsistent. An investigation revealed that the translator wasn't translating; he was making it all up out of a fertile imagination and some knowledge of what was of current intelligence interest. The reports were withdrawn and the translator fired. On withdrawing the reports, we learned a basic rule of intelligence: The surest way to get a customer to read a report is to retract it.

Two lessons emerge from this example: First, if the source or a person in the communications channel has something to gain by providing interesting material, be wary. In this case the translator earned recognition and a promotion. Second, intelligence that sparks interest is more likely to be used. In this case the lesson comes from the customers, who would cite the reports for years because they were so interesting and provocative. When the customers were told that the reports were not valid, their response was typically, "Well, they should be!"

Evaluating the Credentials of Evidence

The major credentials of evidence, as noted earlier, are credibility, reliability, and inferential force. *Credibility* refers to the extent to which we can believe something. *Reliability* means consistency or replicability. *Inferential force* means that the evidence carries weight, or has value, in supporting a conclusion. The credibility of tangible evidence depends on its authenticity, accuracy, and reliability. The credibility of testimonial evidence depends on the veracity, objectivity (and memory), and observational sensitivity of the testifier.[13]

U.S. government intelligence organizations have established a set of definitions to distinguish levels of credibility of intelligence:

- *Fact.* Verified information, something known to exist or to have happened.
- *Direct information.* The content of reports, research, and reflection on an intelligence issue that helps to evaluate the likelihood that something is factual and thereby reduces uncertainty. This is information that can be considered factual because of the nature of the source (imagery, signal intercepts, and similar observations).

- *Indirect information.* Information that may or may not be factual because of some doubt about the source's reliability, the source's lack of direct access, or the complex (nonconcrete) character of the contents (hearsay from clandestine sources, foreign government reports, or local media accounts).[14]

This division sounds suspiciously like the "primary" and "secondary" source construct used in business intelligence. It downplays the real-world situation: that intelligence has a continuum of credibility, and that "direct information" such as signal intercepts or imagery can be misleading or false due to denial and deception.

In weighing evidence, the usual approach is to ask three questions that are embedded in the oath that witnesses take before giving testimony in U.S. courts:

- Is it true?
- Is it the whole truth?
- Is it nothing but the truth? (Is it relevant or significant?)

Is It True?

Is the evidence factual or opinion (someone else's analysis)? If it is opinion, question its validity unless the source quotes evidence to support it.

How does it fit with other evidence? The relating of evidence—how it fits in—is best done in the synthesis phase. The data from different collection sources are most valuable when used together. The synergistic effect of combining data from many sources both strengthens the conclusions and increases the analyst's confidence in them.

- HUMINT and COMINT data can be combined with ELINT data to yield a more complete picture of a radar.
- HUMINT and OSINT are often melded together to give a more comprehensive picture of people, programs, products, facilities, and research specialties. This is excellent background information to interpret data derived from COMINT and IMINT.
- Data on environmental conditions during weapons tests, acquired through specialized technical collection, can be used with ELINT and COMINT data obtained during the same test event to evaluate the capabilities of the opponent's sensor systems.
- Identification of research institutes and their key scientists and researchers can be initially made through HUMINT, COMINT, or OSINT. Once the organization or individual has been identified by one intelligence collector, the other ones can often provide extensive additional information.
- Successful analysis of COMINT data may require correlating raw COMINT data with external information such as ELINT and IMINT, or with knowledge of operational or technical practices.

One of the best examples of synthesis comes from the extensive efforts U.S. intelligence made during the 1960s through the 1980s to assess the performance of Soviet ballistic missiles. Satellite photography was compared with telemetry to check hypotheses about the weight and size of missiles. Photography of missiles on a launch pad could be used to alert telemetry collectors. Radar tracking of the boost phase could be cross-checked with telemetry to determine booster performance, and the same cross-checks on reentry vehicles could be used to estimate reentry vehicle size and weight more confidently.[15]

Is It the Whole Truth?

When asking this question, it is time to do source analysis. In HUMINT, this means looking at such things as past reporting history or psychological profile. (Is the source loose-lipped? A conniver? Or a straight shooter?) We all have *ad hoc* profiles on the people we deal with based on such things as first impressions or reputation. Sometimes we need more—a psychological profile, for example.

An incomplete picture can mislead as much as an outright lie. During the Cold War, Soviet missile guidance and control experts regularly visited their counterparts in the United States to do some informal elicitation. Alerted to yet another impending Soviet visit, U.S. intelligence, working with a leading U.S. expert, set up an elaborate display of a new and highly accurate missile guidance system in the expert's office. The Soviet visitors were impressed with the new technology, and the entire visit centered on the details of the guidance system and how it was manufactured. What the U.S. expert did not mention was that for the system to work some components had to be machined to a precision that was beyond U.S. or Soviet capabilities. It was a failed design, but the problem would not become apparent until (as we heard later) the Soviets had spent many months and much money trying to replicate the design. The U.S. expert told no lies—he simply omitted a critical truth.

Is It Nothing but the Truth?

It is worthwhile at this point to distinguish between data and evidence. *Data* become *evidence* only when the data are relevant to the problem or issue at hand. The simple test of relevance is whether it affects the likelihood of a hypothesis about the target. Does it help answer a question that has been asked? Or does it help answer a question that *should* be asked? The preliminary or initial guidance from customers seldom tells what they really need to know—an important reason to keep them in the loop through the target-centric process.

Medical doctors often encounter the relevance problem. They must synthesize evidence (symptoms and test results) to make a diagnosis: a model of the patient's present state. Doctors encounter difficulties when they must deal with a patient who has two pathologies simultaneously. Some of the symptoms are relevant to one pathology, some to the other. If the doctor tries to fit all of the symptoms into one diagnosis, he or she is apt to make the wrong call. This is a severe enough problem for doctors, who must deal with relatively few symptoms. It is a much worse problem for intelligence analysts, who typically deal with a large volume of data, most of which is irrelevant.

As a simple example of the relevance problem, suppose that the port authorities in Naples, Italy, discover a cache of arms and explosive devices in a cargo container on the docks. COMINT reporting later indicates that six members of a known terrorist group had met in a Naples harbor café on the day that the illicit cargo was discovered. An analyst might be inclined to put the two facts together in the same target model of a planned terrorist act. But the two facts could be completely unrelated.

The converse problem of fitting evidence into the model is the risk of discarding relevant evidence. Avoid discarding evidence simply because it doesn't seem to fit the model. Such anomalies may indicate that something is wrong with the model, or another model is more appropriate. Alternatively, as with the two-pathologies problem above, the evidence should be partitioned and fit into two distinct models.

Pitfalls in Evaluating Evidence

There are many pitfalls to avoid in weighing evidence. Seven that are especially important in intelligence are described in the sections that follow.

Vividness Weighting

In general, the channel for communication of intelligence should be as short as possible; but when could a short channel become a problem? If the channel is too short, the result is *vividness weighting*—the phenomenon that evidence that is experienced directly is strongest ("seeing is believing"). Customers place the most weight on evidence that they collect themselves—a dangerous pitfall that senior executives fall into repeatedly and that makes them vulnerable to deception. Strong and dynamic leaders are particularly vulnerable: Franklin Roosevelt, Winston Churchill, and Henry Kissinger are examples of statesmen who occasionally did their own collection and analysis, sometimes with unfortunate results. Michael Herman tells how Churchill, reading Field Marshal Erwin Rommel's decrypted cables during World War II, concluded that the Germans were desperately short of supplies in North Africa. Basing his interpretation on this raw COMINT traffic, Churchill pressed his generals to take the offensive against Rommel. Churchill did not realize what his own intelligence analysts could have readily told him: Rommel consistently exaggerated his shortages in order to bolster his demands for supplies and reinforcements.[16]

There is a danger in judging any evidence by its presentation, yet everyone does it. Statistics are the least persuasive form of evidence; abstract (general) text is next; concrete (specific, focused, exemplary) text is a more persuasive form still; and visual evidence, such as imagery or video, is the most persuasive. Of course, vividness can work to the advantage of a good analyst. Why not use the persuasive force of certain types of evidence to make the presentation of her conclusions more effective with the customer?

Numerous examples exist of the powerful impact that vivid evidence can have. One such was the murder of *Wall Street Journal* reporter Daniel Pearl in Pakistan in February 2002. The videotape of the murder and decapitation of Pearl evoked a strong public reaction. In August 2014, Daesh released videos of the beheading of U.S. journalist James Foley; in January 2015, they released a video of the beheading of Japanese journalist Kenji Goto; and in February 2015, they videotaped the captured Jordanian pilot Muath Al-Kasaesbeh being burned alive. All evoked strong reactions in the United States, Japan, Jordan, and other countries. Sometimes decision makers can be unduly affected by such vivid evidence. It can be argued that the subsequent measures taken against Daesh were more intense than would have been the case if the killings had been done without being videotaped.

Weighing Based on the Source

One of the most difficult traps for an analyst to avoid is that of weighing evidence based on its source. HUMINT operatives repeatedly value information gained from clandestine sources—the classic spy—above that from refugees, émigrés, and defectors. COMINT gained from an expensive emplaced telephone tap is valued (and protected from disclosure) above that gleaned from high-frequency radio communications (which almost anyone can monitor). The most common pitfall, however, is to devalue the significance of open-source material; being the most readily available, it is often deemed to be the least valuable. Using open sources well is a demanding analytic skill, and it can pay high dividends to those who have the patience to master it. Collectors may understandably make the mistake of equating source with importance. Having spent a sizable portion of their organization's budget in collecting the material, they may believe that its value can be measured by the cost of collecting it. No competent analyst should ever make such a mistake.

Favoring the Most Recent Evidence

Analysts often give the most recently acquired evidence the most weight. One caution on the danger of doing this is taken from the second law of thermodynamics, discussed earlier. For weighing evidence, the second law of thermodynamics has a different meaning. As Figure 7-3 suggests, the value of information or the weight given it in a report tends to decrease with time. The freshest intelligence—crisp, clear, and the focus of the analyst's attention—often gets more weight than the fuzzy and half-remembered (but possibly more important) information that has had to travel down the long lines of time. The analyst has to remember this tendency and compensate for it. It sometimes helps to go back to the original (older) intelligence and reread it to bring it more freshly to mind.

Favoring or Disfavoring the Unknown

It is hard to decide how much weight to give to answers when little or no information is available for or against each one. Some analysts give an answer too much weight where evidence is absent; some give it too little. Former CIA analyst Richards J. Heuer Jr. cited this "absence of evidence" problem in the example of two groups of automobile mechanics who were given a choice of reasons why a car would not start, with the list of choices ending in "other." The mechanics were told to estimate what percentage of failures was attributable to each reason. One group was given a list that omitted several of the reasons; they tended to over-weight the remaining reasons and under-weight the category "other."[17]

Trusting Hearsay

The chief problem with much of HUMINT (not including documents) is that it is hearsay evidence; and as noted earlier, the judiciary long ago learned to distrust hearsay for good reasons, including the biases of the source and the collector. Sources may deliberately distort or misinform because they want to influence policy or increase their value to the collector. Moreover, the analyst doesn't have the nonverbal details of the conversation—the setting, the context, facial and body expressions—to aid judgment. The hearsay problem had severe consequences in the case of Curveball's reporting on Iraqi biological weapons programs that was discussed earlier. U.S. intelligence officers were not able to directly interrogate Curveball and observe his demeanor during interrogation. Had they been allowed to do so, they likely would have reached quite different conclusions about the validity of his reporting.

COMINT reporting, like HUMINT, is hearsay and has to be evaluated carefully for three reasons. First, much interpretation goes into a COMINT report, and the COMINT analyst who translates and interprets the conversation may not properly guard against subjectivity. Second, some COMINT targets know they are being monitored and deliberately use the collector as a conduit for information. Finally, and most important, *people can be misinformed or lie.* COMINT can only report what people say, not the truth about what they say. So intelligence analysts have to use hearsay, but they must also weigh it accordingly.

Unquestioning Reliance on Expert Opinions

Expert opinion is often used as a tool for analyzing data and making estimates. Any intelligence community must often rely on its nation's leading scientists, economists, and political and social scientists for insights into foreign developments. These experts can and do make valuable contributions, and calls have been made to increase the U.S. intelligence community's use of outside experts.[18] But outside experts often have issues with objectivity. With experts, an analyst gets not only their expertise, but also their biases; there are those experts who have axes to grind or egos that convince them there is only one right way to do things (their way). British counterintelligence officer Peter Wright once noted that "on the big issues, the experts are very rarely right."[19] The fallibility of experts has been noted in many cases. They can be useful in pointing out flaws in logic; and their understanding of political, social, and economic situations in other countries often is superior to that of their intelligence community counterparts. But studies have found that experts are no better than simple statistical models at making predictions.[20]

More than a few scientific experts consulted by intelligence organizations have been guilty of report inflation at one time or another. Experts used as evaluators have the same problem. Analysts should treat expert opinion as HUMINT and be wary when the expert makes extremely positive comments ("that foreign development is a stroke of genius!") or extremely negative ones ("it can't be done").

The negative comments frequently stem from what former British intelligence officer R. V. Jones described as "principles of impotence." An expert will find it more reassuring to decide that something is impossible than to conclude that it is possible but that he or she failed to accomplish it. Having made such a judgment, an expert will always defend it vigorously (Analysis Principle 7-3).

Jones was the assistant director of Britain's Royal Air Force Intelligence Section during World War II and is widely regarded as the founder of the scientific intelligence discipline. He encountered several examples of principles of impotence during his tenure, such as, "It is impossible to make a bulletproof fuel tank"; "radio waves cannot be generated in the centimeter band (above 3,000 MHz)"; and "photoconductive materials cannot be made to detect wavelengths longer than two microns."[21] All of these "impossibilities" later became realities.

During 1943–1944, aerial photography of the German rocket test center at Peenemünde revealed the existence of a rocket about 45 feet long and 6 feet in diameter. As was the case with many other interesting analytic issues of World War II, this one fell to Jones to puzzle through.

British experts of the time were familiar only with rockets that burned cordite in a steel case. A simple calculation showed that a cordite-burning rocket of this size would weigh approximately 80 tons and would have to have a warhead weighing on the order of 10 tons to be worthwhile. To the British cabinet, the prospect of rockets as heavy as railroad locomotives carrying 10 tons of high explosives and landing on London was appalling.

In June 1944 a V-2 rocket crashed in Sweden, and British intelligence officers had an opportunity to examine the fragments. They reported that two liquids fueled the rocket and that liquid oxygen was one of the fuels. Armed with this evidence, Jones was able to sort through the volume of conflicting HUMINT reports about the German rocket and to select the five reports that mentioned liquid oxygen. All five were consistent in attributing light weights to the rocket and warhead. Jones subsequently (and correctly) reported to the

British war cabinet—over the objections of British rocket experts—that the V-2 weighed 12 tons and carried a 1-ton warhead.[22]

Analysis Principle 7-3 •————————————————————————————

Principles of Impotence

Fundamental limits are well known and valid in physics: It is generally accepted that one can neither travel faster than the speed of light nor reduce the temperature of an object to absolute zero. R.V. Jones described such postulates as "principles of impotence" and pointed out that they pose a special danger for scientific experts. Having tried an experiment or development and failed, the expert is strongly tempted to invoke a principle of impotence and say, "It can't be done."

Although experts have generally taken a beating in this section and perhaps frequently led us astray, their contribution has on the whole been positive. Some say that experts are harder to deceive. In the words of one author, "It is hard for one specialist to deceive another for very long."[23] By this view, deception, which is discussed in chapter 8, can be beaten more easily with expert help. Maybe. Many experts, particularly scientists, are not mentally prepared to look for deception, as intelligence officers should be. It is simply not part of the expert's training. A second problem, as noted earlier, is that experts often are quite able to deceive themselves without any help from opponents.

Varying the way expert opinion is used is one way to attempt to head off the problems cited here. Using a panel of experts to make analytic judgments is a common method of trying to reach conclusions or to sort through a complex array of interdisciplinary data. Such panels have had mixed results. One former CIA office director observed that "advisory panels of eminent scientists are usually useless. The members are seldom willing to commit the time to studying the data to be of much help."[24] The quality of the conclusions reached by such panels depends on several variables, including the panel's

- Expertise
- Motivation to produce a quality product
- Understanding of the problem area to be addressed
- Effectiveness in working as a group

A major advantage of the target-centric approach is that it formalizes the process of obtaining independent opinions. It also lends itself readily to techniques, such as the *Delphi method*, for avoiding negative group dynamics. Delphi is a systematic version of the panel consensus designed to eliminate some of the traditional panel shortcomings. It uses anonymous inputs to help obtain an objective consensus from initially divergent expert opinion. One objective of the Delphi method is the encouragement, rather than the suppression, of conflicting or divergent opinions—specifically, the development of alternative target models. Participants explain their views, and others review these explanations absent the personality, status, and debating skills that are brought to bear in conferences. The Delphi method arrives at a consensus by pooling the two separate items involved in any estimate:

- Expert information or knowledge
- Good judgment, analysis, and reasoning

Although a Delphi participant may not initially be well informed on a given question, that person still can contribute judgment, analysis, and reasoning of the information and arguments that other respondents advance.

Where panels are used, several other techniques are available to make the panel input more effective. In general, the techniques apply whenever collaborative analytic efforts are used, as they inevitably will be when the target-centric approach is applied.

If the analysis is a group effort and qualitative, a method for combining the various opinions must be determined in advance and approved by the participants. The analysis may be as simple as providing a list of all comments by participants or as difficult as reducing variance among opinions to the point that one combined opinion can be generated. If the analysis is quantitative, decide whether each participant's vote will be averaged or whether the group will be asked to come to consensus.

In determining the voting method, consider the level of expertise of each voter. Often, analyses include persons from different organizations with varying viewpoints and levels of expertise. But it is rarely feasible politically to accord a greater weight to those voters who are better informed. Instead, seek consensus among voters. In this process, each person's vote is posted before the group. All votes are then viewed to determine a median or mode. If there appears to be great dispersion among the votes, a mediator intervenes and asks voters on opposing ends to explain their positions to each other. In many cases, a disparity in knowledge is the cause of the polarized opinions.

Premature Closure and Philosophical Predisposition

In chapter 1, we discussed the failures caused by premature closure. It breaks several tenets of good problem-solving procedures, in particular the tenet of postponing evaluation and judgment until all relevant data are available. Both single-source and all-source analysts have to guard against falling into the trap of reaching conclusions too early. ELINT, COMINT, and IMINT analysts can too easily focus on one explanation for an intercept or an image and exclude the others.

Premature closure also has been described as "affirming conclusions," based on the observation that people are inclined to verify or affirm their existing beliefs rather than modify or discredit those beliefs. It has been observed that "once the Intelligence Community becomes entrenched in its chosen frame, its conclusions are destined to be uncritically confirmed."[25]

The Iraqi WMD Commission identified what it described as a "textbook example" of premature closure. Iraq was attempting to acquire aluminum tubes, ostensibly for its Medusa rocket, and a CIA officer suggested that the CIA determine the precise rocket dimensions to determine if the tubes were in fact intended for the rockets. The CIA rejected the request because it had already concluded that Iraq was acquiring the tubes for gas centrifuges to support its nuclear weapons program.[26]

The primary danger of premature closure is not that one might make a bad assessment because the evidence is incomplete. Rather, the danger is that when a situation is changing quickly or when a major, unprecedented event occurs, the analyst will become trapped by the judgments already made. Chances increase that he or she will miss indications of change, and it becomes harder to revise an initial estimate, as intelligence analysts found during the Cuban missile crisis in 1962 (discussed in more detail in chapter 8).

Few intelligence successes make headlines. Failures make headlines. One exception was the Cuban missile crisis, in which U.S intelligence services obtained information and made assessments that helped policymakers act in time to make a difference. The assessments would have been made sooner, however, except for the difficulty in changing a conclusion once reached and the tendency to ignore the Cuban refugees who "cried wolf" too often.

For some time before 1962, Cuban refugees had flooded Western intelligence services, embassies, and newspapers with reports of missiles being hidden in Cuba. When the reports about the deployment of medium-range ballistic missiles began to sift into the CIA and the Defense Intelligence Agency in 1962, they were by and large disregarded—intelligence analysts had heard such false reports too many times. Only as the weight of evidence from several independent sources, including photographic evidence and ship movement patterns, began to grow was it possible to change the collective mind of the intelligence community.[27]

The Cuban missile crisis illustrates the problem that Princeton University professor Klaus Knorr described as "philosophical predisposition," meaning a situation in which expectations fail to apply to the facts.[28] Before 1962 the Soviets had never deployed nuclear weapons outside their direct control, and U.S. analysts assumed that they would not do so by deploying nuclear warhead-equipped missiles in Cuba. Thus the analysts discounted information that contradicted this assumption. The counterintelligence technique of deception thrives on this tendency to ignore evidence that would disprove an existing assumption (a subject to which we return in chapter 8). Furthermore, once an intelligence agency makes a firm estimate, it has a propensity in future estimates to ignore or explain away conflicting information. Denial and deception succeed if one opponent can get the other to make a wrong initial estimate.

Fortunately, several problem-solving approaches help to prevent premature closure and overcome the bias of philosophical predisposition in the sifting of data. We return to this point in the discussion of alternative models in subsequent chapters. Understanding the ways to combine different types of evidence, as discussed next, helps.

Combining Evidence

In almost all cases, intelligence analysis involves combining disparate types of evidence. Analysts have to have methods for weighing the combined data to help them make qualitative judgments as to which conclusions the various data best support.

Convergent and Divergent Evidence

Two items of evidence are said to be conflicting or *divergent* if one item favors one conclusion and the other item favors a different conclusion. They are said to be *convergent* if they favor the same conclusion.

For example, a HUMINT cable reports that the Chinese freighter *Kiang Kwan* left Shanghai bound for the Indian Ocean. A COMINT report on radio traffic from the *Kiang Kwan* as she left port states that the ship's destination is Colombia. Ships seldom sail from Shanghai to Colombia via the Indian Ocean, so the two reports point to two different conclusions; they are divergent. Note that both items of divergent evidence can be true (for example, the ship could make an intermediate stop at an Indian Ocean port); they simply lead to differing conclusions. The evidence that Iraq was acquiring aluminum tubes that fit the dimensions of its Medusa rocket, cited earlier, diverged from the conclusion that the tubes were for gas centrifuges; but both conclusions nevertheless could have been true. The Iraqis could have purchased the tubes for both purposes.

In contrast, two items of evidence are *contradictory* if they say logically opposing things. A COMINT report says that the *Kiang Kwan* left Shanghai yesterday at 1800 hours; a HUMINT report says that the ship was in Singapore this morning. Given the distance between these ports and the maximum speed of merchant ships, only one report can be true.

Redundant Evidence

Convergent evidence can also be *redundant*. To understand the concept of redundancy, it helps to understand its importance in communications theory. We know that information comes to an analyst by several different channels. It often is incomplete, and it sometimes arrives in garbled form. As discussed in Analysis Principle 7-2, entropy takes its toll on any information channel. In communications theory, redundancy is one way to improve the chances of getting the message right.

Redundant, or duplicative, evidence can have corroborative redundancy or cumulative redundancy. In both types, the weight of the evidence piles up to reinforce a given conclusion. A simple example illustrates the difference.

Corroborative Redundancy

An analyst following clandestine arms transfer networks receives two reports. A COMINT report indicates that a Chinese freighter carrying a contraband arms shipment will be at coordinates 05-48S, 39-52E on June 13 to transfer the arms to another boat. A separate HUMINT report says that the Chinese freighter *Kiang Kwan* will rendezvous for an arms transfer south of Pemba Island on June 13. Both reports say the same thing; a quick map check confirms that the coordinates lie near Pemba Island, off the Tanzanian coast; so no new information (except the ship's name) is gained by the second report. The second report has value for confirmatory purposes and helps establish the validity of both sources of information.

The analogy in communications theory might occur when dealing with a noisy teletype channel. Message errors are not a concern when dealing with text only, because text has inherent redundancy. If "Chinese freighter will rendezvous" is sent, but the recipient gets the printout "Chinese frei3hter will rentezvous," the message will probably be understood in spite of the errors. The coordinates of the rendezvous point, however, have less inherent redundancy. Some redundancy does exist in geographic coordinates—a message that has the coordinates "5 degrees 88 minutes South," clearly has an error, since minutes of latitude and longitude never exceed 59. However, it is unclear what the correct latitude should be. It is common practice to spell out or repeat numbers in such a message, or even to repeat the entire message, if a chance of a garble exists; that is, the sender introduces corroborative redundancy to ensure that the correct coordinates are received.

Cumulative Redundancy

Now, suppose instead that the HUMINT report in the previous example says that a Chinese freighter left port in Shanghai on May 21 carrying AK-47 rifles and ammunition destined for Tanzanian rebels. The report does not duplicate information contained in the COMINT report, but it adds credibility to both reports. Furthermore, it leads to a more detailed conclusion about the nature of the illicit arms transfer.

The second report, in this case, adds cumulative redundancy to the first report. Both reports are given more weight, and a more complete estimate can be made than if only one report had been received.

Formal Methods for Combining Evidence

The preceding sections describe some informal methods for evidence combination. It often is important to combine evidence and demonstrate the logical process of reaching a conclusion based on that evidence by careful argument.[29] The formal process of making that argument is called *structured argumentation*. Such formal structured argumentation approaches have been around at least since the seventeenth century. Two of these are discussed in the next section. A number of other structured argumentation methods are used in prediction: Chapter 12 discusses influence trees and influence diagrams; scenario creation is covered in chapter 14.

Structured Argumentation

Structured argumentation is an analytic process that relies on a framework to make assumptions, reasoning, rationales, and evidence explicit and transparent. The process begins with breaking down and organizing a problem into parts so that each one can be examined systematically, as discussed in earlier chapters. As analysts work through each part, they identify the data requirements, state their assumptions, define any terms or concepts, and collect and evaluate relevant information. Potential explanations or hypotheses are formulated and evaluated with empirical evidence, and information gaps are identified.

Formal graphical or numerical processes for combining evidence are time consuming to apply and are not widely used in intelligence analysis. They are usually reserved for cases in which the customer requires them because the issue is critically important, because the customer wants to examine the reasoning process, or because the exact probabilities associated with each alternative are important to the customer. Two such formal processes of structured argumentation are Wigmore's charting method and Bayesian analysis.

Wigmore's Charting Method

John Henry Wigmore was the dean of the Northwestern University School of Law in the early 1900s and author of a ten-volume treatise commonly known as *Wigmore on Evidence*. In this treatise he defined some principles for rational inquiry into disputed facts and methods for rigorously analyzing and ordering possible inferences from those facts.[30]

Wigmore argued that structured argumentation brings into the open and makes explicit the important steps in an argument, and thereby makes it easier to judge both their soundness and their probative value.[31] One of the best ways to recognize any inherent tendencies one may have in making biased or illogical arguments is to go through the body of evidence using Wigmore's method.

The method is complex and is not detailed here. It is, however, a powerful tool for comparing alternative models or hypotheses. It requires the construction of elaborate diagrams that incorporate all important evidence and have the following main features, a few of which are illustrated in Figure 7-4:

- Different symbols are used to show varying kinds of evidence: explanatory, testimonial, circumstantial, corroborative, undisputed fact, and combinations.

- Relationships between symbols (that is, between individual pieces of evidence) are indicated by their relative positions (for example, evidence tending to prove a fact is placed below the fact symbol).
- The connections between symbols indicate the probative effect of their relationship and the degree of uncertainty about the relationship. For example, a double arrowhead on the connector indicates strong credit is given to the relationship; a question mark next to the connector signifies doubt about the probative effect of the connection; a zero on the connector indicates a negating effect.[32]

Wigmore intended his approach to be used by trial lawyers. But the trial lawyers basically ignored him because his diagrams were too hard to prepare.[33] His approach has fared no better with intelligence analysts. Even proponents admit that it is too time-consuming for most practical uses, especially in intelligence analysis, where the analyst typically has limited time.

Recognizing this shortcoming, Wigmore proposed a narrative form (listing rather than charting the evidence) to simplify the process and make it more readily usable by a novice.[34] But even the narrative approach runs into trouble when dealing with the large mass of data that is typical of complex problems. Nevertheless, making Wigmore's approach, or something like it, widely usable in intelligence analysis would be a major contribution. His method brings into the open and makes explicit the important steps in an argument and thereby makes it easier to evaluate the soundness of any conclusion.

Bayesian Techniques for Combining Evidence

By the early part of the eighteenth century, mathematicians had solved what is called the "forward probability" problem: When all of the facts about

Figure 7-4   Example of Wigmore's Charting Method

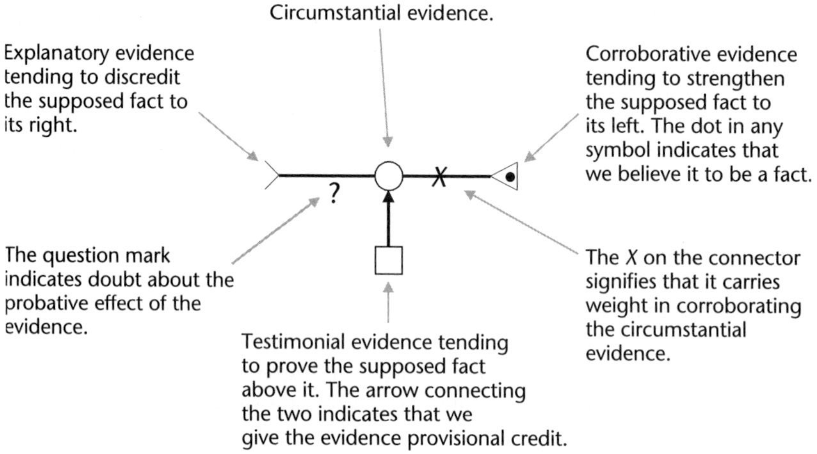

Circumstantial evidence.

Explanatory evidence tending to discredit the supposed fact to its right.

Corroborative evidence tending to strengthen the supposed fact to its left. The dot in any symbol indicates that we believe it to be a fact.

The question mark indicates doubt about the probative effect of the evidence.

The X on the connector signifies that it carries weight in corroborating the circumstantial evidence.

Testimonial evidence tending to prove the supposed fact above it. The arrow connecting the two indicates that we give the evidence provisional credit.

a situation are known, what is the probability of a given event happening? For example, if you know the number of black and white balls in a bag, it is easy to determine the probability of drawing a black ball out of the bag. In the middle of that century, British mathematician and Presbyterian minister Thomas Bayes dealt with the "inverse problem": Given that an event has occurred, what can be determined about the situation that caused the event? Continuing our bag of balls example, if you draw three black balls and one white ball out of a bag, what estimate can you make about the relative number of black and white balls in the bag? And how does your estimate change if you then draw a white ball out? Intelligence analysts find this problem of far more interest than the forward probability problem, because they often must make judgments about an underlying situation from observing the events that the situation causes. Bayes developed a formula for the answer that bears his name: Bayes' rule.

The application of Bayes' rule is called Bayesian analysis. It uses incoming data to modify previously estimated probabilities. It therefore can be used to narrow the error bounds on estimates. Each new piece of information may be evaluated and combined with prior historical or subjective assessments of the probability of an event to determine whether its occurrence has now been made more or less likely and by how much. Bayesian analysis can also be used to compute the likelihood that the observed data are attributable to particular causes. One advantage claimed for Bayesian analysis is its ability to blend the subjective probability judgments of experts with historical frequencies and the latest sample evidence.

To explain how Bayesian analysis works, let us assume that we know how often a given event normally occurs. We can assign that event a probability: $P(\text{event})$. Assume also that we have previously made an intelligence conclusion and given it a likelihood, or probability, of $P(\text{conclusion})$. Finally, we are fairly sure that, if our conclusion is true, it changes the probability $P(\text{event})$. We call this changed probability $P(\text{event} \mid \text{conclusion})$, which is read as "probability that the event will occur, given that the conclusion is true."

Now, suppose that the event does occur. Its occurrence changes the probability of our conclusion to a new probability $P(\text{conclusion} \mid \text{event})$, which is read as "probability that our conclusion is true, given that the event has occurred." The new probability is given by Bayes' rule, which is expressed by the following formula:

$$P(\text{conclusion} \mid \text{event}) = \frac{P(\text{event} \mid \text{conclusion}) \times P(\text{conclusion})}{P(\text{event})}$$

A simple illustration will help make Bayes' rule clear. Suppose an analyst has previously made an estimate based on existing evidence that a particular bank is laundering narcotics funds and has given the estimate a probability P(conclusion) = .4. The analyst knows that the probability of similar banks making profits in excess of 12 percent is .2 if the bank operates legally. The bank in question, however, recently made a profit of 20 percent, which certainly looks suspicious. The analyst concludes that there is a 30 percent (.3) chance of the bank making this much profit if it is in the fund-laundering business. The probability that the bank is laundering funds has increased:

$$P(\text{event} \mid \text{conclusion}) = (.3) \times (.4) = .12$$

$$P(\text{event}) = P(\text{event} \mid \text{conclusion}) \times P(\text{conclusion}) + P(\text{event} \mid \text{conclusion is wrong}) \times P(\text{conclusion is wrong})$$

$$\text{or } .3 \times .4 + .2 \times .6 = .24.$$

Dividing the P(event | conclusion) by P(event) gives the new probability of .5 instead of .4 that the bank is in the fund-laundering business.

While Bayesian analysis can be a powerful tool for fitting new intelligence into an existing model, it has been observed that

> Bayes seems difficult to teach. It is generally considered to be "advanced" statistics and, given the problem that many people (including intelligence analysts) have with traditional elementary probabilistic and statistical techniques, such a solution seems to require expertise not currently resident in the intelligence community or available only through expensive software solutions.[35]

The acceptance and wider use of Bayesian analysis may indeed depend on its availability as a software tool that is easy for analysts to apply to any intelligence problem.

A Note about the Role of Information Technology

It may be impossible for new analysts today to appreciate the markedly different work environment that their counterparts faced 40 years ago. Incoming intelligence arrived at the analyst's desk in hard copy, to be scanned, marked up, and placed in file drawers. Details about intelligence targets—installations, persons, and organizations—were often kept on 5" × 7" cards in card catalog boxes. Less tidy analysts "filed" their most interesting raw intelligence on their desktops and cabinet tops, sometimes in stacks over 2 feet high.

Information technology (IT) has dramatically altered that work environment for at least the government intelligence services. IT systems allow analysts to acquire raw intelligence material of interest (incoming classified cable traffic and open source) and to search, organize, and store it electronically. Such IT capabilities have been eagerly accepted and used by analysts because of their advantages in dealing with the information explosion.

A major consequence of this information explosion is that we must deal with what is called "big data" in collating and analyzing intelligence. Big data has been defined as "datasets whose size is beyond the ability of typical database software tools to capture, store, manage, and analyze."[36] It is about more than just size, though; the challenge is to deal with datasets so large *and* complex that they become difficult to process using existing database management tools or traditional data-processing applications.

The challenge of dealing with big data is not new, though the name is. The intelligence community has for decades collected more raw intelligence than could be analyzed or even stored for later analysis. Big data has been described as

> not a revolution but an evolution whose catalyst is the digitization of everything. Unfathomable amounts of resulting data must be stored and processed. And we are still using analytics to synthesize that data into information with meaning and value, just like we always have.[37]

For intelligence, it is more than just the "digitization of everything." The new source material provided by social media, cell phone communications, and imaging systems, for example, has flooded intelligence data banks. Intelligence analysts have had to move from dealing primarily with structured data (tables, relational data) and unstructured data (raw text, images, video, and audio) to dealing with metadata (data about data). Although the flood is not readily dealt with, the payoff is high. We can extract intelligence from these new sources that simply could not be acquired with the limited sources of previous years.

Analysts, inundated by the flood, have turned to IT tools for extracting meaning from the data. A wide range of such tools exists, including ones for visualizing the data and identifying patterns of intelligence interest, ones for conducting statistical analysis, and ones for running simulation models. Analysts with responsibility for counterterrorism, organized crime, counternarcotics, counterproliferation, or financial fraud can choose from commercially available tools such as Palantir, CrimeLink, Analyst's Notebook, NetMap, Orion, or VisuaLinks to produce matrix and link diagrams, timeline charts, telephone toll charts, and similar pattern displays.[38] Tactical intelligence units, in both the military and law enforcement, find geospatial analysis tools to be essential.

Some intelligence agencies also have in-house tools that replicate these capabilities. Depending on the analyst's specialty, some tools may be more relevant than others. All, though, have definite learning curves and their database structures are generally not compatible with each other. The result is that these tools are used less effectively than they might be, and the absence of a single standard tool hinders collaborative work across intelligence organizations.

In a completely different category are IT tools to support structured argumentation. Efforts have been made in recent years to incorporate a structured argumentation process into software to aid intelligence analysts. These tools promise to make structured argumentation useful for dealing with complex intelligence problems. Under Project GENOA, the Defense Advanced Research Projects Agency (DARPA) developed a tool named SEAS[39] that was well conceived but did not gain wide acceptance. Subsequently, a proprietary tool to support the analysis of competing hypotheses, called ACH, was developed for the U.S. intelligence community. An open-source version of ACH called Analysis of Competing Hypotheses is available online.[40] Use of ACH tools may be increasing, at least in the U.S. intelligence community; it is too early to tell. Like Wigmore's charting method, they may ultimately be too unwieldy for the average analyst to use.

Summary

In gathering information for synthesizing the target model, analysts should start by reviewing existing finished and raw intelligence. This provides a picture of the current target model. It is important to do a key assumptions check at this point: Do the premises that underlie existing conclusions about the target seem to be valid?

Next, the analyst must acquire and evaluate raw intelligence about the target, and fit it into the target model—a step often called collation. Raw intelligence is viewed and evaluated differently depending on whether it is literal or nonliteral. Literal sources include open source, COMINT, HUMINT, and cyber collection. Nonliteral sources involve several types of newer and highly focused collection techniques that depend heavily on processing, exploitation, and interpretation to turn the material into usable intelligence.

Once a model template has been selected for the target, it becomes necessary to fit the relevant information into the template. Fitting the information into the model template requires a three-step process:

- Evaluating the source, by determining whether the source (a) is competent, that is, knowledgeable about the information being given; (b) had the access needed to get the information; and (c) had a vested interest or bias regarding the information provided.
- Evaluating the communications channel through which the information arrived. Information that passes through many intermediate points becomes distorted. Processors and exploiters of collected information can also have a vested interest or bias.
- Evaluating the credentials of the evidence itself. This involves evaluating (a) the credibility of evidence, based in part on the previously completed source and communications channel evaluations; (b) the reliability; and (c) the relevance of the evidence. Relevance is a particularly important evaluation step; it is too easy to fit evidence into the wrong target model.

As evidence is evaluated, it must be combined and incorporated into the target model. Multiple pieces of evidence can be convergent (favoring the same conclusion) or divergent (favoring different conclusions and leading to alternative target models). Convergent evidence can also be redundant, reinforcing a conclusion.

In the ongoing target-centric process, the picture will always be incomplete after the available information is incorporated into the target model. This means that gaps exist, and new collection must be undertaken to fill the gaps. How that is done is the subject of chapter 20.

A large number of analytic methodologies are available to the analyst. Some of the most useful fall into the two broad categories of structured argumentation and alternative or competitive analysis. A third category, predictive methodologies, is discussed in chapters 12–15.

Structured argumentation is a formal process of combining evidence graphically or numerically. It brings into the open and makes explicit the important steps in an argument and thereby makes it easier to evaluate the soundness of the conclusions reached. But it is time consuming to apply and, therefore, is often ignored in favor of informal evidence combination methods. Two of the most enduring formal methods are Wigmore's evidence charting method and Bayesian analysis.

Information technology has provided a major boost to analyst productivity and to the quality of analysis. Tools to acquire, organize, search, store, and retrieve raw intelligence are widely available and enthusiastically accepted by analysts. Tools to extract meaning from data, for example, by relationship, pattern, and geospatial analysis, are used by analysts where they add value that offsets the cost of "care and feeding" of the tool. Tools to support structured argumentation are available and can significantly improve the quality of the analytic product, but whether they will find serious use in intelligence analysis is still an open question.

Notes

1. Rob Johnson, *Analytic Culture in the U.S. Intelligence Community* (Washington, D.C.: Center for the Study of Intelligence, CIA, 2005), 22.
2. Michael Herman, *Intelligence Power in Peace and War* (Cambridge, U.K.: Cambridge University Press, 1996), 82.
3. CIA, *A Tradecraft Primer: Structured Analytic Techniques for Improving Intelligence Analysis* (Washington, D.C.: Author, March 2009).
4. Bertrand Russell, *A History of Western Philosophy* (New York: Simon & Schuster, 1945), 472.
5. John Evangelist Walsh, *Moonlight: Abraham Lincoln and the Almanac Trial* (New York: St. Martin's Press, 2000).
6. "Report of the Commission on the Intelligence Capabilities of the United States Regarding Weapons of Mass Destruction," March 31, 2005, 97.
7. Alfred Price, *Instruments of Darkness* (London: William Kimber, 1967).
8. John Braithwaite, *Corporate Crime in the Pharmaceutical Industry* (London: Routledge and Kegan Paul, 1984).
9. "Report of the Commission on the Intelligence Capabilities of the United States," 125.
10. David A. Schum and Jon R. Morris, "Assessing the Competence and Credibility of Human Sources of Intelligence Evidence: Contributions from Law and Probability," *Law, Probability and Risk*, 6, no. 1-4 (March/December 2007): 247–274.

11. Claude E. Shannon, *The Mathematical Theory of Communication* (Urbana: University of Illinois Press, 1963).

12. "Report of the Commission on the Intelligence Capabilities of the United States," 10, 49.

13. David A. Schum, "On the Properties, Uses, Discovery, and Marshaling of Evidence in Intelligence Analysis," Lecture to the SRS Intelligence Analysis Seminar, Tucson, Ariz., February 15, 2001.

14. CIA Directorate of Intelligence, *A Compendium of Analytic Tradecraft Notes* (Washington, D.C.: Author, February 1997), http://www.oss.net/dynamaster/file_archive/040319/cb27cc09c84d 056b66616b4da5c02a4d/OSS2000-01-23.pdf.

15. John Prados, *The Soviet Estimate* (Princeton, N.J.: Princeton University Press, 1987), 203.

16. Michael Herman, *Intelligence Power in Peace and War* (Cambridge, U.K.: Cambridge University Press, 1996), 96.

17. Richards J. Heuer Jr., *Psychology of Intelligence Analysis* (McLean, Va.: Center for the Study of Intelligence, CIA, 1999), 119.

18. William J. Lahneman, *The Future of Intelligence Analysis*, Center for International and Security Studies at Maryland, Final Report, Vol. I (March 10, 2006), iii.

19. Peter Wright, *Spycatcher* (New York: Viking Penguin, 1987), 12.

20. Johnson, *Analytic Culture in the U.S. Intelligence Community*, 64.

21. R. V. Jones, "Scientific Intelligence," *Research*, 9 (September 1956): 350.

22. Ibid.

23. Roy Godson, *Intelligence Requirements for the 1990s* (Lanham, Md.: Lexington Books, 1989), 17.

24. David S. Brandwein, "Maxims for Analysts," *Studies in Intelligence*, 22, no. 4 (Winter 1978): 31–35.

25. Matthew Herbert, "The Intelligence Analyst as Epistemologist," *International Journal of Intelligence and CounterIntelligence*, 19 (2006): 678.

26. "Report of the Commission on the Intelligence Capabilities of the United States," 68.

27. Prados, *The Soviet Estimate*, 133.

28. Klaus Knorr, "Failures in National Intelligence Estimates: The Case of the Cuban Missiles," *World Politics*, 16 (April 1964): 455–467.

29. David A. Schum, *The Evidential Foundations of Probabilistic Reasoning* (Evanston, IL: Northwestern University Press, 1994), 161.

30. Terence Anderson and William Twining, *Analysis of Evidence* (Evanston, IL: Northwestern University Press, 1991), xxiv.

31. Ibid., 119.

32. Ibid., 112.

33. Ibid., 164–166.

34. Ibid., 156.

35. Kristan J. Wheaton, Jennifer Lee, and Hemangini Deshmukh, "Teaching Bayesian Statistics to Intelligence Analysts: Lessons Learned," *Journal of Strategic Security*, 2, no. 1 (2009): 39–58.

36. McKinsey Global Institute, "Big Data: The Next Frontier for Innovation, Competition, and Productivity," May 2011, http://www.mckinsey.com/insights/business_technology/big_data_ the_next_frontier_for_innovation.

37. David Williams, "If 'Big Data' Simply Meant Lots of Data, We Would Call It 'Lots of Data'," *Forbes*, September 19, 2012, http://www.forbes.com/sites/davidwilliams/2012/09/19/if-big-data-simply-meant-lots-of-data-we-would-call-it-lots-of-data/.

38. Jennifer Schroeder, Jennifer Xu, Hsinchun Chen, and Michael Chau, "Automated Criminal Link Analysis Based on Domain Knowledge," *Journal of the American Society for Information Science and Technology*, 56, no. 6 (2007): 842–855.

39. See the description of SEAS, the Structured Evidential Argumentation System, at http://www .ai.sri.com/project/GENOA.

40. Visit Palo Alto Research Center, http://www2.parc.com/istl/projects/ach/ach.html, or Pherson Associates, www.pherson.org, to download a copy of the tool.

8

Denial, Deception, and Signaling

There is nothing more deceptive than an obvious fact.

Sherlock Holmes, in
"The Boscombe Valley Mystery"

In evaluating evidence and developing a target model, an analyst must constantly take into account the fact that evidence may have been deliberately shaped by an opponent. That is, the analyst is seeing (or not seeing) what the opponent wants him to see (or not see). This means considering the possibility of denial and deception. Denial and deception are major weapons in the counterintelligence arsenal of a country or organization. They may be the only weapons available for many countries to use against highly sophisticated technical intelligence (such as against IMINT and SIGINT).

At the opposite extreme, the opponent may intentionally shape what the analyst sees, not to mislead but rather to send a message or signal. It is important to be able to recognize signals and to understand their meaning.

Denial

Denial and deception come in many forms. Denial is somewhat more straightforward. Some examples include the following:

- Communications and radar signals can be denied to SIGINT by operational practices such as intermittent operation or use of land lines instead of radio—practices commonly known as emissions control (EMCON). More technically sophisticated opponents use encryption or a wide range of technical approaches known collectively as low-probability-of-intercept (LPI) techniques. Signals can also be denied by the more aggressive tactic of jamming the opponent's SIGINT system with interfering signals.
- Denial against IMINT may take the form of camouflage netting, obscuring or masking techniques, or placing sensitive operations in underground facilities (protecting them against attack at the same

time); blinding sensors with lasers; conducting operations during darkness or cloud cover to hide military force movements or illegal activity; and moving units frequently to prevent their being targeted.

- Denial of spectral imagery collection could include scrubbing gas emissions (cleaning them up by removing telltale chemicals) and processing effluents to conceal the nature of the process at a plant.

Deception

Deception techniques are limited only by our imagination. Passive deception might include using decoys or having the intelligence target emulate an activity that is not of intelligence interest—making a chemical or biological warfare plant look like a medical drug production facility, for example. Decoys that have been widely used in warfare include dummy ships, missiles, and tanks.

Active deception includes misinformation (false communications traffic, signals, stories, and documents), misleading activities, and double agents (agents who have been discovered and "turned" to work against their former employers), among others.

Illicit groups (for example, terrorists) conduct most of the deception that intelligence must deal with. Illicit arms traffickers (known as gray arms traffickers) and narcotics traffickers have developed an extensive set of deceptive techniques to evade international restrictions. They use intermediaries to hide financial transactions. They change ship names or aircraft call signs en route to mislead law enforcement officials. One airline changed its corporate structure and name overnight when its name became linked to illicit activities.[1] Gray arms traffickers use front companies and false end-user certificates.[2] The following are some of the standard deception techniques that illicit arms carrier aircraft use:

- Registering the aircraft in one country, then chartering it by companies registered in another, with crews that are hired in yet other countries and basing the aircraft somewhere else
- Using another aircraft's call sign
- Flying into an airport with one registration number and then flying out with a different one
- Making an unscheduled landing on the way to the approved destination and unloading illicit cargo
- Making an unscheduled landing to load illicit cargo en route, and then shipping the additional load under cover of the legal cargo

In another actual example, a pilot was told to give the destination of his aircraft as N'Djamena in Chad, but when he arrived in Cairo he was told to file a new flight plan giving his destination as Muscat, Oman. Once the plane was on its way to Oman, the crew were told to divert to Mukalla Airport, near Riyan, in Yemen, and then to fly a specific, circuitous route over Saudi Arabian airspace.[3]

Commercial entities also engage in deception to mislead competitors, but companies must usually tread a fine line in conducting such deception. The objective is to mislead the competitor without misleading the public (in countries such as the United States, misinformation can result in lawsuits) and without doing anything illegal. In a number of areas, though, such as positioning for competitive contract bidding and in mergers and acquisitions, deception is a common and accepted part of the game.

Defense against denial and deception (D&D) starts with one's own denial effort, that is, the protection of sources and methods of collecting and analyzing intelligence.

Defense against Denial and Deception: Protecting Intelligence Sources and Methods

In the intelligence business, it is axiomatic that if you need information, someone will try to keep it from you. And we have noted repeatedly that if an opponent can model a system, he can defeat it. So your best defense is to deny your opponent an understanding of your intelligence capabilities. Without such understanding, the opponent cannot effectively conduct D&D.

For small governments, and in the business intelligence world, protection of sources and methods is relatively straightforward. Selective dissemination of and tight controls on intelligence information are possible. But a major government has too many intelligence customers to justify such tight restrictions. Thus these bureaucracies have established an elaborate system to simultaneously protect and disseminate intelligence information. This protection system is loosely called *compartmentation*, because it puts information in "compartments" and restricts access to the compartments.

There are two levels of protection for intelligence information. The levels distinguish between the *product* of intelligence and the *sources and methods*; usually the product is accorded less protection than the sources and methods. Why? The product, if lost, reveals only itself and not how it was obtained. Information about the product is typically classified "Secret" or below, though "Top Secret" reports are used to protect especially sensitive information. Information that might reveal the identity of the source (such as the identity of an agent) is given the highest level of protection. Loss of this information often results in the person being imprisoned or killed; the source is lost permanently and other potential sources are discouraged from coming forward.

In the U.S. intelligence community, the intelligence product, sources, and methods are protected by the sensitive compartmented information (SCI) system. The SCI system uses an extensive set of compartments to protect sources and methods. Only the collectors and processors have access to many of the compartmented materials. Much of the product, however, is protected only by standard markings such as "Secret," and access is granted to a wide range of people.

Under the SCI system, protection of sources and methods is extremely high for two types of COMINT. Clandestine COMINT—usually acquired through taps on telecommunications systems—is heavily protected because it is expensive to set up, it provides high-quality intelligence, and its loss has a severe and often permanent impact. COMINT based on decryption is the second highly protected type. Successes at breaking encryption are tightly compartmented because an opponent can readily change the encryption code, and breaking the new code is laborious.

Most IMINT, by contrast, has no special controls, because the information needs to be made available quickly to field commanders. Very little protection of sources and methods is needed anyway, because when a reconnaissance aircraft flies overhead, it is obvious to the enemy that you are taking their pictures. Most aerial photography has been classified "Secret" or below, and a substantial amount of satellite photography is now unclassified. High security protection is reserved for the unusual IMINT—unique capabilities that are not obvious to the opponent.

Open-source intelligence has little or no protection because the source material is unclassified. However, the techniques for exploiting open-source material, and the specific material of interest for exploitation, can tell an opponent much about an intelligence service's targets. For this reason, intelligence agencies that translate open source often restrict its dissemination, using markings such as "Official Use Only." A restrictive marking also allows a government to avoid copyright laws while limiting use of the material. Corporations make use of similar restrictive markings on material that is translated or reproduced for in-house use for the same reasons—concealment of their interest and avoidance of copyright problems.

An important reason for protecting open-source methods is that if an opponent knows what the intelligence target materials are, it is easier for the opponent to take deceptive countermeasures. For example, the United States has long been aware that many intelligence services translate and avidly read *Aviation Week and Space Technology*. When the Defense Department wishes to mislead or deceive another country about U.S. aerospace capabilities and intentions, this magazine would be a logical place to plant a misleading story.

The protection given to specialized technical collection varies greatly across the many collection types. ELINT is classified "Secret" or below. When opponents use a radar, they have to assume that someone will intercept it, and denial is very difficult. In contrast, the value of FISINT depends on concealing any successes in identifying the purpose of each telemetry channel that is collected. FISINT therefore resembles COMINT—the processing part is accorded tight compartmentation protection. The results of cyber collection are given a high degree of protection for a similar reason; collection can be defeated or used in deception if its success becomes known to an opponent.

Higher Level Denial and Deception

A few straightforward examples of denial and deception were cited earlier. But sophisticated deception must follow a careful path; it has to be very subtle (too-obvious clues are likely to tip off the deception) yet not so subtle that your opponent misses it. It is commonly used in HUMINT, but today it frequently requires multi-INT participation or a "swarm" attack to be effective. Increasingly, carefully planned and elaborate multi-INT D&D is being used by various countries. Such efforts even have been given a different name—*perception management*—that focuses on the end result that the effort is intended to achieve.

Perception management can be effective against an intelligence organization that, through hubris or bureaucratic politics, is reluctant to change its initial conclusions about a topic. If the opposing intelligence organization makes a wrong initial estimate, then long-term deception is much easier to pull off. If D&D are successful, the opposing organization faces an *unlearning* process: its predispositions and settled conclusions have to be discarded and replaced. Highly adaptive organizations have the capacity to unlearn and are therefore less vulnerable to D&D than are more structured organizations. Large, bureaucratic organizations find unlearning very difficult.

The best perception management results from highly selective targeting, intended to get a specific message to a specific person or organization. This requires knowledge of that person's or organization's preferences in intelligence—a difficult feat to accomplish, but the payoff of a successful perception management effort is very high. It can result in an opposing intelligence service making a miscall or causing it to develop a false sense of security. If you are armed with a well-developed model of the three elements of a foreign intelligence strategy described in chapter 5—targets, operations, and linkages—an effective counterintelligence counterattack in the form of perception management or covert action is possible, as the following examples show.

The Man Who Never Was

During World War II, the British had a very good model of German intelligence, including a good understanding of the German operations in Spain and the close linkages between German and Spanish intelligence. Armed with this knowledge, they were able to plant on the Spanish coastline the body of an apparent British staff officer carrying documents that indicated the targets of the next Allied invasion. The deception effort, nicknamed "Operation Mincemeat," was first revealed in Ewen Montagu's book (later a motion picture) entitled *The Man Who Never Was*.[4] It involved dressing a corpse as a British Royal Marines officer. To the corpse was attached a briefcase with documents indicating that the upcoming Allied invasion of southern Europe would take place in Greece or Sardinia. The corpse and briefcase were then released from a submarine near the coast of Spain, where it was expected that it would be found and the briefcase's contents shared with German intelligence. The deception succeeded because the British had an excellent model of how the German and Spanish services worked together, and they knew what form of information the Germans were likely to believe. A fake operations plan probably would have aroused German suspicions. Instead, the key document was a masterpiece of subtlety, in the form of a personal letter hinting that the next invasions would hit Sardinia and Greece, and that Sicily (the actual invasion target) was a feint.

Nevertheless, the plan had a number of potentially serious flaws. Fortunately for the Allies, these were overlooked by both the Spanish and the German intelligence. The body was released in a coastal area known to have strong pro-Axis sentiments, but the documents wound up in the control of the Spanish Navy—the least pro-Axis of possible recipients. The Spanish coroner who examined the body was, contrary to British expectation, an expert pathologist who had long experience in examining drowning victims. He noticed several suspicious features about the body. No fish or crab bites, shiny instead of dull hair, and clothing that wasn't shapeless, all indicated that the body had not been in the water as long as the briefcase's documents indicated; but the state of decay indicated that the body had been in the water longer than the documents indicated.[5] Furthermore, a large number of people knew of the operation (apparently including the Soviets), increasing the chances of a leak.

The point is that complex deception efforts are very difficult to pull off, even with a good model of the opposing services such as the British had. In the end, the success of the British effort depended on a few lucky breaks.

Operation Fortitude

In planning for the Normandy invasion during World War II, the Allies fabricated elaborate invasion preparations in an effort to convince the Germans that the invasion target was the Pas-de-Calais, directly across the English Channel from Britain. The deception operation was called Operation Fortitude.

The deception involved creating a fictional invasion force in the region around Dover, publicly identified as General Patton's 1st U.S. Army Group. It used large numbers of dummy tanks, military vehicles, and other equipment that appeared to be assembling for an invasion across the Channel. The dummy equipment made use of inflatables that were highly detailed and looked real when photographed by an overflying Luftwaffe reconnaissance aircraft.

Operation Fortitude, in combination with several other deception operations, was a success; the Germans allocated much of their defenses to the Pas-de-Calais, well away from the real invasion in Normandy.[6]

The Cuban Missile Crisis

In early 1962 the Soviets decided to emplace nuclear-equipped SS-4 and SS-5 ballistic missiles in Cuba to counter the increasing U.S. edge in ballistic missiles aimed at the Soviet Union. The deployment was to be hidden from U.S. intelligence by an elaborate D&D program that combined HUMINT, IMINT, open-source, and diplomatic deception:

- Soviet military units designated for the Cuban assignment were told that they were going to a cold region. They were outfitted with skis, felt boots, fleece-lined parkas, and other winter equipment.
- Officers and missile specialists traveled to Cuba as machine operators, irrigation specialists, and agricultural specialists.
- Missiles were shipped from eight Soviet ports to hide the size of the effort; the missiles were loaded under cover of darkness.
- The missile crates and launchers were shielded with metal sheets to defeat infrared photography.
- Ordinary automobiles, tractors, and harvesters were placed on the top decks to convey the impression that the ships were carrying only agricultural equipment.
- The ships' captains made false declarations when exiting the Black Sea and the Bosporus. They altered the cargo records and declared tonnage well below what was being carried. They often listed Conakry, Guinea, as their destination.
- In Cuba, anything that resembled agricultural equipment was unloaded in the daytime. Weaponry was unloaded only at night, and moved directly to the missile bases along back roads at night.
- Radio Moscow regularly reported that the Soviet Union was supplying Cuba with "machine tools, wheat, and agricultural machinery . . . and fertilizer."
- In what proved to be a brilliant move, the Soviets leaked accurate information about the deployment to mask it. They funneled accurate details through counterrevolutionary Cuban organizations in the United States. The CIA discounted the information because they did not regard the groups as credible, and dismissed the subsequent stream of reporting from Cubans, tourists, and foreign diplomats in Cuba—some of which were valid—as simply more of the same.
- During September, Soviet diplomats gave repeated assurances to top U.S. officials (including President John Kennedy) that they had no intention of putting offensive weaponry in Cuba.[7]

The deception was not perfect. There were some slips:

- The Soviets used the freighter *Poltava* to carry missiles. Some U.S. experts speculated that the ship might be carrying ballistic missiles, because the Soviets used large-hatch ships such as the *Poltava* to deliver such missiles.
- Had a vessel experienced mechanical failure en route, the captains were told to explain to any ships offering assistance that they were

exporting automobiles. If such an encounter had occurred, it would have been a tipoff to analysts that something was amiss, because the Soviet Union was not an automobile exporter at the time.

- Once deployed, the units were not well concealed from aerial reconnaissance. They had a characteristic imagery signature that the Soviets did not change, and that led to the U.S. discovery of the San Cristobal missile site in October—and the beginning of the Cuban missile crisis.[8]

In summary, the deception was a remarkably well-crafted multi-INT D&D effort that succeeded for a long time because the Soviets had a very good understanding of U.S. intelligence capabilities and predispositions.

The Farewell Dossier

Detailed knowledge of an opponent is the key to successful counterintelligence, as the "Farewell" operation shows. In 1980 the French internal security service *Direction de la Surveillance du Territoire* (DST) recruited a KGB lieutenant colonel, Vladimir I. Vetrov, codenamed "Farewell." Vetrov gave the French some four thousand documents, detailing an extensive KGB effort to clandestinely acquire technical know-how from the West, primarily from the United States. In 1981 French president François Mitterrand shared the source and the documents (which DST named "the Farewell Dossier") with U.S. president Ronald Reagan.

The documents revealed a far-reaching and successful intelligence operation that had already acquired highly sensitive military technology information about radars, computers, machine tools, nuclear weaponry, and manufacturing techniques. But the specific targets on the list provided the needed guidance for an effective counterstrike.

In early 1982 the U.S. Department of Defense, the Federal Bureau of Investigation, and the CIA began developing a counterattack. Instead of simply improving U.S. defenses against the KGB efforts, the U.S. team used the KGB shopping list to feed back, through CIA-controlled channels, the items on the list—augmented with "improvements" that were designed to pass acceptance testing but would fail randomly in service. Flawed computer chips, turbines, and factory plans found their way into Soviet military and civilian factories and equipment. Misleading information on U.S. stealth technology and space defense flowed into the Soviet intelligence reporting. The resulting failures were a severe setback for major segments of Soviet industry. The most dramatic single event resulted when the United States provided gas pipeline management software that was installed in the trans-Siberian gas pipeline. The software had a feature that would, at some time, cause the pipeline pressure to build up to a level far above its fracture pressure. The result was the Soviet gas pipeline explosion of 1982, described as the "most monumental non-nuclear explosion and fire ever seen from space."[9]

Mounting a deception campaign often requires extensive effort, but sometimes it is worth the payoff. The Farewell operation was expensive to run but produced many benefits; it may have hastened the end of the Cold War.

In many ways, the Farewell operation was the perfect counterintelligence response. Even its subsequent exposure did not reduce the effectiveness of the operation, since the exposure called into question all of the successful KGB technology acquisitions and discredited the KGB's technology collection effort within the Soviet Union.[10] The operation would not have been possible without the detailed knowledge that Vetrov provided that allowed the United States to create detailed models of the KGB targets; the nature of the KGB operations; and the linkages—that is, the use of other Warsaw Pact country intelligence services in the technology acquisition effort.

Farewell also was a model of collaboration—not only within U.S. intelligence, but also of collaboration with allied governments and with industry. The operation would have been far less successful without the assistance provided by manufacturers in several countries.

Rabta

In late 1988, with extensive foreign assistance, Libya completed construction of a chemical warfare production complex at Rabta. During three years of operation, the facility produced at least 100 metric tons of mustard gas and the nerve agent sarin.[11]

In 1990 the United States publicized the details of the Rabta operation and its production of chemical weapons. The Libyans responded with an elaborate deception operation, fabricating evidence of a fire to make the Rabta facility appear to be damaged and possibly inoperative.[12] The fabrication reportedly involved painting burn marks on buildings and burning stacks of tires to create the perception of a fire for imagery collectors.

Libya subsequently switched from deception to denial. The Libyans closed the Rabta plant later in 1990. To replace it, they constructed a large underground chemical warfare plant near Tarhunah, a mountainous region about 60 kilometers southeast of Tripoli. Putting the facility underground masked its activities and increased its survivability in case of an attack.[13]

The Indian Nuclear Test

Unfortunately, other intelligence services often learn of U.S. collection capabilities through the actions of policymakers. Demarches[14] and public statements that are based on intelligence results inevitably reveal something about intelligence capabilities. India used such knowledge in developing a strategic deception plan to cover its nuclear device test on May 11, 1998. On that date, the Indians conducted three underground nuclear tests at their Pokhran nuclear test site in the country's northwestern desert. The test came as a complete surprise to the U.S. government.

The deception plan succeeded because the Indian government had an excellent understanding of the keys that U.S. imagery analysts used to detect test preparations. The U.S. government had succeeded in deterring an earlier plan by India to stage the tests. In December 1995, U.S. reconnaissance satellites had observed test preparations at the Pokhran site, including the movement of vehicles and the deployment of testing equipment. The U.S. ambassador to India showed the imagery to top Indian officials in a successful demarche to persuade them not to test.[15] However, what happened next is an illustrative example of unintended consequences.

Using the knowledge they gained from the demarche, the Indians were able to plan an elaborate D&D campaign to conceal preparations for the 1998 tests. The denial campaign was many-faceted, aimed at protecting the operation from HUMINT and IMINT:[16]

- The effort was protected by extensive secrecy measures within the Indian government. Few knew of the plan; the decision to test was not disclosed even to senior cabinet ministers.
- Work was done at night, and heavy equipment was always returned to the same parking spot at dawn with no evidence it had been moved.
- Piles of dug-out sand were shaped to mimic the wind-aligned and shaped dune forms in the desert area.
- The shafts were dug under a netting of camouflage.
- When cables for sensors were laid, they were carefully covered with sand and native vegetation replaced to conceal the digging.

The deception campaign had several elements, making it an excellent example of multi-INT deception:

- All technical staff at the range wore military fatigues, so that in satellite images they would appear as military personnel charged with maintenance of the test range.
- All scientists involved in the operation left in groups of two or three on the pretext of attending a seminar or a conference. Tickets were bought for some location other than Pokhran under false names and after arriving at their destination, the group would secretly leave for Pokhran. After finishing their part of the work, the group would go back, retracing their path. Then another group would leave for the range, employing similar means to do their part of the work on the bombs.
- The Indian government issued a number of public statements just prior to the test, designed to reassure Washington that no nuclear test was contemplated. Indian diplomats also categorically told their U.S. counterparts that "there would be no surprise testings."

- At the same time, Indian leaders began an effort to focus U.S. attention elsewhere. They started preparations for what appeared to be a ballistic missile test at their Chandipur missile test range, more than a thousand miles from the Pokhran site. The Indians actually tested a Trishul surface-to-air missile (which was of relatively low intelligence interest), but they moved additional equipment into the test range so that the preparations appeared to be for a test of the Agni intermediate range ballistic missile (which was of high intelligence interest).[17]

As a result, U.S. reconnaissance satellites reportedly were focused on the Chandipur missile site, with only minimal coverage of the nuclear test site at the time of the test.[18] The deception was helped along by the U.S. government's mindset that, since India wanted to improve trade relations, the country would not provoke a crisis by testing a nuclear weapon.[19]

Countering Denial and Deception

In recognizing possible deception, an analyst must first understand how deception works. Four fundamental factors have been identified as essential to deception: truth, denial, deception, and misdirection.[20]

- *Truth*—All deception works within the context of what is true. Truth establishes a foundation of perceptions and beliefs that are accepted by an opponent and can then be exploited in deception. Supplying the opponent with real data establishes the credibility of future communications that the opponent then relies on.
- *Denial*—It's essential to deny the opponent access to some parts of the truth. Denial conceals aspects of what is true, such as your real intentions and capabilities. Denial often is used when no deception is intended; that is, the end objective is simply to deny knowledge. One can deny without intent to deceive, but not the converse.
- *Deceit*—Successful deception requires the practice of deceit.
- *Misdirection*—Deception depends on manipulating the opponent's perceptions. You want to redirect the opponent away from the truth and toward a false perception. In operations, a feint is used to redirect the adversary's attention away from where the real operation will occur. Operation Fortitude in 1944 and the 1998 Indian nuclear weapon test, discussed earlier, are examples of misdirection.

The first three factors allow the deceiver to present the target with desirable, genuine data while reducing or eliminating signals that the target needs to form accurate perceptions. The fourth provides an attractive alternative that commands the target's attention.

It is essential that these four factors of deception—truth, denial, deceit, and misdirection—be considered while creating the model, to tip off the likelihood of deception.

Many of the standard techniques for countering D&D were developed during World War II, and they continue to work with new twists and new technologies. However, when collection becomes too predictable—as can happen in large intelligence organizations—tactics for countering D&D no longer work. If opponents can model the collection process, they can defeat it. U.S. intelligence learned that lesson in HUMINT against numerous Soviet targets after some painful losses. There is a tendency to believe that overhead (satellite) IMINT and SIGINT are less vulnerable to countermeasures. However, critics have pointed out that not only denial, but also effective deception, is possible against both IMINT and SIGINT if the opponent knows enough about the collection system.[21] The effectiveness of hostile D&D is a direct reflection of the predictability of collection.

Collection Rules

The best way to defeat D&D is for all of the stakeholders in the target-centric approach to work closely together. The two basic rules for collection, described here, form a complementary set. One rule is intended to provide incentive for collectors to defeat D&D. The other rule suggests ways to defeat it.

The first rule is to establish an effective feedback mechanism. *Relevance* of the product to intelligence questions is the correct measure of collection effectiveness, and analysts and customers—not collectors—determine relevance. The system must enforce a content-oriented evaluation of the product, because content is used to determine relevance. This implies that a strong feedback system exists between analyst and collector and generally that collectors have established close links to the analysts. The link has to work both ways. Collectors need to see clearly how their product was used to modify the target model.

At one point in history, intelligence services did very well at countering D&D. During World War II, both the British and the Germans had efficient systems for identifying D&D techniques and countering them. (The successful Allied deception that covered the 1944 Normandy invasion was a notable exception; but that worked, in part, because the Germans had a very poor "analyst" in Adolf Hitler.) Few D&D tactics worked for very long. Britain and Germany owed their World War II success to a tight feedback loop in their intelligence processes. Intelligence analysts interacted constantly with IMINT and SIGINT collectors to develop counter-countermeasures. As a result, there existed a constant action-counteraction process, much like what has existed in the electronic warfare and radar communities since the outbreak of WWII.

The second rule is to make collection smarter and less predictable. There exist several tried-and-true tactics for doing so:

- *Don't optimize systems for quality and quantity; optimize for content.* One might, for example, move satellite-based collectors to less desirable orbits to achieve surprise or to keep opponents off balance. At the opposite extreme in sophistication, in collecting discarded papers (TRASHINT), don't keep coming back to the same dumpster every day at the same time.
- *Apply sensors in new ways.* Analysis groups often can help with new sensor approaches in their areas of responsibility. Also, techniques for defeating D&D that have been developed for one problem (counternarcotics, for example) may be applicable to others (weapons proliferation).
- *Consider provocative techniques against D&D targets.* In the U.S. Air Force airborne reconnaissance programs dating back to the 1950s, provocation was used effectively to overcome the practice of emissions control by the Soviets. In EMCON, one keeps all nonessential signals off the air until the SIGINT collector has left the area. The U.S. response was to send an aircraft on a penetration course toward the Soviet border, for example, and turn away at the last minute, after the Soviets had turned on their entire air defense network to deal with the threat. Probing an opponent's system and watching the response is a useful tactic for learning more about the system. Even so, probing may have its own set of undesirable consequences: The Soviets would occasionally chase and shoot down the reconnaissance aircraft to discourage the probing practice.
- *Hit the collateral or inferential targets.* If an opponent engages in D&D about a specific facility, then supporting facilities may allow inferences to be made or to expose the deception. Security measures around a facility and the nature and status of nearby communications, power, or transportation facilities may provide a more complete picture.
- *Finally, use deception to protect a collection capability.* Military tacticians claim that the best weapon against a tank is another tank, and the best weapon against a submarine is another submarine. Likewise, the best weapon against D&D is to mislead or confuse opponents about intelligence capabilities, disrupt their warning programs, and discredit their intelligence services.

In analysis, the first defense against D&D involves maintaining alternative target models, as discussed in chapter 7. Another important step is to continually develop new techniques for sensor fusion or synthesis of intelligence data. An analyst can often beat D&D simply by using several types of intelligence—HUMINT, COMINT, and so on—in combination, simultaneously, or successively. It is relatively easy to defeat one sensor or collection channel. It is more difficult to defeat all types of intelligence at the same time. Hyperspectral imaging, for example, is a valuable weapon against IMINT deception because it can be used to measure so many different aspects (signatures) of a target. Increasingly, opponents can be expected to use "swarm" D&D, targeting several INTs in a coordinated effort like that used by the Soviets in the Cuban missile crisis and the Indian government in the Pokhran deception. Such complex operations, however, as in those examples, inevitably have their weak points. The analyst has only to find them. Which leads us to the most effective method of countering D&D—the experienced and inquiring analyst.

The Information Instrument

Analysts, whether single- or all-source, are the focal points for identifying D&D. In the types of conflicts that analysts now deal with, discussed in chapter 2, opponents have made effective use of a weapon that relies on deception: using both traditional media and social media to paint a misleading picture of their adversaries. Nongovernmental opponents (insurgents and terrorists) have made effective use of this information instrument. The usual approach is to produce videos designed to increase hostility toward the United States and its allies, to facilitate recruitment of new members to incite sympathizers to taking action, or to increase media sympathy for their cause.

This use of the information instrument for deception is not new; the Soviets used it often and with effect against the United States in South Asia, Africa, and Latin America, planting disinformation such as forged documents that portrayed the United States as a greedy, malicious world power intent on overthrowing existing governments. But the prevalence of media reporters in all conflicts, and the easy access to social media, have given the information instrument more utility. Media deception has been used repeatedly by opponents to portray U.S. and allied "atrocities" during military campaigns in Kosovo, Iraq, Afghanistan, and Syria. It has been used against the Israelis in Gaza and Lebanon. And several parties to the conflict in Syria have used it. As examples of the technique, in Kosovo, the Serbs posted dramatic photographs of the same blood-stained doll in their reporting of several alleged atrocities in different locations. In Afghanistan, Taliban forces took journalists on a night convoy to an alleged mass casualty site while coalition airstrikes were ongoing in the area, apparently for the purpose of drawing coalition fire with resulting media casualties.[22]

Signaling

Signaling is the opposite of denial and deception. It is the process of deliberately sending a message, usually to an opposing intelligence service. It is included here because, like D&D, its use depends on a good knowledge of how the opposing intelligence service obtains and analyzes knowledge. Recognizing and interpreting an opponent's signals is one of the more difficult challenges an analyst must face. Depending on the situation, signals can be made verbally, by actions, by displays, or by very subtle nuances that depend on the context of the signal.

In negotiations, signals can be both verbal and nonverbal. True signals often are used in place of open declarations, to provide information while preserving the right of deniability.

One signal that has gained use with the increase in satellite imagery is the purposeful display of items in an imaged area to send a message. Massing troops on a frontier as an intimidation tactic is one example of signaling. It is such a well-known tactic that in July 1990, Saddam Hussein's massing of troops on the Kuwaiti border initially was interpreted as a signal, putting pressure on Kuwait to obtain economic concessions in upcoming negotiations.

In business, signals are often conveyed by actions rather than by words. A competitor's price increase or decrease, an acquisition, a new product line, or a major reorganization, among others, can signal the company's future intentions in the market.

Analyzing signals requires examining the content of the signal and its context, timing, and source. Statements made to the press are quite different from statements made through diplomatic channels—the latter usually carry more weight. As an example of context, a statement made by the Egyptian ambassador to a U.S. military attaché at an embassy function could easily be a signal; the ambassador knows that he is speaking to an intelligence officer.

Signaling between members of the same culture can be subtle, with high success rates of the signal being understood. Two U.S. corporate executives can signal to each other with confidence; they both understand the rules. A U.S. executive and an Indonesian executive would face far greater risks of misunderstanding each other's signals. The cultural differences in signaling can be substantial. Cultures differ in their reliance on verbal and nonverbal signals to communicate their messages. The more people rely on nonverbal or indirect verbal signals and on context, the higher the complexity. For instance, the Japanese and the Chinese rely heavily on implicitly understood communications, and the context of any communication is also highly significant. As Figure 8-1 indicates, the Swiss are at the opposite extreme; their messages are explicitly stated and often independent of context.

The importance of both implicit messages and context is illustrated in the final note submitted by Japanese diplomats to U.S. secretary of state Cordell Hull, on December 7, 1941. Negotiations between the U.S. and the Japanese governments to resolve differences had reached an impasse, and the key parts of the note read:

> [H]ope to preserve and promote the peace of the Pacific through cooperation with the American Government has finally been lost . . . in view of the attitude of the American Government [Japan] cannot but consider that it is impossible to reach an agreement through further negotiations.

This is a *declaration of war.* But most Americans, less sensitive to context and more accustomed to explicit communication than the Japanese, would not

Figure 8-1   Cultural Differences in Signaling

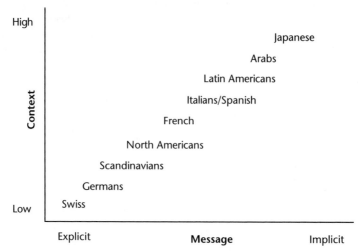

Source: Adapted from Edward T. Hall, *Beyond Culture* (New York: Anchor, 1976).

read it as such. It might simply indicate a new phase in the negotiation, such as verbally upping the level of rhetoric. In no part of the message was the word *war* used. (To his credit, Secretary of State Hull did recognize the implications of the message; he had considerable past experience in negotiating with the Japanese government.)

Signaling is an art, and interpreting signals is an art. Failure to understand the signals can have severe consequences. In the Pearl Harbor case, Hull understood the signal, but nothing could be done; the attack was underway before he was presented with the note. Two more recent examples illustrate the consequences of both failure to understand an opponent's signals and failure to understand that *you* are signaling the opponent:

- During the Korean War, as U.S. and U.N. forces advanced north of the thirty-eighth parallel, China decided that a North Korean defeat was unacceptable. China's leaders moved aggressively on several fronts to signal their intention to intervene militarily if the advances continued. Diplomatic notes, press releases, and overt troop movements all were used to send that signal. U.S. policymakers and military leaders either dismissed or failed to understand the signals, and the Chinese intervention came as a surprise.[23]
- In July 1990 the U.S. State Department unintentionally sent several signals that Saddam Hussein apparently interpreted as a green light to attack Kuwait. State Department spokesperson Margaret Tutwiler said, "[W]e do not have any defense treaties with Kuwait. . . ." The next day,

Ambassador April Glaspie told Saddam Hussein, "[W]e have no opinion on Arab-Arab conflicts like your border disagreement with Kuwait." And two days before the invasion, Assistant Secretary of State John Kelly testified before the House Foreign Affairs Committee that there was no obligation on our part to come to the defense of Kuwait if it were attacked.[24]

The Kuwait example illustrates the other side of signaling—and intelligence analysts can and should help their customers in this regard. Clearly, it is important to be able to tell a policymaker what the opponent's signals are and to interpret them. But it is equally important to let policymakers know how their signals, whether intentional or not, are likely to be interpreted by the opponent.

Analytic Tradecraft in a World of Denial and Deception

Writers often use the analogy that intelligence analysis is like the medical profession.[25] Analysts and doctors weigh evidence and reach conclusions in much the same fashion. In fact, intelligence analysis, like medicine, is a combination of art, tradecraft, and science.[26] Different doctors can draw different conclusions from the same evidence, just as different analysts do.

But intelligence analysts have a different type of problem than doctors do. Scientific researchers and medical professionals do not routinely have to deal with denial and deception. Though patients may forget to tell them about certain symptoms, physicians typically don't have an opponent who is trying to deny them knowledge.[27] In medicine, once doctors have a process for treating a pathology, it will in most cases work as expected. The human body won't develop countermeasures to the treatment.[28] But in intelligence, your opponent may be able to identify the analysis process and counter it. If analysis becomes standardized, an opponent can predict how you will analyze the available intelligence, and then D&D become much easier to pull off. Consider, for example, the effect of the Soviet "leak" during the Cuban missile crisis discussed previously. Intelligence collection and analysis, by their nature, have to evolve. One cannot establish a process and retain it indefinitely.

Intelligence analysis within the context of D&D is in fact analogous to being a professional poker player, especially in the games of Seven Card Stud or Texas Hold 'em. You have an opponent. Some of the opponent's resources are in plain sight, some are hidden. You have to observe the opponent's actions (bets, timing, facial expressions, all of which incorporate art and tradecraft) and do pattern analysis (using statistics and other tools of science). There are lots of poker "methodologies," just as there are lots of intelligence methodologies. No single one works universally, and all can be defeated once they are understood.

Some underlying principles are common to intelligence analysis and poker. In poker, you create a model of your opponents, based on observations of their past behavior; and you create a model of their current hand, based on the model of your opponents, evidence of their behavior during the current hand, plus a statistical analysis of what can be observed (for example, the exposed cards). You analyze those models, and make judgments. In intelligence analysis, you do the same—the stakes are much higher, of course.

Summary

In evaluating raw intelligence, analysts must constantly be aware of the possibility that they may be seeing material that was deliberately provided by the opposing side. Most targets of intelligence efforts practice some form of denial. Deception—providing false information—is less common than denial because it takes more effort to execute, and it can backfire.

Defense against D&D starts with your own denial of your intelligence capabilities to opposing intelligence services. Some collection sources and methods have to be heavily protected, or they will become vulnerable to D&D. Names of HUMINT sources, the nature of COMINT or many types of technical collection, and the decryption of encrypted messages all fall into this category. In contrast, the information that a source provides is accorded less protection than details about the source itself, because the information provided needs to go to many intelligence customers. IMINT and open sources usually receive less source protection than do HUMINT, COMINT, or specialized technical collection.

Where one intelligence service has extensive knowledge of another service's sources and methods, more ambitious and elaborate D&D efforts are possible. Often called *perception management*, these involve developing a coordinated multi-INT campaign to get the opposing service to make a wrong initial estimate. Once this happens, the opposing service faces an unlearning process, which is difficult. A high level of detailed knowledge also allows for covert actions to disrupt and discredit the opposing service.

A collaborative target-centric process helps to stymie D&D by bringing together different perspectives from the customer, the collector, and the analyst. Collectors can be more effective in a D&D environment with the help of analysts. Working as a team, they can make more use of deceptive, unpredictable, and provocative collection methods that have proven effective in defeating D&D.

The opposite of D&D, yet closely related, is the practice of signaling: deliberately sending a message to the opposing intelligence service. Like D&D, its success depends on a good understanding of the opponent to whom a signal is sent. Signals can be verbal, or by actions or displays. Analysts have to be alert to the presence of signals and adept at interpreting their meaning. When signals must be sent between different cultures, it's important to consider how they may be misinterpreted or missed altogether.

Intelligence analysis is a combination of art, tradecraft, and science. In large part, this is because analysts must constantly deal with denial and deception, and dealing with D&D is primarily a matter of artfully applying tradecraft.

Notes

1. Brian Wood and Johan Peleman, *The Arms Fixers* (Oslo: International Peace Research Institute [PRIO], 1999), http://www.nisat.org/publications/armsfixers, chapter 5.
2. International legal protocol surrounding the shipment of lethal weapons requires that the shipper have a certificate of "end use," in which the buyer declares that the weapons are for its use only, and will not be trans-shipped.
3. Wood and Peleman, *The Arms Fixers*, chapter 5.
4. Ewen Montagu, *The Man Who Never Was* (Annapolis, Md.: Naval Institute Press, 1953).
5. Ben Macintyre, *Operation Mincemeat* (New York: Harmony Books, 2010), 201–202.
6. Huw Hopkins, "D-Day 70–Pt.17–Operation FORTITUDE: Allied Deception Tactics," June 4, 2014, http://www.globalaviationresource.com/v2/2014/06/04/d-day-70-pt-17-operation-fortitude-allied-deception-tactics/.
7. James H. Hansen, "Soviet Deception in the Cuban Missile Crisis," *Studies in Intelligence*, 46, no. 1 (2002), http://www.cia.gov/csi/studies/vol46no1/article06.html.
8. Ibid.
9. Thomas C. Reed, *At the Abyss: An Insider's History of the Cold War* (Novato, Calif.: Presidio Press, 2004).
10. Gus W. Weiss, "The Farewell Dossier," *CIA: Studies in Intelligence,* 39, no. 5 (1996), http://www.cia.gov/csi/studies/96unclass.
11. U.S. Department of Defense, "Proliferation: Threat and Response," April 1996, https://www2.gwu.edu/~nsarchiv/NSAEBB/NSAEBB372/docs/Document09.pdf.
12. Ibid.
13. Ibid.
14. A demarche is a political or diplomatic step, such as a protest or diplomatic representation made to a foreign government.
15. Tim Weiner and James Risen, "Policy Makers, Diplomats, Intelligence Officers All Missed India's Intentions," *New York Times,* May 25, 1998.
16. Ibid.
17. "Strategic Deception at Pokhran Reported," *Delhi Indian Express* in English, May 15, 1998, 1.
18. Weiner and Risen, "Policy Makers, Diplomats, Intelligence Officers."
19. Ibid.
20. Edward Waltz and Michael Bennett, *Counterdeception Principles and Applications for National Security* (Boston, Mass.: Artech House, 2007).
21. Angelo Codevilla, *Informing Statecraft* (New York: Free Press, 1992), 159–165.
22. U.S. Department of Defense, "Background Briefing on Enemy Denial and Deception," October 24, 2001, http://www.defense.gov/transcripts/transcript.aspx?transcriptid=2162.
23. P. K. Rose, "Two Strategic Intelligence Mistakes in Korea, 1950," *CIA: Studies in Intelligence* (Fall/Winter 2001), http://www.cis.gov/csi/studies/fall_winter_2001/article06.html.
24. Jude Wanniski, "Where Did Saddam Hussein Come From?" *Wall Street Journal*, February 19, 1998.
25. Steven Marin, "Intelligence Analysis: Turning a Craft into a Profession," https://analysis.mitre.org/proceedings/Final_Papers_Files/97_Camera_Ready_Paper.pdf.
26. Rob Johnson, *Analytic Culture in the U.S. Intelligence Community* (Washington, D.C.: Center for the Study of Intelligence, CIA, 2005), 43.
27. Doctors must routinely deal with patients who conceal embarrassing information. But the patient seldom if ever is trying to lead the doctor to an incorrect diagnosis.
28. This analogy has its limits, of course; microbes do develop resistance to antibiotics over time.

9

Systems Modeling and Analysis

Believe what you yourself have tested and found to be reasonable.

Buddha

In chapter 3, we described the target as three things: as a complex system, as a network, and as having temporal and spatial attributes. In fact, any entity having the attributes of structure, function, and process can be described and analyzed as a system, as noted in previous chapters. Air defense systems, antisubmarine weaponry, transportation networks, welfare systems—all of these and many others have been the object of systems modeling and analysis.

Many of the formal applications of systems analysis were pioneered in the U.S. Department of Defense during the 1960s. Systems analysis has since then been used in assessing both U.S. and foreign weapons systems—ballistic missiles, combat aircraft, naval vessels—and smaller systems and subsystems such as radars.

This chapter discusses modeling the target as a system. It focuses on weapons systems modeling and analysis, but the basic principles apply in modeling political and economic systems, as well. Systems analysis can be applied to analyze both existing systems and those under development.

A government can be considered a system and analyzed in much the same way—by creating structural, functional, and process models. So can an insurgency: The following example from the Soviet-Afghan war illustrates that point. It also illustrates the importance of considering the system from a broad perspective, and of doing performance analysis.

Analyzing an Existing System: The Mujahedeen Insurgency

During the 1980s, the CIA engaged in a covert operation to supply the Afghans with resources to fight the Soviet occupation of Afghanistan. The agency planned to supply a stockpile of rifles to the mujahedeen who were leading the insurgency. A military systems analyst with the program, Michael Vickers, analyzed the total Afghan resistance effort. Vickers argued that supplying rifles alone would be counterproductive. The Afghans didn't have enough ammunition for the rifles they already had. Unless the CIA could supply a very high volume of ammunition, more rifles would hinder, not help, the resistance. The real problem was that the insurgents had to feed their families and care for their wounded, and that hindered their ability to put pressure on the Soviet forces. Vickers put together a complete systems package that included ammunition, food for the families, and medical kits to keep the mujahedeen in the field year-round.[1]

Vickers's Afghan resistance assessment illustrates a key point about systems analysis: Analysis of any complex system is, of necessity, multidisciplinary. Systems analysts often have problems in dealing with multidisciplinary aspects; they are more comfortable sticking to the technical aspects, primarily performance analysis. In its national intelligence estimate on Iraqi weapons of mass destruction, the WMD Commission observed, "The October 2002 NIE contained an extensive technical analysis . . . but little serious analysis of the socio-political situation in Iraq, or the motives and intentions of the Iraqi leadership. . . . [T]hose turn out to be the questions that could have led the Intelligence Community closer to the truth."[2] That criticism is frequently valid; technical analysis of complex systems is often done in a vacuum, with no consideration of political, economic, and social factors. Such was not the case with the Vickers analysis.

Vickers's second brilliant systems analysis achievement came in assessing the mix of weapons needed to defeat the Soviet HIND attack helicopter, which was the most effective and feared weapon against mujahedeen fighters. Representative Charlie Wilson, the covert action's key supporter, wanted to supply Swiss Oerlikon heavy machine guns for the mujahedeen to use against the HIND. Vickers told Wilson that this was the wrong way to look at the problem. The Oerlikon was too heavy to be moved around in large parts of Afghanistan. And a single weapon can be defeated, as in this case, by tactics. But the proper mix of antiair weaponry could not. The mix here included surface-to-air missiles (SA-7s, British Blowpipes, and Stinger missiles) and machine guns (Oerlikons and captured Soviet Dashika machine guns). The Soviet helicopter operators could defend against some of these, but not all simultaneously. SA-7s were vulnerable to flares; Blowpipes were not. The HINDs could stay out of range of the Dashikas, but then they would be at an effective range for the Oerlikons.[3] Unable to know what they might be hit with, Soviet pilots were likely to avoid attacking or rely on defensive maneuvers that would make them almost ineffective—which is exactly what happened.

Analyzing a Developmental System: Methodology

The mujahedeen example illustrates two applications of systems analysis to an existing system. In intelligence, we also are concerned about modeling a system that is under development. The first step in modeling a developmental system, and particularly a future weapons system, is to identify the system(s) under development. Two approaches traditionally have been applied in weapons systems analysis, both based on reasoning paradigms drawn from the writings of philosophers: deductive and inductive.

- The deductive approach to prediction is to postulate desirable objectives, in the eyes of the opponent; identify the system requirements; and then search the incoming intelligence for evidence of work on the weapons systems, subsystems, components, devices, and basic research and development (R&D) required to reach those objectives.
- The opposite, an inductive or synthesis approach, is to begin by looking at the evidence of development work and then synthesize the advances in systems, subsystems, and devices that are likely to follow.[4]

A number of writers in the intelligence field have argued that intelligence uses a different method of reasoning—*abduction*, which seeks to develop the best hypothesis or inference from a given body of evidence. Abduction is much like induction, but its stress is on integrating the analyst's own thoughts and intuitions into the reasoning process. Abduction has been described as "an instinct for guessing right."[5] Like induction, abduction has the difficulty that different analysts can come to different conclusions using the same set of facts. So both induction and abduction are inherently probabilistic.[6]

The deductive approach can be described as starting from a hypothesis and using evidence to test the hypothesis. The inductive approach is described as evidence-based reasoning to develop a conclusion.[7] Evidence-based reasoning is applied in a number of professions. In medicine, it is known as evidence-based practice—applying a combination of theory and empirical evidence to make medical decisions.

Both (or all three) approaches have advantages and drawbacks. In practice, though, deduction has some advantages over induction or abduction in identifying future systems development. If only one weapons system is being built, it is not too difficult to identify the corresponding R&D pattern and the indicators in the available information, and from that to synthesize the resulting systems development. The problem arises when two or more systems are under development at the same time. Each system will have its R&D process, and it can be very difficult to separate the processes out of the mass of incoming raw intelligence. This is the "multiple pathologies" problem that was introduced in chapter 7: When two or more pathologies are present in a patient, the symptoms are mixed together, and diagnosing the separate illnesses becomes very difficult. Generally, the deductive technique works better for dealing with the multiple pathologies issue in future systems assessments.

Once a system has been identified as being in development, analysis proceeds to the second step: answering customers' questions about it. These questions usually are about the system's functional, process, and structural characteristics—that is, about performance, schedule, risk, and cost.

At the highest level of national policy, details on how a future weapons system may operate are not as important as its general characteristics and capabilities and a fairly accurate time scale.[8] As the system comes closer to completion, a wider group of customers will want to know what specific targets the system has been designed against, in what circumstances it will be used, and what its effectiveness will be. These matters typically require analysis of the system's performance, including its suitability for operating in its environment or in accomplishing the mission for which it has been designed. The schedule for completing development and fielding the system, as well as associated risks, also become important. In some cases, the cost of development and deployment will be of interest. Let's consider each in turn.

Performance

Performance analyses are done on a wide range of systems, varying from simple to highly complex multidisciplinary systems. Determining the performance of a narrowly defined system, such as a surface-to-air missile, is straightforward. More challenging is assessing the performance of a complex system such as an air defense network or a narcotics distribution network. Most complex system performance analysis is now done by using simulation, a topic to which we will return.

Much systems analysis for both policymakers and the military is focused on weapons systems performance. Weapons systems analysts operate in a different environment from political, military, and economic analysts—their conclusions are less often challenged by customers. Policymakers and military leaders seldom have the technical expertise to engage weapons systems analysts at the detailed level. That does not necessarily make the weapons systems analyst's life easier; it's not uncommon for the customer to turn to outside experts who don't have an intelligence background, as some of the examples in this chapter illustrate.

Two techniques are frequently used to assess system performance: comparative modeling and simulation. Sometimes the two are used together. Let's look at the more straightforward method of comparative modeling first.

Comparative Modeling

Comparative modeling is similar to benchmarking, introduced in chapter 6, but the focus is on analysis of one group's system or product performance, versus an opponent's.

Comparing your country's or organization's developments with those of an opponent can involve four distinct fact patterns. Each pattern poses challenges that the analyst must deal with. The first possible pattern is that country A has developed a certain capability (for example, a weapon, a technology, or a factory process) and so has opponent country B. In this case the analyst from country A has the job of comparing country B's capability with that of country A. The other three possible patterns are that country A has developed a particular capability, but country *B* has not; that country *A* has not developed a particular capability, but country *B* has; or that neither country has developed the capability. In short, the possibilities can be described as follows:

- We did it—they did it.
- We did it—they didn't do it.
- We didn't do it—they did it.
- We didn't do it—they didn't do it.

There are many examples of the "we did it—they did it" sort of intelligence problem, especially in industries in which competitors typically develop similar products. The United States developed intercontinental ballistic missiles (ICBMs); the Russians developed ICBMs. Both sides developed antiballistic missile systems and missile-firing submarines. Many countries build aircraft, cruise missiles, tanks, electric power distribution systems, computers, and so on. In these cases the intelligence officer's analysis problem is not so difficult because she can turn to her own country's or organization's experts on that particular system or product for help.

For example, in World War II both the British and the Germans developed and used radar. So when in 1942 a British reconnaissance aircraft photographed a bowl-shaped antenna near the French coast, British intelligence could determine, with help from their experts, that it was a radar. Because the radar, which was later nicknamed the Würzburg, posed a threat to British aircraft attacks on Germany, the British undertook some rather direct materiel collection means to gather additional information about the radar. They assembled a company of paratroops to make an airborne assault on a Würzburg radar located near the coast in Bruneval, France. The assault team made off with the feed antenna for the radar dish, the receiver, and display equipment.

The subsequent analysis of the Würzburg also provides a good example of the mirror-imaging problem that can exist when a country uses its own experts. The Würzburgs were typically deployed in pairs; one radar in a pair had one to three searchlights collocated with it. British radar experts believed that the second radar was a spare, to be used when the first radar was inoperative, since this was the normal British practice. British intelligence officer R. V. Jones, however, argued that the Würzburg with searchlights was intended to track bombers, whereas the second radar had the job of tracking fighters that would be guided to the bomber. British experts disagreed, since this would require accuracy in coordinate transformation that was beyond their technical skill at the time. They failed to appreciate the accuracy with which German radars operated as a matter of course. As it turned out, Jones, armed with a better understanding of the German way of building defense systems, was correct.

In the second case, "we did it—they didn't do it," the intelligence officer runs into a real problem: It is almost impossible to prove a negative in intelligence. The fact that no intelligence information exists about an opponent's development cannot be used to show that no such development exists.

After the British created the magnetron (a microwave transmitter tube widely used in radar) and discovered what wonders it could do for a radar system, their constant worry was that the Germans would make a similar discovery and that the British would have to face radars with capability equal to their own. In fact, the Germans learned about the magnetron only when they captured one from a downed British aircraft late in the war, but the threat kept British intelligence on edge.

The third pattern, "we didn't do it—they did it," is the most dangerous type that we encounter. Here the intelligence officer has to overcome opposition from skeptics in his country, because he has no model to use for comparison. Jones faced a case like this when he pieced together the operating principles of a new German aircraft navigation system called Knickebein.

Knickebein was a radio beam system that the Germans used to guide their bombers at night to their bomb drop point (usually London). At one point, when Jones was attempting to convince top government officials to send radio-equipped aircraft aloft to search for the Knickebein signal, he was opposed by Britain's leading authority on radio wave propagation—Thomas Eckersley of the Marconi Company. Eckersley argued that radio waves would not propagate sufficiently far at 30 megahertz to be observed over London. Fortunately for Jones, the ELINT search aircraft collected the signal before its flights could be halted.

The central premise of the movie *The Hunt for Red October* is another example of this type. In the movie, the Soviets had developed a low-noise caterpillar drive for their submarine, the *Red October*, making it almost undetectable when under way. The United States had no equivalent development, so understanding the submarine's quiet performance was difficult.

The "we didn't do it—they did it" case presents analysts with an opportunity to go off in the wrong direction analytically. Such was the case with the Caspian Sea Monster.

In the 1960s, U.S. intelligence analysts obtained satellite imagery of a massive aircraft in the Caspian Sea near the port of Kaspiysk. Nearly 100 meters in length, it was the largest aircraft in the world at the time and was promptly nicknamed the "Caspian Sea Monster." The vehicle appeared to be a seaplane, but it quickly posed problems for the analysts trying to identify its mission and performance. Its short, stubby wings could not support it as an aircraft in conventional flight. After much system performance modeling and simulation, analysts concluded that it was a "ground effect" or "wing in ground effect" vehicle, designed to fly a short distance above the water to take advantage of the additional lift provided by flying close to the surface.

The question of the monster's mission remained. Analysis focused on what the United States would do with such a craft—classic mirror imaging—and the major candidates for a mission were off the mark. The answer came only many years later. The craft was originally intended as a very high speed transport for troops and military equipment. A smaller variant later was developed to carry antiship cruise missiles; it now sits rusting in the water at the Kaspiysk naval base.

Flying very close to the water is of course a risky affair, and the original monster crashed on takeoff in 1980. The vehicle was too heavy to be recovered from its watery graveyard.

"We didn't do it—they didn't do it"—this seems to be a ridiculous case. After all, if we haven't developed a weapon and they haven't developed a weapon, who cares? The answer is that people do care, and intelligence analysts spend a great deal of their time on just this sort of problem. One historical example is the case of the German engine killer.

Back in World War II, British intelligence received reports about classified testing going on at a secret installation inside Germany. According to the reports, automobiles driving near this installation would suddenly stall and could not be started again. After a while a German sentry would step out of the nearby woods, tell the automobile drivers they could proceed, and the automobiles would start again and run normally.

As one might imagine, the thought of a weapon that could stall internal combustion engines caused British intelligence some concern, since British tanks, trucks, and airplanes relied on such engines. While the threat was a continuing concern to British intelligence, in the postwar period it was found that the order of events had become transposed in reports. What actually happened is that the Germans were testing very sensitive radio equipment that was vulnerable to automobile ignition noise. When testing was under way, German sentries throughout the area around the plant would force all automobiles to stop and shut down their ignitions until testing was over.

This sort of transposition of cause and effect is not uncommon in human source reporting. Part of the skill required of an intelligence analyst is to avoid the trap of taking sources too literally. Occasionally, intelligence analysts must spend more time than they should on problems that are even more fantastic or improbable than that of the German engine killer. In chapter 11 we discuss the particle beam weapon scare of the 1970s. The particle beam weapon appears to have been a classic case of "we didn't do it—they didn't do it." The United States didn't build one and neither did the Soviets; in fact, no one could.

Simulation

Simulation is discussed in detail in chapter 15. Here we introduce it for its application to performance modeling. Performance simulation typically is a parametric, sensitivity, or "what if" type of analysis; that is, the analyst needs to try a relationship between two variables (parameters), run a computer analysis and examine the results, change the input constants, and run the simulation again. Such systems simulations must be interactive; the analyst has to see what the results look like and make changes as new ideas surface.

In weapons systems performance simulations, analysts sometimes tend to get lost in the details and lose sight of the main objective. It's a matter of professional pride for engineers to run simulations that compute the thrust of a rocket to within a pound, or to go to fractions of a decibel on radar performance analysis. The customers usually don't care.

At times, though, a relatively small performance difference can be critical. In the case of the Backfire bomber, it was.

Throughout the 1960s, U.S. Air Force intelligence had consistently predicted that the Soviets would develop a new heavy bomber capable of striking U.S. targets. In 1969, photos of a plant at Kazan revealed the existence of a new bomber, subsequently codenamed "Backfire." Two alternative missions for Backfire became the center of an intelligence analysis controversy. Air Force analysts took the position that Backfire could be used for intercontinental attack. CIA analysts argued that the aircraft's mission was peripheral attack— that is, attack of ground or naval targets near the Soviet mainland.

Over the next several years, national intelligence estimates shifted back and forth on the issue. The critical evaluation criterion was the aircraft's range. A range of 5,500 miles or more would allow Backfires to strike U.S. targets from Soviet bases on one-way missions. A range of less than 5,000 miles would not allow such strikes, unless the Backfire received inflight refueling. The answer was important for the U.S. Department of Defense and particularly for the Air Force, because the longer range meant that Backfires were a threat to the United States that would have to be countered.

The Air Force and the Defense Intelligence Agency (DIA) produced simulations from McDonnell Douglas engineers that showed the Backfire had a range between 4,500 and 6,000 miles. The CIA produced estimates from a different set of McDonnell Douglas engineers that showed a range of between 3,500 and 5,000 miles. Each side accused the other of slanting the evidence.

The issue of the range of the Backfire bomber became even more important because it became enmeshed in Strategic Arms Limitation Talks (SALT). A Soviet intercontinental bomber would have to be counted in the Soviet array of strategic weaponry. The Russians eventually agreed as part of the SALT II process to produce no more than thirty Backfires a year and not to equip them for inflight refueling; the United States agreed not to count Backfires as intercontinental bombers. In later years, evidence became clear that the Backfire was in fact a somewhat overdesigned peripheral attack bomber, never intended for intercontinental attack missions.

The Backfire bomber case illustrates some of the analytic traps discussed in chapter 7: premature closure, in that analysts were trapped by previous predictions that the Soviets would develop a new intercontinental bomber, and "cherry picking"—preferring the evidence that supports your hypothesis. It also illustrates the need for doing multidisciplinary analysis in systems analysis. A serious consideration of Soviet systems designs and requirements, and of what the Soviets foresaw as threats at the time, would likely have led analysts to zero in more quickly on the Backfire's mission of peripheral attack.

The case also illustrates the common systems analysis problem of presenting the worst-case estimate: National security plans often are made on the basis of a systems estimate; out of fear that policymakers may become complacent, an analyst will tend to make the worst case that is reasonably possible. In a more recent example, the WMD Commission noted that "the Intelligence Community made too much of an inferential leap, based on very little hard evidence, in judging that Iraq's unmanned aerial vehicles were being designed for use as biological warfare delivery vehicles and that they might be used against the United States"[9]—a case of moving to the most disturbing conclusion.

The Backfire bomber example illustrates the importance of having alternative target models. It also is a good example of applying both techniques of performance analysis: comparative performance analysis and simulation.

The Mirror-Imaging Challenge

Both comparative modeling and simulation have to deal with the risks of mirror imaging. The opponent's system or product (such as an airplane, a missile, a tank, or a supercomputer) may be designed to do different things or to serve a different market than expected. U.S. Air Force analysts in the Backfire bomber case tended to compare the Backfire to the slightly larger U.S. B-1A, which was an intercontinental bomber under development at the time.

The risk in all systems analysis is one of mirror imaging, which is much the same as the mirror-imaging problem in decision-making discussed in chapter 6. U.S. analysts of Soviet military developments made a number of bad calls on systems performance during the Cold War years as a result of mirror imaging. It is useful to review some of the major differences we observed in the Soviet case.

Unexpected Simplicity

In effect, the Soviets applied a version of Occam's razor (choose the simplest explanation that fits the facts at hand) in their industrial practice. Because they were cautious in adopting new technology, they tended to keep everything as simple as possible. They liked straightforward, proven designs. When they copied a design, they simplified it in obvious ways and got rid of the extra features that the United States tends to put on its weapons systems. The Soviets made maintenance as simple as possible, because the hardware was going to be maintained by people who did not have extensive training.

In a comparison of Soviet and U.S. small jet engine technology, the U.S. model engine was found to have 2.5 times as much materials cost per pound of weight. It was smaller and lighter than the Soviet engine, of course, but it had 12 times as many maintenance hours per flight-hour as the Soviet model, and overall the Soviet engine had a life cycle cost half that of the U.S. engine.[10] The ability to keep things simple was the Soviets' primary advantage over the United States in technology, especially military technology. This was a major pitfall in comparing the Backfire bomber to U.S. bombers; a U.S. bomber of Backfire's size and configuration could easily have had intercontinental range.

A Narrowly Defined Mission

The Soviets built their systems to perform specific, relatively narrow (by U.S. standards) functions. The MIG-25 is an example of an aircraft built this way—overweight and inefficient by U.S. standards but simple and effective for its intended mission. The Backfire also was designed for a very specific mission—countering U.S. naval forces in the North Atlantic. The United States tends to optimize its weapons systems for a broad range of missions.

Quantity May Replace Quality

U.S. analysts often underestimated the number of units that the Soviets would produce. The United States needed fewer units of a given system to perform a mission, since each unit had more flexibility, quality, and performance ability than its Soviet counterpart. The United States forgot a lesson that it had learned in World War II—U.S. Sherman tanks were inferior to the German Tiger tanks in combat, but the United States deployed a lot of Shermans and overwhelmed the Tigers with numbers.

Schedule

The intelligence customer's primary concern about systems under development usually centers on performance, as discussed previously. But sometimes, schedule becomes a critical factor, as it was during negotiations about Iran's nuclear weapons potential during 2006–2015.

In 2006 a group of six world powers referred to as P5+1 (the U.N. Security Council's five permanent members—the P5—plus Germany) joined together in diplomatic efforts to constrain Iran from producing nuclear weapons. The negotiations focused on maximizing Iran's time to "breakout," which is defined as the amount of time that it would take Iran to produce sufficient weapons-grade uranium or plutonium for one nuclear weapon.

To produce weapons-grade material, uranium needs to be enriched (in the Iranian case, with centrifuges) to more than 90 percent of its U-235 isotope. The amount of enriched material required for one weapon is defined by the International Atomic Energy Agency as approximately 27 kilograms of uranium.[11] So the subsequent agreement limited the number of centrifuges that Iran could have, to lengthen the breakout time.

Readers who are familiar with the issue decomposition method described in chapter 4 will recognize a *seeming* flaw in this focus on breakout time. Producing bomb-grade material is just one step in creating a nuclear weapons system. The entire systems development process includes designing a bomb; configuring it to fit into a missile warhead; and developing a missile (including reentry vehicle and guidance system) with the range, accuracy, and throw weight to carry the warhead.

The Iranians emphasized the need for these steps in arguing that the real time was measured in years, instead of in months, as estimated by the P5+1 negotiators. The Iranians argued that production of enough material for a bomb would actually take them eighteen months; conversion of the material to pure uranium metal, twelve months; molding into an explosive device, six months; developing a warhead around the device and mating to a missile, an unknown time because Iran claims no experience in building nuclear warheads and fitting them to delivery systems.[12]

It's a specious argument, though. The remaining steps after the production of enough fissile material would be difficult for the P5+1 group to monitor, and even more difficult to stop. The P5+1 negotiators apparently recognized that their best bet was to control nuclear material production. The Iranian negotiations also are an excellent example of the importance, in intelligence, of understanding the customer's perspective—a topic to which we'll return in chapter 19.

The Iranian example illustrates the importance of the systems *development* process, which is one of the many types of processes we deal with in intelligence. Before returning to the development process and its importance in intelligence analysis, let's look at process modeling generally.

Process Models

The functions of any system are carried out by processes. The processes will be different for different systems. That's true whether you are describing an organization, a weapons system, or an industrial system. Different types of organizations, for example—civil government, law enforcement, military, and commercial organizations—will have markedly different processes. Even similar types of organizations will have different processes, especially in different cultures. The processes used by a terrorist organization such as Al Qaeda are quite different from those used by the Tamil Tigers of Sri Lanka.

There are a correspondingly large number of analytic techniques for analyzing processes, many of which are industry or weapons systems specific. Analysts tend over time to develop process methodologies that are unique to their area of responsibility. Political, military, economic, and weapons systems analysts all use specialized process-analysis techniques. In this chapter we address a few that are widely used.

A process model is one that describes a sequence of events or activities that produce results. It can be an open or closed loop, with feedback being the difference, as Figure 9-1 illustrates. Most processes and most process models have feedback loops. Feedback allows the system to be adaptive, that is, to adjust its inputs based on the output. Even simple systems such as a home heating/air conditioning system provide feedback via a thermostat. For complex systems, feedback is essential to prevent the process from producing undesirable output. Feedback is such an important part of both synthesis and analysis that it receives detailed treatment in chapter 13.

Process models are frequently used in simulation modeling, discussed in detail in chapter 15. Now let's return to the specific issue of the development process.

Figure 9-1 A Simple Process Model

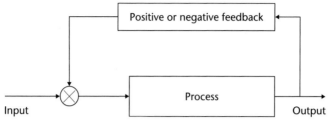

Note: The circled *X* shows where the input and the feedback combine before they feed into the process.

Figure 9-2 Example Development Process Model

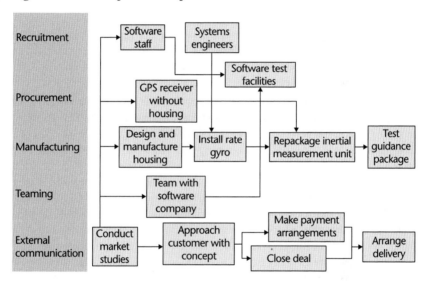

Development Process Models

In determining the schedule for a systems development, we concentrate on examining the development process and identifying the critical points in that process.

An example development process model is shown in Figure 9-2. In this display, the process nodes are separated by function into "swim lanes" to facilitate analysis. This model shows the process of a hypothetical European electronics manufacturer that is building a missile guidance system destined for shipment to a Middle Eastern country.[13]

Chapter 6 introduced the iterative process of model improvement using new intelligence. Figure 9-3 shows how this sort of iterative modeling can be done using a process model. In this example, the model shown in

Figure 9-3 Analysis of a Revised Process Model

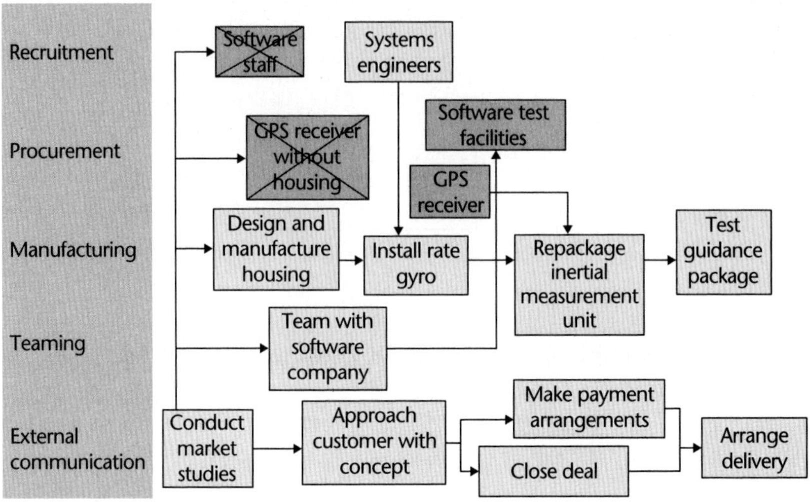

Figure 9-2 envisioned the electronics manufacturer as hiring software staff to support software development and purchasing a Global Positioning System (GPS) receiver from an external source. Suppose that the analyst later receives evidence that the company is neither hiring software staff nor trying to acquire a GPS receiver externally. The analyst then revises the model, as shown in Figure 9-3, to delete these two blocks and add a new one showing the analyst's estimate of internal manufacture of a GPS receiver. The analyst then must estimate whether software test facilities will be procured or whether the manufacturer will rely on those of its partner software company. In any event, the result will affect schedule—and likely cost and performance, as well.

We previously discussed the Iranian nuclear agreement negotiations. Two alternative process models for building a nuclear weapon exist. Figure 9-4 shows the two processes as they would be carried out by known Iranian facilities. The faster development results in a warhead with U-235 fuel. This alternative requires uranium enriched to greater than 90 percent U-235, as the figure indicates. Another approach is to use a combination of U-238 and at least 20 percent U-235, and convert the U-238 to plutonium-239 in a heavy water reactor. This approach, as the figure suggests, is a longer-term process.

The Program Cycle Model

The process models shown in Figures 9-2 through 9-4 are just one part—albeit an important part—of the larger systems process model known as the program cycle. A new system—whether a banking system, a weapons system, or computer software—develops and evolves through a process commonly

Figure 9-4   Process Model for an Iranian Nuclear Weapon

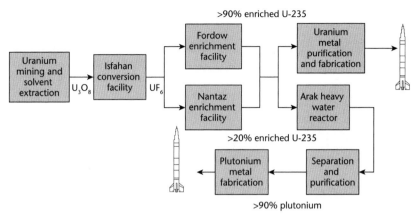

Source: Figure drawn using information in Mansouor Ahmed, "The Iranian Nuclear Conundrum and the NPT," *South Asian Voices*, January 7, 2015, http://southasianvoices.org/the-iranian-nuclear-conundrum-and-the-npt/

known as the program cycle or the system life cycle. Beginning with the system requirement and progressing to production, deployment, and operations, each phase bears unique indicators and opportunities for collection and synthesis/analysis. Customers of intelligence often want to know where a major system is in this life cycle.

Each country, industry, or company has its own version of the program cycle. Figure 9-5 illustrates the major components of a generic program cycle. Different types of systems may evolve through different versions of the cycle, and product development differs somewhat from systems development. It is therefore important for the analyst to first determine the specific names and functions of the cycle phases for the target country, industry, or company and then determine exactly where the target program is in that cycle. With that information, analytic techniques can be used to predict when the program might become operational or begin producing output.

It is important to know where a program is in the cycle in order to make accurate predictions. In assessing both Libya's and Iraq's WMD capabilities, analysts tended to equate procurement actions as indicating that a weapons capability existed—though the two occur at quite different phases in the program cycle. This tendency was partially a result of getting a large volume of procurement-related intelligence, possibly leading analysts to overestimate its importance.[14]

A general rule of thumb is that the more phases in the program cycle, the longer the process will take, all other things being equal. Countries and organizations with large, stable bureaucracies typically have many phases, and the process, whatever it may be, takes that much longer.

Figure 9-5   The Generic Program Cycle

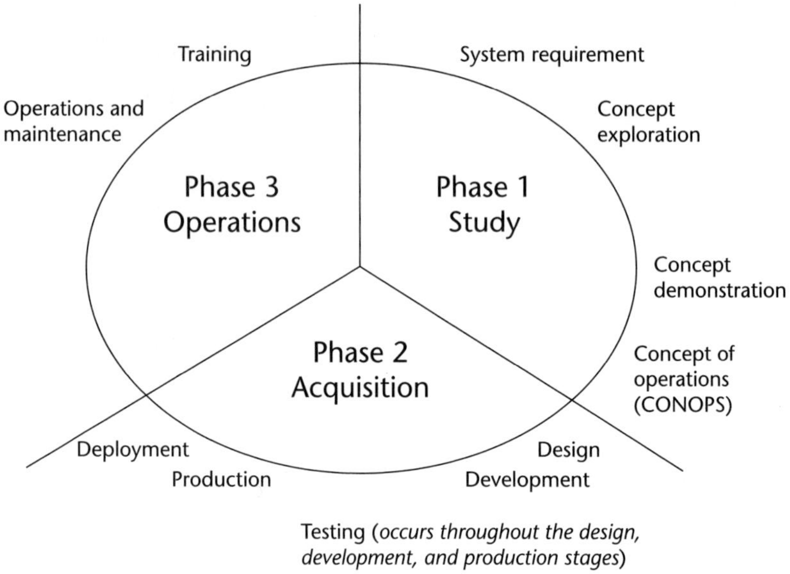

Testing (*occurs throughout the design, development, and production stages*)

Program Staffing

The duration of any stage of the cycle shown in Figure 9-5 is determined by the type of work involved and the number and expertise of workers assigned. Fred Brooks, one of the premier figures in computer systems development, defined four types of projects in his book *The Mythical Man-Month.*[15] Each type of project has a unique relationship between the number of workers needed (the project loading) and the time it takes to complete the effort.

The graph at the upper left of Figure 9-6 shows the time-labor profile for a perfectly partitionable task—that is, one that can be completed in half the time by doubling the number of workers. It is referred to as the "cotton-picking curve": Twice as many workers can pick a cotton field in half the time. Few projects fit this mold, but it is a common misperception of management that people and time are interchangeable on any given project, such that a project that could be done in ten months by one person could be completed in one month by ten. Brooks notes that this is the dangerous and deceptive myth that gave his book its title.

A second type of project involves the unpartitionable task, and its profile is shown in the upper right of Figure 9-6. The profile is referred to here as the "baby production curve," because no matter how many women are assigned to the task, it takes nine months to produce a baby.

Most small projects fit the curve shown in the lower left of the figure, which is a combination of the first two curves. In this case a project can be

Figure 9-6 The Brooks Curves for Projects

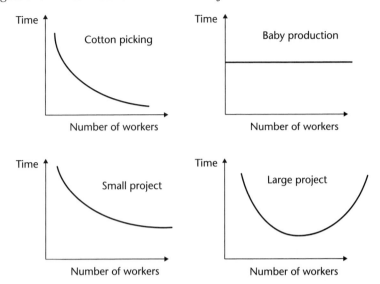

partitioned into subtasks, but the time it takes for people working on different subtasks to communicate with one another will eventually balance out the time saved by adding workers, and the curve levels off.

Large projects tend to be dominated by communication. At some point, shown as the bottom point of the lower right curve, adding additional workers begins to slow the project because all workers have to spend more time in communication. The result is simply another form of the familiar bathtub curve. Failure to recognize this pattern, or to understand where a project is on the curve, has been the ruin of many large projects. As Brooks observed, adding workers to a late project makes it later.[16]

All of these development curves can have wider applications in intelligence than those Brooks described. They can be used with other parameters besides workers. In the Iranian nuclear case, for example, U-235 production was defined by the cotton-picking curve, with number of centrifuges replacing number of workers. Doubling the number of centrifuges would halve the time required for nuclear breakout.

The Technology Factor

Technology is another important factor in any development schedule; and technology is neither available nor applied in the same way everywhere. An analyst in a technologically advanced country, such as the United States, tends to take for granted that certain equipment—test equipment, for example—will be readily available and will be of a certain quality. This can be a bad assumption with respect to the typical state-run economy.

It took some time to recognize how low the productivity of Soviet engineers could be, but the reasons had nothing to do with their competence. They often had to build their own oscilloscopes and voltmeters—items that were available in the United States at a nearby Radio Shack. Sometimes plant engineers would be idle for weeks waiting for a resistor so that they could finish the oscilloscope needed to test the microwave tube for the radar they were supposed to build.

As a result, Soviet weapons systems might be designed quite differently from those in the United States to take advantage of their technology strengths and compensate for weaknesses. For example, the United States and the Soviet Union took strikingly different paths in ballistic missile development. U.S. missiles had simple rocket engines operating at fixed thrust with very sophisticated guidance systems using onboard computers. The Soviets could build good rocket engines but had problems building guidance systems for their missiles. So they used more sophisticated variable-thrust engines with simple guidance systems having almost no onboard computation capability. The Soviet approach had the advantages of simplicity and quick achievement of satisfactory reliability.[17]

There is also a definite schedule advantage to not being the first to develop a system. A country or organization that is not a leader in technology development has the advantage of learning from the leader's mistakes, an advantage that entails being able to keep research and development costs low and avoid wrong paths. A basic rule of engineering is that you are halfway to a solution when you know that there is a solution, and you are three-quarters there when you know how a competitor solved the problem. It took much less time for the Soviets to develop atomic and hydrogen bombs than U.S. intelligence had predicted. The Soviets had no principles of impotence or doubts to slow them down. They knew that the bombs would work. The development time for nuclear weaponry has become even more compressed in the years since. And as the Iranian nuclear negotiations illustrate, the time factor has become one of high intelligence significance.

The previous section was about system *function*, that is, how well the system performs its function. This section concerned *process* and its effect on the development schedule. The next two sections on risk and cost analysis, are about *structure*.

Risk

Analysts often assume that the programs and projects they are evaluating will be completed on time and that the target system will work perfectly. They would seldom be so foolish in evaluating their own projects or the performance of their own organizations. Risk analysis needs to be done in any assessment of a target program. It is typically difficult to do and, once done, difficult to get the customer to accept. But it is important to do because intelligence customers, like many analysts, also tend to assume that an opponent's program will be executed perfectly. The Iranian nuclear breakout issue, discussed previously, might be an example of such a worst-case analysis.

One fairly simple but often overlooked approach to evaluating the probability of success is to examine the success rate of similar ventures. In planning the 1980 Iranian hostage rescue attempt, the Carter administration could have looked at the Vietnam prisoner of war rescue attempts, only 21 percent of which succeeded. The Carter team did not study those cases, however, deeming them irrelevant, though the Iranian mission was more complex.[18] Similar miscalculations are made every day in the world of information technology. Most software projects fail. The failure rate is higher for large projects, although the failures typically are covered up.

Risk analysis, along with a project-loading review, is a common tool for predicting the likely success of programs. Risk analysis is an iterative process in which an analyst identifies and prioritizes risks associated with the program, assesses the effects of the risks, and then identifies alternative actions to reduce the risks. Known risk areas can be readily identified from past experience and from discussions with technical experts who have been through similar projects. The risks fall into four major categories—programmatic, technical, production, and engineering. Analyzing potential problems requires identifying specific potential risks from each category. Some of these risks include the following:

- *Programmatic*: funding, schedule, contract relationships, political issues
- *Technical*: feasibility, survivability, system performance
- *Production*: manufacturability, lead times, packaging, equipment
- *Engineering*: reliability, maintainability, training, operations

Risk assessment assesses risks quantitatively and ranks them to establish those of most concern. A typical ranking is based on the *risk factor*, which is a mathematical combination of the probability of failure and the consequence of failure. This assessment requires a combination of expertise and software tools in a structured and consistent approach to ensure that all risk categories are considered and ranked.

Risk management is the definition of alternative paths to minimize risk and set criteria on which to initiate or terminate these activities. It includes identifying alternatives, options, and approaches to mitigation. Examples are initiation of parallel developments (for example, funding two manufacturers to build a satellite, where only one satellite is needed), extensive development testing, addition of simulations to check performance predictions, design reviews by consultants, or focused management attention on specific elements of the program. A number of decision analysis tools are useful for risk management. The most widely used tool is the Program Evaluation and Review Technique (PERT) chart, which shows the interrelationships and dependencies among tasks in a program on a timeline.

Risk management is of less concern to the intelligence analyst than risk assessment; but one factor in evaluating the likelihood of a program failure is how well the target organization can assess and manage its program risks.

Cost

Systems analysis usually doesn't focus heavily on cost estimates. The usual assumption is that costs will not keep the system from being completed. Sometimes, though, the costs are important because of their effect on the overall economy of a country. The costs to the Soviets of building the Siberia-to-Western Europe natural gas pipeline were significant enough to merit a CIA estimate in 1982.[19]

Estimating the cost of a system usually starts with comparative modeling. That is, you begin with an estimate of what it would cost your organization or an industry in your country to build something. You multiply that number by a factor that accounts for the difference in costs of the target organization (and they will always be different). The result is a fairly straightforward cost estimate that is only as good as your understanding of the differences in the way the two firms build a system. As noted in the preceding section on comparative performance analysis, there is much room for error in this understanding, especially when the two firms are located in different countries.

Another way to estimate cost is to start by applying the issue decomposition methodology of chapter 4 to the system, breaking it down into its component parts. The analyst then produces estimates for building each component of the system and for each phase of the system development process shown in Figure 9-5. In more sophisticated versions of this approach, the analyst can run multiple simulations of each component cost, in effect "building" the system on a computer repeated times to get a most likely cost. This simulation process is used by the U.S. intelligence community on most major hardware development programs.

When several system models are being considered, cost-utility analysis may be necessary. Cost-utility analysis is an important part of decision prediction. Many decision-making processes, especially those that require resource allocation, make use of cost-utility analysis. For an analyst assessing a foreign military's decision whether to produce a new weapons system, it is a useful place to start. But the analyst must be sure to take "rationality" into account. As noted earlier, what is "rational" is different across cultures and from one individual to the next. It is important for the analyst to understand the logic of the decision maker—that is, how the opposing decision maker thinks about topics such as cost and utility. Chinese leaders' decision to implement a manned space program can be subjected to cost-utility analysis, but doing such an analysis illustrates the pitfalls. Hardware and launch costs can be estimated fairly well. Utility is measurable to some extent—by most standards, it is low. The benefits in prestige and advancements in Chinese space technology have to be quantified subjectively, but these factors probably were dominant in the decision-making process.

In performing cost-utility analysis, the analyst must match cost figures to the same time horizon over which utility is being assessed. This will be a difficult task if the horizon reaches past a few years away. Life-cycle costs should be considered for new systems, and many new systems have life cycles in the tens of years.

Operations Research

A number of specialized methodologies are used to do systems analysis. Operations research is one of the more widely used ones.

Operations research is a specific type of performance simulation that objectively compares alternative means of achieving a goal, or alternative means of solving a problem, and selecting an optimum choice. It is widely used to help design complex systems. Operations research techniques grew out of the military sciences in World War II. One of the first applications was in antisubmarine warfare against German U-boats. Analysts looked at the effectiveness of searching from aircraft and surface ships, the disposition of escorts around a convoy, and methods of attacking submarines. They subsequently formulated a model of U-boat operations in the North Atlantic.[20] Operations research has been used since then to predict bombing effectiveness, to compare weapons mixes, and to assess military strategies.[21] In the communications arena, operations research techniques have helped planners and decision makers select transmitter locations and satellite orbits, to provide competitive services that stay within goals for efficiency and costs, and to increase overall system reliability.

Operations research techniques are valuable in intelligence for solving problems such as those described in this chapter. But they have special value in dealing with the problem definition phase described in chapter 4. Operations research has a rigorous process for defining problems that can be usefully applied in intelligence. As one specialist in the discipline has noted, "It often occurs that the major contribution of the operations research worker is to decide what is the real problem."[22] Understanding the problem often requires understanding the environment and/or system in which an issue is embedded, and operations researchers do that well.

After defining the problem, the operations research process requires representing the system in mathematical form. That is, the operations researcher builds a computational model of the system and then manipulates or solves the model, using computers, to come up with an answer that approximates how the real-world system should function.[23] Systems of interest in intelligence are characterized by uncertainty, so probability analysis is a commonly used approach.

Two widely used operations research techniques are linear programming and network analysis. They are used in many fields, such as network planning, reliability analysis, capacity planning, expansion capability determination, and quality control. Linear programming is useful in assessing factory production, as the next example illustrates.

Linear Programming

Linear programming involves planning the efficient allocation of scarce resources, such as material, skilled workers, machines, money, and time.[24] Linear programs are simply systems of linear equations or inequalities that are solved in a manner that yields as its solution an optimum value—the best way to allocate limited resources, for example.[25] The optimum value is based on some single-goal statement (provided to the program in the form of what is called a *linear objective function*). Linear programming is often used in intelligence for estimating production rates, though it has applicability in a wide range of disciplines.

Suppose that an analyst is trying to establish the maximum number of tanks per day that can be produced by a tank assembly plant. Intelligence indicates that the primary limits on tank production are the availability of skilled welders and the amount of electricity that can be supplied to the plant. These two limits are called *constraints* in linear programming. The plant produces two types of tanks:

- The T-76 requires 30 hours of welder time and 20 kilowatt-hours of electricity per tank.
- The T-81 requires 40 hours of welder time and 5 kilowatt-hours of electricity per tank.

The plant has 100 kilowatt-hours of electricity and 410 hours of welder time available per day. The goal statement, or objective function, is to determine the maximum possible number of tanks produced per day, where

Tanks per day = (# of T-76s) + (# of T-81s)

subject to two constraints, represented by inequalities. It takes four times as much power to produce a T-76 than a T-81, so one inequality is:

20 (# of T-76s) + 5 (# of T-81s) ≤ 100 kilowatt-hours.

And a T-76 takes only three-quarters as many welder hours to produce as does a T-81, so the second inequality is:

30 (# of T-76s) + 40 (# of T-81s) ≤ 410 welder hours.

The solution to the linear program is observed most easily in a graph, as shown in Figure 9-7. The two constraints are shown as solid lines. Both are inequalities that define a limit; an acceptable solution must lie below and to the left of both lines to satisfy both inequalities. According to the lines, the plant could produce ten T-81s and no T-76s or five T-76s and no T-81s. The objective function or goal statement is shown as a dotted line representing the total number of tanks produced. Anywhere on this dotted line, the total

Figure 9-7 Linear Programming Solution for Tank Production

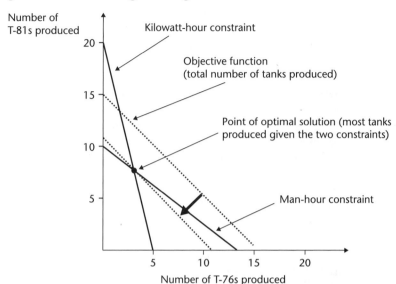

number of tanks produced is a constant, which changes as the line is moved up and to the right or down and to the left. We start the line at a total of fifteen tanks produced, and move it down and left, as indicated by the large arrow, until it touches a point that meets both constraints. This point— approximately eight T-81s and three T-76s, for a total of eleven tanks— represents the optimal solution to the problem.

Network Analysis

Another operations research technique widely used in intelligence is network analysis. In chapter 10 we'll investigate the concept of network analysis as applied to relationships among entities. Network analysis in an operations research sense is not the same. Here, networks are interconnected paths over which things move. The things can be automobiles (in which case we are dealing with a network of roads), oil (with a pipeline system), electricity (with wiring diagrams or circuits), information signals (with communication systems), or people (with elevators or hallways).

In intelligence against networks, we frequently are concerned with things like maximum throughput of the system, the shortest (or cheapest) route between two or more locations, or bottlenecks in the system. Such network analysis, like the network analysis discussed in the next chapter, is frequently used to identify the points in a complex system that are vulnerable to attack or subject to countermeasures.

Summary

Any entity having the attributes of structure, function, and process can be described and analyzed as a system. Systems analysis is used in intelligence extensively for assessing foreign weapons systems performance. But it also is used to model political, economic, infrastructure, and social systems.

Modeling the structure of a system can rely on an inductive, a deductive, or an abductive approach. The deductive approach postulates an opponent's objectives, and then searches for evidence of systems development to meet the objectives. The inductive approach starts from intelligence reporting and identifies likely systems development that follows from the evidence. The abductive approach starts from the inductive approach and incorporates the analyst's intuition based on experience with the issue.

Functional assessments typically require analysis of a system's performance. Comparative performance analysis is widely used in such assessments. Simulations, discussed in chapter 15, are used to prepare more sophisticated predictions of a system's performance.

Process analysis is important for assessing organizations and systems in general. Organizational processes vary by organization type and across cultures. Process analysis also is used to determine systems development schedules and in looking at the life cycle of a program. Program staffing and the technologies involved are other factors that shape development schedules.

Intelligence also is commonly interested in measuring programs' probabilities of success. Risk assessments are frequently used to measure these probabilities. Cost-utility analysis is often used to support predictions about an opponent's program decisions. Most leaders go through some form of cost-utility analysis in making major decisions; the trick is to apply the proper cultural and individual biases to both cost and utility. What appears to be a high cost in the analyst's culture can appear to be very modest in the target's culture.

Operations research techniques are useful for many types of process analysis. Linear programming is used to establish optimum values for a process. Network analysis is used to define flows and vulnerable points within a physical network such as a communications or transportation network.

Notes

1. George Crile, *Charlie Wilson's War* (New York: Atlantic Monthly Press, 2003), 300–301.
2. "Report of the Commission on the Intelligence Capabilities of the United States Regarding Weapons of Mass Destruction," March 31, 2005, 13.
3. Crile, *Charlie Wilson's War*, 303–305.
4. Herbert C. Rothenberg, "Identifying the Future Threat," *Studies in Intelligence*, 12, no. 4 (Fall 1968): 13–21.
5. Stéphane J. Lefebvre, "A Look at Intelligence Analysis," Poster Presentation TC99, February 27, 2003, International Studies Association Conference, Portland, Ore., p. 25.
6. Roger Z. George and James B. Bruce, *Analyzing Intelligence* (Washington, D.C.: Georgetown University Press, 2008), 175–176.

7. Jeffrey R. Cooper, "Curing Analytical Pathologies," Center for the Study of Intelligence, December 2005, http://www.fas.org/irp/cia/product/curing.pdf.

8. Rothenberg, "Identifying the Future Threat."

9. "Report of the Commission on the Intelligence Capabilities of the United States," 143.

10. Arthur J. Alexander, "The Process of Soviet Weapons Design," Technology Trends Colloquium, U.S. Naval Academy, Annapolis, Md., March 29–April 1, 1978.

11. Olli Heinonen, "Iran's Nuclear Breakout Time: A Fact Sheet," Belfer Center for Science and International Affairs, Harvard University, March 28, 2015, http://belfercenter.ksg.harvard.edu/publication/25174/irans_nuclear_breakout_time.html.

12. Kambiz Foroohar, "Iran's Zarif Warns Nuclear Talks May Be Derailed on Centrifuges," BloombergBusiness, June 11, 2014, http://www.bloomberg.com/news/articles/2014-06-11/iran-s-zarif-warns-nuclear-talks-may-be-derailed-on-centrifuges.

13. Michael C. O'Guin and Timothy Ogilvie, "The Science, Not Art, of Business Intelligence," *Competitive Intelligence Review*, 12, no. 4 (2001): 15–24.

14. "Report of the Commission on the Intelligence Capabilities of the United States," 261.

15. Frederick P. Brooks Jr., *The Mythical Man-Month* (Reading, Mass.: Addison-Wesley, 1975), 16–25.

16. Ibid., 16–19.

17. David S. Brandwein, "Interaction in Weapons R&D, *Studies in Intelligence*, 12, no. 1 (Spring 1968): 13–20.

18. Hossein Askari, "It's Time to Make Peace with Iran," *Harvard Business Review* (September–October 1993): 13.

19. Gerald K. Haines and Robert E. Leggett, eds., "CIA's Analysis of the Soviet Union, 1947–1991," 2001, https://nomorebiggov.files.wordpress.com/2008/11/cias-analysis-of-the-soviet-union-1947-1991.pdf, 219.

20. Brian McCue, *U-Boats in the Bay of Biscay* (Washington, D.C.: National Defense University Press, 1990).

21. Theodore J. Gordon and M. J. Raffensperger, "The Relevance Tree Method for Planning Basic Research," in *A Practical Guide to Technological Forecasting*, ed. James R. Bright and Milton E. F. Schoeman (Englewood Cliffs, N.J.: Prentice Hall, 1973), 129.

22. Edward H. Kaplan, "Operations Research and Intelligence Analysis," in *Intelligence Analysis: Behavioral and Social Scientific Foundations*, ed. Baruch Fischoff and Cherie Chauvin (Washington, D.C.: National Academies Press, 2011), 39.

23. "What Is Operations Research," Cornell University School of Operations Research and Engineering, 2015, http://www.orie.cornell.edu/about/whatis.cfm.

24. Ibid.

25. The two sides of an equation are connected by an "equals" or "=" sign. The two sides of an inequality are connected by an inequality sign, such as "is less than (<)" or "is equal to or less than (≤)."

10

Network Modeling and Analysis

*Future conflicts will be fought more by networks than by hierarchies,
and whoever masters the network form will gain major advantages.*

John Arquilla and David Ronfeldt,
RAND Corporation

In intelligence, we're concerned with many types of networks: communications, social, organizational, and financial networks, to name just a few. The basic principles of modeling and analysis apply across most different types of networks. As noted in chapter 2, intelligence has the job of providing an advantage in conflicts by reducing uncertainty. That consistently requires assessing the opposing network, but it often requires assessing neutral and friendly networks as well.

One of the most powerful tools in the analyst's toolkit is network modeling and analysis. It has been used for years in the U.S. intelligence community against targets such as terrorist groups and narcotics traffickers. The netwar model of multidimensional conflict between opposing networks, described in chapter 3, is more and more applicable to all intelligence, and network analysis is our tool for examining the opposing network.

This chapter is about network modeling and analysis. But network models are derived from the simpler link model form, and they use many of the same concepts as link models. So let's start with a brief introduction to link models. First, though, a few definitions:

- *Network*—that group of elements forming a unified whole, also known as a system
- *Node*—an element of a system that represents a person, place, or physical thing
- *Cell*—a subordinate organization formed around a specific process, capability, or activity within a designated larger organization
- *Link*—a behavioral, physical, or functional relationship between nodes[1]

Link Models

Link modeling has a long history; the Los Angeles police department report-edly used it first in the 1940s as a tool for assessing organized crime networks. Its primary purpose was to display relationships among people or between people and events. Link models demonstrated their value in discerning the complex and typically circuitous ties between entities. They are closely related to hierarchy models; in fact, some types of link diagrams are referred to as *horizontal relevance trees.*[2] Their essence is the graphical representation of (a) nodes and their connection patterns or (b) entities and relationships.

Most humans simply cannot assimilate all the information collected on a topic over the course of several years. Yet a typical goal of intelligence synthe-sis and analysis is to develop precise, reliable, and valid inferences (hypothe-ses, estimations, and conclusions) from the available data for use in strategic decision-making or operational planning. Link models directly support such inferences.

For decades, link modeling was routinely used in government intelligence and law enforcement to identify narcotics trafficking groups, terrorists, and espionage groups. It has been applied in sociology and anthropology, and in the analysis of communications networks.

Before the 1970s, link modeling was an arduous and time-consuming endeavor because graphical trees had to be constructed on paper. Computer software subsequently contributed to the expansion of link synthesis and analysis. Software tools simplified the process by allowing the relational stor-age of data as it comes in and by graphically displaying different types of relationships among the entities.

The primary purpose of link modeling is to facilitate the organization and presentation of data to assist the analytic process. A major part of many assessments is the analysis of relationships among people, organizations, loca-tions, and things. Once the relationships have been created in a database system, they can be displayed and analyzed quickly in a link analysis pro-gram. Figure 10-1 illustrates part of a link display that was drawn from an actual case study of funds-laundering operations involving Citibank private bank accounts belonging to Mohammed, Ibrahim, and Abba Sani Abacha. The three men are sons of the late general Sani Abacha, the dictator who controlled Nigeria from 1993 until his death in 1998. General Abacha is believed to have taken more than $3.5 billion from the Nigerian treasury dur-ing the five years that he was in power.[3] The figure illustrates some of the relationships involved in laundering the funds that were stolen. Note that this link model includes more than just people; it also includes banks, companies, government organizations, and bank accounts—a point we'll return to later, in discussing target networks.

Figure 10-1 shows the importance of being able to see second- and third-order links in pattern synthesis and analysis. Connections that are not apparent

Figure 10-1   Financial Relationships in a Link Model

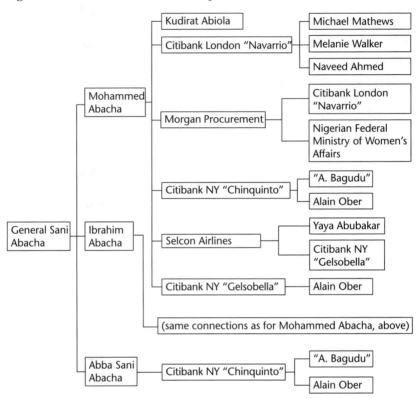

when each piece of evidence is examined separately become obvious when link displays are used.

To be useful in intelligence analysis, the links should not only identify relationships among data items but also show the nature of their ties. A subject-verb-object display has been used in the intelligence community for several decades to show the nature of such ties, and it is sometimes used in link displays. A typical subject-verb-object relationship from Figure 10-1 would read: "Mohammed Abacha (subject) owns (verb) Selcon Airlines (object)." This is a positive relationship and needs to be distinguished from negative ones such as the one between Mohammed Abacha and Kudirat Abiola (Abacha was charged with Abiola's murder).

Quantitative and temporal (date stamping) relationships have also been used when the display software has a filtering capability. Filters allow the user to focus on connections of interest and can simplify by several orders of magnitude the data shown in a link display. For example, the user could select "Morgan Procurement" in Figure 10-1 as the root (that is, the start, or left side, of the link diagram) and display a link chart of all the group and personal associations of Morgan Procurement. The user could then use filters and display the Morgan Procurement network of associations for a specific date range (say, 1995 to 1998) and associations only with Swiss banks, to make the display more useful for analysis.

Link modeling has been replaced almost completely by network modeling, discussed next, because it offers a number of advantages in dealing with complex networks.

Network Models

Most modeling and analysis in intelligence today focuses on networks. The remainder of the chapter is about network modeling, though the same principles apply to link modeling.

Network modeling has been successfully applied in the U.S. intelligence community to assess problems of terrorism, WMD proliferation, insurgencies, and narcotics trafficking as well as to address clandestine arms traffic and weapons systems development. It has become an indispensable tool in military intelligence for targeting and for planning combat strategies and tactics.

Figure 10-2 is a modified version of the financial relationships link model in Figure 10-1, redrawn as a network model with some additional information

Figure 10-2   Financial Relationships in a Network Model

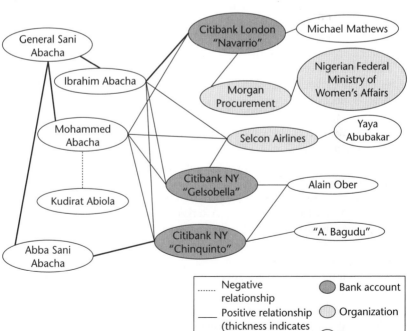

Figure 10-3   Network Diagram Features Used in Law Enforcement
Intelligence

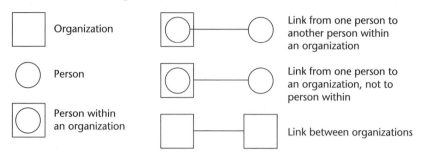

that has analytic value. Nodes are shaded to indicate type—bank accounts and
bank employees in gray, persons unshaded, and organizations in light gray.
Relationships are shown as either positive (solid links) or negative (dashed
links). Strength of relationship is shown by the thickness of the linkage line.
Additional techniques can convey more information—making the links dotted
to indicate a suspected relationship, for example, or making nodes larger or
smaller to indicate relative importance in the model.

Law enforcement intelligence units have developed a special notation for
network diagrams to meet their particular needs. All intelligence units are
concerned about relationships among persons and organizations. But in dealing with organized crime, the law enforcement community has a requirement
to highlight whether a relationship is to an organization, or just to a person
within the organization. So the law enforcement community has developed an
efficient method of drawing network diagrams to make relationships more
apparent, as shown in Figure 10-3.

Some Network Types

With that introduction to networks, let's examine some specific types that are
used in modeling and analysis. There are a number of other types besides
those considered here, but these are some of the most common networks of
intelligence interest.

All of these are *target networks*, from an intelligence viewpoint. That doesn't
mean that they are always hostile. A target network can include friendly or
allied entities (for example, U.S. allies have been the United Kingdom in the
1982 Falklands war between the United Kingdom and Argentina, or Saudi
Arabia during the 2015 conflict in Yemen). It can include neutrals that your
customer wishes to influence—either to become an ally or to remain neutral.

Social Networks

When intelligence analysts talk about network analysis, they often mean
social network analysis (SNA). SNA involves identifying and assessing the

relationships among people and groups—the nodes of the network. The links show relationships or transactions between nodes. So a social network model provides a visual display of relationships among people, and SNA provides a visual or mathematical analysis of the relationships.[4] SNA is used to identify key people in an organization or social network and to model the flow of information within the network.[5]

Organizational Networks

Management consultants often use SNA methodology with their business clients, referring to it as organizational network analysis.[6] It is a method for looking at communication and social networks within a formal organization. Organizational network modeling is used to create statistical and graphical models of the people, tasks, groups, knowledge, and resources of organizations.

Commercial Networks

In competitive intelligence, network analysis tends to focus on networks where the nodes are organizations. As Babson College professor and business analyst Liam Fahey noted, competition in many industries is now as much competition between networked enterprises (companies such as Cisco and Wal-Mart that have created collaborative business networks) as it is between individual stand-alone firms.[7] Fahey has described several such networks and defined five principal types:

- *Vertical networks.* Networks organized across the value chain; for example, 3M Corporation goes from mining raw materials to delivering finished products.
- *Technology networks.* Alliances with technology sources that allow a firm to maintain technological superiority, such as the CISCO Systems network.
- *Development networks.* Alliances focused on developing new products or processes, such as the multimedia entertainment venture DreamWorks SKG.
- *Ownership networks.* Networks in which a dominant firm owns part or all of its suppliers, as do the Japanese *keiretsu*.
- *Political networks.* Those focused on political or regulatory gains for its members, for example, the National Association of Manufacturers.[8]

Hybrids of the five are possible, and in some cultures such as in the Middle East and Far East, families can be the basis for a type of hybrid business network.

Financial Networks

Financial networks tend to feature links among organizations, though individuals can be important nodes, as in the Abacha family funds-laundering case. These networks focus on topics such as credit relationships, financial exposures between banks, liquidity flows in the interbank payment system, and funds-laundering transactions. The relationships among financial institutions, and the relationships of financial institutions with other organizations and individuals, are best captured and analyzed with network modeling.

Financial network modeling and analysis have been used on a micro scale to identify white-collar crime such as fraud; illicit funds transfers to terrorist groups; and financial transfers connected to gray arms, stolen goods, sex slavery, and narcotics trafficking. It is useful on a macro scale in assessing high-volume financial risks and identifying potential financial crises. Global financial markets are interconnected and therefore amenable to large-scale modeling. Analysis of financial system networks helps economists to understand systemic risk and is key to preventing future financial crises. Olivier Blanchard, the International Monetary Fund's chief economist, has identified breakdowns in supply chain networks as helping to explain the difficulties that East European transition economies encountered in the early 1990s. Blanchard also identified financial network problems as contributing to an economic recession in advanced economies.[9]

Threat Networks

Military and law enforcement organizations define a specific type of network, called a *threat network*. These are networks that are *opposed to friendly networks*. They fit the description depicted in Figure 3-4. Such networks have been defined as being "comprised of people, processes, places, and material—components that are identifiable, targetable, and exploitable."[10]

Threat networks take many forms. Today they seldom are comprised of states, though they may have state backing. They include insurgents, violent global jihadists, and international criminal organizations such as human smugglers and narcotics traffickers.

A premise of threat network modeling is that all such networks have vulnerabilities that can be exploited. Intelligence must provide an understanding of how the network operates so that customers can identify actions to exploit the vulnerabilities.

Some threat networks are territorially based. An example is the largest known criminal group in the world, a Japanese criminal syndicate called the Yamaguchi-Gumi. It is one of several such syndicates collectively referred to in Japan as "Yakuza"—an expression that is roughly equivalent to the American use of "Mafia." The Yamaguchi-Gumi earn money primarily from drug trafficking, gambling, and extortion.[11]

At the other extreme are transnational threat networks. Central and South American narcotics traffickers such as the Sinaloa drug cartel exemplify these networks. Some of the most powerful are the Russian Mafia groups (Solntsevskaya Bratva) that have roots in Russia but function across the globe—operating in Europe, southwestern Asia, and North and South America.[12] One of these groups—the Vory v Zakone ("thieves in law") dates back nearly a century. The Vory now engage in narcotics trafficking, funds laundering, and prostitution and have ties with the American Mafia and Colombian drug cartels.

Threat networks, no matter their type, can access political, military, economic, social, infrastructure, and information resources. They may connect to social structures in multiple ways (kinship, religion, former association, and history)—providing them with resources and support. They may make use of the global information networks, especially social media, to obtain recruits and funding and to conduct information operations to gain recognition and international support.

Other Network Views

Target networks can be a composite of the types described so far. That is, they can have social, organizational, commercial, and financial elements, and they can be threat networks. But target networks can be labeled another way. They generally take one of the following relationship forms:

- *Functional networks.* These are formed for a specific purpose. Individuals and organizations in this network come together to undertake activities based primarily on the skills, expertise, or particular capabilities they offer. Commercial networks, crime syndicates, and insurgent groups all fall under this label. The U.S. Joint Forces Command calls these "specialized networks." Most networks of intelligence interest are functional networks.

- *Family and cultural networks.* Some members or associates have familial bonds that may span generations. Or the network shares bonds due to a shared culture, language, religion, ideology, country of origin, and/or sense of identity. Friendship networks fall into this category as do proximity networks—where the network has bonds due to geographic or proximity ties (such as time spent together in correctional institutions). The Yakuza and many terrorist groups fit into this category, but they also are functional networks.

- *Virtual network.* This is a relatively new phenomenon. In these networks, participants seldom (possibly never) physically meet, but work together through the Internet or some other means of communication. Networks involved in online fraud, theft, or funds laundering are usually virtual networks. Social media often are used to operate virtual networks.[13]

A target network can be any combination of these, and it's not uncommon for the network to have more than one of these forms. It is possible, in fact, for a network to be functional, family, cultural, proximity, *and* virtual. Generally, however, it is important to know which of these forms, or combinations of forms, that you're dealing with, because different network forms have different strengths and vulnerabilities.

Modeling the Network

Target networks can be modeled manually, or by using computer algorithms to automate the process.

Manual Modeling

When network modeling was first developed as an analytic methodology, the target network models were created manually, drawing circles and links on large sheets of paper. Some network models created for intelligence purposes still are created manually. Using open-source and classified HUMINT or COMINT, an analyst typically goes through the following steps in manually creating a network model:

- *Understand the environment.* You should start by understanding the setting in which the network operates. That may require looking at all six of the PMESII factors that constitute the environment, and almost certainly at more than one of these factors. This approach applies to most networks of intelligence interest, again recognizing that "military" refers to that part of the network that applies force (usually physical force) to serve network interests. Street gangs and narcotics traffickers, for example, typically have enforcement arms.
- *Select or create a network template.* Pattern analysis, link analysis, and social network analysis are the foundational analytic methods that enable intelligence analysts to begin templating the target network.[14] To begin with, are the networks centralized or decentralized? Are they regional or transnational? Are they virtual, familial, or functional? Are they a combination? This information provides a rough idea of their structure, their adaptability, and their resistance to disruption.
- *Populate the network.* If you don't have a good idea what the network template looks like, you can apply a technique that is sometimes called "snowballing." You begin with a few key members of the target network. Then add nodes and linkages based on the information these key members provide about others. Over time, COMINT and other collection sources (open source, HUMINT) allow the network to be fleshed out. You identify the nodes, name them, and determine the linkages among them. You also typically need to determine the nature of the link. For example, is it a familial link, a transactional link, or a hostile link (such as the one between Mohammed Abacha and Kudirat Abiola in Figure 10-2)?

Computer-Assisted and Automated Modeling

Although manual modeling is still used, commercially available network tools such as Analyst's Notebook and Palantir are now available to help. One option for using these tools is to enter the data manually but to rely on the tool to create and manipulate the network model electronically.

To the extent possible, we'd like to automate the process completely, that is, to have network models created directly from raw data. Considerable progress has been made in doing just that. In the early 2000s, DARPA created the evidence extraction and link discovery program. It was intended to demonstrate the feasibility of extracting relationships from text. The program developed technologies and tools for automated discovery, extraction, and linking of sparse evidence contained in large amounts of classified and unclassified data sources such as phone call records, Internet histories, or bank records. Because of privacy concerns, Congress suspended the program in 2003. But the technology for automating link discovery and network creation continues in the private sector and in other parts of government. Automated creation of social network models now is possible using data- and text-mining techniques on open sources; e-mails; telephone conversations; and social network sites such as Facebook and Twitter.

One example is the algorithm developed at Columbia University that was applied to the e-mail dataset of the Enron Corporation. Enron in 2001 became infamous for its institutionalized and systematic accounting fraud that led to the company's bankruptcy and imprisonment of key executives. The algorithm subsequently was used to recognize and rank key officers, groups, and individuals by e-mail relationships, and to graphically draw an organizational chart that approximated the actual social hierarchy in the company.[15]

Considerable effort has gone into developing systems that can learn from analysts and create network models from data. But an analyst will always need to evaluate sources and validate the results. Any system that purports to organize massive amounts of data also will generate massive false alarms.[16]

Analyzing the Network

Analyzing a network involves answering the classic questions—who-what-where-when-how-why—and placing the answers in a format that the customer can understand and act upon, what is known as "actionable intelligence." Analysis of the network pattern can help identify the *what, when,* and *where.* Social network analysis typically identifies *who.* And nodal analysis can tell *how* and *why.*

In network analysis, we want to evaluate the importance of individuals or organizations within networks and the assets available to them. Specifically, are they connected to a large number of other individuals or organizations? Who would provide them access to financial, political, equipment, or other resources? What is their role in the network, for example, as brokers or intermediaries? How close are they on average to other actors in the networks? Do they have the power to easily share information in the network? The answer to such questions helps to identify the individuals we would want to focus on and to determine the nature of the power they hold.[17] Getting to the answers depends on the use of one or more of the types of analysis discussed next.

Nodal Analysis

As noted throughout this book, nodes in a target network can include persons, places, objects, and organizations (which also could be treated as separate networks). Where the node is an organization, it may be appropriate to assess the role of the organization in the larger network—that is, to simply treat it as a node.

Sometimes, nodal analysis involves assessing performance of an object—an aircraft, an improvised explosive device (IED), a missile, or a radar, for example. A large military force is comprised of many people, objects, and organizations. Some of the objects (military equipment) may be critical components to the success or failure of the military force. The HIND attack helicopter and the Oerlikon heavy machine gun discussed in chapter 9 are examples. The HIND was a critical component of the Soviet forces in Afghanistan; the Oerlikon alone was not the key to countering the HIND.

The usual purpose of nodal analysis is to identify the most critical nodes in a target network. This requires analyzing the properties of individual nodes, and how they affect or are affected by other nodes in the network. So the analyst must understand the behavior of many nodes and, where the nodes are organizations, the activities taking place within the nodes.

Social Network Analysis

Social network analysis, in which all of the network nodes are persons or groups, is widely used in the social sciences, especially in studies of organizational behavior. In intelligence, as noted earlier, we more frequently use *target network analysis*, in which almost anything can be a node. The Abacha funds-laundering network discussed earlier illustrates the need to include entities such as banks, airlines, and bank accounts as nodes. However, the basic techniques of SNA apply to target network analysis as well.

A social network is a set of individuals referred to as *actors* (shown graphically as nodes on Figure 10-4) that are connected by some form of relationship (shown as lines in Figure 10-4). Such networks can comprise few or many actors with different bonds between actors. To understand a social network, we need a full description of the social relationships in the network. Ideally, we would know about every relationship between each pair of actors in the network.

We rely heavily on graphics to depict social network data because the graphics suggest things that we might look for in our data—things that might not have occurred to us if we described the network using only words. It is fairly easy to see, in Figure 10-4, that removing node A will have the most impact on the network. It might not be so obvious if all the relationships were described textually.

In summary, SNA is a tool for understanding the internal dynamics of a target network and how best to attack, exploit, or influence it. Instead of

Figure 10-4   Social Network Analysis Diagram

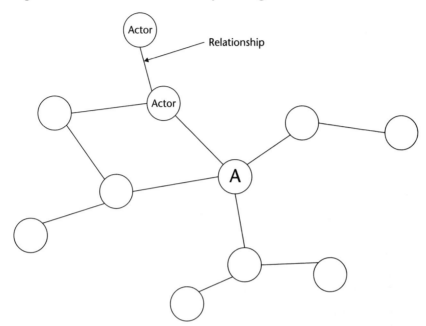

assuming that taking out the leader will disrupt the network, SNA helps to identify the distribution of power in the network and the influential nodes—those that can be removed or influenced to achieve a desired result. SNA also is used to describe how a network behaves and how its connectivity shapes its behavior.

The result of a well-executed SNA against military opponents occasionally appears in the headlines. On May 15–16, 2015, the U.S. Army's special forces attempted to capture Daesh commander Abu Sayyaf during a raid at al-Omar in eastern Syria. The Daesh commander was killed while fighting capture. Abu Sayyaf was the key person directing the terrorist organization's illicit oil, gas, and financial operations, according to U.S. secretary of defense Ashton Carter. Because of the importance of these operations in financing Daesh operations, Abu Sayyaf represented a critical—possibly irreplaceable—node in the Daesh network. The raw intelligence (computers, cell phones, and documents) seized in the raid were a bonus and probably one expected by the raid planners, given the importance of that node.

Several analytic concepts that come along with SNA also apply to target network analysis. The most useful concepts are *centrality* and *equivalence*. These are used today in the analysis of intelligence problems related to terrorism, arms networks, and illegal narcotics organizations.

Centrality refers to the sources and distribution of power in a social structure. The network perspective suggests that the power of an individual actor arises from relationships with other actors. In fact, it is generally known that power arises from occupying an advantageous position in a social network. An actor's position in the network tells the analyst much about the extent to which that actor may be constrained by, or may be able to constrain, others. To understand networks and their participants, we have to assess the location of actors in the network, that is, the centrality of any actor. This measure gives us insight into the various roles and groupings in a network—who the leaders or connectors are, where the clusters are and who is in them, who is in the core of the network, and who is on the periphery.[18]

So the extent to which an actor can reach others in the network is a major factor in determining the power that the actor wields. Three basic sources of this advantage are *high degree, high closeness,* and *high betweenness.*

The more ties an actor has to other actors, the more power (higher degree) that actor has. In Figure 10-5, actor A has degree five (ties to five other actors); all other actors have degree one (ties to just one other actor). Actor A's high degree gives him more opportunities and alternatives than other actors in the network. If any actor chooses not to work with A, then that actor cannot effectively work with the network. But actor A still has the rest of the network available to work with. Actors who have many network ties have greater opportunities because they have choices. Their rich set of choices makes them less dependent than those with fewer ties and hence more powerful.

The second reason why actor A is more powerful than other actors in the "star network" depicted in Figure 10-5 is that actor A is closer (high closeness) to more actors than anyone else. Power can be exerted by direct bargaining and exchange, but power also comes from being a center of attention and

Figure 10-5   Social Network Analysis: A Star Network

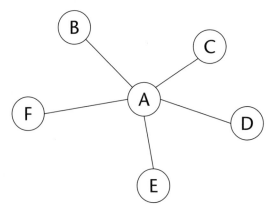

being able to communicate directly with more actors. Actors who are able to reach others by shorter paths, or who are more reachable by other actors through shorter paths, have favored positions. Such a structural advantage can be translated into power.

The third reason that actor A is advantaged is that he lies between all other pairs of actors (high betweenness)—no other actors lie between A and other actors. If A wants to contact F, A may do so directly. If F wants to contact B, she must do so by way of A. This gives actor A the capacity to broker contacts among other actors—to extract "service charges" and to isolate actors or prevent contacts.

In the star network, all these advantages are held by one actor.

The Yakuza, introduced earlier, are examples of star networks. Yakuza are probably the most centralized of organized crime networks. Beneath the head, or *oyabun*, are subordinate *kobun*, each of whom forms a lower-level star network in what is an elaborate hierarchy. The Yakuza organization contrasts with that of East Asian gangs such as the Chinese Triads, which are a loose conglomeration of criminals bonded together mostly by familial relations.

Let's look at a terrorist network to illustrate the concept of centrality. In seeking to disrupt terrorists, one obvious approach is to identify the central players and then target them for assessment, surveillance, or removal. The network centrality of the individuals removed will determine the extent to which the removal impedes continued operation of the activity. Thus centrality is an important ingredient (but by no means the only one) in considering the identification of network vulnerabilities.

A second analytic concept that accompanies SNA is equivalence. The disruptive effectiveness of removing one individual or a set of individuals from a network (such as by making an arrest or hiring a key executive away from a business competitor) depends not only on the individual's centrality but also on some notion of his uniqueness, that is, on whether or not he has *equivalents*. The notion of equivalence is useful for strategic targeting and is tied closely to the concept of centrality. If nodes in the social network have a unique role (no equivalents), they will be harder to replace. The most valuable targets will be both central and without equivalents. Continuing the example of a terrorist network, the network leader may have equivalents, for example, a strong subordinate who can take over. But the accountant, with his unique expertise and knowledge, may be the irreplaceable part of the network by virtue of his centrality and lack of equivalents.

Network analysis literature offers a variety of concepts of equivalence. Three in particular are quite distinct and, between them, seem to capture most of the important ideas on the subject. The three concepts are *substitutability, stochastic equivalence*, and *role equivalence*. Each can be important in specific analysis and targeting applications.

Substitutability is easiest to understand; it can best be described as interchangeability. Two objects or persons in a category are substitutable if they have identical relationships with every other object in the category. If a target individual has no substitute, her removal will cause more damage to the operation of the network than it would if a substitute existed. If another individual can take over the same role and already has the same connections, an opponent who wants to damage the network has to remove or incapacitate not only the target individual but all other substitutable individuals as well. Individuals who have no network substitutes usually make the most worthwhile targets for removal.

Substitutability also has relevance to detecting the use of aliases. The use of an alias by a criminal will often show up in a network analysis as the presence of two or more substitutable individuals (who are in reality the same person with an alias). The interchangeability of the nodes actually indicates the interchangeability of the names.

Stochastic equivalence is a slightly more sophisticated idea. Two network nodes are stochastically equivalent if the probabilities of their being linked to any other particular node are the same. Narcotics dealers working for one distribution organization could be seen as stochastically equivalent if they, as a group, all knew roughly 70 percent of the group, did not mix with dealers from any other organizations, and all received their narcotics from one source.

Role equivalence means that two individuals play the same role in different organizations, even if they have no common acquaintances at all. Substitutability implies role equivalence, but not the converse. As an example, the chief financial officer (CFO) of company *A* can be mapped onto the CFO of company *B* if companies *A* and *B* are similar enough (the two CFOs have similar roles and responsibilities). Or, an explosives expert in terrorist group *A* can be mapped onto a biological weapons expert in terrorist group *B* if group *A* specializes in the use of explosives against its target and group *B* specializes in the use of biological terrorism. Stochastic equivalence and role equivalence are useful in creating generic models of target organizations and in targeting by analogy— for example, the explosives expert is analogous to the biological expert in planning collection, analyzing terrorist groups, or attacking them.

Organizational Network Analysis

Organizational network analysis is a well-developed discipline for analyzing organizational structure. The traditional hierarchical description of an organizational structure does not sufficiently portray entities and their relationships. Consider the network model created using e-mails by employees of Enron Corporation mentioned earlier. That network model highlighted the relationships that revealed the true social hierarchy of the company over the course of time—which was significantly different from the official Enron hierarchy.[19]

Chapter 9 discussed systems modeling and analysis, focusing on weapons systems. But the typical organization also is a system that can be viewed (and analyzed) from the same three perspectives discussed in chapter 9: structure, function, and process. *Structure* here refers to the components of the organization, especially people and their relationships; this chapter deals with that. *Function* refers to the outcome or results produced and tends to focus on decision making, a topic of discussion in chapter 14. *Process* describes the sequences of activities and the expertise needed to produce the results or outcome. Fahey, in his assessment of organizational infrastructure, described four perspectives: structure, systems, people, and decision-making processes.[20] Whatever their names, all three (or four, following Fahey's example) perspectives must be considered.

For the analyst, one goal of network analysis is to understand the strengths and weaknesses of the target organization. Another goal is predictive: to forewarn of changes in the target organization's structure, function, or process that arise from changing forces. Policy-oriented customers can use the analysis in planning strategy; operations units can use it to adversely affect the target, possibly with information warfare. Depending on the goal, an analyst may need to assess the network's mission, its power distribution, its human resources, and its decision-making processes. The analyst might ask questions such as, Where is control exercised? Which elements provide support services? Are their roles changing? Network analysis tools are valuable for this sort of analysis.

An analyst identifies vulnerable points in the target organization so that intelligence customers—the decision makers—can select the appropriate target to act on; that is, to identify where perception management or coercive techniques would be most effective. For example, the analyst's customers may want to know how to convey to the organization's leadership that it can expect strong retaliatory actions if it behaves in a certain way.

Threat Network Analysis

We want to develop a detailed understanding of how a threat network functions by identifying its constituent elements, learning how its internal processes work to carry out operations, and seeing how all of the network components interact. So assessing threat networks requires, among other things, looking at the

- *Command-and-control structure.* Threat networks can be decentralized, or flat. They can be centralized, or hierarchical. The structures will vary, but they are all designed to facilitate the attainment of the network's goals and continued survival.
- *Closeness.* This is a measure of the members' shared objectives, kinship, ideology, religion, and personal relations that bond the network and facilitate recruiting new members.
- *Expertise.* This includes the knowledge, skills, and abilities of group leaders and members.
- *Resources.* These include weapons, money, social connections, and public support.

- *Adaptability*. This is a measure of the network's ability to learn and adjust behaviors and modify operations in response to opposing actions.
- *Sanctuary*. These are locations where the network can safely conduct planning, training, and resupply.[21]

Such networks have several strengths, and the analyst must assess these. Primary is the ability to adapt over time, specifically to blend into the local population and to quickly replace losses of key personnel and recruit new members. The networks also tend to be difficult to penetrate because of their insular nature and the bonds that hold them together. They typically are organized into cells in a loose network where the loss of one cell does not seriously degrade the entire network.

Threat networks also may have weaknesses that can be exploited, once identified. They have a tendency to follow a standard operating pattern based on what has worked in the past. Some must compete with similar groups for resources, support, markets (narcotics traffickers), or territory (gangs). They must communicate between cells and with their leadership, exposing the network to discovery and mapping of links. To carry out the network's functions, they must engage in activities that expose parts of the network to countermeasures.

Target Network Analysis

As we have said, in intelligence work we usually apply an extension of social network analysis that retains its basic concepts. So the techniques described earlier for SNA work for almost all target networks. But whereas all of the entities in SNA are people, again, in target network analysis they can be anything. If we are charting a target network diagram for a terrorist organization, it is important to include associated organizations, weapons, locations, and means of conducting terrorist activities (vehicles, types of explosives). The purpose of such target network displays is usually to reveal, for example, the patterns of operations, likely future targets, and weaponry. Target network analysis thereby includes some aspects of functional analysis and process analysis.

Target networks come in many forms, but they typically fall into three types:

- They may be threat networks that must be countered, requiring analysis of strengths and vulnerable points in the network.
- They may be neutrals who must either be influenced to join your side or maintain their neutrality.
- They may be friendlies or allies, whose goals and capability to support your network need to be assessed.

The job of assessing all three network types traditionally has been one for intelligence. During and immediately after World War I, British intelligence relied on the human terrain knowledge and diplomatic skills of T. E. Lawrence (known as Lawrence of Arabia) and Gertrude Bell in assessing the tribal networks of Arabia and Iraq. Without the intelligence that they furnished about neutral and friendly networks, the British probably would have had considerably less success militarily and diplomatically during and after the war.[22]

Automating the Analysis

Target network analysis has become one of the principal tools for dealing with complex systems, thanks to new, computer-based analytic methods. One tool that has been useful in assessing threat networks is the Organization Risk Analyzer (called *ORA) developed by the Computational Analysis of Social and Organizational Systems (CASOS) at Carnegie Mellon University. *ORA is able to group nodes and identify patterns of analytic significance. It has been used to identify key players, groups, and vulnerabilities, and to model network changes over space and time.[23]

Intelligence analysis relies heavily on graphical techniques to represent the descriptions of target networks compactly. The underlying mathematical techniques allow us to use computers to store and manipulate the information quickly and more accurately than we could by hand. Suppose we had information about trade flows of fifty different commodities (such as corn, coal, tea, copper, and bauxite) among 150 nations in a given year. Here, the 150 nations can be thought of as nodes, and the amount of each commodity exported from each nation to each of the other 149 can be thought of as the strength of a direct tie from the exporting nation to the other. An intelligence analyst might be interested in how the networks of trade in metal ores differ from networks of trade in grain. To answer this fairly simple question requires a huge amount of data manipulation. That could take years to do by hand; a computer can do it in less than a minute.

Summary

One of the most powerful tools in the analyst's toolkit is network modeling and analysis. It is widely used in analysis disciplines. It is derived from link modeling, which organizes and presents raw intelligence in a visual form such that relationships among nodes (which can be people, places, things, organizations, or events) can be analyzed to extract finished intelligence.

In intelligence, we're concerned with many types of networks. Network modeling and analysis always are about the most general type, called a target network—where "target" means a target of intelligence interest, not necessarily an opponent. Target networks can be

- *Social.* The nodes are all people or groups of people.
- *Organizational.* Diagrams are used to assess the communication and social networks within a formal organization.
- *Commercial.* These can be structured as vertical, technology, development, ownership, political, or a hybrid.

- *Financial.* These are networks among financial organizations, typically banks and other financial institutions.
- *Threat.* These are opponent networks, comprising people, processes, places, and material components that can be targeted or exploited in conflicts. They can be social, organizational, commercial, or financial as well.

Target network models can be created manually, but the process of creating and updating them is tedious and time-consuming. We prefer to have network models created and updated automatically from raw intelligence data by software algorithms. Although some software tools exist for doing that, the analyst still must evaluate the sources and validate the results.

Intelligence analysis looks at network patterns and nodes. It can take several forms:

- Social network analysis is a tool for understanding the internal dynamics of a network and how best to attack, exploit, or influence it. Within the network structure, relationship analysis is of high interest to the intelligence customer. Structural position confers power. A powerful individual has high centrality, meaning high degree (many ties to other members), high closeness (being close to many other members), and high betweenness (being the only connection between members). Another important measure of an individual in the organization is his or her uniqueness, that is, whether the individual has equivalents.
- Organizational network analysis overlaps with the systems analysis of chapter 9. It is concerned with structure, function, and process, and it looks at power centers, decision making, and vulnerable points in the organization. Threat network analysis is quite similar. It includes identifying the network's constituent elements, understanding how its internal processes work to carry out operations, and understanding how all of the network components interact.
- Target network analysis, the most general type, can include all of the analytic methods discussed above. Some computer-based methods show promise for identifying patterns of significance to assist analysis.

Notes

1. U.S. Joint Forces Command, *Commander's Handbook for Attack the Network* (Suffolk, Va.: Joint Warfighting Center, 2011).
2. William L. Swager, "Perspective Trees: A Method of Creatively Using Forecasts," in *A Guide to Practical Technological Forecasting*, ed. J. R. Bright and M. E. F. Schoeman (Englewood Cliffs, N.J.: Prentice Hall, 1980), 165.
3. "Minority Staff Report for Permanent Subcommittee on Investigations—Hearing on Private Banking and Money Laundering: A Case Study of Opportunities and Vulnerabilities," November 9, 1999, http://levin.senate.gov/issues/psireport2.htm.
4. "Social Network Analysis, A Brief Introduction," Orgnet.com, 2013, http://www.orgnet.com/sna.html.

5. Kristan J. Wheaton and Melonie K. Richey, "The Potential of Social Network Analysis in Intelligence," January 9, 2014, http://www.e-ir.info/2014/01/09/the-potential-of-social-network-analysis-in-intelligence/.
6. "Social Network Analysis, A Brief Introduction."
7. Liam Fahey, *Competitors* (New York: Wiley, 1999), 237.
8. Ibid., 238.
9. Carmelia Minoiu and Sanjay Sharma, "Financial Networks Key to Understanding Systemic Risk," *IMF Survey Magazine*, May 28, 2014, http://www.imf.org/external/pubs/ft/survey/so/2014/RES052314A.htm.
10. U.S. Joint Forces Command, *Commander's Handbook*, III-1.
11. Chris Matthews, "Fortune 5: The Biggest Organized Crime Groups in the World," *Fortune*, September 14, 2014, http://fortune.com/2014/09/14/biggest-organized-crime-groups-in-the-world/.
12. Ibid.
13. U.S. Joint Forces Command, *Commander's Handbook*.
14. Ibid., III-1.
15. German Creamer, Ryan Rowe, Shlomo Hershkop, and Salvatore J. Stolfo, "Segmentation and Automated Social Hierarchy Detection through Email Network Analysis," Columbia University, no date, http://ids.cs.columbia.edu/sites/default/files/hierarchyv3.pdf.
16. See Defense Advanced Research Projects Agency, "DARPA Evidence Extraction and Link Discovery pamphlet," November 22, 2002, http://www.darpa.mil/iso2/EELD/BAA01-27PIP.htm.
17. Anasuya Raj and Jean-François Arvis, "How Social Connections and Business Ties Can Boost Trade: An Application of Social Network Analysis," *The World Bank*, April 28, 2014, http://blogs.worldbank.org/trade/how-social-connections-and-business-ties-can-boost-trade-application-social-network-analysis.
18. "Social Network Analysis, A Brief Introduction."
19. Creamer, Rowe, Hershkop, and Stolfo, "Segmentation and Automated Social Hierarchy Detection."
20. Fahey, *Competitors*, 403.
21. U.S. Joint Forces Command, *Commander's Handbook*.
22. Janet Wallach, *Desert Queen* (New York: Anchor Books, 2005).
23. Carnegie Mellon University, "*ORA," http://www.casos.cs.cmu.edu/projects/ora/.

11

Geospatial and Temporal Modeling and Analysis

*Go up from here through the Negev, then ascend to the hill country.
See what the land is like. Observe whether the people who live
there are strong or weak, or whether they're few or numerous.
Look to see whether the land where they live is good or bad, and
whether the cities in which they live are merely tents or if they're
fortified. Examine the farmland, whether it's fertile or barren, and
see if there are fruit-bearing trees in it or not.*

Moses's guidance to his spies,
the Bible, Numbers 13:17–20

In intelligence, we usually need to discern our target's geographic location
and observe what happens there over time in order to predict what may
occur next. Although there are all sorts of new terms for how we accomplish
that, the analytic concept is very old.

Sun Tzu in his *Art of War,* published in about 500 B.C.E., advocated reliance
on geospatial models in planning military movements. He observed that "[w]e
are not fit to lead an army on the march unless we are familiar with the face of
the country—its mountains and forests, its pitfalls and precipices, its marshes
and swamps."[1] In Alexandria in approximately 200 B.C.E., a Greek astronomer
named Eratosthenes produced the first chart of the Mediterranean "world" and
used astronomical techniques to create a model of the Earth itself—estimating
the Earth's circumference to within 200 kilometers. And, of course, the quote
that begins this chapter is probably the oldest known example of detailed
guidance on geospatial intelligence collection.

Spatial and temporal modeling and analysis have been practiced by military commanders, government leaders, and commercial entities for thousands
of years, as some of the examples in this chapter illustrate. But, there is something new today—the speed, accuracy, detail, and persistence with which they
can be done. New and better collection sensors and communications systems

have driven this change and made the intelligence product far more useful to customers. Collection assets have shifted from relying on reconnaissance (periodic observations of a target) to surveillance (continuous observations of a target). Along with this success, the umbrella term *geospatial intelligence*, or GEOINT, has arisen. There are academic debates over what should or should not be included in the definition of GEOINT, but Darryl Murdock, vice president of professional development for the United States Geospatial Intelligence Foundation (USGIF), has articulated the most salient one for the target-centric approach to analysis:

> GEOINT is the professional practice of integrating and interpreting all forms of geospatial data to create historical and anticipatory intelligence products used for planning or that answer questions posed by decision-makers.[2]

This definition incorporates the key ideas of an intelligence mission: all-source analysis and modeling *in both space and time* (from "historical and anticipatory"). These models are frequently used in analysis; insights about networks are often obtained by examining them in spatial and temporal ways.

Some definitions of GEOINT are more narrow. They often focus on imagery as an essential component. In fact, it is possible to produce geospatial intelligence without reference to imagery at all. A few examples will illustrate the point:

- During World War II, although the Germans maintained censorship as effectively as anyone else, they did publish their freight tariffs on all goods, including petroleum products. Working from those tariffs, a young U.S. Office of Strategic Services analyst, Walter Levy, conducted geospatial modeling based on the German railroad network to pinpoint the exact location of the refineries, which were subsequently targeted by allied bombers.[3]
- Every day, thousands of communications transmitters and radars are geolocated around the world using only the geolocation capabilities of SIGINT systems such as France's ELISA satellite.
- Every day, the ships and submarines in the Atlantic and Pacific Oceans are located and their movements tracked using the Integrated Underwater Sound System (IUSS)—a MASINT sensor.
- Aircraft, ships, and satellites are continuously tracked by numerous radars—airborne, ship-based, and land-based—worldwide.
- Underground explosions and earthquakes are routinely located around the globe and distinguished from each other by seismic event monitoring stations—which are MASINT sensors.

Geospatial intelligence relies heavily on both imagery and maps, of course. But as the above examples illustrate, neither are required to produce GEOINT.

The rest of this chapter discusses where geospatial models and analysis are of most value in intelligence. The point to remember is that in all of these examples, we are concerned with what is happening in a specific location over a period of time and that the events typically include human actors and objects. Although we sometimes are interested in a geospatial or temporal snapshot, the vast majority of intelligence now revolves around assessing activity in a location over time. So we'll start with static spatial (or geospatial) models, touch briefly on purely temporal models, and then focus on the combination of the two, which is the most general case of GEOINT.

Static Geospatial Models

In the most general case, geospatial modeling is done in both space and time. But sometimes only a snapshot in time is needed. For that purpose, geospatial modeling typically uses electronically stored maps (of the world, of regions, of cities) to display geographically oriented data. These displays are valuable for visualizing complex spatial relationships. Networks often can be best understood by examining them in geospatial terms. Geospatial modeling is a very old analytic technique, as noted earlier. Let's look at a more recent example from the Korean War, followed by a completely different example that is still in process today.

The Inchon Landing

In July 1950, invading North Korean forces pushed South Korean and U.S. forces into the southeastern corner of the Korean peninsula. General Douglas MacArthur, commanding the allied forces, decided on a counterstrike that required U.S. naval forces to land at Inchon, a major port on Korea's Yellow Sea coast. From Inchon, MacArthur reasoned, the Allies could mount a major ground offensive to cut off North Korean forces in the south.

The North Koreans believed that the Inchon area was entirely unsuitable for a major amphibious operation. Tides rose and fell an average of 32 feet daily, producing strong currents in the narrow, winding waterways; the harbor approaches were easy to mine, lined by defensible islands, and marked by extensive mud flats, high seawalls, and dominating hills. The harbor facilities were rudimentary, with little room for logistics ships.

The allied planning effort was a model of both geospatial intelligence analysis and intelligence preparation of the battlespace. It made good use of overhead imagery from aircraft, debriefings of former inhabitants, and on-the-ground reconnaissance by naval special warfare teams. The intelligence allowed planners to select the best water approach, set the time for the amphibious assaults, and identify the North Korean Army line of communication as a critical vulnerability.

The amphibious landing on September 15 took the North Koreans completely by surprise. Two weeks later, the 1st Marine Division captured Seoul, and a large portion of the North Korean forces to the south were caught in a trap.[4]

There have been many examples since Inchon of geospatial modeling to support military operations—the support to Desert Storm planning discussed in chapter 2, for example. But geospatial modeling is applied more widely in commercial enterprises, many of which have intelligence significance. The following example is an illustration.

The Natural Gas Pipeline

Geospatial models can be very complex, with many associated submodels or collateral models. Figure 11-1 presents a geospatial model of a complex system—the Trans-Afghanistan pipeline (also known as the Turkmenistan-Afghanistan-Pakistan-India pipeline, or TAPI). TAPI is proposed to carry natural gas from fields in Turkmenistan to customers in Pakistan and India. Afghanistan, Turkmenistan, Pakistan, and India signed an agreement in July 2014 to move forward with the 1,700-kilometer, $7.5 billion project. The pipeline itself is a complex system that includes a number of political issues (implementation agreements that have to be executed; the requirement for an unprecedented level of cooperation among traditionally hostile powers in the region); technical issues (specific route selection, design and construction of the pipeline); security issues (the pipeline is an obvious target for terrorists); economic and commercial issues (pricing terms for gas; agreements regarding which companies and middlemen get what benefits). When built and in operation, the pipeline would significantly change the economies in the region by providing investment and trading opportunities.

The effects of such a pipeline would reach far beyond South Asia. A number of companies would compete to build it. Commercial firms that stand to gain or lose from the pipeline construction would conduct their own intelligence efforts. When built, it would change the patterns of gas distribution worldwide—more gas would flow to customers in South Asia, and less to other regions. So governments (and their intelligence services) worldwide—not just in South Asia—would be interested in the progress of the pipeline because of its political, economic, and military implications. The relevant system for analysis in this example would be global and complex.[5]

Figure 11-1 shows a simple structural view of the system.[6] A functional view would address the economic changes that the pipeline would cause. A process model could show the patterns of gas extraction and delivery, the political processes to reach a pipeline agreement, and the security processes to protect it, among others. These topics involve social, economic, political, infrastructure, and military (for example, pipeline security) models. As discussed in chapter 6, there would be many submodels or collateral models of the system.

Human Terrain Modeling

U.S. ground forces in Iraq and Afghanistan in the past few years have rediscovered and refined a type of static geospatial model that was used in the

Figure 11-1   Trans-Afghanistan Natural Gas Pipeline

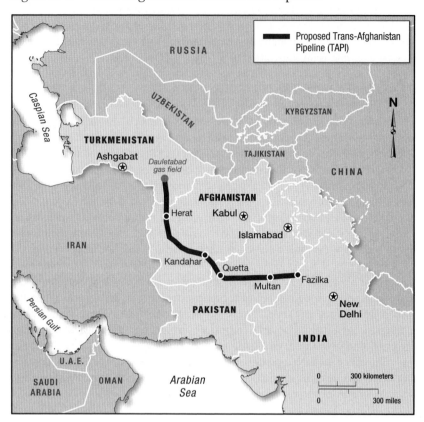

Source: Public domain map produced by the U.S. Government Energy Information Administration (2014), http://199.36.140.204/countries/analysisbriefs/India/images/natural_gas_ infrastructure_map.png.

Vietnam War, though its use dates far back in history. Military forces now generally consider what they call "human terrain mapping" as an essential part of planning and conducting operations in populated areas.[7] In combating an insurgency, military forces have to develop a detailed model of the local situations that includes political, economic, and sociological information as well as military force information. It involves acquiring the following details about each village and town:

- The boundaries of each tribal area (with specific attention to where they adjoin or overlap)
- Location and contact information for each sheik or village mukhtar and for government officials
- Locations of mosques, schools, and markets

- Patterns of activity such as movement into and out of the area; waking, sleeping, and shopping habits
- Nearest locations and checkpoints of security forces
- Economic driving forces including occupation and livelihood of inhabitants; employment and unemployment levels
- Anti-coalition presence and activities
- Access to essential services such as fuel, water, emergency care, and fire response
- Particular local population concerns and issues[8]

Human terrain mapping, or more correctly human terrain modeling, is an old intelligence technique. Once again, looking at ancient history, Sun Tzu understood and advocated it, and Moses's guidance to his spies was, in effect, to obtain the human terrain on the land of Canaan. Though Moses's HUMINT mission failed because of poor analysis by the spies, it remains an excellent example of specific collection tasking as well as of the history of human terrain mapping.

Human terrain modeling was a major feature of the "Great Game" in India in the nineteenth century. This was a competition for control of the balance of power and influence in the buffer states between the British and Russian empires. Beginning in 1878 the Intelligence Branch of the Quartermaster General's Department in India developed human terrain models from various sources, including gazetteers, route books, personality reports, political assessments, and intelligence reports submitted by political and military officials in the field, travelers, and locally engaged clandestine agents.[9] The term "great game" is attributed to a British intelligence officer in India, but it was popularized by Rudyard Kipling in his novel *Kim*. In Kipling's book, an intelligence unit called the Ethnological Survey did the human terrain modeling.

Human terrain modeling has a history in supporting international deliberations. Following are two historical examples of its use to support negotiations.

1919 Paris Peace Conference

In 1917 President Woodrow Wilson established a study group to prepare materials for peace negotiations that would conclude World War I. He eventually tapped geographer Isaiah Bowman to head a group of 150 academics to prepare the study. It covered the languages, ethnicities, resources, and historical boundaries of Europe. With support from the American Geological Society, Bowman directed the production of over three hundred maps per week during January 1919. One example of a human terrain product that was used in the negotiations is the ethnicity map shown in Figure 11-2.

Maps such as the one in the figure were important in establishing the boundaries of the new nations that were established at the peace conference. The other delegations at the 1919 Versailles Peace Conference were envious of the expertise, data, analysis, and production capabilities that Bowman's team provided.

Figure 11-2 The "Human Terrain" of Europe, 1914

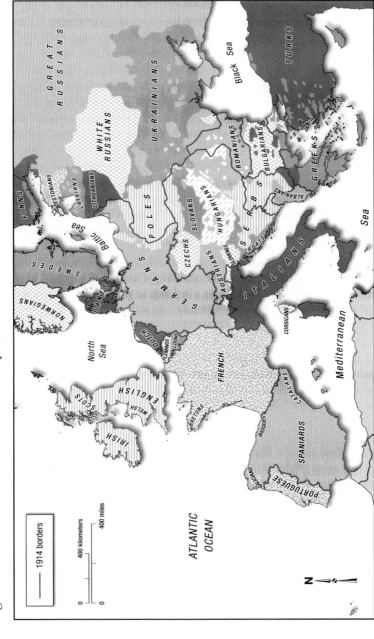

Source: Adapted from "Languages, Peoples and Political Divisions of Europe [1800 to 1914]," http://www.srpska-mreza.com/MAPS/Ethnic-groups/map-Times-1978.html. Used with permission.

The Dayton Peace Accords

During November 1995, representatives from the warring factions in Yugoslavia met in Dayton, Ohio, to negotiate what would become the Dayton Peace Accords. The U.S. participants were supported by a team from the Defense Mapping Agency and the U.S. Army Topographic Engineering Center. The team provided, in near real time, the human terrain in the form of maps from the CIA and other sources of the disputed Balkans areas that included cultural and economic data. Three-dimensional imagery of the disputed areas permitted cartographers to guide negotiators on a virtual tour of the terrain. Figure 11-3 illustrates the sort of map product provided in support of the negotiations.[10]

The Tools of Human Terrain Modeling

Today, human terrain modeling is used extensively to support military operations in Syria, Iraq, and Afghanistan. Many tools have been developed to create and analyze such models. The ability to do human terrain mapping and other types of geospatial modeling has been greatly expanded and popularized by Google Earth and by Microsoft's Virtual Earth. These geospatial modeling tools provide multiple layers of information. The layers are in the form of collateral models (as discussed in chapter 6) that provide details about a location such as building photographs, three-dimensional models of buildings, virtual tour videos that include interaction with locals, and textual material. It is an easy step to include detailed models of the building interiors, including blueprints or CAD/CAM models. This unclassified online material has a number of intelligence applications. For intelligence analysts, it permits planning HUMINT and COMINT operations. For military forces, it supports precise targeting. For terrorists, it facilitates planning of attacks.

Temporal Models

Pure temporal models are used less frequently than the dynamic geospatial models discussed next, because we typically want to observe activity in both space and time—sometimes over very short times. Timing shapes the consequences of planned events. In sales campaigns, military campaigns, and political campaigns, among others, timing is critical to making an impact. The importance of temporal models was illustrated in the Iranian nuclear negotiations discussed in chapter 9. There are a number of different temporal model types; this chapter touches on two of them—timelines and pattern-of-life modeling and analysis.

Timelines

An opponent's strategy often becomes apparent only when seemingly disparate events are placed on a timeline.[11] Consider, for example, the chronological model shown in Figure 11-4. The timeline shows the expected actions of an intelligence target discussed in chapter 9: the hypothetical European electronics manufacturer that is building a missile guidance system destined for shipment to a Middle Eastern country.

Figure 11-3   The "Human Terrain" of Former Yugoslavia, 1991

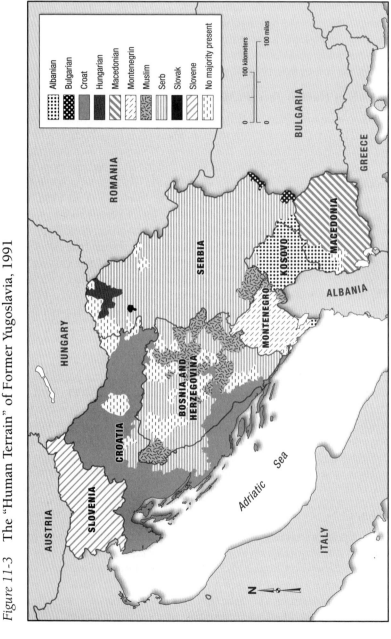

Source: Public domain map produced by CIA in 1992. Retrieved from http://www.lib.utexas .edu/maps/europe/yugoslav.jpg.

Figure 11-4   Chronological Model of a Firm's Expected External Actions

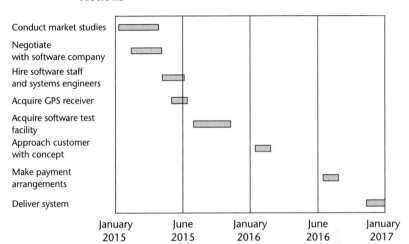

Such a model can be used to predict an opponent's actions and to time future counteractions. In the example of Figure 11-4, the model could be used by the analyst country's government to block shipment of the guidance system or to disrupt the payment arrangements. Similar timelines have been used in the U.S. intelligence community for decades to assess foreign weapons development trends.

Event-time patterns such as Figure 11-4 tell analysts a great deal; they allow analysts to infer relationships among events and to examine trends. Activity patterns of a target network, for example, are useful in determining the best time to collect intelligence. An example is a plot of total telephone use over twenty-four hours—the plot peaks about 11 a.m., which is the most likely time for a person to be on the telephone.

Figure 11-5 shows an example of a type of timeline that is useful in satellite-based SIGINT or IMINT collection planning. The horizontal axis is calibrated in months over the period of one year; the vertical axis is calibrated in hours of the day over a twenty-four-hour period (in Greenwich Mean Time, or GMT). The dark areas show the visibility from a specific low-orbiting satellite to Bermuda during the year, and the horizontal curved lines near 1100 and 2300 GMT show the points of sunrise and sunset in Bermuda during the year, establishing the limits of daylight. If the satellite were carrying a visible-imaging camera, the shaded areas during daylight would indicate opportunities for imagery collection (or, conversely, the unshaded areas would indicate when operations in Bermuda could be carried out unobserved). Such time pattern correlations are best done with the help of computers. Several commercial software packages are well designed for computing and displaying time-series data.

Pattern-of-Life Modeling and Analysis

Pattern-of-life (POL) analysis is a method of modeling and understanding the behavior of a single person or group by establishing a recurrent pattern of actions over time in a given situation. It has similarities to the concept of activity-based intelligence (ABI) discussed in the next section, but it differs somewhat from ABI in that POL analysis typically is targeted and collection is done to answer specific intelligence questions. The resulting model can be used to assess future activity by the targeted individual or group. And where ABI generally relies at least in part on video surveillance, POL analysis can be done entirely by nonvisual surveillance—focusing on Internet browsing habits, telephone calls, or financial transactions, for example. In finance, POL analysis might identify patterns left by a particular kind of criminal. It is useful for white-collar crime analysis. Patterns of fraud such as embezzlement and insurance fraud are uncovered by application of POL techniques.[12]

Dynamic Geospatial Models

A dynamic variant of the geospatial model is the space-time model. Many activities, such as the movement of a satellite, a vehicle, a ship, or an aircraft, can best be shown spatially—as can population movements. A combination of geographic and time synthesis and analysis can show movement patterns, such as those of people or of ships at sea. For example, merchant ships radio their geographic positions at least daily. If a ship begins to transmit false position data, as revealed by independent means such as ELINT or radar geolocation, it becomes a target of intelligence interest. If the ship's track does not fit a normal operating profile—for example, if it takes several days to move only

Figure 11-5   Satellite Visibility and Set over Bermuda—Day versus
              Hour

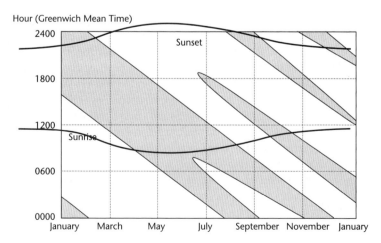

a few miles—then alert analysts will begin to investigate whether the ship could have conducted illicit activity in the area or reached a nearby port for an unannounced stop in that time frame.

Dynamic geospatial modeling and analysis has been described using a number of terms. Three that are commonly used in intelligence are described in this section: movement intelligence, activity-based intelligence, and geographic profiling. Though they are similar, each has a somewhat different meaning. Dynamic modeling is also applied in understanding intelligence enigmas.

Movement Intelligence

Intelligence practitioners sometimes describe space-time models as movement intelligence, or "MOVINT" as if it were a collection "INT" instead of a target model. The name "movement intelligence" for a specialized intelligence product dates roughly to the wide use of two sensors for area surveillance. One was the moving target indicator (MTI) capability for synthetic aperture radars. The other was the deployment of video cameras on intelligence collection platforms. MOVINT has been defined as "an intelligence gathering method by which images (IMINT), non-imaging products (MASINT), and signals (SIGINT) produce a movement history of objects of interest."[13]

MOVINT therefore relies heavily on the collection of what is called wide-area motion imagery, which can be obtained from certain types of electro-optical imagers or synthetic aperture radars. Wide-area motion imagery provides high-resolution images that allow tracking of vehicle and pedestrian movements across a large city. For smaller areas of coverage, full motion video (FMV) provides movement intelligence. But MOVINT depends on more than the detection of motion and change with an area. It also requires *a priori* detailed knowledge of the terrain (to include urban areas) and the normal behavior of targets that move on that terrain. The term *MOVINT* is less commonly used today, having been absorbed into the idea of activity-based intelligence.

Figure 11-6 shows an example of movement intelligence that fits into the definition, but relies on radar and communications rather than on imagery. On July 17, 2014, Malaysia Airlines Flight 17, en route from Amsterdam to Kuala Lumpur, was shot down over Eastern Ukraine, killing all 283 passengers and 15 crew on board. Based on the space-time model shown in the figure and on collateral intelligence, American and German intelligence sources concluded that the aircraft was shot down by pro-Russian insurgents in Ukraine. The collateral intelligence included sensors that traced the path of the missile, analysis of shrapnel patterns in the wreckage, voice print analysis of separatists' conversations in which they claimed credit for the strike, as well as photos and other data from social media sites. Images released by the Office of the Director of National Intelligence claimed to show the location of a surface-to-air missile (SAM) launcher that fired the missile.[14] The figure shows the flight profile of MH17 and Singapore Airlines Flight 351, which was in the area at the time of the shootdown.

Figure 11-6   Flight Profile of Malaysia Airlines Flight MH17

Source: Adapted from "MH17 Flight Route (en)" © User: PM3 / Wikimedia Commons / CC BY 3.0. http://creativecommons.org/licenses/by/3.0/. Flight data from Flightradar24; restricted airspace zones as to NOTAMs A1383/14 and A1492/14.

A subsequent Dutch investigation team concluded that Flight MH17 was shot down by a Buk-M1-2 SAM probably crewed by Russian military personnel. Photographic and video evidence, along with witness interviews, indicate that the SAM battery was brought across the border from Russia into Ukraine shortly before the incident.[15]

Activity-Based Intelligence

Activity-based intelligence, or ABI, has been defined as "a discipline of intelligence where the analysis and subsequent collection is focused on the activity and transactions associated with an entity, population, or area of interest."[16] So ABI is a form of situational awareness that focuses on interactions over time. It has three characteristics:

- Raw intelligence information is constantly collected on activities in a given region and stored in a database for later metadata searches.

- It employs the concept of "sequence neutrality," meaning that material is collected without advance knowledge of whether it will be useful for any intelligence purpose.
- It also relies on "data neutrality," meaning that any source of intelligence may contribute; in fact, open source may be the most valuable.[17]

The U.S. director of national intelligence has defined ABI as an inherently multi-INT approach to activity and transactional data analysis to resolve unknowns, develop object and network knowledge, and drive collection.[18] Patrick Biltgen, a senior engineer in the intelligence and security sector at BAE Systems, has described the development of ABI as a result of *failure of the traditional intelligence cycle*:

> ABI came out of the realization that the scheduled, targeted, one-thing-at-a-time, stove-piped analysis and collection paradigm was not relevant to non-nation-state and emergent threats. We are breaking this one-thing-after-another paradigm because information is flowing . . . all the time and we don't know what to do with it because if you've stopped to try and collect it, you've missed everything else that's coming.[19]

ABI therefore is a variant of the target-centric approach, focused on the activity of a target (person, object, or group) within a specified target area. So it includes both spatial and temporal dimensions. At a higher level of complexity, it can include network relationships as well. It differs from the analysis approach discussed in chapters 3 and 4 in one important respect: *One can come up with an answer without first specifically defining the intelligence issue.* So ABI involves discovery of targets of intelligence interest from observations, rather than identifying a *specific* target and then observing it.[20] And the observations depend on the fact that opponents are identified by their actions, that is, by temporal and visual activity patterns that indicate hostile or nefarious intent.[21]

Scott White, former associate deputy director of the CIA, has observed that "ABI is not a new concept. It's been used in the past in the Intelligence Community. . . ."[22] In fact, SIGINT, MASINT, and IMINT were used together for decades to monitor the normal activity patterns at Soviet missile test sites; deviations from the norm then indicated possible missile test launch preparations. And the unidentified facilities discussed in the next section undoubtedly were the targets of ABI modeling to identify their purpose. The difference is that today, imagery surveillance of an area is possible, whereas in the past, only reconnaissance was possible—and this still is the case in denied areas where unmanned aerial vehicles cannot operate. But many targets of ABI—nonstate actors such as criminal networks and insurgent groups—don't have the protection of operating in an area denied to aerial surveillance.

Social media have provided a powerful tool for modeling behavior in space and time, especially for ABI. Such models can identify patterns of sentiment such as pro-terrorist or anti-Shiite attitudes in a region. ABI can also tip off major population shifts, such as the flight from Ramadi, Iraq, during fighting there, as illustrated in Figure 11-7.

Though the term *ABI* is of recent origin and is tied to the development of surveillance methods for collecting intelligence, the concept of solving intelligence problems by monitoring activity over time has been applied for decades. It has been the primary tool for dealing with geographic profiling and intelligence enigmas.

Geographic Profiling

Geographic profiling is a term used in law enforcement for geospatial modeling, specifically a space-time model, that supports serial violent crime or sexual crime investigations. Such crimes, when committed by strangers, are difficult to solve. Their investigation can produce hundreds of tips and suspects, resulting in the problem of information overload. Geographic profiling—really, a form of POL modeling—provides police with an effective method of managing and prioritizing the information they collect. The profiling process analyzes the locations connected to a series of crimes to determine the area where the offender probably lives. The result helps focus an investigation, prioritize tips and suspects, and suggest new strategies to complement traditional methods.

Intelligence Enigmas

Geospatial modeling and analysis frequently must deal with unidentified facilities, objects, and activities. These are often referred to by the term *intelligence enigmas*. For such targets, a single image—a snapshot in time—is insufficient.

Figure 11-7   Population Flees Ramadi, 2015

Ramadi Social Media Footprint (November 2014–May 8, 2015)	Ramadi Social Media Footprint (May 9, 2015–May 18, 2015)

Source: Figure courtesy of SCORPION social media analytics software developed by Courage Services, Inc.

The key typically is to observe the facility, object, or activity over time. Two examples involve targets located in the Soviet Union/Russia: URDF-3 and Yamantau Mountain.

URDF-3

During the 1970s, U.S. satellite reconnaissance images of the Soviet nuclear test site at Semipalatinsk showed the construction of an unusual facility. Several possible purposes of the facility were proposed and discussed within the intelligence community. The facility became a subject of heated debate when Air Force major general George Keegan in 1977 claimed publicly that the Soviets had constructed a huge particle beam weapon at the site— called PNUTS (Possible Nuclear Underground Test Site) by the Defense Department and URDF-3 (Unidentified Research and Development Facility-3) by the CIA. During the 1970s and early 1980s the United States expended considerable intelligence and scientific research effort in the suspicion that the Soviet Union was building a particle beam weapon capable of destroying ballistic missile warheads in flight.[23]

After the fall of the Soviet Union in 1991, it was discovered that URDF-3 was in fact an attempt to develop a nuclear thermal rocket similar to the United States' Nuclear Engine for Rocket Vehicle Application (NERVA) project, with the objective of powering space exploration missions. The United States had ended the NERVA program in 1972, so a nuclear rocket development was not one of the alternative models considered by intelligence analysts. Had it been, that probably would have been selected as the most likely explanation, because it was consistent with observations of the facility. As it was, some analysts and scientists called in to consult about the facility force-fit the evidence into the particle beam weapon model—identifying the rocket test stands as beam weapons, the reactor assembly as a nuclear accelerator, and the liquid hydrogen tanks as nuclear pulse generators.[24]

Yamantau Mountain

Another unidentified Russian facility that has received much attention from the U.S. government is located at Yamantau Mountain in the Urals. It was under construction prior to the end of the Cold War. According to one U.S. official, the complex is "as big as the Washington area inside the Beltway," or approximately 400 square miles, constructed inside the mountain. Because the facility appears to be hardened to withstand a nuclear attack, U.S. officials reportedly have speculated that it is a survivable command-and-control center, a survivable weapons production center, or a weapons storage area. Because of its location relatively close to Russia's main nuclear weapons laboratory called Chelyabinsk-70 and the extensive rail network serving the facility, some observers suspect that the underground complex will be a nuclear warhead and missile storage site.[25]

Russia appears to have engaged in a campaign to deliberately mislead the United States about the purpose of the Yamantau Mountain project. Russian officials have made several conflicting claims about the purpose of the facility over the years. Some are far-fetched: that it is a mining and ore-processing complex or an underground warehouse for food and clothing. Others seem plausible: that Yamantau Mountain is to become a shelter for the Russian national leadership in case of nuclear war.[26]

Summary

One of the most powerful combination models is the geospatial model, which combines all sources of intelligence into a visual picture (often on a map) of a situation. One of the oldest of analytic products, geospatial modeling today is the product of all-source analysis that can incorporate OSINT, IMINT, HUMINT, COMINT, and advanced technical collection methods. This product is referred to as geospatial intelligence, or GEOINT. GEOINT is most properly defined as the professional practice of integrating and interpreting all forms of geospatial data to create historical and anticipatory intelligence products used for planning or that answer questions posed by decision makers.

GEOINT models can be static, that is, a snapshot in time—maps and imagery, for example. Static GEOINT products called human terrain models are used extensively by governments to support military operations and international negotiations. The commercial availability of tools such as Google Earth and Microsoft's Virtual Earth allows human terrain modeling to support nongovernmental operations as well.

Many GEOINT models are dynamic; they show temporal changes. This combination of geospatial and temporal models is perhaps the single most important trend in GEOINT. Dynamic GEOINT models are used to observe how a situation develops over time and to extrapolate future developments. They have several names that focus on specific features or uses of the basic concept:

- Movement intelligence, or MOVEINT, is usually concerned with tracking the movement of an object—a vehicle or person, for example—over time.
- Activity-based intelligence (ABI) is a form of situational awareness that identifies and catalogues interactions over time of an entity, of a population, or in an area of interest. It is a variant of the target-centric approach that is focused on discovery of targets of intelligence interest based on their activity patterns.
- Geographic profiling is a term used in law enforcement for geospatial modeling, where pattern analysis focuses on the locations of criminal activity.

Purely temporal models are used to address intelligence issues where timing is a critical factor—as it often is in military campaign planning and in assessing new systems development. The product often takes the form of a timeline. An example is pattern-of-life (POL) modeling and analysis: a method of understanding the behavior of a single person or group by establishing a recurrent pattern of actions in a given situation. POL modeling can be done as either a temporal model or as a dynamic geospatial model.

Notes

1. Sun Tzu, *The Art of War*, ed. James Clavell (New York: Dell Publishing, 1983), 9.
2. Darryl Murdock and Robert M. Clark, "Geospatial Intelligence," in *The Five Disciplines of Intelligence Collection*, ed. Mark M. Lowenthal and Robert M. Clark (Thousand Oaks, Calif.: Sage/CQ Press, 2015), 114.
3. Walter Laqueur, *The Uses and Limits of Intelligence* (Somerset, N.J.: Transaction Publishers, 1993), 43.
4. U.S. Navy, *Naval Doctrine Publication 2: Naval Intelligence*, no date, http://www.dtic.mil/doctrine/jel/service_pubs/ndp2.pdf.
5. Marc Grossman, "The Trans-Afghan Pipeline Initiative: No Pipe Dream," *YaleGlobal*, 28 (August 2014), http://yaleglobal.yale.edu/content/trans-afghan-pipeline-initiative.
6. BBC News, "South Asia Gas Pipeline Talks End," July 13, 2005, http://news.bbc.co.uk/1/hi/world/south_asia/4674301.stm; Shamila N. Chaudhary, "Iran to India Natural Gas Pipeline," *TED Case Studies*, 11, no. 1 (January 2001).
7. U.S. Department of Defense, Defense Science Board, "Counterinsurgency (COIN) Intelligence, Surveillance, and Reconnaissance (ISR) Operations," February 2011, http://www.acq.osd.mil/dsb/reports/ADA543575.pdf, 58.
8. Jack Marr, John Cushing, Brandon Garner, and Richard Thompson, "Human Terrain Mapping: A Critical First Step to Winning the COIN Fight," *Military Review* (March–April 2008): 18–24.
9. Penelope Tuson, *British Intelligence on Russia in Central Asia, c. 1865–1949* (Leiden, Netherlands: Brill, 2005), http://www.brill.com/british-intelligence-russia-central-asia-c-1865-1949.
10. National Geospatial-Intelligence Agency, "Dayton Accords," in *The NGA in History*, no date, https://www.nga.mil/About/History/NGAinHistory/Pages/DaytonAccords.aspx.
11. M. S. Loescher, C. Schroeder, and C. W. Thomas, *Proteus: Insights from 2020* (Utrecht, Netherlands: The Copernicus Institute Press, 2000), 24.
12. Gabriel Miller, "Activity-Based Intelligence Uses Metadata to Map Adversary Networks," Defensenews.com, July 8, 2103, http://archive.defensenews.com/print/article/20130708/C4ISR02/307010020/Activity-based-intelligence-uses-metadata-map-adversary-networks.
13. Erik P. Blasch, Stephen Russell, and Guna Seetharaman, "Joint Data Management for MOVINT Data-to-Decision Making," 14th International Conference on Information Fusion, Chicago, Illinois, July 5–8, 2011, http://www.nrl.navy.mil/itd/imda/sites/www.nrl.navy.mil.itd.imda/files/pdfs/Fusion11_JDM_110126.pdf, 176.
14. Greg Miller, "U.S. Discloses Intelligence on Downing of Malaysian Jet," *Washington Post*, July 22, 2014, http://www.washingtonpost.com/world/national-security/us-discloses-intelligence-on-downing-of-malaysian-jet/2014/07/22/b178fe58-11e1-11e4-98ee-daea85133bc9_story.html.
15. Reuben F. Johnson, "Dutch Investigation Concludes MH17 Downed by Buk Missile from Russian Battery," *IHS Jane's 360*, March 19, 2015, http://www.janes.com/article/50075/dutch-investigation-concludes-mh17-downed-by-buk-missile-from-russian-battery.
16. Miller, "Activity-Based Intelligence Uses Metadata."
17. Ibid.
18. Office of the Director of National Intelligence, "Proposed ODNI Activity-Based Intelligence (ABI) Lexicon," August 2013.
19. Miller, "Activity-Based Intelligence Uses Metadata."
20. Note, though, that you must still identify a general target; the definition of ABI requires identifying an "entity, population, or area of interest."
21. Edwin C. Tse, Chief Technologist, Ground Systems Business Unit, Office of Technology, Northrop Grumman Information Systems, "Activity Based Intelligence Challenges," PowerPoint presentation to the IMSC Spring Retreat, March 7, 2013.

22. Kristen Quinn, "A Better Toolbox," *Trajectory* (Winter 2012): 11–15.
23. John Pike, "The Death Beam Gap: Putting Keegan's Follies in Perspective," e-Print, October 1992, http://www.fas.org/spp/eprint/keegan.htm.
24. Michael Dobbs, "Deconstructing the Death Ray," *Washington Post*, October 17, 1999, F01.
25. Michael R. Gordon, "Despite Cold War's End, Russia Keeps Building a Secret Complex," *New York Times*, April 16, 1996, http://www.nytimes.com/1996/04/16/world/despite-cold-war-s-end-russia-keeps-building-a-secret-complex.html.
26. *Congressional Record*, June 19, 1997, p. H3943, http://fas.org/spp/starwars/congress/1997/h970619_a.htm.

Part II

The Estimative Process

Part I of this book concentrated on the analysis process and how to do analysis, taking the target-centric view. Part II focuses on estimative modeling. This involves creating target models of the future. Chapter 12 defines the basic methodology. Chapter 13 describes some major forces that shape future events and situations. Chapters 14 and 15 explain how to apply two powerful methodologies for producing estimates: scenario creation and simulation modeling. Chapters 12 through 15 also discuss some specific structured analytic methodologies that are focused primarily on prediction.

12

Predictive Analysis

Your problem is that you are not able to see things before they happen.

Wotan to Fricka, in Wagner's opera *Die Walküre*

Describing a past event is not intelligence analysis; it is reciting history. The highest form of intelligence analysis requires structured thinking that results in an estimate of what is likely to happen. True intelligence analysis is always predictive. The previous chapters focused mostly on models of current or past situations. Now, we consider models of possible futures. This requires that we think about forces that shape the future.

The value of a model of possible futures is in the insights that it produces. Those insights prepare customers to deal with the future as it unfolds. The analyst's contribution lies in the assessment of the forces that will shape future events and the state of the target model. If an analyst accurately assesses the forces, she has served the intelligence customer well, even if the prediction derived from that assessment turns out to be wrong. Competent customers may make their own assessments anyway, but identifying the forces helps them to make a more reasoned assessment and to refine it as new events unfold. In the ideal case, the analyst's prediction will not come true because the customer will act on the intelligence to change the predicted outcome to a more favorable one.

However, policymaking customers tend to be skeptical of predictive analysis unless they do it themselves. They believe that their own opinions about the future are at least as good as those of intelligence analysts. So when an analyst offers an estimate without a compelling supporting argument, he or she should not be surprised if the policymaker ignores it.

By contrast, policymakers and executives will accept and make use of predictive analysis if it is well reasoned, and if they can follow the analyst's logical development. This implies that we apply a formal methodology, one that the customer can understand, so that he or she can see the basis for the conclusions drawn.

Former national security adviser Brent Scowcroft observed, "What intelligence estimates do for the policymaker is to remind him what forces are at work, what the trends are, and what are some of the possibilities that he has to consider."[1] Any intelligence assessment that does these things will be readily accepted. This chapter and the three following chapters discuss how to prepare such assessments. This chapter introduces the three basic predictive methodologies—extrapolation, projection, and forecasting. It then goes into detail on how the three are applied in predictive analysis.

Introduction to Predictive Analysis

Intelligence can usually deal with near-term developments. Extrapolation—the act of making predictions based solely on past observations—serves us reasonably well in the short term for situations that involve established trends and normal individual or organizational behaviors.

Long-term predictions are considerably more challenging because they encounter the effects of the second law of thermodynamics that was introduced in chapter 7: Entropy (chaos, randomness) always increases with time. And when you reach a turning point, a major shift of some kind, then the future becomes uncertain. We do not readily grasp fundamental changes and are skeptical of those who claim to have done so. To go beyond description to prediction, an analyst must be able to apply a proven methodology and bring multidisciplinary understanding to the problem. Understanding a narrow technical specialty may be useful for simple target modeling, but it is insufficient beyond that.

Adding to the difficulty, intelligence estimates can also affect the future that they predict. Often, the estimates are acted on by policymakers—sometimes on both sides. CIA reports released to the press by Congress and by President Jimmy Carter warned that Soviet oil production was likely to plateau by the early 1980s and then decline to the point where the Soviet Union would become a net importer of oil. Production did in fact fall, but the Soviets—likely warned by the published CIA estimate—shifted investment to their energy sector and changed their extraction and exploration policies to avert the worst.[2] As another example, the publication of the Yugoslavia national intelligence estimate in 1990 (see Appendix I) probably hastened the breakup of Yugoslavia that it predicted.

The first step in making any estimate is to consider the phenomena that are involved, in order to determine whether prediction is even possible.

Convergent and Divergent Phenomena

In chapter 7 we discussed convergent and divergent evidence. Items of evidence were convergent if they tended to reinforce the same conclusion and divergent if they pointed to different conclusions. In examining trends and possible future events, we use the same terminology: Convergent phenomena make prediction possible; divergent phenomena frustrate it.

So a basic question to ask at the outset of any predictive attempt is, Does the principle of causation apply? That is, are the phenomena we are to examine and prepare estimates about governed by the laws of cause and effect? One of the basic principles of classical physics is that of causation. The behavior of any system can be predicted from the average behavior of its component parts. Scientist and Nobel laureate Irving Langmuir defined such behavior as *convergent* phenomena.

The events leading up to World War I, which Barbara Tuchman superbly outlines in *The Guns of August*, had an inevitable quality about them, as befits convergent phenomena.[3] World War I was predictable; many astute observers at the time saw it as almost inevitable. No one person or event actually "started" World War I; the assassination of Archduke Franz Ferdinand and his wife, Sophie, in Sarajevo merely triggered a process for which groundwork had been laid over many years.

Likewise, a war between the United States and Japan was predictable (and both sides foresaw it) throughout most of 1941. The Japanese aggression in China and Indochina, the consequent U.S. imposition of a petroleum embargo on Japan, the freezing of funds by both sides, the steady deterioration in American-Japanese relations during the fall of 1941—all events converged toward war.[4]

Similarly, a pattern of continued Al Qaeda terrorist attacks on U.S. interests worldwide were predictable and had been predicted before September 11, 2001, when terrorists flew airplanes into the Pentagon and the World Trade Center.

In the late 1940s U.S. ambassador George Kennan identified perhaps the most significant convergent phenomenon of the last century in defining his "containment" policy for the United States to pursue against the Soviet Union. He argued that, if contained, the Soviet Union would eventually collapse due to its overdeveloped military and underdeveloped economic system. It took over forty years for the collapse to happen, but successive U.S. administrations basically followed the containment policy.

In contrast to the above examples, many phenomena are not governed by the laws of cause and effect. Quantum physics deals with the individual atom or basic particles and tells us that the behavior of such particles is as unpredictable as the toss of a coin; they can be dealt with only by the laws of probability.[5] Such behavior can, from a small beginning, produce increasingly large effects—a nuclear chain reaction, for example. Langmuir defined such phenomena as *divergent*. In the terms of chaos theory, such phenomena are the result of *strange attractors*—those creators of unpredictable patterns that emerge out of the behavior of purposeful actors.[6] When dealing with divergent phenomena, we have an almost insurmountable difficulty making estimates.

To contrast the effect of the two phenomena, consider three major events that have occurred in Russia since 1997. CIA analysts warned policymakers of Russia's looming economic crisis two months before the August 1998 ruble crash; they subsequently identified the economic rebound in the Russian economy long before business and academic experts did.[7] Both events involved convergent phenomena and were predictable. In contrast, the CIA was unable to predict the rise of Vladimir Putin to the Russian presidency until his handling of the Chechen war dramatically increased his popularity. But in early 1999, Putin himself probably did not foresee this happening.[8] It was a divergent phenomenon.

A good example of a divergent phenomenon in intelligence is the coup d'état. Policymakers often complain that their intelligence organizations have failed to warn of coups. But a coup event is conspiratorial in nature, limited to a handful of people, and dependent on the preservation of secrecy for its success. If a foreign intelligence service knows of the event, then secrecy has been compromised and the coup is almost certain to fail—the country's internal security services will probably forestall it. The conditions that encourage a coup attempt can be assessed and the coup likelihood estimated by using probability theory, but the timing and likelihood of success are not "predictable."

The failed attempt to assassinate Adolf Hitler in 1944, for example, had more of the "what if?" hypothetical quality that characterizes a divergent phenomenon. Assassinations, like that of Israeli prime minister Yitzhak Rabin in 1995, are simply not predictable. Specific terrorist acts, such as those on September 11, 2001, similarly are not predictable in detail, though some kind of terrorist attempt was both predictable and predicted. In all such divergent cases, from the Sarajevo assassination to the 9/11 attack, some tactical warning might have been possible. An agent within the Serbian terrorist organization Black Hand could have warned of the Sarajevo assassination plan. An agent within Al Qaeda might have warned of the attack planned for September 11, 2001. But tactical warning is not the same as estimation. All such specific events can be described by probabilities, but not predicted in the same fashion as the larger events they were immersed in—World War I, the collapse of Nazi Germany, and the increasing conflict between the United States and Al Qaeda.

One of the watershed moments in personal computing was clearly a divergent phenomenon. In 1980, IBM was searching for software to run on its planned Personal Computer (PC) and had zeroed in on a small startup company named Microsoft Corporation, located in Bellevue, Washington. Microsoft could provide the languages that programmers would use to write software for the PC, but IBM wanted more; it needed an operating system. Microsoft did not have an operating system and was not positioned to write one, so Bill Gates, Microsoft's president, steered IBM to Intergalactic Digital Research (later known as DRI).

An intelligence analyst assessing the likely future of personal computing in 1980 would have placed his bets on DRI. DRI built the CP/M operating system, at that time the most popular operating system for computers, using the Intel processor. It had the basic features IBM needed. Gates arranged an appointment between the IBM team and Gary Kildall, DRI's president, in Pacific Grove, California.

Instead of meeting with the IBM team, however, Kildall chose to take a flight in his new airplane. Miffed, the IBM team told Gates to find or write an operating system himself. Gates found one from a small software company in the Seattle area, and called it the Disk Operating System (DOS), which later became the most widely used personal computer operating system and a major contributor to Microsoft's dominance of the personal computer business. A single event, a decision made not to keep an appointment, shaped the future of personal computing worldwide.[9]

In summary, the principles of causation apply well to convergent phenomena, and estimates are made possible. Divergent phenomena, such as the actions of an individual person, are not truly predictable and must be handled by different techniques, such as those of probability theory or high-impact/low-probability analysis, discussed later in this chapter. Where estimation is possible, analysts typically consider the forces involved, which we discuss in this chapter.

The Estimative Approach

The target-centric approach to prediction follows an analytic pattern long established in the sciences, in organizational planning, and in systems synthesis and analysis. In intelligence analysis, we are concerned with describing the past and the current states of the target in order to make an assessment about its future state.

Estimates are as old as engineering. No large projects—temples, aqueducts, pyramids—were undertaken without some type of estimative process. Many estimative techniques have evolved over the past five centuries as mathematics and science have evolved.[10] They frequently reappear with new names, even though their underlying principles are centuries old.

The synthesis and analysis process discussed in this chapter and the next is derived from an estimative approach that has been formalized in several professional disciplines. In management theory, the approach has several names, one of which is the Kepner-Tregoe Rational Management Process.[11] In engineering, the formalization is called the Kalman Filter. In the social sciences, it is called the Box-Jenkins method. Although there are differences among them, all are techniques for combining complex data to create estimates. They all require combining data to estimate an entity's present state and evaluating the forces acting on the entity to predict its future state.

This concept—to identify the forces acting on an entity, to identify likely future forces, and to predict the likely changes in old and new forces over time, along with some indicator of confidence in these judgments—is the key to successful estimation. It takes into account redundant and conflicting data as well as the analyst's confidence in these data. It can be made quantitative if time permits and if confidence in the data can be quantified. But the concept can be applied qualitatively by subjectively assessing the forces acting on the entity. Figure 12-1 shows an overview of the methodology. The key is to start from the present target model (and preferably, also with a past target model) and move to one of the future models, using an analysis of the forces involved as a basis. Other texts on estimative analysis describe these forces as issues, trends, factors, or drivers.[12] All those terms have the same meaning: They are the entities that shape the future.[13] Something to note is that, in most cases, the future target models will be in the form of scenarios, as Figure 12-1 indicates.

The methodology relies on three predictive mechanisms: extrapolation, projection, and forecasting. Those components and the general approach are defined here; later in the chapter, we delve deeper into "how-to" details of each mechanism. All three mechanisms involve assessing forces that act on the entity. An extrapolation assumes that these forces do not change between the present and future states, a projection assumes they do change, and a forecast assumes they change and that new forces are added. The analysis follows these steps:

1. Determine at least one past state and the present state of the entity. In intelligence, this entity is the target model, and it can be a model of almost anything—a terrorist organization, a government, a clandestine trade network, an industry, a technology, or a ballistic missile.

2. Determine the forces that acted on the entity to bring it to its present state. In Figure 12-1, these forces (Forces 1 and 2) are shown, using the thickness of the arrow to indicate strength. These same forces, acting unchanged, would result in the future state shown as an extrapolation (Scenario 1).

3. To make a projection, estimate the changes in existing forces that are likely to occur. In the figure, a decrease in one of the existing forces (Force 1) is shown as causing a projected future state that is different from the extrapolation (Scenario 2).

4. To make a forecast, start from either the extrapolation or the projection and then identify the new forces that may act on the entity, and incorporate their effect. In the figure, one new force is shown as coming to bear, resulting in a forecast future state that differs from both the extrapolated and the projected future states (Scenario 3).

5. Determine the likely future state of the entity based on an assessment of the forces. Strong and certain forces are weighed most heavily in this prediction. Weak forces, and those in which the analyst lacks confidence (high uncertainty about the nature or effect of the force), are weighed least.

Figure 12-2 shows how the process of Figure 12-1 works in practice: It is iterative. In this figure, we are concerned with a target (technology, system, person, organization, country, situation, industry, or some combination) that changes over time. We want to describe or characterize the entity at some

Figure 12-1   The Estimative Methodology

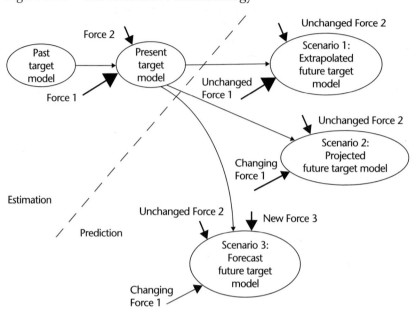

Note: Arrows vary in thickness to indicate the strength of their respective forces. Thicker arrows represent stronger forces; thinner arrows, weaker ones.

future point. We might want to establish the future performance of an aircraft or missile, the future state of a country's economy, the future morale and effectiveness of a terrorist organization, or the future economic health of an industry. The models are created in an iterative process, each one building on the results of the previous ones. They become more difficult to create as you move upward in the figure.[14]

Designing good predictive scenarios requires such an iterative process, as Figure 12-2 indicates. In fact, iteration is the key to dealing with complex patterns and complex models.[15] Again, the basic analytic paradigm is to create a model of the past and present state of the target, followed by alternative models of its possible future states, usually created in scenario form. Following are two brief historical anecdotes illustrating the outcomes of the process:

- The CIA's Office of Soviet Analysis in late 1987 estimated that Moscow could not effectively counter the U.S. Strategic Defense Initiative (SDI) without severely straining the Soviet economy, discounting Moscow's assertions that it could do so quickly and cheaply. The estimate was based on a straightforward extrapolation of the state of the Soviet economy without Soviet attempts to counter SDI. It concluded that the Soviets had no margin for increased rates of investment in the economy.

Figure 12-2 Applying an Iterative Approach to the Methodology

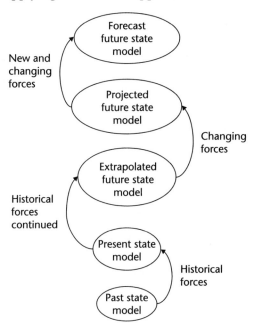

That was followed by a projection (adding in a new force—the burden on the economy of countering SDI). The analysts correctly predicted the alternative outcome: that Moscow instead would push arms control measures to gain U.S. concessions on SDI.[16]

- A CIA assessment of Mikhail Gorbachev's economic reforms in 1985–1987 correctly estimated that his proposed reforms risked "confusion, economic disruption, and worker discontent" that could embolden potential rivals to his power.[17] This projection was based on assessing the changing forces in Soviet society along with the inertial forces that would resist change.

The process we've illustrated in these examples has many names—*force field analysis* and *system dynamics* are two.[18] It is a technique for prediction that involves finding out what the existing forces are, how they are changing, in what direction, and how rapidly (see Analysis Principle 12-1). Then, for forecasting, the analyst must identify new forces that are likely to come into play. Most of the chapters that follow focus on identifying and measuring these forces. One of the most important forces comes from the feedback mechanism, which is discussed in chapter 13. An analyst can (wrongly) shape the outcome by concentrating on some forces and ignoring or downplaying the significance of others.

Analysis Principle 12-1 ●————————————————————————

Force Analysis According to Sun Tzu

Factor or force analysis is an ancient predictive technique. Successful generals have practiced it in warfare for thousands of years, and one of its earliest known proponents was Sun Tzu. He described the art of war as being controlled by five factors, or forces, all of which must be taken into account in predicting the outcome of an engagement. He called the five factors Moral Law, Heaven, Earth, the Commander, and Method and Discipline. In modern terms, the five would be called social, environmental, geospatial, leadership, and organizational factors.

The simplest approach to both projection and forecasting is to do it qualitatively. That is, an analyst who is an expert in the subject area begins the process by answering the following questions:

1. What forces have affected this entity (organization, situation, industry, technical area) over the past several years?[19]

2. Which five or six forces had more impact than others?

3. What forces are expected to affect this entity over the next several years?

4. Which five or six forces are likely to have more impact than others?

5. What are the fundamental differences between the answers to questions two and four?

6. What are the implications of these differences for the entity being analyzed?

The answers to those questions shape the changes in direction of the extrapolation or the projection shown earlier in Figure 12-1. At more sophisticated levels of qualitative synthesis and analysis, the analyst might examine adaptive forces (feedback forces) and their changes over time.

It is also possible to create a projection or forecast quantitatively. The methodology in fact has been implemented in simulation models. One example, described in chapter 15, is a model based on game theory and developed by New York University professor Bruce Bueno de Mesquita. It has successfully developed projections, based on changing forces, and forecasts, by identifying emerging forces, of political developments in several countries.

High-Impact/Low-Probability Analysis

Projections and forecasts focus on the most likely outcomes. But customers also need to be aware of the unlikely outcomes that could have severe adverse effects on their interests. Creating such awareness is the objective of high-impact/low-probability analysis. It is useful for sensitizing both customers and analysts to think about the consequences of unlikely developments—events that typically arise from the divergent phenomena discussed in chapter 7 and earlier in this chapter. These are typically unexpected and come as unpleasant surprises—to some customers, at least. The events of the Arab Spring in 2011, the rise of Daesh in Iraq and Syria, and the Russian incursion into Crimea and Eastern Ukraine all are events that fit into this category. Possible but unlikely future events that could fit into this category are the implosion of China or Iran; an India-Pakistan nuclear exchange; or the release of a genetically engineered, lethal and highly contagious disease organism into a populated region.

The analysis requires describing how such a development might plausibly start and considering its consequences. This provides indicators that can be monitored to warn that the development actually may occur. It therefore takes the form of a scenario (discussed in chapter 14). The CIA's tradecraft manual describes the analytic process as follows:

- Define the high-impact outcome clearly. This definition will justify examining what most analysts believe to be a very unlikely development.
- Devise one or more plausible explanations for or "pathways" to the low-probability outcome. This should be as precise as possible, as it can help identify possible indicators for later monitoring.
- Insert possible triggers or changes in momentum if appropriate. These can be natural disasters, sudden health problems of key leaders, or new economic or political shocks that might have occurred historically or in other parts of the world.
- Brainstorm with analysts having a broad set of experiences to aid the development of plausible but unpredictable triggers of sudden change.
- Identify for each pathway a set of indicators or "observables" that would help you anticipate that events were beginning to play out this way.
- Identify factors that would deflect a bad outcome or encourage a positive outcome.[20]

The product of high-impact/low-probability analysis is a type of scenario called a *demonstration scenario*, which is discussed in more detail in chapter 14.

We now visit in more detail the three approaches introduced earlier for predicting the future state of a target: extrapolation, projection, and forecasting. Different terms for these three approaches are used in different books. Liam Fahey uses the term "simple projection" to refer to extrapolation, and "complex projection" to refer to both projection and forecasting.[21] Projection and forecasting are addressed separately in this text, to emphasize that different forces are involved. To reiterate: An extrapolation predicts future events by assuming that the *current* forces influencing the target go unchanged, and it does not consider new forces. A projection assumes current forces will change. A forecast begins from either an extrapolation or a projection, and considers what *new* forces may come to bear.

Two important types of bias can exist in predictive analysis: *pattern, or confirmation, bias*—looking for evidence that confirms rather than rejects a hypothesis; and *heuristic bias*—using inappropriate guidelines or rules to make predictions.[22] This chapter addresses how to deal with both—the first, by having alternative models for outcomes; the second, by defining a set of appropriate guidelines for making predictions, amplified on in succeeding chapters.

Two points are worth noting at the beginning of the discussion:

- One must make careful use of the tools in synthesizing the model, as some will fail when applied to prediction. Expert opinion, for example, is often used in creating a target model; but experts' biases, egos, and narrow focuses can interfere with their predictions. (A useful exercise for the skeptic is to look at trade press or technical journal predictions that were made more than ten years ago that turned out to be way off base. Stock market predictions and popular science magazine predictions of automobile designs are particularly entertaining.)
- Time constraints work against the analyst's ability to consistently employ the most elaborate predictive techniques. Veteran analysts tend to use analytic techniques that are relatively fast and intuitive. They can view scenario development, red teams (teams formed to take the opponent's perspective in planning or assessments), competing hypotheses, and alternative analysis as being too time-consuming to use in ordinary circumstances.[23] An analyst has to guard against using just extrapolation because it is the fastest and easiest to do. But it is possible to use shortcut versions of many predictive techniques and sometimes the situation calls for that. This chapter and the following one contain some examples of shortcuts.

Extrapolation

An *extrapolation* is a statement, based only on past observations, of what is expected to happen. Extrapolation is the most conservative method of prediction. In its simplest form, an extrapolation, using historical performance as the basis, extends a linear curve on a graph to show future direction. When there is little uncertainty about the present state of a target model, and when an analyst is confident that he or she knows what forces are acting on the target, the prediction begins from the present and propagates forward along the direction of an unchanged system (straight-line extrapolation). In this low-uncertainty, high-confidence situation, new information is given relatively low weight. But when uncertainty about the state of the model is high, new information is accorded high value; when uncertainty about the forces acting on the target is high, prediction uncertainty is high.

Extrapolation is usually accurate in the short run, assuming an accurate starting point and a reasonably accurate understanding of the direction of movement. The assumption is that the forces acting on the target do not change. Inertia (the tendency to stay on course and resist change, discussed in chapter 13) is what typically causes a straight-line extrapolation to work. Where inertial effects are weak, extrapolation has a shorter "lifetime" of accuracy. Where they are strong, extrapolation can give good results over time.

Let's look at some examples of extrapolation. Everyone in the digital age has encountered Moore's law—the observation that, over the history of computing hardware, the number of transistors that can be placed in an integrated circuit has doubled approximately every two years. American inventor and futurist Ray Kurzweil has extended the basic idea of Moore's law backward in time, by plotting the speed (in instructions per second) per $1,000 (in constant dollars) of forty-nine well-known calculators and computers spanning the twentieth century.[24] The result is shown in Figure 12-3.

The graph reinforces the point made about a pitfall of a trend extrapolation. The apparent exponential growth shown in Figure 12-3 could be the early part of the S curve (illustrated earlier, in Figure 6-3). In such a case, the curve will not continue its climb indefinitely but will level off. Many industry observers recently have argued that is exactly what is happening.

Figure 12-3   Kurzweil's Extrapolation of Moore's Law

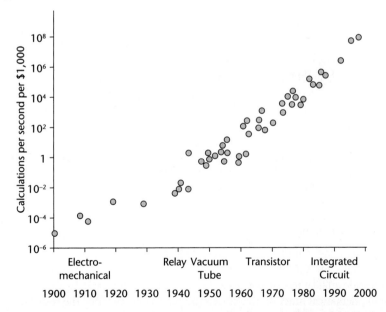

Source: "Moore's Law: The Fifth Paradigm," courtesy of Ray Kurzweil and Kurzweil Technologies, Inc. / Wikimedia Commons / CC BY 1.0. http://creativecommons.org/licenses/by/1.0/.

Figure 12-4   Homicides in the United States per 100,000 Persons, 1900–2012

Homicides per 100,000 people

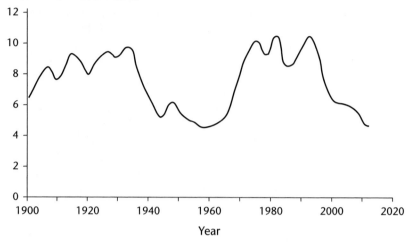

Year

Source: Data drawn from David Solinsky, *Homicide and Suicide in America, 1900–1998* (Macon, Ga.: Hacienda Publishing, 2001), http://haciendapublishing.com/medicalsentinel/homicide-and-suicide-america-1900-1998, and U.S. Department of Justice, Bureau of Justice Statistics, http://www.bjs.gov/index.cfm?ty=pbdetail&iid=2221.

Figure 12-4 shows a type of extrapolation that is used to predict periodic (repeating) phenomena. The technique used, called *autocorrelation*, works well when one is dealing with a cyclical (sinusoidal) behavior such as wave action. Cyclical behavior is a familiar concept to economists. Economic cycles and the cycle of automobile and lawnmower sales are examples. The curve in Figure 12-4 shows a different type of cyclical behavior. This pattern of homicides over a century plus is intriguing because it appears to have two cycles superimposed; a shorter (approximately eight- to ten-year) pattern and a "long wave" spanning about seventy years. The curve would be useful in an analysis to identify the driving forces that may shape the increases and declines.

Extrapolation also makes use of correlation and regression techniques. *Correlation* is a measure of the degree of association between two or more sets of data, or a measure of the degree to which two variables are related. *Regression* is a technique for predicting the value of some unknown variable based only on information about the current values of other variables. Regression makes use of both the degree of association among variables and the mathematical function that is determined to best describe the relationships among variables. If values from only one independent variable are used to predict values for another, dependent variable, then the process is referred to as *bivariate regression. Multivariate regression* involves using values from more than one independent variable to predict values for a dependent variable.

Figure 12-5 illustrates the use of correlation. It supports the argument that corruption is strongly correlated with the existence of excessive business regulation. The figure shows the rankings for 175 countries using Transparency International's Corruption Perceptions Index (CPI) versus the World Bank's rankings on ease of doing business (DB 2014). High CPI scores indicate less corruption; high DB 2014 scores indicate a favorable business climate. As the figure indicates, the more bureaucracy and red tape involved in doing business, the more corruption is likely in the country. The correlation coefficient is nearly .80, indicating a high level of correlation. Graphics such as this are useful in extrapolating the effects of government actions, for example, the likely reduction in corruption that would result from a government's easing restrictions on doing business.

Extrapolation often is a valuable predictive methodology. But it must be used properly and its limitations recognized. First, it usually is inaccurate in the long run because it is narrowly focused and assumes that the static forces that operate on the model will continue unchanged, with no new forces being added. As noted earlier, the method depends on inertia. Second, extrapolation will be inaccurate if the original target model is inaccurate. If the extrapolation starts from the wrong point, it will almost certainly be even farther off as it is

Figure 12-5   Correlation of Perceived Corruption with Ease of Doing Business

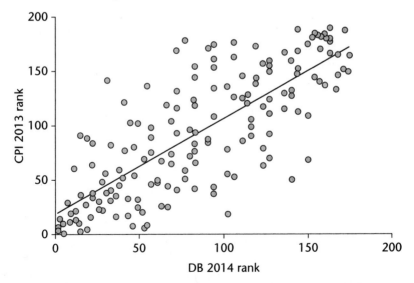

Source: Augusto Lopez-Claros, "What Are the Sources of Corruption," The World Bank, February 10, 2014, http://blogs.worldbank.org/futuredevelopment/what-are-sources-corruption.

extended forward in time. Both problems were present in the national intelligence estimates predicting the future development of Soviet military forces from 1974 to 1986. They all overestimated the rate at which Moscow would modernize its strategic forces.[25] All these estimates relied on extrapolation, without fully considering restraining forces, and used starting points that were, at best, shaky.

Projection

Before moving on to projection and forecasting, let's reinforce the differentiation from extrapolation. An extrapolation is a simple assertion about what a future scenario will look like. In contrast, a projection or a forecast is a *probabilistic* statement about some future scenario. The underlying form of such a statement is, "If *A* occurs (plus some allowance for unknown or unknowable factors), then we can expect *B* or something very much like *B* to occur, or at least *B* will become more probable."

Projection is more reliable than extrapolation. It predicts a range of likely futures based on the assumption that forces that have operated in the past will change, whereas extrapolation assumes the forces do not change. The changing forces produce a deviation from the extrapolation line, as shown by Figure 12-1.

Projection makes use of two major analytic techniques. One technique, *force analysis*, was discussed earlier in this chapter. After a qualitative force analysis has been completed, the next technique is to apply *probabilistic reasoning* to it. *Probabilistic reasoning* is a systematic attempt to make subjective estimates of probabilities more explicit and consistent. It can be used at any of several levels of complexity (each successive level of sophistication adds new capability and completeness). But even the simplest level of generating alternatives, discussed next, helps to prevent premature closure and adds structure to complicated problems.

Generating Alternatives

The first step to probabilistic reasoning is no more complicated than stating formally that more than one outcome is possible. One can generate alternatives simply by listing all possible outcomes to the issue under consideration. Remember that the possible outcomes can be defined as alternative scenarios.

Ideally the alternatives should be mutually exclusive (only one can occur, not two or more simultaneously) and exhaustive (nothing else can happen; one of the listed alternatives must occur).[26] For instance, suppose that an analyst is tracking an opponent's research and development on a revolutionary new technology. The analyst could list two outcomes only:

- The technology is used in producing a product (or weapons system).
- The technology is not used.

This list is mutually exclusive and exhaustive. If a third option, "The technology will be used within two years," were added, the mutually exclusive principle will have been violated (unless the first outcome has been reworded to "The technology is used after two years").

This brief list of outcomes may or may not be very useful with just two alternative outcomes. If the analyst is interested in more details, then the outcome can (and should) be decomposed further. A revised list containing four alternative outcomes might be as follows:

- The technology is used:
  — successfully.
  — but the result is a flawed product.
- The technology is not used:
  — and no new technology is introduced into the process.
  — but a variant or alternative technology is used.

This list illustrates the way that specifying all possible (relevant) outcomes can expand one's perspective. The expanded possibilities often can generate useful insights into problems. For example, the alternative that a different technology is used in lieu of the technology in question suggests that intelligence analysis should focus on whether the target organization has alternative research and development under way.

The key is to list all the outcomes that are meaningful. It is far easier to combine multiple outcomes than it is to think of something new that wasn't listed or to think of separating one combined-event outcome into its subcomponents. The list can serve as both a reminder that multiple outcomes can occur and as a checklist to decide how any item of new intelligence might affect an assessment of the relative likelihoods of the diverse outcomes listed. The mere act of generating a complete, detailed list often provides a useful perspective on a problem.

When generating a set of possible outcomes, one should beware of using generic terms (such as "other"). As the story of the automobile mechanics in chapter 7 illustrates, we do not easily recall the vast number of things that could fall under that seemingly simple label. A catchall outcome label should be included only when a complete list of all alternatives cannot be generated first. In intelligence, it is rare that all possible future states can be included. Also, you should not overlook the possibility of nothing happening. For instance, if an analyst is creating a list of all the things that the French government might do regarding a tariff issue, one item on the list should be "Nothing at all."

Influence Trees or Diagrams

A list of alternative outcomes is the first step. A simple projection might not go beyond this level. But for more rigorous analysis, the next step typically is to identify the things that influence the possible outcomes and indicate the interrelationship of these influences. This process is frequently done by using an influence tree. Influence trees and diagrams represent a systematic approach to the force analysis introduced earlier.

For instance, let's assume that an analyst wants to assess the outcome of an ongoing African insurgency movement. There are three obvious possible outcomes: The insurgency will be crushed, the insurgency will succeed, or there will be a continuing stalemate. Other outcomes may be possible, but we can assume that they are so unlikely as not to be worth including. The three outcomes for the influence diagram are as follows:

- Regime wins
- Insurgency wins
- Stalemate

The analyst now describes those forces that will influence the assessment of the relative likelihoods of each outcome. For instance, the insurgency's success may depend on whether economic conditions improve, remain the same, or become worse during the next year. It also may depend on the success of a new government poverty relief program. The assumptions about these "driver" events are often described as *linchpin premises* in U.S. intelligence practice, and these assumptions need to be made explicit.[27]

After listing all of the influencing or driver events, the analyst next focuses on two questions:

- Do any of the influencing events influence each other?
- Is it possible to assess the relative likelihood of the outcomes of the influencing events directly, or do the outcomes of these events depend in turn on other influencing events (and outcomes)?

If the answer to the first question is that the events influence each other, the analyst must define the direction of influence. In the case at hand, we have two influencing events—economic conditions and the poverty relief program. One can argue that each event influences the other to some extent; but it seems reasonable that the poverty relief program will have more influence on economic conditions than the converse. So we are left with the following relationship:

Poverty relief program influences economic conditions, which influence the outcome of the insurgency.

Having established the uncertain events that influence the outcome, the analyst proceeds to the first stage of an influence tree, which is shown in Figure 12-6. This tree simply shows all of the different outcomes in the hierarchy of dependency.

Figure 12-6   An Influence Tree for Insurgency

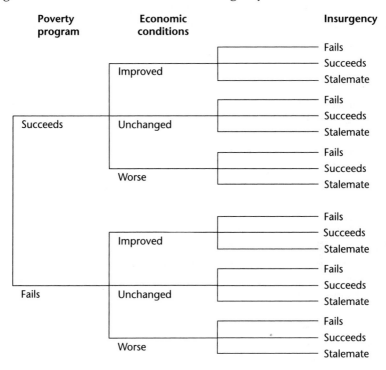

The thought process that is invoked when generating the list of influencing events and their outcomes can be useful in several ways. It helps identify and document factors that are relevant to judging whether an alternative outcome is likely to occur. The analyst may need to document the process (create an audit trail) by which he or she arrived at the influence tree. The audit trail is particularly useful in showing colleagues what the analyst's thinking has been, especially if he desires help in upgrading the diagram with things that may have been overlooked. Software packages for creating influence trees allow the inclusion of notes that create an audit trail.

In the process of generating the alternative lists, the analyst must address the issue of whether the event (or outcome) being listed actually will make a difference in his assessment of the relative likelihood of the outcomes of any of the events being listed. For instance, in the economics example, if the analyst knew that it would make no difference to the success of the insurgency whether economic conditions improved or remained the same, then there would be no need to differentiate these as two separate outcomes. The analyst should instead simplify the diagram.

The second question, having to do with additional influences not yet shown on the diagram, allows the analyst to extend this pictorial representation of influences to whatever level of detail is considered necessary. Note, however, that the analyst should avoid adding unneeded layers of detail. Making things more detailed than necessary can degrade, rather than improve, the usefulness of this diagramming technique.

The thought process also should help identify those events that contain no uncertainty. For example, the supply of arms to both government and insurgent forces will have a strong influence on the outcomes. We assume that, in this problem, these are not uncertain events because intelligence officers have high confidence in their estimates of the future arms supply. They are not linchpins. The analyst will undoubtedly take these influences into account in the analysis. In fact, the analyst would make use of this information when assessing the relative likelihoods of the main event (insurgency) outcome, which will be done next, but the information does not need to be included in the diagram of uncertain events.

Probabilistic reasoning is used to evaluate outcome scenarios. A relative likelihood must be assigned to each possible outcome in the influence tree in Figure 12-6. We do this by starting at the left and estimating the likelihood of the outcome, given that all of the previous outcomes in that branch of the tree have occurred. This is a subjective process, done by evaluating the evidence for and against each outcome using the evaluative techniques discussed in chapter 7. Figure 12-7 shows the result. Note that the sum of the likelihoods for each branch in the tree equals 1.00 and that the cumulative likelihood of a particular outcome (on the far right) is the product of the probabilities in the branches that reach that point. (For example, the outcome probability of the poverty program succeeding, economic conditions improving, and the insurgency failing is $.224 = .7 \times .4 \times .8$.)

The final step in the evaluation is to sum the probabilities on the right in Figure 12-7 for each outcome—"fails," "succeeds," and "stalemate." When we do this we find the following probabilities:

Insurgency fails	.631
Insurgency succeeds	.144
Stalemate	.225

This influence tree approach to evaluating possible outcomes is more convincing to customers than would be an unsupported analytic judgment about the prospects for the insurgency. Human beings tend to do poorly at such complex assessments when they are approached in a totally unaided, subjective manner; that is, by the analyst mentally combining the force assessments in an unstructured way. Conversely, though, numerical methods such as the influence tree have the inherent disadvantage of implying (merely because numbers are used) a false degree of accuracy. The numbers are precise

Figure 12-7   Influence Tree with Probabilities

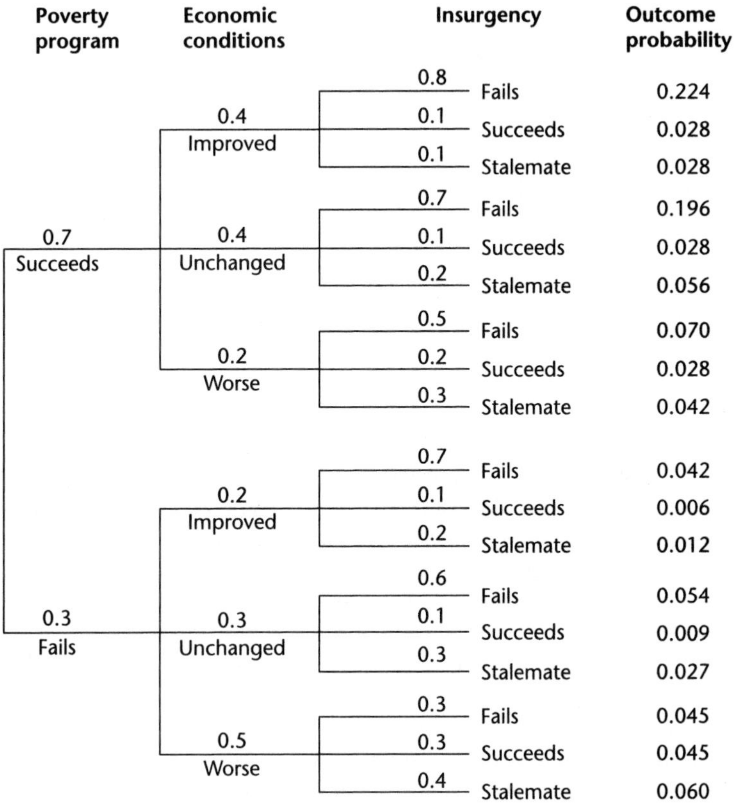

Poverty program	Economic conditions	Insurgency		Outcome probability
		0.8	Fails	0.224
	0.4	0.1	Succeeds	0.028
	Improved	0.1	Stalemate	0.028
		0.7	Fails	0.196
0.7	0.4	0.1	Succeeds	0.028
Succeeds	Unchanged	0.2	Stalemate	0.056
		0.5	Fails	0.070
	0.2	0.2	Succeeds	0.028
	Worse	0.3	Stalemate	0.042
		0.7	Fails	0.042
	0.2	0.1	Succeeds	0.006
	Improved	0.2	Stalemate	0.012
		0.6	Fails	0.054
0.3	0.3	0.1	Succeeds	0.009
Fails	Unchanged	0.3	Stalemate	0.027
		0.3	Fails	0.045
	0.5	0.3	Succeeds	0.045
	Worse	0.4	Stalemate	0.060

and unambiguous in meaning, but they are no more accurate than the subjective judgments they represent.

The probability calculations and the tree structuring technique demand that feedback loops do not exist, or that the feedback is so small that it can be ignored. A feedback loop would exist if, for example, the economic conditions significantly affect the poverty relief program, or if a continuing insurgency stalemate affects economic conditions. If feedback loops emerge and are needed in influence diagrams, the analyst will need to use techniques designed to handle dynamic feedback situations, such as simulation modeling.

Influence Nets

Influence net modeling is an alternative to the influence tree. It is a powerful tool for projection of complex target models where the influence tree would be too cumbersome for practical use. Influence net modeling is a combination of two established methods of decision analysis: Bayesian inference

Figure 12-8   **An Example Influence Net Model**

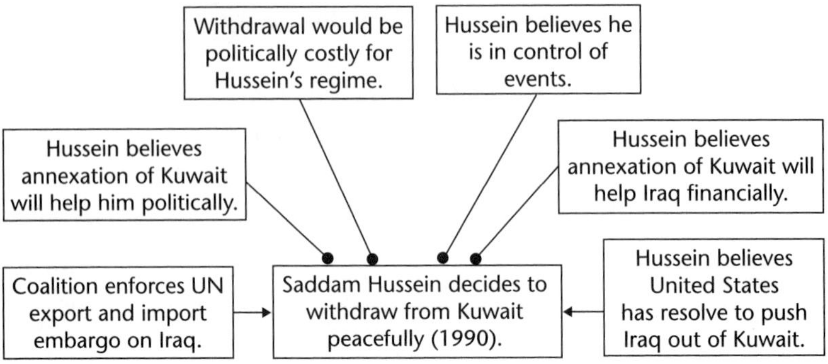

Withdrawal would be politically costly for Hussein's regime.		Hussein believes he is in control of events.

| Hussein believes annexation of Kuwait will help him politically. | | Hussein believes annexation of Kuwait will help Iraq financially. |

| Coalition enforces UN export and import embargo on Iraq. | Saddam Hussein decides to withdraw from Kuwait peacefully (1990). | Hussein believes United States has resolve to push Iraq out of Kuwait. |

Source: Julie A. Rosen and Wayne L. Smith, "Influencing Global Situations: A Collaborative Approach," *Air Chronicles* (Summer 1996).

net analysis, originally employed by the mathematical community, and influence diagramming techniques, such as the insurgency example, that were originally employed by operations researchers. Influence net modeling is an intuitive, graphical method.

To create an influence net, the analyst defines *influence nodes*, which depict events that are part of cause-effect relationships within the target model. The analyst also creates "influence links" between cause and effect that graphically illustrate the causal relation between the connected pair of events. The influence can be either positive (supporting a given decision) or negative (decreasing the likelihood of the decision), as identified by the link "terminator." The terminator is either an arrowhead (positive influence) or a filled circle (negative influence). The resulting graphical illustration is called the "influence net topology." An example topology, showing some of the influences on Saddam Hussein's decision whether to withdraw from Kuwait in 1990, is pictured in Figure 12-8.[28] The decision is stated as "Hussein decides to withdraw from Kuwait peacefully."

The influence net is one of the most important tools in implementing the target-centric approach. It can be shared with customers, and it encourages customers to provide feedback from their knowledge of the target—adding influencing factors, and increasing or decreasing the influence of existing factors in the diagram. (A variant that is useful for this purpose is to make the influence link lines larger or smaller to indicate the weight given to a factor.)

Making Probability Estimates

Probabilistic projection is used to predict the probability of future events for some time-dependent random process, such as the health of the Japanese economy. A number of these probabilistic techniques are used in industry for projection. Two techniques that we use in intelligence analysis are as follows:

- *Point and interval estimation.* This method attempts to describe the probability of outcomes for a single event. An example would be a country's economic growth rate, and the event of concern might be an economic depression (the point where the growth rate drops below a certain level).
- *Monte Carlo simulation.* This method simulates all or part of a process by running a sequence of events repeatedly, with random combinations of values, until sufficient statistical material is accumulated to determine the probability distribution of the outcome. Monte Carlo simulations are discussed in chapter 15.

Most of the predictive problems we deal with in intelligence use subjective probability estimates. We routinely use subjective estimates of probabilities in dealing with broad issues for which no objective estimate is feasible. An estimate about the probability of a major terrorist attack occurring somewhere in the United Kingdom next week, for example, would inevitably be subjective; there would not be enough hard data to make a formal quantitative estimate. In contrast, an estimate of the probability that the Chinese economy will grow by more than 5 percent next year could be made by using formal quantitative techniques, because quantitative data are available.

Even if a formal probability estimate is used, it will always have a subjective element. A subjective component is incorporated into every estimate of future probability; it is a basis for the weighting of respective outcomes to which no numerical basis can be assigned.

Sensitivity Analysis

When a probability estimate is made, it is usually worthwhile to conduct a sensitivity analysis on the result. For example, the occurrence of false alarms in a security system can be evaluated as a probabilistic process. The effect of introducing alarm maintenance procedures can be included in the evaluation by means of sensitivity analysis.

The purpose of sensitivity analysis is to evaluate the relative importance or impact of changes in the values assigned to influencing event outcomes. The inputs to the estimate are varied in a systematic manner to evaluate their effect on possible outcomes. This process lets an analyst identify variables whose variation has little or no effect on possible outcomes.

A number of tools and techniques are available for sensitivity analysis. Most of them are best displayed and examined graphically. Figure 12-9 shows the results of an analysis of the likelihood of a manufacturer successfully creating a new biological warfare virus. Three possibilities are assumed to exist: The process will create the new virus, the process will fail, or the manufacturer will abandon the project before it is completed. These three possibilities add up to a likelihood of 1.0 at any point on Figure 12-9.

One of the elements in the analysis is the probability that a new genetic engineering technology will be developed to aid the development of the

Figure 12-9   Sensitivity Analysis for Biological Warfare Virus
Prediction

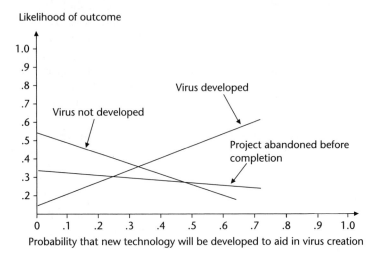

biological warfare virus (the horizontal axis in the figure). The sensitivity analysis indicates that success in producing the virus is relatively sensitive to the genetic engineering technology (the success line goes up sharply with an increase in the probability that the technology works). If the probability of success for the new technology is above .55, the process is more likely to succeed (likelihood of new virus creation above .5 on the vertical scale); it is more likely to fail if the probability of success is less than .55. The figure also indicates that the manufacturer's possible decision not to complete the project is relatively insensitive to the technology's success, because the project abandonment likelihood does not change much as the probability of technology success increases; such a decision might be made for political or economic reasons, for example, rather than technical reasons. The chart is simplistic, of course; in fact, the straight lines would typically be curves with sharp "knees" at points where the probabilities start changing at different rates.

Forecasting

Projections often work out better than extrapolations over the medium term. But even the best-prepared projections often seem very conservative when compared to reality years later. New political, economic, social, technological, or military developments will create results that were not foreseen even by experts in a field. Typically, these new developments are described as disruptive technologies or disruptive events. To take these disruptive developments into account, we are forced to move to forecasting techniques. Forecasting uses many of the same tools that projection relies on—force analysis and probabilistic reasoning, for example. But it presents a stressing intellectual challenge, because of the difficulty in identifying and assessing the effect of new forces.

A major objective of forecasting in intelligence is to define alternative futures of the target model, not just the most likely future. These alternative futures are usually scenarios, which are covered in chapter 14. The development of alternative futures is essential for effective strategic decision-making. Since there is no single predictable future, customers need to formulate strategy within the context of alternative future states of the target. To this end, it is necessary to develop a model that will make it possible to show systematically the interrelationships of the individually forecast trends and events. A forecast attempts to identify new forces that will affect the target— to consider the possible effects of new developments in distantly related fields, such as new technologies in the realm of artificial intelligence, or new constraints posed by the sociological impact of pollution, or new forms of life created through genetic engineering—and to present them to the customer as possibilities. In forecasting, one also must look at forces such as inertia, countervailing forces, contamination, synergy, and feedback—all discussed in chapter 13.

Customers generally prefer to have the highest possible level of predictive analysis (forecasting) be provided so that they can be aware of possible outcomes for a situation and the forces driving toward those outcomes.

A forecast is not a blueprint of the future, and it typically starts from extrapolations or projections. Forecasters then must expand their scope to admit and juggle many additional forces or factors. They must examine key technologies and developments that are far afield but that nevertheless affect the subject of the forecast.

The Nonlinear Approach to Forecasting

Obviously, a forecasting methodology requires analytic tools or principles. But for any forecasting methodology to be successful, analysts who have significant understanding of many PMESII factors and the ability to think about issues in a nonlinear fashion are also required. Just as the intelligence process discussed in chapter 3 is not linear, an analyst cannot effectively approach forecasting in a linear manner—gathering data, analyzing it, and formulating a solution. Such a linear and mechanistic view of the universe has never served well for forecasting, and it is inappropriate for dealing with complex targets. Futuristic thinking examines deeper forces and flows across many disciplines that have their own order and pattern. In predictive analysis, we may seem to wander about, making only halting progress toward the solution. This nonlinear process is not a flaw; rather it is the mark of a natural learning process when dealing with complex and nonlinear matters. The natural pattern of thinking about the future appears chaotic on the surface, but it is chaos with a purpose.

The sort of person who can do such multidisciplinary analysis of what is likely to happen in the future has a broad understanding of the principles that cause a physical phenomenon, a chemical reaction, or a social reaction to occur. People who are multidisciplinary in their knowledge and thinking can pull together concepts from several fields and assess political, economic, and social, as well as technical, factors. Such breadth of understanding recognizes the similarity of principles and the underlying forces that make them work. It might also be called "applied common sense," but unfortunately it is not very common. Analysts instead tend to specialize, because in-depth expertise is highly valued by both intelligence management and the intelligence customer. The CIA, for example, once had a Soviet canned-goods analyst and a Soviet timber analyst.[29]

The failure to do multidisciplinary analysis is often tied closely to mind-set. Chapter 1 illustrated this relationship in the examples of the Yom Kippur War and the Soviet incursion into Afghanistan. The mindset of the Israeli and Soviet leadership constrained their consideration of the broader forces acting on Egyptian president Anwar Sadat and in Afghani society.

Similarly, in 1950, U.S. intelligence had two major failures in prediction in six months, as a result of a combination of mindset and failure to do multidisciplinary analysis. On June 25 of that year, the North Korean People's Army invaded South Korea. The United Nations (UN) forces intervened to defend South Korea and pushed the invading forces back into the North. In October and November, responding to the impending defeat of the North Koreans, The Chinese People's Liberation Army attacked and drove UN forces back into South Korea. Both the North Korean and the Chinese attacks were surprises.

The belief in Washington that permeated political, military and intelligence thinking at the time was that the Soviet Union was the dominant communist state, exercising near-absolute authority over other communist states. The resulting perception was that only the Soviet Union could order an invasion by its "client" states, and that such an act would be a prelude to a world war. Washington was confident that Moscow was not ready to take such a step; so no attack was expected. This mindset persisted after the invasion, with the *CIA Daily Summary* reporting the invasion was a "clear-cut Soviet challenge to the United States." As evidence mounted of a subsequent Chinese intervention, CIA analyses continued to insist that the Soviets would have to approve any Chinese action in Korea.[30]

In fact, quite the opposite was true. Moscow opposed Chinese intervention, fearing that it could lead to a general war involving the Soviet Union. The U.S. mindset of Soviet decision-making supremacy was abetted by the failure of the CIA to consider the multidisciplinary factors that led to both invasions. Cultural, historic, and nationalistic factors in fact dominated the North Korean and Chinese decision-making processes. Kim Il-sung, North Korea's leader, was determined to unify Korea under his leadership; he apparently believed that the South Korean population would rise up to support the invasion and that the United States would not intervene.[31] After the U.S. advance into North Korea, China's strategic interests were threatened by the possibility of a hostile Korea on its border. The CIA analyses took none of this into account.

Techniques and Analytic Tools of Forecasting

Both projection and forecasting use the tools described in this and succeeding chapters. Chapter 5 introduced the idea of a conceptual model. The conceptual model on which projection and forecasting are based is the assessment of the dynamic forces acting on the entity being studied. Forecasting is based on a number of assumptions, among them the following:

- The future cannot be predicted, but by taking explicit account of uncertainty, one can make probabilistic forecasts.
- Forecasts must take into account possible future developments in such areas as organizational changes, demography, lifestyles, technology, economics, and regulation.[32]

For policymakers and executives, the aim of defining alternative futures is to try to determine how to create a better future than the one that would materialize if we merely keep doing what we're currently doing. Intelligence analysis contributes to this definition of alternative futures, with emphasis on the likely actions of others—allies, neutrals, and opponents.

Forecasting starts through examination of the changing political, military, economic, and social environments. We first select issues or concerns that require attention. These issues and concerns have component forces that can be identified using a variant of the strategies-to-task methodology. Forecasts of changes to these forces (mostly in the form of trends and events) are generated and subsequently interrelated through techniques such as cross-impact analysis. The result is a "most likely" forecast future created in a scenario format from the trend and event forecasts. In complex forecasts, a technique called cross-impact modeling, discussed in chapter 14, is sometimes used.

If the forecast is done well, these scenarios stimulate the customer of intelligence—the executive—to make decisions that are appropriate for each scenario. The purpose is to help the customer make a set of decisions that will work in as many scenarios as possible.[33]

Evaluating Forecasts

Forecasts are judged on the following criteria:

- *Clarity*. Can the customer understand the forecast and the forces involved? Is it clear enough to be useful? For example, users may not be able to accurately define "gross national product" or "the strategic nuclear balance," but they still can deal with forecasts on these subjects. Alternatively, they may not understand that there is a difference between households and families and thus be puzzled by forecasts in this area.

- *Credibility*. Do the results make sense to the customer? Do they appear valid on the basis of common sense?
- *Plausibility*. Are the results consistent with what the customer knows about the world outside the scenario and how this world really works or is likely to work in the future?
- *Relevance*. To what extent will the forecasts affect the successful achievement of the customer's mission?
- *Urgency*. To what extent do the forecasts indicate that, if action is required, time is of the essence in developing and implementing the necessary changes?
- *Comparative advantage*. To what extent do the results provide a basis for customer decision-making, compared with other sources available to the customer?
- *Technical quality*. Was the process that produced the forecasts technically sound? Are the alternative forecasts internally consistent?[34]

A "good" forecast is one that meets all or most of these criteria. A "bad" forecast is one that does not. The analyst has to make clear to customers that forecasts are transitory and need constant adjustment to be helpful in guiding thought and action. Customers typically have a number of complaints about forecasts. Common complaints are that the forecast is obvious; it states nothing new; it is too optimistic, pessimistic, or naïve; or it is not credible because it overlooks obvious trends, events, causes, or consequences. Such objections are actually desirable; they help to improve the product. There are a number of appropriate responses to these objections: If something important is missing, add it. If something unimportant is included, get rid of it. If the forecast seems either obvious or counterintuitive, probe the underlying logic and revise the forecast as necessary.

Summary

Intelligence analysis, to be useful, must be predictive. Some events or future states of a target are predictable because they are driven by convergent phenomena. Some are not predictable because they are driven by divergent phenomena.

Intelligence estimates may not come true. But a good estimate—one that accurately describes the forces acting on a target model and the assumptions about those forces—has lasting value for the intelligence customer. As a situation develops, the customer can revise the prediction if the intelligence analyst gets the forces right.

Predictive analysis must take into account unlikely events that could have severe adverse effects on customer interests. To do that, we make use of high-impact/low-probability analysis. It sensitizes customers and analysts to the consequences of unlikely developments. The analysis product—a demonstration scenario—describes how such a development might plausibly start and identifies its consequences. This provides indicators that can be monitored to warn that the improbable event is actually happening.

Analysis involves predicting the future state of a target by using one of three means—extrapolation (unchanging forces), projection (changing forces), and forecasting (changing and new forces). The task is to assess, from the present state of the intelligence target, the transition process that takes the target to its future state and the forces that shape the transition.

Extrapolation is the easiest of the three methods, because it simply assumes that the existing forces will not change. Over the short term, extrapolation is usually reliable, but it seldom gives an accurate picture over the medium to long term, because forces do change. Extrapolation can be used to predict both straight-line and cyclic trends. Correlation and regression are two frequently used types of extrapolation.

For analysts predicting systems developments as many as five years into the future, extrapolations work reasonably well; for those looking five to fifteen years into the future, projections usually fare better. Projection assumes a probability that the forces will change, and it uses several techniques to evaluate the probabilities and the effects of such changes. This probabilistic reasoning relies on techniques such as influence trees and influence nets. Sensitivity analysis can help the customer to identify the significance of changes in the probabilities that go into a projection.

Forecasting is the most difficult predictive technique. It must include the probabilities of changing forces, as projection does. It must also identify possible new forces from across the political, economic, social, and technical arenas and assess their likely impact. Because of the resulting complexity of the problem, most forecasting relies on the use of scenarios. Forecasting, like projection, also takes into account the effects of shaping forces, which are discussed in the next chapter.

Notes

1. Quoted in Woodrow J. Kuhns, "Intelligence Failures: Forecasting and the Lessons of Epistemology," in *Paradoxes of Strategic Intelligence: Essays in Honor of Michael Handel*, ed. Richard K. Betts and Thomas G. Mahnken (London: Frank Cass Publishers, 2003), 96.
2. CIA Center for the Study of Intelligence, "Watching the Bear: Essays on CIA's Analysis of the Soviet Union," Conference, Princeton University, March 2001, https://www.cia.gov/library/center-for-the-study-of-intelligence/csi-publications/books-and-monographs/watching-the-bear-essays-on-cias-analysis-of-the-soviet-union/, Chapter II.
3. Barbara W. Tuchman, *The Guns of August* (New York: Random House, 1962).
4. Roberta Wholstetter, *Pearl Harbor: Warning and Decision* (Stanford, Calif.: Stanford University Press, 1962).
5. Irving Langmuir, "Science, Common Sense, and Decency," *Science*, 97 (January 1943): 1–7.
6. Jamshid Gharajedaghi, *Systems Thinking: Managing Chaos and Complexity* (Boston: Butterworth-Heinemann, 1999), 52.

7. CIA Center for the Study of Intelligence, "Watching the Bear," 11.
8. Ibid.
9. Paul Carroll, *Big Blues* (New York: Crown Publishers, 1993), 18.
10. George Likourezos, "Prologue to Image Enhanced Estimation Methods," *Proceedings of the IEEE*, 18 (June 1993): 796.
11. Thomas Kepner and B. B. Tregoe, *The New Rational Manager* (Princeton, N.J.: Princeton Research Press, 1981).
12. M. S. Loescher, C. Schroeder, and C. W. Thomas, *Proteus: Insights from 2020* (Utrecht, Netherlands: The Copernicus Institute Press, 2000), A-iv.
13. Andrew Sleigh, ed., *Project Insight* (Farnborough, U.K.: Centre for Defence Analysis, Defence Evaluation and Research Agency, 1996), 17.
14. Figure 12-2 assumes that the existing forces change to produce a projection. It is possible that existing forces don't change, and that only new forces come into play. In that case, you would iterate directly from the extrapolation to the forecast.
15. Gharajedaghi, *Systems Thinking*, 51.
16. CIA Center for the Study of Intelligence, "Watching the Bear," Chapter II.
17. Ibid.
18. Gharajedaghi, *Systems Thinking*, 122.
19. The time frame for most predictions extends over years. On a fast-developing situation, the appropriate time frame for force analysis may be months or even days, not years.
20. CIA Directorate of Intelligence, *A Compendium of Analytic Tradecraft Notes* (Washington, D.C.: Author, February 1997), http://www.oss.net/dynamaster/file_archive/040319/cb27cc09c84d056b66616b4da5c02a4d/OSS2000-01-23.pdf.
21. Liam Fahey, *Competitors* (New York: Wiley, 1999), 448.
22. Rob Johnson, *Analytic Culture in the U.S. Intelligence Community* (Washington, D.C.: CIA Center for the Study of Intelligence, 2005), 66.
23. Ibid., 15.
24. Ray Kurzweil, "The Law of Accelerating Returns," March 7, 2001, http://www.kurzweilai.net/the-law-of-accelerating-returns.
25. CIA Center for the Study of Intelligence, "Watching the Bear," 5.
26. This will permit later extension to more sophisticated analyses, such as Bayesian analysis, discussed in chapter 7.
27. Jack Davis, *Intelligence Changes in Analytic Tradecraft in CIA's Directorate of Intelligence* (Washington, D.C.: CIA, 1995), 8.
28. Julie A. Rosen and Wayne L. Smith, "Influencing Global Situations: A Collaborative Approach," *Air Chronicles* (Summer 1996).
29. CIA Center for the Study of Intelligence, "Watching the Bear," 7.
30. P. K. Rose, "Two Strategic Intelligence Mistakes in Korea, 1950," *Studies in Intelligence* (Fall/Winter 2001), http://www.cis.gov/csi/studies/fall_winter_2001/article06.html.
31. William Stueck, *The Korean War: An International History* (Princeton, N.J.: Princeton University Press, 1995).
32. James L. Morrison and Thomas V. Mecca, "Managing Uncertainty: Environmental Analysis/Forecasting in Academic Planning," January 12, 2003, http://horizon.unc.edu/courses/papers/Mang.asp.
33. Ibid.
34. W. I. Boucher, *Technical Advisors' Final Report: Chapters Prepared by Benton International, Inc.*, prepared for the Futures Team of the Professional Development of Officers Study (PDOS), Office of U.S. Army Chief of Staff (Torrance, Calif.: Benton International, 1984).

13

Estimative Forces

Estimating is what you do when you don't know.

Sherman Kent,
former chief of CIA's Office
of National Estimates; often described
as the "father of intelligence analysis"

Chapter 12 introduced the idea of force analysis. The factors or forces that have to be considered in estimation—primarily PMESII factors—vary from one intelligence problem to another. I do not attempt to catalog them in this book; there are too many. But an important aspect of critical thinking, discussed earlier, is thinking about the underlying forces that shape the future. This chapter deals with some of those forces.

The CIA's tradecraft manual describes an analytic methodology that is appropriate for identifying and assessing forces. Called "outside in" thinking, it has the objective of identifying the critical external factors that could influence how a given situation will develop. According to the tradecraft manual, analysts should

> develop a generic description of the problem or the phenomenon under study. Then, analysts should:
>
> - List all the key forces (social, technological, economic, environmental, and political) that could have an impact on the topic, but over which one can exert little influence (e.g., globalization, social stress, the Internet, or the global economy).
> - Focus next on key factors over which an actor or policymaker can exert some influence. In the business world this might be the market size, customers, the competition, suppliers or partners; in the government domain it might include the policy actions or the behavior of allies or adversaries.

- Assess how each of these forces could affect the analytic problem.
- Determine whether these forces actually do have an impact on the particular issue based on the available evidence.[1]

In our analytic construct, what the CIA manual calls a "generic description of the problem" is the model described in Figure 12-1 (see preceding chapter). Starting with the key forces that the CIA manual cites (social, technological, economic, environmental, and political), let's expand them using the more inclusive set described in this book—the PMESII forces or factors. We'll then focus on those that our customers can influence, recognizing that the ones that cannot be much affected by customer actions nevertheless will shape the eventual state of affairs. But first, an historical example.

Political and military factors are often the focus of attention in assessing the likely outcome of conflicts. But the other factors can turn out to be dominant. In the developing conflict between the United States and Japan in 1941, Japan had a military edge in the Pacific. But the United States had a substantial edge in these factors:

- *Political.* The United States could call on a substantial set of allies. Japan had Germany and Italy.
- *Economy.* Japan lacked the natural resources that the United States and its allies controlled.
- *Social.* The United States had almost twice the population of Japan. Japan initially had an edge in the solidarity of its population in support of the government, but that edge was matched within the United States after Pearl Harbor.
- *Infrastructure.* The U.S. manufacturing capability far exceeded that of Japan and would be decisive in a prolonged conflict (as many Japanese military leaders foresaw).
- *Information.* The prewar information edge favored Japan, which had more control of its news media, while a segment of the U.S. media strongly opposed involvement in war. That edge also evaporated after December 7, 1941.

Japan's military edge gave it an early advantage in the consequent war, but the infrastructural and economic factors shifted the military advantage to the United States within a year after December 7, 1941.

There are some forces that can fit under any of the PMESII factors and should be considered in analytic estimates. They tend to shape or temper events and other forces. These forces are mostly social or environmental. An analyst should start a predictive effort by asking which of these forces are relevant to the problem under consideration. The five forces discussed here are inertia, countervailing forces, contamination, synergy, and feedback.

Inertia

One force that has broad implications is inertia, the tendency to stay on course and resist change. Newton's first law of motion (Analysis Principle 13-1) says that bodies at rest tend to stay at rest, and that bodies in motion tend to remain in motion.

Analysis Principle 13-1 •

Newton's First Law: Inertia

Newton's first law (liberally translated) says that

1. Bodies at rest tend to remain at rest; and

2. Bodies in motion tend to remain in motion, *unless* you place them in the real world, where friction applies; then

3. Bodies in motion tend to come to rest; and then you go back to rule 1.

Inertia is important because organizations don't deal well with change in any of the PMESII factors. Military organizations have a tendency to refight the last war. Religious (social) organizations have a history of referring to attempted changes as heresy. It has been observed that

> Historical inertia is easily underrated . . . the historical forces molding the outlook of Americans, Russians, and Chinese for centuries before the words capitalism and communism were invented are easy still to overlook.[2]

Opposition to change is a common reason for organizations' coming to rest. Opposition to technology in general, for example, is an inertial matter; it results from a desire of both workers and managers to preserve society as it is, including its institutions and traditions. The price of inertia is illustrated in the history of the Bessemer steelmaking process in America.

The Bessemer process was invented at about the same time (1856) by two men, each working independently—Henry Bessemer, an Englishman, and William Kelly, an American. The process involved blowing air under pressure into the bottom of a crucible of molten iron. Within a few years the Bessemer process almost completely replaced the conventional crucible method of steelmaking. It lowered the price of producing steel and was the basis for the modern steel industries. It was one of the foundations of the Industrial Revolution.

Between 1864 and 1871, ten companies in the United States began using the Bessemer process to make steel. All but one of them, the Cambria Company, imported English workers familiar with the process. By 1871, Cambria dominated the industry. Although the company had begun at a disadvantage, its workers were able to adapt to changes and improvements in the process that took place between 1864 and 1871. The British steel workers at the other companies, secure in the tradition of their craft, resented and resisted all change, and their companies did not adapt.

A common manifestation of the law of inertia is the "not-invented-here," or NIH, factor, in which the organization opposes pressures for change from the outside. It was a powerful force in the old Soviet technical bureaucracies. The Soviet system developed a high level of stability as a result of central economic planning. But all societies resist change to a certain extent. The societies that succeed seem able to adapt while preserving that part of their heritage that is useful or relevant.

A textbook example of resistance to innovation is the story of the U.S. Navy and Lieutenant William Sims. A century ago, the standard gunnery method used a highly trained gun crew to manipulate the heavy set of gears that aimed naval guns at an opposing ship. Because both ships would be moving, and the gun platform would also move with the pitch and roll of the ship, naval gunnery became an art, and accuracy depended on professionalism and teamwork.

In the early 1900s, a young naval officer, Sims, developed a new method that made use of the movement of the ship. He was able to simplify the aiming gear set and remove the gunnery sight from the gun's recoil so that the operator could keep his eye on the gunsight and move the gears at the same time. His tests demonstrated that the new method would markedly improve the accuracy of naval gunnery.

Sims then attempted to attract the attention of U.S. Navy headquarters and was told that the Navy was not interested. Sims persisted, however, and the Navy finally consented to a test with some conditions: Sims's aiming device had to be strapped to a solid block in the Washington Naval Yard. Deprived of the ship's movement, the aiming device failed, proving to the Navy that continuous-aim firing was impractical.

Sims, however, was as persistent and bold as the person he next contacted with his idea—President Theodore Roosevelt. Roosevelt forced the Navy to take the device and give it a fair test. Sims's device was subsequently adopted and significantly improved naval gunnery accuracy.[3]

The organizational resistance to change that Sims encountered is common in all organizations. The structure of the U.S. Navy is that of a highly organized society, and Sims's innovation directly threatened the society by making some skills less essential. The Navy resisted his innovation, and it took someone outside the society—the president of the United States—to force the change. Organizations are societies just as a U.S. Navy ship's crew is a society. They possess a basic antipathy to changes that threaten their structure. Most research and development groups restrict their members' freedom to innovate: Ideas that don't fit the mold of the group are unwelcome.

From an analyst's point of view, inertia is an important force in prediction. Established factories will continue to produce what they know how to produce. In the automobile industry, it is no great challenge to predict that next year's autos will look much like this year's. A naval power will continue to build ships for some time even if a large navy ceases to be useful.

Inertia is also a warning flag to watch for in intelligence analysis. It has been noted that

> the mere fact of a unit's published record creates analytic inertia—an argument at rest tends to stay at rest and one in motion (i.e., ambiguous or uncertain) tends to stay in motion. (A variation of this includes groupthink.)[4]

Countervailing Forces

All forces are likely to have countervailing or resistive forces that must be considered. The principle is summarized well by another of Newton's laws of physics: For every action there is an equal and opposite reaction (Analysis Principle 13-2).[5]

Analysis Principle 13-2 •

Newton's Third Law (the Dialectic)

Newton's third law states that whenever one body exerts a force on another, the second always exerts on the first a force that is equal in magnitude but oppositely directed. In the social sciences, Hegel's dialectic is the philosophical equivalent of Newton's third law. Hegel describes a process of thesis-antithesis-synthesis, by which views of one type lead, by their internal contradictions, to the creation of views of the opposite type.

This analysis principle indicates that no entity (country, organization, initiative, or project) can expand unopposed. Opponents will always arise. Harvard historian David Landes wrote that "all innovations of thought and practice elicit an opposite if not always equal reaction."[6] If the force reaction is initially not equal, as Landes posits, then a change in momentum (in physics) or in the situation (in the social sciences) takes place until the action and reaction balance. Thus every action ultimately creates an equal and opposite reaction.

Applications of this principle are found in all organizations and groups, commercial, national, and civilizational. As Samuel P. Huntington noted,

"[W]e know who we are . . . often only when we know who we are against."[7] The rallying cry of Japan's Komatsu Corporation, and the definition of its being, was summed up in its slogan, "Beat Caterpillar"—Caterpillar Inc., being Komatsu's chief competitor worldwide.

In Isaac Asimov's brilliant short story *The Last Trump*, the archangel Gabriel sounds the last trumpet and judgment day arrives (on January 1, 1957, to be precise). Earth's residents (and former residents, who are coming back to life on a featureless Earth in their last corporeal form) slowly realize that boredom, not the fire and ice of Dante's *Inferno*, is the ultimate hell. Etheriel, Earth's guardian angel, meanwhile is appealing to a higher court—the Almighty—for an *ex post facto* reversal of the judgment day order. Finally, Etheriel, realizing who has actually won the final battle for the souls of human-kind, asks, "Is then the Adversary your servant also?" God invokes Newton's third law in his reply: "Without him I can have no other . . . for what is Good but the eternal fight against Evil?"[8]

A predictive analysis will always be incomplete unless it identifies and assesses opposing forces. All forces eventually meet counterforces. An effort to expand free trade inevitably arouses protectionist reactions. One country's expansion of its military strength always causes its neighbors to react in some fashion. If laws bar access to obscenity online, you can count on offshore evasion of restrictions and growing pressures for free speech.

Counterforces need not be of the same nature as the force they are countering. A prudent organization is not likely to play to its opponent's strengths. Today's threats to U.S. national security are asymmetric; that is, there is little threat of a conventional force-on-force engagement by an opposing military, but there is a threat of an unconventional yet lethal attack by a loosely organized terrorist group, as the events of September 11, 2001, and more recently the Boston Marathon bombing, demonstrated.[9] Asymmetric counterforces are common in industry as well. Industrial organizations try to achieve cost asymmetry by using defensive tactics that have a large favorable cost differential between their organization and that of an opponent.[10] Any intelligence assessment of the consequences of a policy-maker's or field commander's decision should take into account countervailing forces, because the opponents will react and smart ones are likely to react asymmetrically.

Contamination

Contamination is the degradation of any of the six factors—political, military, economic, social, infrastructure, or information (PMESII factors)—through an infection-like process (Analysis Principle 13-3). Corruption is a form of political and social contamination. Funds laundering and counterfeiting are forms of economic contamination. The result of propaganda is information contamination.

Analysis Principle 13-3 •─────────────────────────────

Gresham's Law of Currency

Gresham's law of currency is based on the observation that when currencies of different metallic content but the same face value are in circulation at the same time, people will hoard the more valuable currency or use it for foreign purchases, leaving only the "bad" money in domestic circulation. The law explains a major disadvantage of a bimetallic currency system. Gresham's law is generally summarized as "the bad drives out the good."

Irving Langmuir described the contamination phenomenon in this story about a glycerin refinery:

> Glycerin is commonly known as a viscous liquid, even at low temperatures. Yet if crystals are once formed, they melt only at 64 degrees Fahrenheit. If a minute crystal of this kind is introduced into pure glycerin at temperatures below 64 degrees Fahrenheit, the entire liquid gradually solidifies.
>
> A glycerin refinery in Canada had operated for many years without having any experience with crystalline glycerin. But suddenly one winter, without exceptionally low temperatures, the pipe carrying the glycerin from one piece of apparatus to another froze up. The whole plant and even the dust on the ground became contaminated with nuclei, and although any part of the plant could be temporarily freed from crystals by heating above 64 degrees, it was found that whenever the temperature anywhere fell below 64 degrees crystals would begin forming. The whole plant had to be shut down for months until outdoor temperatures rose above 64 degrees.[11]

Contamination phenomena can be found throughout organizations as well as in the scientific and technical disciplines. Once such an infection starts, it is almost impossible to eradicate. It keeps poisoning its host, and there are too many little bits to stamp out entirely—like the crystals of glycerin or metastasizing cancerous cells. For example, in the U.S. electronics industry, a company's microwave tube production line suddenly went bad. With no observable change in the process, the tubes no longer met specifications. Somehow, the line had become contaminated. Attempts to find or correct the problem failed, and the only solution was to close down the production line and rebuild it completely.

Contamination phenomena have analogies in the social sciences, organization theory, and folklore. Folklore tells us that "One bad apple spoils the barrel." At some point in organizations, contamination can become so thorough that only drastic measures will help—such as shutting down the glycerin plant or rebuilding the microwave tube plant. Predictive intelligence has to consider the extent of such social contamination in organizations, because contamination is a strong restraining force on an organization's ability to deal with change.

The effects of social contamination are hard to measure, but they are often highly visible. Large sectors of industry in Russia reached a high level of contamination during the Soviet era, and recovery has proved to be very difficult. Indications of contamination can be seen in the production results, but there are also other visible symptoms. For example, most Japanese plants are clean and neat, with grass and flowers even in unlikely areas, such as underneath drying kilns. Even today a Russian factory is likely to have a dirty, cluttered environment; buildings with staggering losses of energy; and employees with chronic absenteeism and alcohol problems. The environment in the Japanese plant reinforces the positive image. The environment in the Russian plant reinforces and prolongs the contamination. Such contamination can be reversed—the cleanup of New York City in the 1990s is an example—but a reversal typically requires a massive effort.

The contamination phenomenon has an interesting analogy in the use of euphemism in language. It is well known that if a word has or develops negative associations, it will be replaced by a succession of euphemisms. Such words have a half-life, or decay rate, that is shorter as the word association becomes more negative. In older English, the word *stink* meant "to smell." The problem is that most of the strong impressions we get from scents are unpleasant ones; so each word for olfactory senses becomes contaminated over time and must be replaced. *Smell* has a generally unpleasant connotation now, and words such as *scent, aroma,* and *bouquet* are replacing it, to fall in their turn. Similarly, words that denote any socially, mentally, or physically disadvantaged group seem to become contaminated over time; words such as *deaf, blind,* and *retarded* were replaced by *handicapped,* and then by *physically/mentally challenged,* then *special needs* or *people with disabilities,* and most recently, *people with special abilities,* reflecting the negative associations that attach to the words as contamination sets in.

The phenomenon of contamination in language can be especially useful for the intelligence analyst in assessing the effectiveness of programs, whether social, political, or technical—and of hardware also. *We don't rename our successes.* Ford Motor Company since 1964 has kept the name "Mustang" for its most beloved automobile, but there will never be another Edsel or, for that matter, another Pinto. The renaming of a program or project is a good signal that the program or project is in trouble—especially in Washington, D.C., but the same rule holds in any culture.

Synergy

As discussed in chapter 12, predictive intelligence analysis almost always requires multidisciplinary understanding. Therefore, it is essential that the analysis organization's professional development program cultivate a professional staff that can understand a broad range of concepts and function in a multidisciplinary environment. One of the most basic concepts is that of synergy: The whole can be more than the sum of its parts due to interactions among the parts. Synergy is therefore, in some respects, the opposite of the countervailing forces discussed earlier.

Synergy is not really a force or factor as much as a way of thinking about how forces or factors interact. Synergy can result from cooperative efforts and alliances among organizations (synergy on a large scale). It can be the consequence of a combination of social, economic, political, and technological forces on a grand scale, such as caused the Industrial Revolution.[12] Netwar, as discussed in chapter 2, is an application of synergy. Synergy can also result from interactions within a physical system, as the following example shows.

When the U.S. Nike Hercules surface-to-air missile system was deployed in the 1950s, its target tracking radar proved to be very difficult for attacking aircraft to defeat in combat training exercises. The three standard techniques for defeating such radars at the time were rapid maneuvers, radar decoys, and noise jamming. None of the three techniques worked very well against the Nike Hercules radar:

- Maneuvers had no effect.
- Radar decoy material known as chaff (thin strips of aluminum foil that cause a radar signal resembling an aircraft) did not work, because the radar tracking system could discriminate between slow-moving chaff and a fast-moving aircraft.
- Conventional noise jamming was ineffective because of the radar's antijam circuits.

The U.S. Air Force's Strategic Air Command (SAC) put its electronic warfare planners on the problem, because the Nike Hercules capabilities could be expected to appear in hostile radars that SAC's B-52s would face. SAC's planners found that a combination of the three techniques—noise jamming with an S maneuver in which chaff was dropped when the aircraft track was perpendicular to the radar bearing—consistently defeated the tracking radar. The secret to the success of what became called the "side-step" maneuver was synergy.

In electronics warfare, it is now well known that a weapons system may be unaffected by a single countermeasure; however, it may be degraded by a combination of countermeasures, each of which fail individually to defeat it. The same principle applies in a wide range of systems and technology developments: The combination may be much greater than the sum of the components taken individually.

An example of synergy on a large scale is in the fields of computers and communications. These once distinct technical areas merged over several decades during the past century as we expanded our ability to use one to enhance performance of the other. Managing the merger of these two required technical knowledge in both, plus an understanding of political issues (regulation in communications), economic issues (cost-performance tradeoffs of central versus distributed computing), and social issues (willingness of large numbers of people to adopt advanced technologies, as people have done in using networks such as the Internet, social networking technologies, and cloud computing).

Synergy is the foundation of the "swarm" approach that military forces have applied for centuries—the coordinated application of overwhelming force. The massed English longbows at the Battle of Crécy in 1346 were more lethal than the sum of many single longbows might indicate. In chapter 9, we discussed the effectiveness of synergy in Michael Vickers's plan for defeating the HIND helicopter in Afghanistan. The solution that was used—a combination of several surface-to-air missiles and several heavy machine guns—was far more effective than any one of these weapons would have been alone.

Synergy is equally effective in the commercial world. In planning a business strategy against a competitive threat, a company will often put in place several actions that, each taken alone, would not succeed. But the combination can be very effective. As a simple example, a company might use several tactics to cut sales of a competitor's new product: start rumors of its own improved product release, circulate reports on the defects or expected obsolescence of the competitor's product, raise buyers' costs of switching from its own to the competitor's product, and tie up suppliers by using exclusive contracts. Each action, taken separately, might have little impact, but the synergy—the "swarm" effect of the actions taken in combination—might shatter the competitor's market.

In intelligence support to policymakers, the same rule holds. A combination of policy actions may be much more effective than any single action. The policymaker or executive usually identifies the possible combinations and, in the end, selects one combination. The usual job of the intelligence analyst is to evaluate the likely effects of a given combination, though in some cases he may also formulate likely combinations for the executive.

Most of the major innovations and changes that make straight-line extrapolation fail over the long term occur because of some form of synergy. Synergy was a major factor in the spread of television, citizens band (CB) radio, and personal computing. It should be on the analyst's mind constantly as she evaluates the factors going into a forecast.

Feedback

In examining any complex system, it is important for the analyst to evaluate the system's feedback mechanism. Feedback is the mechanism whereby the system adapts—that is, learns and changes itself. The following discussion provides more detail about how feedback works to change a system.

Many of the techniques for prediction depend on the assumption that the process being analyzed can be described, using systems theory, as a closed-loop system. Under the mathematical theory of such systems, feedback is a controlling force in which the output is compared with the objective or standard, and the input process is corrected as necessary to bring the output toward a desired state, as shown in Figure 13-1 (which is identical to Figure 9-1). The results (the output) are evaluated and the result of the evaluation fed back as an input to the system at the point shown in the figure. The feedback function therefore determines the behavior of the total system over time. Only one feedback loop is shown in the figure, but many feedback loops can exist, and usually do in a complex system.

The model shown in Figure 13-1 is a generalized one and is used extensively in electrical engineering to describe the operation of mechanical and electrical control systems. It also has been found to represent many social processes, especially how organizations adapt. Although its general validity is untested formally, the model is accepted here as having some validity in predicting the future state of the system.

An analyst should not consider a prediction complete until she has assessed the potential effects of feedback. This assessment requires that the analyst predict the nature and extent of feedback. Feedback can be positive and encourage more output, or it can be negative and encourage less output. Feedback can also be strong and have a greater effect on output, or be weak and have less of an effect. Finally, feedback can be immediate and thus reflected immediately in the output, or its effect can be delayed, so that it changes the output at some future time.

The Indian Nuclear Test deception, described in chapter 8, is an example of how feedback works in the world of national policy and intelligence. The U.S. State Department's demarche about India's test preparation contained detailed (though unintended) feedback to New Delhi on how to prepare for a test the next time around. The Indian government altered its process accordingly in its next test preparations. The output (or result) was highly satisfactory for India but less so for the United States.

Figure 13-1 The Feedback Process

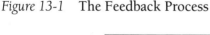

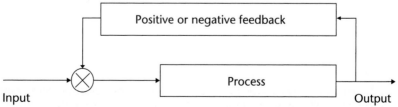

Note: The circled *X* shows where the input and the feedback combine before they flow into the process.

Strength

Most systems are adaptive. Feedback causes changes in the input and should also cause the management assessment and innovation parts of a process to change. The measure of this adaptivity is the strength of feedback. In most systems, a change in the output (type, quantity, and so on) changes the input due to an evaluative process. In positive feedback systems, where benefits outweigh costs, the output causes a reinforcement of the input, and the output therefore tends to grow at a rate determined in part by the amount of positive feedback. In negative feedback systems, where costs outweigh benefits, output is fed back in such a manner as to decrease input, and the output tends to stabilize or decrease.

The rate of change in forces that is due to feedback is a result of weighing observed benefits of a development (positive feedback) against the costs (negative feedback). This is the evaluation or decision-making step.

Organizations tend to act to reduce the strength of feedback in two ways. First, because few organizations can readily cope with the uncertainty that comes from adaptivity, organizations try to hold things constant so that they can deal with them. This tendency is a powerful constraint on feedback.[13] Sims's problem with introducing his gunnery innovation is one of many examples of the problem.

Second, feedback must reach decision makers or action takers to be effective. Only when it is accepted by the appropriate people in an organization can it shape future actions. But the organization itself—its administrative layers and staff—diffuses, weakens, misdirects, and delays feedback, effectively reducing its strength. A large bureaucratic organization or a centralized economy, with its relative inflexibility and numerous layers of administrators, keeps feedback at a feeble level. Funding is set through political processes that have only an indirect relation to previous industrial successes and failures. The market provides poor feedback in a centralized or command economy.

National leaders tend to react poorly when they receive negative feedback—for example, if their policies are not turning out well. So negative feedback tends not to reach them at all, or to be so attenuated as to be ignored. In contrast, because they react favorably to positive feedback, it tends to reach these leaders in full strength. This book contains several examples of leaders who didn't get the negative feedback because they didn't want to hear it. Adolf Hitler, Lyndon Johnson, Saddam Hussein, and a succession of Soviet leaders, beginning with Josef Stalin—all failed to receive the negative feedback that they needed at critical times.

Time Delay

All feedback loops, whether in technological or social systems, have inherent delay. The time lag causes a problem when it results in the feedback's sending the wrong signal. Sometimes feedback of positive benefits comes more slowly than does feedback of a negative kind. So in the early stages, the system may receive only negative feedback, though more positive information may be coming later. The benefits of deregulation or free trade agreements, for example, may be much more difficult to identify and take longer to observe than the costs.

It is fairly common, by contrast, for benefits to be perceived more quickly than costs. The drug industry has provided examples of this phenomenon, one of the most dramatic of which occurred with the drug thalidomide. First introduced in Europe in 1956 for use as a sedative and to combat morning sickness in pregnant women, its benefits were realized quickly. But the costs were observed later on; thalidomide was withdrawn from the market in 1961 after it was found to have caused severe birth defects in thousands of infants.[14]

The delayed effects of environmental pollution have provided other examples of such "false positive" feedback. The nuclear power industry, however, has probably provided the most spectacular examples. This industry benefited for some years from extensive government-supported efforts to advance technology. The resulting pace of nuclear power technology development was too rapid to allow adequate mitigation of the risks.[15] As a result, in 1979 the United States suffered from the Three Mile Island reactor incident that released radioactive material into the air near Harrisburg, Pennsylvania, creating widespread panic. In 1986 Russia had its Chernobyl disaster—a reactor meltdown that contaminated a wide area in the Ukraine and caused numerous deaths. In 2011 the Fukushima, Japan, nuclear power plant was hit by a tsunami. The damage resulted in the meltdown of three of the plant's nuclear reactors, releasing substantial amounts of radioactive contamination.

As these examples suggest, delays in negative feedback are a continuing problem in areas of rapid technological advance. The rapid advances depend on technology diffusion mechanisms that work extremely well in the United States, with its efficient communications networks and high mobility of workers. Multinational corporations also provide a powerful technological diffusion mechanism. This fast advance of technology, compared to the technology evaluation process, leads to examples of technology-driven systems in which the constraining effects of regulatory, human resources, organizational, and management factors are too slow to exert much power. The pharmaceutical, communications, and computer industries have provided examples of this technology drive in action for several decades. Genetic engineering is one example of a current technology-driven field that could result in serious problems worldwide in coming decades.

Unintended Consequences

When an organization or person acts, they often focus on solving the highly visible problem and fail to recognize possible adverse consequences of their solution. This is a particularly common problem for national governments.

In part because of slower feedback processes and a more cumbersome structure, governments are generally not as quick on their feet as the opponents they deal with. And in the intervention, governments continually encounter the law of unintended consequences: Actions taken to change a complex system will have unintended, and usually adverse, consequences (Analysis Principle 13-4).

Analysis Principle 13-4 ●————————————————————————

The Law of Unintended Consequences

The law of unintended consequences, simply stated, says that

- Any deliberate change to a complex system will have unintended (and usually unforeseen) consequences; and
- The consequences are usually undesirable.

The classic illustration of the law of unintended consequences dates back to Tudor England. In England before 1535, real property passed by descent to the oldest son on his father's death. At that transfer, a tax was owed to the king. Over the years, feudal lawyers had created a device called the *Use* that allowed trustees to hold legal title to land in trust for the true owner so that, unless all of the trustees died at once, the land could be passed repeatedly from father to son without the requirement that a tax be paid.

The story goes that King Henry VIII, as his financial needs increased, "contemplated the state of his exchequer with great dismay."[16] A survey of the kingdom's assets revealed to Henry how England's landowners were avoiding his taxes through the device of the Use. In 1535 Henry prevailed upon a reluctant Parliament to pass the Statute of Uses.[17] The statute was simple and direct: It vested legal title in the land's true owner, not in the trustee, so that taxes would be due upon the death of the true owner.

The statute is remarkable for two reasons:

- First, it totally failed in its revenue-raising purpose. Within a few years the British lawyers, who were no less clever than tax lawyers are today, had found enough loopholes in the statute to thwart it.
- Second, the *unintended* consequences of this tax-raising statute were vast, so that it has been called the most important single piece of legislation in the Anglo-American law of property. Specifically, the law gave rise to the modern law of trusts and to the modern methods of transferring real estate. The British Parliament's reaction to the Statute of Uses also led to the law of wills as we know it.

The Statute of Uses also is one of the few known exceptions to the rule that unintended consequences are usually undesirable. It had highly beneficial results for succeeding generations, though not for Henry VIII.

The law of unintended consequences has an analogy in the world of data processing. In a modern distributed processing network, or in a complex software package, one cannot predict all the effects of changes. But it is predictable that most of the unintended consequences—system crashes, lockouts, and so forth—will be undesirable ones.

The law of unintended consequences may be merely an elegant expression of Murphy's law (which states that anything that can go wrong, will) or simply an expression of human inability to foretell the outcome of a complex social process. One facet of the law has been described as "counterintuitiveness." One generic model of a welfare system demonstrated that expanding a welfare system to reduce the number of poor families in a community actually (and counterintuitively) increased their numbers.[18] Another model indicated that making drugs illegal as a way to curb drug abuse and reduce other societal problems had the opposite effect.[19]

There are many historical examples of this law in action in international affairs:

- The harsh terms that the Allies imposed on Germany after World War I were one of the root causes of World War II.
- Soviet secrecy during the Cold War forced U.S. defense planners to assume the worst-case scenario and provoked a military buildup that the Soviets did not want.
- The killing of Pablo Escobar (see chapter 3) didn't significantly alter the narcotics problem for the United States. Colombia's Cali cartel expanded to serve the markets that the Escobar cartel had served.
- Many governments and commercial entities pay ransom for the return of hostages or of ships seized by pirates. U.S. government policy is not to pay ransom because the practice simply provides an incentive for more kidnappings and piracy.

Intelligence analysts have an important role to play in dealing with this particular force. They are best positioned to understand how others will react to their customer's actions, and so to identify possible unintended consequences of those actions.

Summary

Predictive analysis relies on assessing the impact of forces that shape organizations, lead to new developments, and motivate people.

- *Inertia*, or resistance to change, is common in established organizations. Organizations naturally seek to establish and maintain a stable state, and to keep doing what they've done in the past.

- *Countervailing forces* will always arise to oppose any significant force, and the countervailing force may be of an asymmetric type.
- *Contamination* phenomena can adversely affect the PMESII assets of a state or organization.
- *Synergy*—the combination of forces to achieve unexpected results— is behind many social and technical advances. Synergy enables the effectiveness of the "swarm" attack that organizations increasingly use to win conflicts.
- *Feedback* is an adaptive force that can be beneficial or detrimental, depending on the strength and time delay. Bad policy decisions can result when there are significant differences in time delays between positive and negative feedback.
- Actions by organizations and individuals often have *unintended consequences*. An important role of the intelligence analyst is to identify possible unintended consequences for the customer before any action is taken.

These shaping forces should be a "first stop" in any estimative analysis about a target model.

Notes

1. CIA Directorate of Intelligence, *A Compendium of Analytic Tradecraft Notes* (Washington, D.C.: Author, February 1997), http://www.oss.net/dynamaster/file_archive/040319/cb27cc09c84d056b66616b4da5c02a4d/OSS2000-01-23.pdf, 30.
2. J. M. Roberts, *The Penguin History of the World* (London: Penguin Books, 1995), xi–xii.
3. Elting Morrison, *Men, Machines, and Modern Times* (Cambridge, Mass.: MIT Press, 1966).
4. Barry G. Silverman, Richard L. Rees, Jozsef A. Toth, Jason Cornwell, Kevin O'Brien, Michael Johns, and Marty Caplan, "Athena's Prism—A Diplomatic Strategy Role Playing Simulation for Generating Ideas and Exploring Alternatives," University of Pennsylvania, 2005, http://repository.upenn.edu/cgi/viewcontent.cgi?article=1321&context=ese_papers.
5. Sir Isaac Newton, *Philosophiae Naturalis Principia Mathematica* (July 5, 1687).
6. David S. Landes, *The Wealth and Poverty of Nations* (New York: Norton, 1998), 201.
7. Samuel P. Huntington, *The Clash of Civilizations and the Remaking of World Order* (New York: Simon & Schuster, 1996), 21.
8. Isaac Asimov, "The Last Trump," in *Isaac Asimov: The Complete Stories*, vol. 1 (New York: Doubleday, 1990), 106–119.
9. Another thoughtful perspective on the use of asymmetric attack against the United States is presented in the book *Unrestricted Warfare* by Chinese People's Liberation Army colonels Qiao Liang and Wang Xiangsui.
10. Michael E. Porter, *Competitive Advantage* (New York: Free Press, 1985), 500.
11. Irving Langmuir, "Science, Common Sense, and Decency," *Science* 97 (January 1943): 1–7.
12. Landes, *The Wealth and Poverty of Nations*, chapters 13 and 14.
13. Donald A. Schon, *Organizational Learning* (Boston, Mass.: Addison-Wesley, 1978).
14. Crohn's and Colitis Foundation of America, "Thalidomide and IBD," March 10, 2003, http://www.ccfa.org/weekly/wkly828.htm.
15. Ibid.
16. John E. Cribbet, *Principles of the Law of Property* (St. Paul, Minn.: Foundation Press, 1975).
17. Ibid.
18. Jamshid Gharajedaghi, *Systems Thinking: Managing Chaos and Complexity* (Boston, Mass.: Butterworth-Heinemann, 1999), 49.
19. Ibid, 48.

14

Scenarios

It's hard to make predictions, especially about the future.

Attributed to Yogi Berra and
physicist Niels Bohr, among others

Chapter 12 introduced fairly advanced estimative concepts. Now let's turn to the primary methodology for applying the estimative approach: scenarios, which are the product of what the CIA's tradecraft manual refers to as *alternative futures analysis*.[1] An exercise at the end of this chapter is provided to help clarify how the scenario methodology works in practice.

Intelligence scenarios are descriptions in story form of a potential future model of the target. They are used primarily for planning and decision making. Each scenario represents a distinct, plausible picture of the future.

Because it is impossible to know the future precisely, the solution is to create several scenarios. These scenarios are in essence specially constructed stories about the future, each one modeling a distinct potential outcome. The resulting scenario set establishes the boundaries of our uncertainty and the limits to credible futures.

Why Use Scenarios?

The purpose of scenarios is to highlight major forces that could shape the future. The scenario development makes these forces visible, so that as they begin to make an impact, the intelligence officer will at least recognize them.[2] Scenario planning thereby helps both the intelligence analyst and the customer to anticipate the future and better respond to subsequent events.

Scenarios have great power to communicate the sense or feel of situations that do not currently and may never exist. They give the user a feel for what might happen if he or she pursues a certain course of action in a complex situation that cannot be quantified. An example scenario might be one that describes the likely pattern of daily life in the future under specified assumptions about nuclear power plant regulation. Depending on the views of the scenario planner, the scenario could be used to support or oppose increased regulation. A supporter of regulation would likely develop scenarios that included a series of Chernobyl or Fukushima disasters absent regulation. An opponent of regulation would be more likely to devise scenarios that showed a world of high electric power costs, atmospheric pollution due to smokestack power plants, and declining economies due to the increasing energy costs of regulation. An intelligence analyst must have the objectivity to avoid such slanted scenarios.

Scenarios are used in strategic planning—for instance, in business—to examine merger candidates or consider a new product line. Such scenarios are often global. Scenarios are used also in tactical or operational planning—for example, for interdicting illicit traffic such as narcotics. In narcotics interdiction, the scenarios would include a geospatial target model of narcotics growing and processing areas and drug trans-shipment routes, possibly with timeline models showing when trans-shipments take place. The scenarios would also include relationship models (link or network diagrams) showing the pattern of funds-laundering. For operational planning, the scenarios would then be modified to show the effect of specific narcotics interdiction actions—for example, deployment of radar surveillance aircraft into the Caribbean or a program to pay farmers not to grow the crop. Because of the analyst's knowledge of the target, she is a key player in incorporating such effects into the scenario.

In an alternative future as depicted by a scenario, a decision maker should be able to make decisions and develop strategies by identifying the following:

- Relationships among forces
- The probable impacts of those forces on an organization or a situation
- The key decision points for taking action

By providing a realistic range of possibilities, the set of alternative scenarios helps the decision maker to identify common features likely to have an impact on the organization, no matter which alternative occurs.

Predicting the future in detail is no more possible than predicting the weather in detail. The details tend to be controlled by divergent phenomena, such as an assassination in Sarajevo. But the dominant forces and trends tend to be convergent phenomena that allow the creation of a few "most likely" outcome scenarios, with indicators that can tell which outcome is more likely. Scenario synthesis and analysis is used to create these scenarios.

Once scenarios are created, the job of the intelligence analyst is to track indicators that point toward a specific scenario (for example, favorable consumer reaction to the new product line or the increased flow of narcotics through a specific location). How the analyst does this is discussed later in this chapter.

Types of Scenarios

Analysts use four basic types of scenarios.[3] *Demonstration scenarios, driving-force scenarios*, and *system-change scenarios* move through time, enabling the user to understand the forces and decision points that lead to the final "scene" of the scenario. The *slice-of-time scenario* is a snapshot; it dwells on the final "scene." All four types are used by science fiction writers (who, after all, write scenarios about alternative futures). Some science fiction writers simply drop the reader into the final scene; others explain the history and developments that lead to the final scene.

Demonstration Scenario

The demonstration scenario in intelligence is the product of high-impact/low-probability analysis, discussed in chapter 12. In creating this scenario, the analyst identifies the high-impact outcome and then defines plausible paths to arrive at that outcome. Intelligence analysts typically use an alternative version of the demonstration scenario, called a *branch-point scenario*. It identifies triggering events along the path—events that represent points at which leaders' decisions or other occurrences shape the outcome. The branch points serve as indicators that a particular scenario is developing.

The main purpose of this scenario is to focus attention on the branch points rather than on the final outcome, because those are the points where the intelligence customer may be able to act to change the high-impact outcome.[4] So the analyst's skill at identifying branch points determines the value of the scenario.

Driving-Force Scenario

The driving-force scenario is basically an implementation of the estimative approach for projection, described in chapter 12. The analyst examines the major forces acting on the target and determines how they are changing. These forces are used to produce a projected future target model.

The usual method is to create multiple driving-force scenarios (alternative outcomes). First, the analyst identifies the key *uncertain* factors or forces that will shape the outcomes. Then he identifies alternative levels of change for each factor or force. Finally, the analyst develops a matrix or "tree" showing the outcomes for each assumed combination of the factors or forces.

An example of this scenario development process is the influence tree described in Figure 12-6. The example there concerned an ongoing African insurgency movement. Three possible outcomes were postulated: regime wins, insurgency wins, and stalemate. Two uncertain forces were identified as shaping the outcome: a poverty program that could either succeed or fail, and economic conditions that could improve, remain unchanged, or worsen. The result was a set of six different possible combinations of the two forces, which in turn led to a set of probabilities for the three possible outcomes.

Another alternative is to select different dominant forces for each scenario. This path was taken in *Proteus*, a book of possible future scenarios sponsored by the U.S. National Reconnaissance Office. In *Proteus*, for example, the scenario "Amazon.plague" has a single dominant force: a series of highly contagious, deadly viruses that sweep the globe.[5]

Driving-force scenarios therefore allow the analyst to describe the effects of changing forces, but with a caveat. Once they are selected, the alternative force levels remain constant. This assumption is consciously made in order to simplify the problem, but it ignores potential events that would affect the strength of forces or introduce new forces. In the insurgency influence tree of Figure 12-6, for example, there is no provision for a poverty program that initially does nothing, then gradually succeeds—or alternatively, initially succeeds, then runs into problems due to corruption.

System-Change Scenario

The system-change scenario is a variant of the driving-force scenario that deals with the caveat identified previously. It takes into account all PMESII forces that may have a significant impact. And it accounts for both changes in existing forces and the introduction of new forces. One method of creating the scenario relies on cross-impact analysis (discussed later in this chapter) to identify interactions among events or developments, and then from these interactions to develop alternative outcomes. This is a very difficult scenario to develop because of the need to examine interrelationships among the forces.

Slice-of-Time Scenario

The slice-of-time scenario starts at a future time, where a synthesis of explicit or assumed forces has created a specific result. It resembles the demonstration scenario in that it describes an end point—but without providing a pathway to the end point. Slice-of-time scenarios are not generally useful in intelligence; they give short shrift to the driving forces that lead to the outcome. They therefore provide few indicators for intelligence analysts or their customers to monitor. They are often seen, though, in policy papers that define a specific future environment—a world of reduced tariffs or of combined high unemployment and inflation, for example—without explaining how the environment came to be.

Scenario Perspectives

Scenarios are models, and like the models discussed in chapter 5, they can be either descriptive or normative. The scenario usually begins in the present and then unfolds from there to some future time. The simplest such scenario is the straight-line extrapolation; it assumes that only current forces and policy choices are allowed to be felt in the future (no technological discoveries or revolutions, for example, are permitted). These extrapolation scenarios are "momentum" scenarios—they are dominated by inertia, and no countervailing forces arise to slow the observed trend.[6] Inertia, as discussed in chapter 13, is the tendency for organizations and other bodies to stay their course and resist change. Most China scenarios tend to be momentum scenarios based on the country's spectacular growth. They don't contemplate a weak divided China of the future (for example, a China ruled by economic or military warlords) in spite of the Soviet example and of Chinese history. Scenarios about Japan's economy created in the early 1980s had a similar momentum pattern and proved to be inaccurate. Because momentum scenarios are straight-line extrapolations, it is prudent not to use them for long-term assessments. An analyst can start with extrapolation but should then look at new and changing forces that create projection and forecast scenarios.

Policymakers often make use of normative scenarios, so intelligence analysts should understand the purposes of such scenarios and may need to help the customer develop them. The normative scenario typically deals with the question of "What outcome do I want to see?" or "What outcome do I want to avoid?" As with a normative model, the purpose is to develop a preferred course of action or avoid an unfavorable end state. Policymakers or decision makers therefore define an outcome such as a stable international political environment, and the sequence of events by which that ideal could be achieved. Or they may specify an unfavorable outcome (for example, increasing international terrorism and governmental instability) and will want to know the sequence of events that lead to this end state. This case—the unfavorable end state—may be a high-impact/low-probability demonstration scenario, for example.

How to Construct Scenarios

Scenario planning is really a variant of the well-known modeling, simulation, and gaming methods. It is an art, not a standardized or systematic methodology. The assumptions on which a scenario is based must be made explicit because of its great potential for misuse.

Peter Schwartz, former head of global planning for Royal Dutch Shell, has described a four-step process of scenario construction: (1) define the problem, (2) identify factors bearing on the problem, (3) identify possible solutions, and (4) find the best (most likely) solution(s).[7]

1. Define the Problem

Scenario planning begins by identifying the focal issue or decision. Rather than trying to explore the entire future, ask yourself, "What question am I trying to answer?" We could tell an infinite number of stories about the future; our purpose is to tell those that matter, that lead our customers to make better decisions. So we begin by agreeing on the issue that we want to address. Sometimes the question is broad (What are the future prospects in the Middle East?); sometimes it's specific (Is a terrorist attack on the U.S. railroad industry likely in the next year?). Either way, the point is to agree on the issues that will be used as a test of relevance as we plan the scenario.[8]

2. Identify Factors Bearing on the Problem

This step is basically an extension of the strategies-to-task approach to a problem breakout that was discussed in earlier chapters. In this step, the analyst identifies the key forces that apply to the scenario. Because scenarios are a way of understanding the dynamics shaping the future, we attempt to identify the primary driving forces at work in the present. These forces fall roughly into the same categories that we've discussed throughout this book:[9]

- *Political.* Electoral (Will the prime minister be reelected?); legislative (Will further safety restrictions be imposed on handguns?); regulatory (Will the German government impose new immigration restrictions?); and litigable (Will the courts accept any new theories on the criminality of terrorist acts?)
- *Military.* The weaponry, capabilities, strategies, and tactics that opponents have or will use to apply armed force (Will transnational criminal groups and local gangs make more use of advanced weapons such as rocket-propelled grenades, counter-air missiles, and UAVs?)
- *Economic.* Macroeconomic trends and forces shaping the economy as a whole (What are the effects of international trade barriers and exchange rates on raw material costs? What are economic sanctions likely to do to our markets?); microeconomics (What might industrial competitors do? How will the defense industry's fundamental structure change?); and forces at work on or within an organization (What is its level of debt, and what are those of potential partners?)
- *Social.* Quantitative, demographic issues (What will be the ethnic mix of country *X* in 2020? Will immigration increase or decrease?); and softer issues of values, lifestyle, demand, or political activism (How is the United States likely to be regarded in Western Europe if it builds a missile defense shield? What is the social impact of a large retiree population?)
- *Infrastructure and information.* These factors tend to deal with technology matters that fall into three categories: direct (How will the genome map affect existing DNA testing?); enabling (Will biochips enable a new cell phone revolution? Is the organization facing a loss of skilled employees? Does it have an up-to-date computer network?); and indirect (How will new web technologies change the need for cyber security measures?)

Next, the analyst isolates the driving forces. Which driving forces are critical to this outcome? Some driving forces affect everyone the same way. Most companies, for instance, are driven by the need to cut costs and incorporate new technologies. But unless one of the target organizations is markedly better or worse than others at doing these things, the differences will not affect the end result. The important thing is to identify any asymmetric forces that may be present.

Then the analyst should rank the driving forces by importance and uncertainty. Some forces carry more consequences than others. Whether a market will grow may not be as important as whether new players will enter the market. Some forces are far more certain than others. Local housing and population patterns usually change fairly slowly. The aging of Japan's population is fairly predictable and over the coming decades will have a similar effect in any scenario. By contrast, some questions are highly uncertain. The driving forces that need to be considered will be those that are both very important and highly uncertain.[10]

3. Identify Possible Solutions

This is probably the most important step. First, the analyst identifies the scenario types to be considered. Three distinct scenario types are typical: the *emergent* scenario (which evolves from an opponent's current strategy); the *unconstrained what-if* scenario (which comes from asking unconstrained questions about completely new strategies); and the *constrained what-if* scenario (which asks what the opponent might do under different environmental conditions or forces).[11]

The analyst then works with the issues, reshaping and reframing them and drawing out their less obvious elements until a consensus emerges about which two or three underlying issues will make a difference in the outcome. This step involves differentiating the scenarios: identifying inconsistencies, finding underlying similarities, and eliminating scenarios that are redundant or implausible.

Now the analyst goes back to all the driving forces and trends considered in step 2 and uses these to flesh out the scenarios. For instance, degree of risk; access to capital; and ability to control costs, raise quality, or extend functionality all might be critical in some scenarios and not so important in others.

There are three commonly used techniques for building scenarios: case-based models, contextual mapping, and cross-impact analysis.

Case-Based Models

Case-based models are the foundation for a type of analysis called case-based reasoning. This technique might be called reasoning by analogy or reasoning by history.

Case-based reasoning means using old experiences to understand and solve new problems. In this instance, an analyst remembers a previous situation similar to the current one and uses that to solve the new problem. This can mean adapting old solutions to meet new demands, using old cases to explain new situations, using old cases to critique new solutions, or reasoning from precedents to interpret a new situation (much as lawyers do) or create an equitable solution to a new problem (much as labor mediators do).[12] The analyst makes inferences based directly on previous cases rather than by the more traditional approach of using general knowledge. He solves a new problem by remembering a previous similar situation (a similar model) and by reusing information and knowledge of that situation (duplicating the model).

We can illustrate case-based reasoning by looking at some typical situations having intelligence implications:

- In 1984, reports indicated that the Soviets were systematically destroying Afghan irrigation systems to drive resistance supporters out of the countryside. This paralleled a Soviet army practice of destroying the irrigation systems in Central Asia during the Soviet Union's war against the Basmachi rebels in the 1920s.[13]
- An analyst of the defense industry, monitoring the possible merger of two defense companies, might be reminded of a recent merger between two competing companies in the pharmaceutical industry. She recalls that the merged companies had problems because of dramatically different marketing approaches, similar to the situation in the merger she is monitoring. She commissions a case study of the pharmaceutical merger to obtain details on these potential problems and to determine how they might apply in her own situation.
- A financial consultant, hired by the defense industry analyst to examine financial aspects of the same merger, is reminded of a combination of financial indicators in a previous merger that resulted in serious financial difficulties for the merged companies. He uses this past case to identify likely difficulties in the present one.
- An engineer responsible for the health of a reconnaissance satellite has experienced two past losses of satellite control. He is quickly reminded of these situations when the combination of critical measurements matches those of the past system breakdowns. He also remembers a mistake he made during both previous failures and thereby avoids repeating the error.

Contextual Mapping

The technique of *contextual mapping* is used to identify plausible sequences of development in a given field and to relate these sequences to potential developments in a different field. The method is at least as useful for forcing a fresh perspective as it is for predicting actual developments. Its use requires experienced experts familiar both with the method and with the topic of inquiry.

Contextual mapping has been used largely in technological forecasting applications. As an example, one might specify expected future developments in miniaturized chips, combined with a projection of future sensor and wide radio frequency bandwidth transmitter technologies, to define a unique small, cheap, video surveillance device of the future. Such future developments are then treated as external forces that alter the likely future state of a system—for example, a crime deterrence system. The output is usually a graphical display, often with timelines, showing the interconnecting paths that lead to the projected development.

Cross-Impact Analysis

Cross-impact analysis supports system-change scenarios. It usually shows interactions among events or developments, specifying how one event will influence the likelihood, timing, and mode of impact of another event in a different but associated field. As a simple example, the development of the Global Positioning System (GPS) enabled the development of relatively cheap and highly precise munitions (bombs and missiles). These developments in turn required increased emphasis on providing the military with very precise real-time geospatial intelligence, driving a demand for continuous battlefield reconnaissance from, for example, UAVs. And the combination of all these developments forced opposing military organizations to create highly mobile force units that move constantly during combat to avoid being hit. It also increased the value of denial and deception.

The essential idea behind a cross-impact analysis is to examine all of the pairwise connections within a set of forecast developments. Specifically, the analyst might ask how the prior occurrence of one event would affect other events or trends in the set. When these relationships have been specified, the analyst creates a scenario by letting events "happen"—either randomly, in accordance with their estimated probability, or in some prearranged way—and assessing how each development affects others in the sequence. Repeating the process with different event sequences creates contrasting scenarios.

Cross-impact analysis has been used extensively to model the interaction of future events and trends. In the 1970s the Futures Group developed a version of it called *trend impact analysis* that became well established and is still in use.[14] Network analysis methodologies, described in chapter 10, naturally support cross-impact analysis.

4. Find the Best (Most Likely) Solution(s)

Having built a set of potential future scenarios, the analyst must examine them in light of the original question. Does the idea of paying farmers not to grow coca crops have favorable outcomes in all of the counternarcotics scenarios? Perhaps a common outcome in the scenarios is that new groups of farmers start growing coca crops in order to qualify for the payments, or a bidding war starts between the drug cartels and the government. (Both of these outcomes, of course, are unintended consequences, as discussed in chapter 13.) The customer of intelligence, the operations people who are informed by the scenarios, need to understand these possible outcomes and to prepare their options accordingly.

The final scenarios need to describe relationships among objects or entities (tanks, missiles, airplanes, and units in a military scenario; companies, governments, technologies, and weapons systems in a nonproliferation scenario; governments, farmers, drug cartels, banks, and drug users in a counternarcotics scenario). In a dynamic scenario, the objects must then change in space and time according to known rules (patterns of business competition;

military doctrine in military scenarios; past patterns of clandestine trade and of systems development in a nonproliferation scenario). A military scenario, which can be well defined by existing scenario definition tools, is quite different from a nonproliferation or counternarcotics scenario. It is not the same in format, content, event descriptions, or types of objects being manipulated. However, the basics remain the same; relationship analysis, for example, is pretty much the same in all scenarios.

Indicators and the Role of Intelligence

The final step in Peter Schwartz's process comes after the scenarios are completed. The job of the intelligence officer becomes one of monitoring. The analyst has to look for the leading indicators that would tell which of the scenarios—or which combination of scenarios—is actually taking place. As Babson College professor Liam Fahey pointed out, indicators will also give important insights into what scenarios are *not* taking place.[15]

The monitoring job may involve watching trends. An intelligence analyst might monitor demographic and economic trends, spread of infectious diseases, changes in pollution levels, or proliferation of terrorist cells. A political or economic analyst might look at the questions that opponents ask and the positions they take in trade negotiations. A military intelligence analyst might monitor troop movements and radio traffic for signals as to which scenario is developing.

These indicators suggest movement toward a particular scenario.[16] They provide a means to decide which options should be the focus of a customer's decisions. Specifically, they help identify which outcomes should be prepared for, possibly by use of some of the instruments of national power, and which potential outcomes can be disregarded.

Scenarios, like target models, serve different purposes for different participants. The purpose of scenarios for executives and intelligence customers is to inform decision making. For intelligence analysts, scenarios also help to identify needs, that is, to support intelligence collection.

Intelligence can have one of two roles in scenarios. If an organization has a planning group that develops scenarios, the intelligence officer should participate in the scenario development. Then the role of intelligence is to draw the indicators from the forces and to tell the planner or decision maker how the scenarios are playing out. We want to know which forces and indicators need to be monitored to give an early signal of approaching change and point to more likely outcomes. The planning culture in many organizations is still heavily biased toward single-point forecasting. In such cases, the intelligence customer is likely to say, "Tell me what the future will be; then I can make my decision." The customer is likely to complain that several "forecasts" are more confusing, and less helpful, than a single one. If no scenario planning group exists, the intelligence officer alone must develop the scenarios to address the questions posed by the decision maker. In this case, intelligence synthesis and analysis generally will focus on more narrowly drawn scenarios than planners use, and they are likely to be more tactical than strategic. For example, an intelligence-generated battlefield scenario would probably involve looking only at enemy forces and predicting what their actions will be, while ignoring the actions that friendly forces might be taking.

The U.S. intelligence community has developed a formal methodology for monitoring these indicators, or what it terms "indicators or signposts of change." The methodology is described in the CIA's tradecraft manual as "Periodically review a list of observable events or trends to track events, monitor targets, spot emerging trends, and warn of unanticipated change."[17] It depends on the analyst's identifying and listing the observable events that would indicate that a particular scenario is becoming more or less likely, regularly reviewing all of the lists (one for each scenario) against incoming intelligence, and selecting the scenario that appears most likely to be developing.[18]

A Scenario Exercise:
The Global Information Environment in 2020

In July 2001 the CIA's Global Futures Partnership published *Are You Ready?*—the product of a workshop that developed four possible global scenarios for the global information environment in the year 2010. The scenarios considered broad forces such as globalization, democratization, and emerging transnational threats.[19] The scenarios were drawn based on what the developers considered the two major shaping factors:

- A world that was more open and cooperative, versus one more closed and conflict-ridden
- A world in which technology development slowed and information was mediated or controlled, versus one of innovative technology development and unconstrained flow of information

From these two shaping factors or forces, the developers created the following four scenarios, giving them evocative names:

- *Mister Rogers' Neighborhood*: People rely for information on trusted intermediaries, which flourish in a positive global environment. Information technology development slows, and electronic networks are one form of global communications out of many.
- *Shattered Dreams*. States remain the key players. Established media dominate global communications. Cultural divisions and authoritarian governments impede the flow of information and technology. Conflicts and a worldwide economic downturn result in slowing technology development.

- *Gated Communities of Interest.* A fragmentation of authority occurs worldwide amid national and organizational tensions. Outside these exclusive communities of interest, information is not considered reliable.
- *Hidden Order.* A fragmentation of authority occurs, but government-NGO coalitions flourish. Amid rapid technological innovation, networks and communities of interest self-organize. Power is determined by ability to hold attention and influence events.

All four scenarios missed the mark to some extent, though elements of each scenario were present in the year 2010, and each remains a possible outcome for the year 2020. Because of an accident of timing (the scenarios were published just before 9/11), they missed the decade in which global conflict with terrorism was a predominant driving force. They also underestimated the impact of social networking. Nevertheless, they provide a good example of the value of predictive scenarios that rely on driving force analysis.

Figure 14-1 illustrates one interpretation of how events played out during the past decade, based on the force analysis discussed earlier in this chapter. The forces or factors that were assumed to shape the future are shown as two sets of opposing arrows in the figure. The Global Futures Partnership report suggested that the world of 2000 was in, or close to, the world of Hidden Order. A straight-line extrapolation (unchanged forces) then would have put the world in Hidden Order in the year 2010; the combination of open and cooperative forces, innovative technology development, and unconstrained information flows would continue unchanged.

The actual situation in 2010, of course, was somewhat different than that predicted by a straight-line extrapolation. Conflicts arising in the aftermath of 9/11 arguably moved the "bubble" shown in Figure 14-1 down toward Gated Communities of Interest. And a worldwide economic downturn in the latter half of the decade, while not slowing technology development, arguably moved the "bubble" somewhat closer to Shattered Dreams.

Now it's time to try an exercise. A straight-line extrapolation from 2010 to 2020, assuming that the forces that got us to 2010 remain dominant and unchanged over the next decade, would have the world in much the same place in 2020 as it is now, as Figure 14-2 indicates. But the forces are unlikely to remain the same, and new ones are likely to arise. Since 2010, for example, the economic stresses worldwide appear to have increased. Social networking continues to play an expanding role in the information environment. And during 2011, the Arab Spring (which developed in large part because of social networking) has had an impact that is still being assessed. Global competition for resources appears to be increasing, adding to the potential for conflict. Where would you put the 2020 "bubble," based on the changes? Can you think of any new forces that are likely to become predominant in this decade and shape the result?

Figure 14-1   Predictive Model of the 2010 Global Information Environment

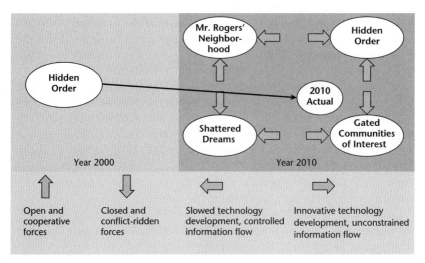

Figure 14-2   Extrapolated Model of the 2020 Global Information Environment

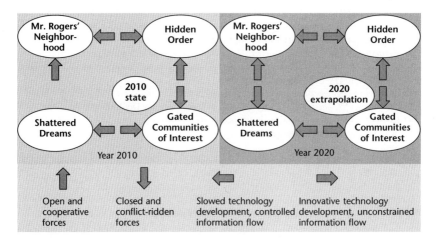

Summary

Most predictive analysis results in some form of scenario—a description of the future state of the target. Typically, the analyst will create several alternative scenarios based on different assumptions about the forces involved. Two scenarios often used in intelligence are the driving-force scenario, a type of projection, and the system-change scenario, a forecast. The demonstration scenario also has application for high-impact/low-probability analysis.

Chapter 13 describes some of the forces to consider in creating a driving-force scenario. System-change scenarios are very demanding to construct; they require cross-impact analysis—that is, looking at how events or developments in one area will affect events or developments in a different area.

Creating a scenario involves four steps that are very similar to the traditional problem-solving process. The first step is problem definition; the focus here is to create a scenario that will be useful to the intelligence customer. The next step is to identify the factors or driving forces that bear on the problem and that will be a part of the scenario. These include all of the PMESII factors. The factors and forces then must be ranked according to their importance in the scenario. The final steps are to identify the possible outcome scenarios and select the most likely ones to present to the customer.

Once scenarios are completed, the analyst's next job is to monitor incoming intelligence. The new intelligence provides indicators that help determine which scenario appears to be developing.

Notes

1. CIA, *A Tradecraft Primer: Structured Analytic Techniques for Improving Intelligence Analysis* (Washington, D.C.: Author, 2009), 34.
2. T. F. Mandel, "Futures Scenarios and Their Use in Corporate Strategy," in *The Strategic Management Handbook*, ed. K. J. Albert (New York: McGraw-Hill, 1983), 10–21.
3. W. I. Boucher, "Scenario and Scenario Writing," in *Nonextrapolative Methods in Business Forecasting*, ed. J. S. Mendell (Westport, Conn.: Quorum Books, 1985), 47–60.
4. Herman Kahn and Anthony Wiener, *The Year 2000* (New York: Macmillan, 1967).
5. M. S. Loescher, C. Schroeder, and C. W. Thomas, *Proteus: Insights from 2020* (Utrecht, Netherlands: The Copernicus Institute Press, 2000).
6. Inertia and countervailing forces are discussed in detail in chapter 13.
7. Peter Schwartz, *The Art of the Long View* (New York: Currency Doubleday, 1996).
8. Lawrence Wilkinson, "How to Build Scenarios," *Wired*, February 12, 2002, http://www.wired.com/wired/scenarios/build.html.
9. Ibid.
10. Liam Fahey, *Competitors* (New York: Wiley, 1999), 452.
11. Ibid., 453.
12. Janet L. Kolodner, "An Introduction to Case-Based Reasoning," *Artificial Intelligence Review*, 6 (1992): 3–34.
13. Angelo Codevilla, *Informing Statecraft* (New York: Free Press, 1992), 217.
14. T. J. Gordon, "The Nature of Unforeseen Developments," in *The Study of the Future*, ed. W. I. Boucher (Washington, D.C.: U.S. Government Printing Office, 1977), 42–43.
15. Fahey, *Competitors*, 415.
16. Andrew Sleigh, ed., *Project Insight* (Farnborough, U.K.: Centre for Defence Analysis, Defence Evaluation and Research Agency, 1996), 13.
17. CIA, *A Tradecraft Primer*, 12.
18. Ibid.
19. CIA, *Are You Ready?* (Washington, D.C.: Global Futures Partnership, July 2001).

15

Simulation Modeling

What is truth?

Pontius Pilate,
the Bible, John 18:38

Simulation models are mathematical descriptions of the interrelationships believed to determine a system's behavior. Simulations differ from other types of models in that the equations that comprise them cannot be solved simultaneously. One usually turns to simulation modeling when it is impossible or impractical to measure all of the variables necessary to solve the set of simultaneous equations that would fully describe a system.

In general, simulation models are most useful in making long-range forecasts where exact numerical estimates are not needed. Simulation models usually are most effective when used to compare the impact of alternative scenarios (resulting from policy decisions or natural phenomena, for example). Following is a discussion of the types of simulations.

But first, some definitions. A *model* is a physical, mathematical, conceptual, or otherwise logical representation of a system, entity, phenomenon, or process. A *simulation*, as used here, is an implementation of the model in a computer program. We'll frequently use the term *simulation model* to refer to a model that is designed to conduct simulations.

Types of Simulations

Simulation may be used in either a deterministic or a stochastic situation. A simple spreadsheet is a deterministic model; the inputs are fixed by the numbers in the spreadsheet cells, only one solution appears, and the input numbers must be changed to get another answer. Where there is uncertainty about the proper input numbers, stochastic simulation is used. The computer "rolls the dice" to assign a value to each uncertain input and obtain an answer; then many repeated "dice rolls" are made to obtain a range of answers. Introduced in chapter 12, the resulting model has been named the *Monte Carlo simulation*, after the gambling capital of Monaco.

The challenge of the Monte Carlo simulation is to select the right type of uncertainty for the input variables. All uncertain variables have a probability distribution. A single six-sided die roll has what is called a uniform distribution: The chance of a 1 coming up is the same as the chance of a 2, or a 3. When two dice are rolled, the distribution is not uniform; 7 is much more likely to occur than 2 or 12. If the wrong probability distribution is chosen for the input, the stochastic simulation will produce the wrong answer.

Simulation models are typically classified as *continuous*, *discrete-event*, or a *hybrid* of the two.

- In *continuous simulations*, the system changes with time. An airplane in flight is an example of a continuous system; changes in the speed, altitude, and direction of the airplane occur continuously with time. This would also be a deterministic simulation, since the airplane speed, altitude, and direction at any time can be predicted by inputs and standard equations.
- In *discrete-event models*, the system changes state as events occur in the simulation. An airplane flight can be modeled as a series of discrete events. One discrete event would be at takeoff, another event occurs when the airplane reaches cruising altitude, and another event occurs when it lands.
- *Hybrid models* are a combination of the two. A simple hybrid model of the airplane flight could have two discrete-event simulations—the beginning and end of the flight—with a continuous simulation of the travel in between.

Creating and Running a Simulation

The process of developing and running a simulation is similar to the analysis process covered in chapters 3 and 4.

Formulate the Issue

Start with intelligence issue definition, discussed in chapter 4. Then identify the parts of the overall issue that can be answered by simulation. As part of this effort, it is almost always necessary to define the desired outputs of the simulation. The outputs measure such things as benefit, impact, effectiveness, or affordability of the system. These analytic measures are often called *measures of effectiveness*, also known as *figures of merit*, and they are used to quantify how well a system meets its objectives. In commercial ventures, return on investment is such a measure. In aircraft performance, top speed is a measure of effectiveness. In an air defense system, probability of kill (P_k) is a measure. Measures of effectiveness are used extensively in systems performance analysis.

Identify the Needed Input Information

Simulation models usually don't work if essential input data are missing. You have to begin by identifying information that is already available; then identify information that it may be possible to collect; and finally identify information that probably will not be available under any circumstances. The answers will help define the model used for the simulation.

Select the Simulation Software

Depending on the topic, the simulation model may already be available commercially, in academia, or within the government. It usually will require some modification to simulate the target system adequately. If no usable model exists, one has to be built. Fortunately, a number of commercial modeling packages can be used to build even very sophisticated models. Many of these require an experienced modeler, but increasingly analysts find packages that they can use without extensive simulation training.

Develop a Valid Model

Once developed, a simulation model has to be validated. That is, you must confirm that the model accurately simulates what it is supposed to simulate. Or, as the quote that begins this chapter illustrates, you must ask, "What is truth?" It is far preferable to use a proven, validated model, that is, one that has had its simulations checked repeatedly against real-world results. If this is not possible, a number of standard methods exist for validating a model. But sophisticated models can be very complex, and independent checks are difficult to run on them. Examining the results to see if they "feel" right may be the best possible check that you have available.

As an example of the validation challenge, it is well known that combat models tend to overrate an opponent's defense. One of the better known examples of this problem is modeling that was done of the offense and defense prior to the B-52 strikes on Hanoi during the Vietnam War. The prestrike model predictions were that enemy fire would inflict significant losses on U.S. forces. In the initial raids, no losses were suffered. A similar disparity existed in models of allied force losses in the Desert Storm operation in Iraq.

These are examples of the observation that models tend to be overbalanced in favor of the defense in the initial stage of any conflict. The reason is that most such models assume a steady state; that is, they assume that both offense and defense have some awareness of what is going to happen. But in the initial stages of an engagement, the offense has a big advantage: It can dictate the rules of engagement, knows what it has to do, and has the advantage of surprise. The defense must prepare for the estimated threat and react. Furthermore, the defense must make every link in the chain strong; the offense needs only to find one weak link in a system and then attack it. Al Qaeda operatives demonstrated the very large advantage of a determined offense in their September 11, 2001, attacks on the World Trade Center and the Pentagon. Islamic militants again demonstrated the attacker's advantage in Great Britain on July 7, 2005, when they killed with no warning 52 London Underground and bus passengers in coordinated suicide bombing attacks. It is difficult for a model to take into account this initial offensive advantage—and the associated defensive disadvantage.

Run the Simulation and Interpret the Results

Once a model has been developed and validated, the analyst runs the simulation and examines the results. Analyzing the results of any modeling effort requires a "sanity check" on the model results. In intelligence simulations, where considerable uncertainty often exists about the input data, it usually will be necessary to make many runs with different possible inputs to do sensitivity analysis and to compare alternative conclusions. Another type of validation becomes important here. A valid model can give invalid results if the inputs are improper. Econometric models, for example, can give almost any desired simulation result simply by choosing different inputs. A smart customer of intelligence knows this and will want to know, not only what model was used, but also what the inputs were.

Simulations Used in Intelligence Analysis

Intelligence analysts use simulation models extensively to assess the performance of foreign economies, weapons systems, military forces, and threat networks, among others. These simulations involve computer programs that solve individual equations or systems of equations and graphically portray the results. They should be interactive. The analyst has to see what the results look like and change the model as new intelligence information is received. Following are some of the most common examples.

Economic Simulations

Economic, or more properly econometric, models can be used to simulate the performance of an entire economy or any segment, for example, of any industry. An econometric model is a quantitative description of an economic system. It incorporates a number of hypotheses on how economic systems function. Econometric models are sets of simultaneous linear equations used for macroeconomic analysis, and the number of equations can be very large. The models are used widely in both the financial and the intelligence communities. Intelligence applications include trade, balance of payments, and worldwide energy analysis models.

Economic simulations also make use of input-output modeling, a procedure in which the output product of an industrial sector is set equal to the input consumption of that product by other industries and consumers. Input-output models are often disaggregated and can, therefore, show more cause-effect relationships than many other models. Input-output models can be interpreted in terms of block diagrams and matrix algebra techniques. Input-output modeling is applied to a variety of economic policy analysis and forecasting problems.

The product of econometric simulation often is displayed as a *linear correlation* or *linear regression* of the sort described in chapter 12. Econometric simulations can produce much more complex displays, but linear regression is still the most frequently used analytic product. Estimating a linear regression on two variables can be visualized as fitting a line through data points representing paired values of the independent and dependent variables. An example is shown in Figure 15-1, which illustrates Okun's law (describing the relationship between GDP growth and unemployment rate). The fitted line is found using regression analysis. It illustrates a rather obvious point—that unemployment increases as GDP declines—but the rate of change is the important item to extract.

Intelligence analysts often run econometric models to support trade negotiations. For example, an analyst can create a simulation of another country's

Figure 15-1   **Linear Regression Model—Unemployment Rate versus GDP Growth**

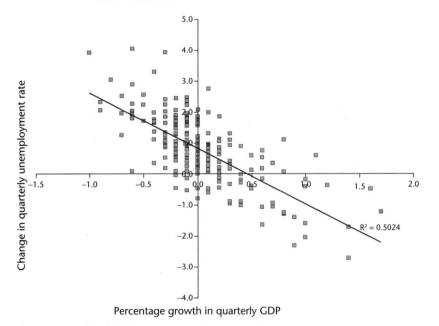

economy to show that his own government's trade proposals will benefit the other country's economy. A particularly effective technique is to obtain and run the other country's econometric model, since it should be more credible with the opposing negotiation team.

Weapons Systems Simulations

Weapons systems simulations range in complexity from simulating the performance of a single entity such as an aircraft to simulating that of an elaborate interconnected system such as an air defense system. Even simulating the performance of a single weapon, though, can be a complicated undertaking. For example, the design of a nuclear weapon requires complex modeling and simulation of the weapon detonation process. High-speed computers and sophisticated simulation codes are necessary. The models used to support one's own nuclear weapons development can be used to assess the performance of another country's nuclear weaponry.

Many simulation models of weapons systems already exist. The U.S. Department of Defense and its contractors possess a large suite of performance models of missiles, ships, submarines, and air and missile defense systems, all used to evaluate their own systems. These models can be modified to simulate the performance of foreign systems, too; the Backfire bomber case described in chapter 9 involved two competing simulation models, both derived from existing models of U.S. aircraft. Commercial simulation models also are available to simulate the performance of radars and communications systems and the orbits of satellites. Both the U.S. and foreign intelligence services, for example, use commercial software to create satellite orbit simulations to identify the occurrences of hostile satellite surveillance in order to conduct denial and deception.

Military Simulations

Also referred to as war gaming, military simulations are closely related to weapons systems simulations and often incorporate them. They are used by defense organizations in planning systems acquisition, for determining force mixes, and for training. Some examples are logistics models, vulnerability and weapons effects models, system reliability models, and force-on-force and campaign models that simulate combat between opposing forces. As with weapons systems simulations, the Defense Department and its contractors possess and regularly use military simulations, and they can be adapted to assessing foreign military systems as well. When models are set up to simulate combat, the intelligence and military operations communities have to work together, applying the target-centric approach: The military operations analysts understand your side, the intelligence analysts understand your opponent, and inputs from both are necessary to make the simulation run effectively.

Military simulations have become familiar parts of the online experience, thanks to the proliferation of online multiplayer war games that are set in past conflicts such as Napoleon's battles, the American Revolution, the Spanish Civil War, and numerous World War II battles.

Network Simulations

Simulations are a powerful tool in modeling and analyzing networks. Carnegie Mellon's *ORA, described in chapter 10, has been used to demonstrate how money, information, disease, or technology can flow through a network.[1] Simulations can be used to assess the impact on the network of removing one or more nodes, which nodes or links are most important to an insurgent or terrorist network's functioning, and the estimated recovery time of the network after removal of a link or node.

Geospatial Simulations

Geospatial simulations take a number of forms. They are used to produce flood models, using high-resolution terrain mapping from laser radar (LIDAR) or synthetic aperture radar (SAR) imagery. They produce trafficability models under different weather conditions. One such model was used to identify optimum locations to build Ebola treatment centers in Liberia during the 2014 outbreak.[2]

One of the most powerful applications of geospatial simulations comes from combining them with network models such as *ORA. The key is to have geographic coordinates associated with each node in the network model. Then

Figure 15-2   Geospatial Network Simulation of Syrian Refugee Movement within Turkey

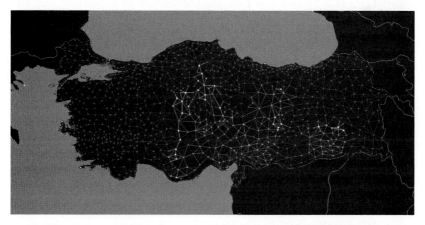

Source: Kristan J. Wheaton and Melonie K. Richey, "The Potential of Social Network Analysis in Intelligence," January 9, 2014, http://www.e-ir.info/2014/01/09/the-potential-of-social-network-analysis-in-intelligence/.

Figure 15-3   Estimate of Syrian Refugee Movement over a 12- to 24-Month Period

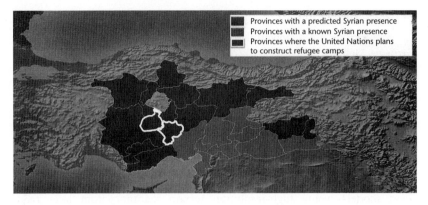

Source: Kristan J. Wheaton and Melonie K. Richey, "The Potential of Social Network Analysis in Intelligence," January 9, 2014, http://www.e-ir.info/2014/01/09/the-potential-of-social-network-analysis-in-intelligence/.

simulations can produce models such as the model of Syrian refugee population movement throughout Turkey that is shown in Figure 15-2.

The combination of network and geospatial simulation can provide valuable analytic insights. Figure 15-3 illustrates one such insight. Based on the results of the simulation, one can predict the areas that Syrian refugees are likely to move into during the next one to two years. That prediction is shown in Figure 15-3. Compare this to the Ramadi social media footprints shown in Figure 11-7. That figure showed the flight of the Ramadi population, but with no indication of where the population went. This model takes a step forward, analytically, in predicting population movement.

Political and Social Simulations

Simulations of political and social systems have been developed to analyze such diverse topics as the interactions of political parties, clashes of cultures, and population migration patterns. The CIA has used a simulation model of political processes, "Policon," to assess topics such as these:

- What policy is Egypt likely to adopt toward Israel?
- What will the Philippines likely do about U.S. bases?
- What stand will Pakistan take on the Soviet occupation of Afghanistan?
- To what extent is Mozambique likely to accommodate with the West?
- What policy will Beijing adopt toward Taiwan's role in the Asian Development Bank?
- How much support is South Yemen likely to give to the insurgency in North Yemen?

- What is the South Korean government likely to do about large-scale demonstrations?
- What will Japan's foreign trade policy look like?
- What stand will the Mexican government take on official corruption?[3]

Simulations have been developed that will search web activity, historical patterns, and social media to warn of possible disasters, disease activity, crimes, and geopolitical events. One such simulation predicted a 2012 cholera outbreak in Cuba a few weeks before the outbreak occurred, based on analyzing past weather and other factors that preceded earlier cholera outbreaks in Africa.[4] Many law enforcement organizations in the United States and Canada use simulations to identify areas in their cities where crimes are likely to be committed each day.[5] Simulations have even found their way into popular use: One interactive simulation, SimCity, has evolved into an educational computer game.

Political and social simulations have not gained the same wide acceptance within the U.S. intelligence community that weapons systems and military simulations enjoy. This is partly a result of the attitudes that the customers of political analysis have, which we will take up in chapter 19.

Political and social simulations are closely related to the topic of decision modeling, as the Policon topics suggest. But decision modeling depends on the inclusion of a number of factors that are difficult to assess, as the next section explains.

Decision Modeling and Simulation

It is frequently important to assess the likely behavior of political and military leaders, specifically to determine what decisions they will make under given conditions. The purpose of behavioral analysis is always predictive: How will the target react to a given situation?

To do this sort of predictive analysis, simulation models of leadership decision-making have been developed and tested. Typically, they simulate the personality, problem-solving styles, values, goals, and environments of individual leaders. One example is Athena's Prism, developed by the University of Pennsylvania. Athena's Prism can be configured to identify likely decisions by real world leaders in different conflict situations, relying on human behavior models from the social sciences.[6]

In all behavioral analysis, but especially in decision prediction, four perspectives of the decision process have to be considered: rational, administrative, cultural, and emotional.[7] We discuss each of these in this section as well as how the decision-making process is played out in groups.

Rational Models

Wharton business school professor Russell Ackoff, in his entertaining book *The Art of Problem Solving: Ackoff's Fables*, tells the story of a household appliance manager who claimed that consumers are often irrational. The manager cited examples of new appliances, such as the dishwasher (manufactured based on research showing that washing dishes was the most hated kitchen task), were not selling. Yet, recently introduced cooktops and ovens had been very successful even though they offered no new features and were more expensive than the traditional all-in-one design. Ackoff and the manager agreed to an experiment—they would put the failed products on one side of the room, the successes on the other, and the two would tour the room together with a fresh eye. Almost immediately after entering the room, the manager retracted his assertion about consumer irrationality. He suddenly saw that consumers could use all of the successful appliances without bending or climbing; conversely, the dishwashers required squatting to load.[8]

Though opponents and consumers may sometimes be irrational, Ackoff rightly pointed out that you are better served by assuming that they are more often simply misunderstood. Rational decision-making is broadly defined as a logical and normally quantitative procedure for thinking about difficult problems. Stated formally, rational decision-making requires the systematic evaluation of costs or benefits accruing to courses of action that might be taken. It entails identifying the choices involved, assigning values (costs and benefits) for possible outcomes, and expressing the probability of those outcomes being realized.

A rational model of decision making is based on the idea of optimal choice: The decision maker will make the choice that will have the best outcome for himself or his organization. It assumes that the decision maker is objective and well informed, and will therefore select the most effective alternative. This approach is based on the assumption that decisions are made on an explicit or implicit cost-benefit analysis, also known as expected utility theory. The theory's origins are in the study of economic decision-making and behavior, notably in the work of John von Neumann and Oskar Morgenstern.[9] The theory views decision making as behavior that maximizes utility. An individual faced with a decision will, consciously or subconsciously, identify the available options, the possible outcomes associated with each option, the utility of each option-outcome combination, and the probability that each option-outcome combination will occur. The decision maker will then choose an option that is likely to yield, in his or her own terms, the highest overall utility. The following assumptions are embedded in this model:

- The decision maker has a number of known alternative courses of action
- Each alternative has consequences that are known and are quantified
- The decision maker has a set of preferences that allows assessing the consequences and selecting an alternative[10]

Using these assumptions, rational decision simulations attempt to identify the most likely option that a decision maker will select in a given situation. A rational decision estimate, based on expected utility theory, is the place to start any decision simulation, but it is not the end point. Some other models should be considered, and they may be more accurate individually or in combination in decision estimation.

Administrative Models

The utility theory (rational) approach is useful in decision estimates, but it must be used with caution. People won't always make the effort to find the optimum action in a decision problem. The complexity of any realistic decision problem dissuades them. Instead, people tend to select a number of possible outcomes that would be "good enough." They then choose a strategy or an action that is likely to achieve one of the good-enough outcomes.[11]

This tendency of leaders to pick suboptimal choices leads to a variant of the rational decision-making model called the *administrative model*. It discards the three assumptions in the rational model and treats decision makers as people having incomplete information, under time pressures, and perhaps beset with conflicting preferences. They consequently look for shortcuts to find acceptable solutions. The decision maker does not try to optimize; he instead identifies and accepts a good-enough alternative. The optimal solution is the alternative with the highest value; but what is called "satisficing" requires no more than finding the first alternative with an acceptable value.[12]

There are limits, though, on how well we can simulate (and therefore predict) decisions based on either the rational or the administrative model. To improve decision estimates, we have to include cultural and emotional factors, discussed in the following sections. They are the factors that often cause an opponent's decision to be labeled "irrational."

Cultural Models

A critical component of decision modeling is the prediction of a single human's behavior, within some bounds of uncertainty. Behavior cannot be predicted with any confidence without putting it in the target's social and cultural context. An analyst needs to understand elements of a culture such as how it trains its youth for adult roles and how it defines what is important in life. In behavioral analysis, culture defines the ethical norms of the collective to which a decision maker belongs. It dictates values and constrains decisions.[13] In general, culture is a constraining social or environmental force. Different cultures have different habits of thought, different values, and different motivations. Straight modeling of a decision-making process without understanding these differences can lead the analyst into the "irrational behavior" trap, which is what happened to U.S. and Japanese planners in 1941.

Before Japan attacked Pearl Harbor, both the United States and Japan made exceptionally poor predictions about the other's decisions. Both sides indulged in mirror imaging—that is, they acted as though the opponent would use a rational decision-making process as *they* defined *rational*.

U.S. planners reasoned that the superior military, economic, and industrial strength of the United States would deter attack. Japan could not win a war against the United States, so a Japanese decision to attack would be irrational.[14]

The Japanese also knew that a long-term war with the United States was not winnable because of the countries' disparities in industrial capacity. But Japan predicted that a knockout blow at Pearl Harbor would encourage the United States to seek a negotiated settlement in the Pacific and East Asia.[15] To validate this assumption, the Japanese drew on their past experience—a similar surprise attack on the Russian fleet at Port Arthur in 1904 had eventually resulted in the Japanese obtaining a favorable negotiated settlement. The Japanese did not mirror image the United States with themselves, but with the Russians of 1904 and 1905. Japan believed that the U.S. government would behave much as the tsarist government had.

Such errors in predicting an opponent's decision-making process are common when the analyst does not take into account cultural factors. Cultural differences cause competitors not to make the "obvious" decision. During the Cold War, U.S. analysts of the Soviet leadership within and without the intelligence community—known as "Kremlinologists"—often encountered a cultural divide in assessing likely Soviet moves. Soviet leader Nikita Khrushchev reportedly disparaged U.S. Kremlinologists, remarking, "They are from a highly educated nation and they look upon us as being highly educated. They don't know that we are dominated by an unimaginative and unattractive bunch of scoundrels."[16]

Practitioners in the field of competitive intelligence encounter the same cultural divide when making estimates. U.S. television manufacturers experienced such a cultural surprise during the 1960s. At that time, all TV manufacturers could foresee a glut of TV sets on the market. U.S. manufacturers responded by cutting back production, assuming that other manufacturers would follow suit. Japanese manufacturers, using different assumptions (giving priority to capturing market share instead of maintaining short-term profit), kept up production. As U.S. manufacturers' market share dropped, they found that their per-unit costs were rising, while the Japanese per-unit costs were dropping due to economies of scale. The U.S. television industry has never recovered.

Emotional Models

The final aspect of the decision process to consider when analyzing behavior is the emotional. We do many things because they are exciting or challenging. Russell Ackoff told the story of a hand-tool manufacturer whose executive team was eager to get into the business of manufacturing the (then) newly discovered transistor—not because they knew what a transistor was, but because they were bored with their existing business and wanted a new challenge.[17] Pride and revenge are also emotional motivators. Business leaders, generals, and even presidents of the United States make some decisions simply because they want to pay back an opponent for past wrongs. The emotional aspect of behavioral prediction cannot be ignored, and personality profiling is one way to grasp it.

Business intelligence analysts have developed a methodology for personality profiling of competitors based on the lesson that personal idiosyncrasies and predisposition will have a greater bearing on an executive's decisions than will a calculated assessment of resources and capabilities.[18] The resulting profile is a model that can be used to assess likely decisions.[19]

In evaluating the likely decision of an executive, it may help to apply the Myers-Briggs model discussed in chapter 6. A decision by one Myers-Briggs type will be predictably different from a decision made by another Myers-Briggs type. An executive who was a linebacker on a college football team will likely have a completely different decision-making style than an executive who was president of the chess club.[20] Former national leaders such as Saddam Hussein and Chile's dictator Augusto Pinochet have been assessed as ESTJ on the Meyers-Briggs scale—a type defined as "The Executive," possessed with confidence about their superior decision-making ability, relative lack of empathy for others, and reluctance to admit mistakes.

Collective Decision-Making Models

The preceding sections assume that a decision of intelligence interest will be made by one person. But decisions are often made by a group. Such cases require a collective decision-prediction approach. It is somewhat easier to estimate what a group will decide than to estimate what an individual will decide—which is not to say that it is easy. In such decision modeling, one must identify the decision makers—often the most difficult step of the process—and then determine the likely decisions.

The collective decision-making model has been referred to as a *political model*. Its dominant features are that

- Power is decentralized; therefore,
- In place of a single goal, value set, or set of interests of a single decision maker, there exist multiple and often competing goals, values, and interests among the decision makers; therefore,
- Decisions result from a bargaining among individuals and coalitions.

So the collective decision-making model is a complex process of conflict resolution and consensus building; decisions are the products of compromises.[21]

In spite of this complexity, some analytic tools and techniques are available to estimate the likely outcome of group decision-making. These tools and techniques are based on the theories of social choice expounded by the Marquis de Condorcet, an eighteenth-century mathematician. He suggested that the prevailing alternative should be the one that is preferred by a majority over each of the other choices in an exhaustive series of pairwise comparisons. Another technique is to start by drawing an influence diagram that shows the persons involved in the collective decision. Collective decisions tend to have more of the rational elements and less of the emotional. But unless the decision participants come from different cultures, the end decision will be no less cultural in nature.

The collective decisions of an organization are usually formalized in its plans, especially its strategic plans. Unless you can acquire the plan itself, the best way to assess a strategic plan is to identify and then attempt to duplicate the target organization's strategic planning process. If the analyst comes from the same culture as the target, a duplication may be relatively easy to do. If that is not the case, it may be necessary to bring in experts from the target culture and have them attempt the duplication. The analyst also can order a collection operation to determine which strategic planning texts the target's planners have read or which approaches they have favored in the past.

Game Theory

In chapter 9, we introduced the discipline of operations research. One branch of that discipline, known as *game theory*, is a powerful tool for decision modeling. Game theory, in brief, is about analyzing the decision processes of two or more parties (referred to as the "players") in conflict or cooperation. It can be applied as a thought exercise or, because it makes use of mathematical models, by using simulations.

The game assumes the existence of two or more interdependent player strategies. Each player must determine how the other players will respond to his current or previous move. Each player next determines how he will respond to the estimated move of the other players, and the game cycle of action and response continues. The idea is for a player to anticipate how his initial decisions will determine the end result of the game. Using this information, a player identifies an initial preferred decision.

The success of game theory depends on understanding the decision processes of the other players. So solid cultural models, as discussed in this chapter, are essential. Game theory usually assumes that the other players will follow a rational decision process. When that is not the case, it becomes even more important to place oneself in the shoes of the other player(s).

The most prominent figure in applying game theory to intelligence issues may be Bruce Bueno de Mesquita, whose model was introduced in chapter 12. Over a thirty-year period, he has developed and refined a simulation model that applies game theory to produce political estimates. The estimates have an impressive success record:

- Five years before the death of Iran's Ayatollah Khomeini in 1989, Bueno de Mesquita identified Khomeini's successor, Ali Khamenei.
- In February 2008 he predicted correctly that Pakistan's president, Pervez Musharraf, would be forced out of office by the end of summer.
- In May 2010 he predicted that Egypt's president, Hosni Mubarak, would be forced from power within a year. Mubarak left the country nine months later, amid massive street protests.[22]

Bueno de Mesquita's estimates are not always on target—no predictive simulations are. But he reportedly has produced a large number of accurate political estimates as a consultant for the U.S. Department of State, the Pentagon, the U.S. intelligence community, and several foreign governments.[23]

As the above examples illustrate, game theory can be used to predict political outcomes. But an opponent can apply game theory as well, and intelligence has a role in identifying the opponent's game moves. Edieal J. Pinker, a Yale University professor of operations research, has applied game theory to the P5+1-Iranian negotiations and developed a hypothesis about the Iranian strategy. According to Pinker,

> Using game theory, we treat the situation as a leader/follower game, like chess, where opponents take turns moving. The first move goes to the West: to choose a threshold for action. The second move goes to Iran: to choose how to manage its weapons development program, taking into account the West's threshold for action.
>
> What is Iran's best strategy, assuming that it wants to develop nuclear weapons? If you're Ayatollah Khamenei and you want to obtain a destructive nuclear military capability, the fastest way to achieve that goal is to do two things in parallel: enrich uranium and develop military delivery systems. But knowing your opponents, the U.S. and Israel, you know that the fastest way is not the best way. You're aware that if you clearly demonstrate your military intentions, they will be forced to attack you. Another piece of intelligence: you know that there isn't very much political support for war in the U.S., especially in the wake of the recent conflicts in Afghanistan and Iraq. Your strategy, therefore, is to not cross the threshold that will compel the United States to act forcefully until the last moment possible.
>
> Therefore your best choice is the slower choice: First, you declare that you are enriching uranium solely for peaceful purposes, like generating energy and providing nuclear materials for treating cancer patients. Second, you refrain from weaponizing the uranium until the very last moment possible. Since your enemies have already shown that they are reluctant to attack, if you don't step across their threshold, you can continue your nuclear program. Once you are ready, you will need to make a mad rush to complete the final steps toward a weapon before the U.S. and Israel react.[24]

The Pinker hypothesis illustrates the value of game theory in assessing the motivation behind an opponent's actions. Interestingly, Bueno de Mesquita in 2008 ran a game theory simulation that came to a different conclusion; it predicted Iran would reach the brink of developing a nuclear weapon and then stop as moderate elements came to power.[25] The part about moderates coming to power did occur when Hassan Rouhani assumed the presidency in 2013. But whether Pinker's hypothesis or Bueno de Mesquita's simulation more accurately describes the Iranian situation remained an open question in 2015.

Checking the Decision Model: Red Team Analysis

The idea of Red Team analysis is to put the analyst in the role of the decision-making individual or group (the target). The methodology can be used to guide simulation, to check the results, or as a stand-alone process (that is, without using a simulation at all). It is intended to avoid the ethnocentric bias (mirror-imaging) problem described in chapter 6.

The methodology requires that a person or team with detailed knowledge of the situation and understanding of the target's decision-making style put themselves in the target's circumstances and react to foreign stimuli as the target would. For that reason, it is especially useful for checking the results of a game theory decision model. The CIA's tradecraft manual recommends these steps for performing Red Team analysis:

- Develop a set of "first-person" questions that the adversary would ask, such as: "How would I perceive incoming information; what would be my personal concerns; or to whom would I look for an opinion?"
- Draft a set of policy papers in which the leader or group makes specific decisions, proposes recommendations, or lays out courses of actions. The more these papers reflect the cultural and personal norms of the target, the more they can offer a different perspective on the analytic problem.[26]

Summary

Simulations have long been a tool to assess the capabilities of an opponent's military hardware such as aircraft, tanks, and naval vessels. Today they are used to assess the performance of larger systems—air defense systems or entire economies, for example. Such complex targets are best analyzed by using simulation models.

Most simulation models are systems of equations that must be solved for different input assumptions. The critical issues in dealing with simulation models are to define the issue, validate the model (ensure that it approximates reality), and select appropriate measures of effectiveness for the output.

Simulation models are also used extensively to describe complex targets. Simulation modeling can range in complexity from the simple equation to a sophisticated econometric model.

Many types of simulation models are used in intelligence; but the major ones are as follows:

- Econometric models, used to assess international economic activity, or the performance of a national economy or some sector of the economy
- Weapons systems models, used to assess the performance of major foreign weapons systems or specific subsystems
- War gaming models, used to simulate military operations
- Network models, used to identify the results of likely actions against the network
- Geospatial models, used in a wide range of military, civil government, and commercial applications
- Political and social simulation models

Simulation modeling is used to predict the decisions of government leaders and leadership groups. Such models must accurately capture the personality, problem-solving styles, values, goals, and environments of individual leaders or of collective leadership. To do that, they typically consider four aspects of the decision process: rational, administrative, cultural, and emotional factors. The cultural and emotional factors are difficult to take into account, yet they can dominate in the decision-making process.

Game theory is a powerful tool for decision modeling. It is used to analyze the decision processes of players in either conflict or cooperative efforts. It can be applied as a thought exercise. Because it makes use of mathematical models, it is frequently used in simulations.

Red Team analysis is a technique for identifying likely decisions by a decision maker. It can be used to guide a decision-modeling process, to check simulation results, or as an independent technique for assessing an opponent's likely actions. It relies on having a person or team with detailed knowledge of the opponent's decision-making style act as a virtual surrogate in reacting to potential events or circumstances.

Notes

1. Kristan J. Wheaton and Melonie K. Richey, "The Potential of Social Network Analysis in Intelligence," January 9, 2014, http://www.e-ir.info/2014/01/09/the-potential-of-social-network-analysis-in-intelligence/.
2. David Brown, "Computer Modelers vs. Ebola," IEEE Spectrum (June 2015): 62.
3. Bruce Bueno de Mesquita, "The Methodical Study of Politics," New York University and Hoover Institution, October 30, 2002, http://www.yale.edu/probmeth/Bueno_De_Mesquita.doc.
4. Susan Karlin, "Kira Radinsky: Using Machine Intelligence and Data Mining, This Entrepreneur Predicts the Future," IEEE Spectrum (June 2015): 25.
5. Tim Mullaney, "Data-Toting Cops," MIT Technology Review, 118, no. 1 (2015): 61.
6. Barry G. Silverman, Richard L. Rees, Jozsef A. Toth, Jason Cornwell, Kevin O'Brien, Michael Johns, and Marty Caplan, "Athena's Prism—A Diplomatic Strategy Role Playing Simulation for Generating Ideas and Exploring Alternatives," University of Pennsylvania, 2005, http://repository.upenn.edu/cgi/viewcontent.cgi?article=1321&context=ese_papers.

7. Jamshid Gharajedaghi, *Systems Thinking: Managing Chaos and Complexity* (Boston, Mass.: Butterworth-Heinemann, 1999), 34.
8. Russell Ackoff, *The Art of Problem Solving* (New York: Wiley, 1978), 62.
9. Oskar Morgenstern and John von Neumann, *Theory of Games and Economic Behavior* (Princeton, N.J.: Princeton University Press, 1980).
10. "Models of Organizational Decision-Making," http://tx.liberal.ntu.edu.tw/~purplewoo/Litera ture/!Theory/MODELS%20OF%20ORGANIZATIONAL%20DECISION%20MAKING.htm.
11. David W. Miller and Marin K. Starr, *Executive Decisions and Operations Research* (Englewood Cliffs, N.J.: Prentice Hall, 1961), 45–47.
12. "Models of Organizational Decision-Making."
13. Gharajedaghi, *Systems Thinking*, 35.
14. Harold P. Ford, *Estimative Intelligence* (Lanham, Md.: University Press of America, 1993), 17.
15. Ibid., 29.
16. Dino Brugioni, *Eyeball to Eyeball: The Inside Story of the Cuban Missile Crisis* (New York: Random House, 1990), 250.
17. Ackoff, *The Art of Problem Solving*, 22.
18. Walter D. Barndt Jr., *User-Directed Competitive Intelligence* (Westport, Conn.: Quorum Books, 1984), 78.
19. Ibid., 93.
20. Comment by Michael Pitcher, vice president of i2Go.com, in *Competitive Intelligence Magazine*, 3 (July–September 2000): 9.
21. "Models of Organizational Decision-Making."
22. Clive Thompson, "Can Game Theory Predict When Iran Will Get the Bomb?" *New York Times*, August 12, 2009, http://www.nytimes.com/2009/08/16/magazine/16Bruce-t.html?_r=0.
23. "Game Theory in Practice," *Economist*, Technology Quarterly, September 3, 2011, http://www.economist.com/node/21527025.
24. Edieal J. Pinker, "What Can Game Theory Tell Us about Iran's Nuclear Intentions," in *Yale Insight* (Yale School of Management), March 2015, http://insights.som.yale.edu/insights/what-can-game-theory-tell-us-about-irans-nuclear-intentions.
25. Thompson, "Can Game Theory Predict When Iran Will Get the Bomb?"
26. CIA Directorate of Intelligence, *A Compendium of Analytic Tradecraft Notes* (Washington, D.C.: Author, February 1997), http://www.oss.net/dynamaster/file_archive/040319/cb27cc09c84d 056b66616b4da5c02a4d/OSS2000-01-23.pdf.

Part III

Systems and Network Views of Analysis

Part I of this book concentrated on the analysis process and how to do analysis, taking the target-centric view. Part II focused on estimative modeling. Part III goes back to the network-versus-network view that was introduced in Figure 3-4, and describes the analyst's network (analysts, customers, and collectors), viewed both as a system and as a network. We'll begin with the systems view in chapters 16–18 (function, process, and structure). Then we'll take a network view that looks at the role of the customer (chapter 19) and the collector (chapter 20).

16

A Systems View: Function

Intelligence research is putting money in the bank; current intelligence is making a withdrawal.

Bruce Clarke, former CIA
deputy director for intelligence

This chapter is about the products of intelligence analysis. Although any intelligence unit could have many different types of products, they mostly fall into three broad classes: intelligence research, current intelligence, and indications and warning. Let's look at each in turn.

Intelligence Research

In this book, we occasionally refer to intelligence research (sometimes referred to as in-depth research) and strategic intelligence as though they were the same. They aren't. Intelligence research involves answering a customer's question, going through the issue definition phase, planning the project, conducting research, and producing a finished intelligence report. Strategic intelligence is about the production of intelligence that is required for forming policy, strategy, and plans in government, the military, law enforcement, and industry. Strategic intelligence is typically a product of intelligence research, though, so the two concepts are closely related.

The strategic intelligence target tends to divide into two major areas: capabilities and plans. This view of strategic intelligence is closely tied to the strategic planning process as it is done in government and industry. Such strategic planning proceeds from the application of the SWOT methodology discussed in chapter 2.

In the SWOT methodology, strengths and weaknesses define *capabilities* and are determined by looking internally, inside the opposing organization. Opportunities and threats shape *plans* and are determined by looking externally— that is, perceiving the situation as the opponent perceives it. The job of strategic intelligence, in this view, is to assess the opposing organization's capabilities (strengths and weaknesses) and its consequent plans (shaped by the opportunities and threats it perceives).

In operational intelligence, an opponent's use of his capabilities to execute plans—specifically, his intentions—becomes important. Intent to launch a military attack, intent to impose an embargo, or intent to break off negotiations are all operational or even tactical. Intelligence about intentions is somewhere between in-depth research and current intelligence. Plans and intentions tend to be lumped together in traditional intelligence definitions, but they are in fact two different targets separated by their time scale: Plans are longer term; intentions, more immediate.

Current Intelligence

Current intelligence deals with issues that require immediate attention. It usually is disseminated quickly, with a minimal level of evaluation or interpretation. Much of this book describes how to handle long-term research, often comprising major analytic efforts that require creating target models that can take anywhere from days to weeks. Current intelligence goes through a similar process, but must proceed quickly and be cut to the essential message.

Intelligence research and strategic intelligence, as noted earlier, are similar concepts. The same is true of current and tactical intelligence; they are closely related but not the same. Both usually concern immediate events. But current intelligence can include anything that may be of interest to the customer. Tactical intelligence is more specific; it provides information that the customer needs in order to make decisions and take action.

Tactical intelligence often is thought of in the context of military actions, that is, responding to the needs of military field commanders so that they can plan for and, if necessary, conduct combat operations. It actually is a much broader concept. Supporting trade negotiations, providing relief to flood or famine victims, enforcing laws, and stopping narcotics or clandestine arms shipments are all examples of the application of tactical intelligence.

At the tactical level, the intelligence process is very fast. The model must already exist or a generic model must do; ideally, it was created in the intelligence research phase in the normal course of things. Incoming intelligence is simply added to refine the model, and an analysis of changes is extracted and reported quickly.

In tactical intelligence the customer wants details. Intelligence has to be fast and highly reactive. A military commander doesn't need to be told, for example, what the tank can do; he already knows that. What he needs to know is where it is and where it is going. At the tactical level in diplomacy, the diplomat worries less about negotiating strategy and more about an opponent's likely reaction to the diplomat's initiatives.

Indications and Warning

The category *indications and warning* (commonly referred to as I&W) for governments involves detecting and reporting time-sensitive information on foreign developments that threaten the country's military, political, or economic interests.

Providing I&W on threats to national security is traditionally an intelligence organization's highest priority. The failure of U.S. intelligence to provide I&W of the Japanese attack on Pearl Harbor, discussed below, is the primary reason that a U.S. intelligence community was formed in 1947. The alleged failure of that community to provide I&W of the 9/11 attack in 2001 led directly to the most significant reorganization of U.S. intelligence since 1947.

The purpose of I&W is to avoid surprise that would damage the organization's or country's interests. Tactical I&W can include warning of enemy actions or intentions, imminent hostilities, insurgency, and terrorist attacks. Indirect and direct threats are targets of I&W, including warnings of coups or civil disorder, third-party wars, and refugee surges, though these examples may not immediately and directly affect the country making the assessment.

Although I&W is typically treated as if it were tactical intelligence, it can also be strategic. Strategic I&W involves identifying and forecasting emerging threats. Warnings about instability or new defense technologies or breakthroughs that could significantly alter the relative advantages of opposing military forces are examples.

For the forty years from 1950 to 1990, U.S. national I&W was dominated by concern about Soviet strategic attack. A secondary focus was persistent world hot spots: the likelihood of Arab-Israeli, India-Pakistan, or Korean conflict. National I&W for many Middle Eastern countries was dominated by the Arab-Israeli situation. Since 2001, I&W has become much more complex—many countries are focusing on the threat of terrorist attack, particularly an attack using WMD. Finally, since fall 2008, many governments have focused their I&W intelligence efforts on a worldwide economic crisis. The category of I&W also is closely related to (and overlaps with) two other categories of intelligence: capabilities, plans, and intentions; and crisis management and operations support.

The traditional approach to I&W has been to develop indicators, or norms, for military force deployments and activity. If a U.S. I&W organization had existed in December 1941, it would have had the following indicators, enumerated by Harold Ford in his book *Estimative Intelligence*, about Japanese plans and intentions that year:

- In January, a HUMINT report from Peru's minister in Tokyo stated that, in the event of trouble between the United States and Japan, the Japanese intended to begin with a surprise attack on Pearl Harbor.
- Intercepts of Japanese Foreign Ministry traffic on November 19 contained the message "East wind rain," which some U.S. intelligence officers interpreted as indicating a decision for war in the near future.
- On November 22, Foreign Minister Togo Shigenori notified Ambassador Nomura Kichisaburo in Washington, D.C., that negotiations had to be settled by November 29, stating, "after that things are going automatically to happen."

- In late November, the Japanese began padding their radio traffic with garbled or redundant messages—a classic tactic to defeat COMINT operations.
- At the beginning of December, the Japanese navy changed its ship call signs, deviating from its normal pattern of changing call signs every six months.
- On December 2, the Japanese Foreign Ministry ordered its embassies and consulates in London, Manila, Batavia, Singapore, Hong Kong, and Washington, D.C., to destroy most codes, ciphers, and classified documents.
- In early December, the locations of Japan's aircraft carriers and submarines were "lost" by U.S. naval intelligence.
- Scattered reports came in of recent Japanese naval air practice torpedo runs against ships anchored in a southern Japanese harbor.[1]

In hindsight these bits of intelligence together clearly indicate an impending Japanese attack on Pearl Harbor. In practice, these bits would have formed a partial picture within a mass of conflicting and contradictory evidence, as Roberta Wohlstetter pointed out in her book *Pearl Harbor: Warning and Decision*.[2] At best, a cautiously worded warning could have been issued as to the likelihood and nature of an attack within days. In 1941, however, no national I&W organization existed.

Since World War II, most countries of any size have created organizations to warn of pending military action and against other types of surprise. Despite some missteps based on poor analysis (for example, the Yom Kippur and Falkland Islands surprises discussed in the introduction in chapter 1), I&W has done reasonably well in warning against conventional military attacks. Charlie Allen, CIA national intelligence officer (NIO) for warning, issued a warning estimating a 60 percent chance of an Iraqi attack against Kuwait on July 25, 1990, more than a week before the war began.[3]

I&W successes, however, have tended to be in predicting the breakout of conventional armed conflict. The indicators of an impending Iraqi attack on Kuwait in 1990 were well established and were sufficient to allow a warning to be given. Warning norms for terrorism, instability, low-intensity conflict, and technological breakthroughs are much more difficult, and the indicators are concealed more easily.

A warning system needs to be able to deal with the unconventional or extraordinary event. The tendency, though, is for intelligence services to "institutionalize" warning through an established set of indicators based on past experience. Such indicators are well established for conventional military attacks. They are nonexistent for a type of attack that has never happened before, and the danger of missing the warning for such attacks is consequently high.

Finally, the problem of pulling a coherent picture out of the mass of available information has not become easier since 1941. Lists of the evidence of an impending terrorist attack on the United States using airplanes have been compiled since the 9/11 attacks on the Pentagon and World Trade Center. Like the Pearl Harbor evidence, they can be judged fairly only when placed with all of the conflicting, contradictory, and often false raw intelligence that the U.S. intelligence community received beforehand.

For commercial organizations, the highest I&W priority is on significant threats to the organization's survival—impending alliances among competitors or a competitor's impending product breakthrough, for example. But I&W has a broader role in business intelligence. Competitors often send out deliberate signals of their intentions. The business intelligence analyst must be attuned to these indicators and ensure that the customer is aware of the signals.[4] Analysis of the meaning of deliberate signals is a special skill that all analysts should possess, because governments send out deliberate signals, too.

I&W intelligence always has had a tradeoff problem. Analysts don't want to miss the indicators and fail to give a warning. This problem is complicated by the opponent's increasing use of denial and deception. By contrast, if the analyst sets the warning threshold too low, false alarms result, and the analyst becomes vulnerable to the "cry wolf" problem; customers become desensitized, and in a genuine crisis the alarm is ignored.[5] The opposite desensitization problem happens to the analyst when a situation worsens gradually over time, or when warning indications persist for some time without the event happening. This desensitization pattern occurs frequently enough that British author Michael Herman has given it a name—"alert fatigue."[6] The trick is to have a set of indicators that is both necessary and sufficient, so that one can successfully navigate between the unfortunate outcomes of false alarms and missed events. Such sets of indicators are pulled together through experience and through accumulated knowledge of common indicators. Some standard indicators of impending military attack, for example, are a stockpiling of whole blood, recall of diplomatic personnel, recall of military personnel on leave and canceling leave, threats made in the press, and movement of warheads out of storage.

The point is that the indicators must exist for warning to be effective. And they must support alternative outcome models, as discussed in the preceding chapters.

What Should an Intelligence Unit Produce?

A basic question that any analysis unit must deal with is, Should we produce intelligence research, current intelligence, or I&W intelligence? Or all three?

Customers want the latter two types—indeed, they *demand* I&W intelligence—but they often need the first type. The analyst typically needs to persuade the customer to look at the strategic analysis product. A common approach is to produce both current intelligence and research, preferably in the same serial product. Customers read the current intelligence, and the in-depth research in the document just may catch their interest.

This is the equivalent of the "teaser" that television news programs use: Putting a high-interest item last in the program and telling viewers about it up front—so that the viewers will watch the whole program.

Analytic managers, for their part, should take care not to send mixed signals to the analysts. This is a recurring problem in intelligence organizations, and one where analysts and managers always seem to have different perspectives. Managers typically have a solid perspective on the mission and goals. They believe that they've shared those goals with their team members. The analysts, in contrast, frequently claim to be uncertain about mission and goals.

A common source of the mixed signals comes from the tension between current intelligence and in-depth intelligence. Managers, for example, will conduct periodic analyst meetings that stress the need for in-depth research, but their day-to-day guidance is focused on responding to current priorities.

All three types of intelligence have their proponents in intelligence organizations and among policymakers. It is not useful to think of them in either-or terms when allocating time and resources, because *all three are needed.* Current intelligence allows analysts to be in close touch with customers and facilitates better understanding between the two. Intelligence research provides the background that allows analysts to make credible judgments in current reporting.

Which area to stress depends on the customers and where they are in operations. Almost all national leaders want current intelligence that is specific.[7] But as former CIA deputy director for intelligence Bruce Clarke once noted, in the quote that begins this chapter, "Intelligence research is putting money in the bank; current intelligence is making a withdrawal." The problem with abandoning in-depth research is that eventually the intelligence models become irrelevant to the problem. Without a clear picture of long-term trends, analysts cannot make short-term predictions. The intelligence outfit becomes bankrupt. It not only cannot provide strategic intelligence; it cannot even produce decent tactical intelligence.

Several incentives favor the production of current intelligence, to the detriment of in-depth research. First, it's easier to do. Second, you have a customer set that depends on the information being delivered in a timely manner. Third, analysts get instant gratification from seeing results, a task completed, and a grateful customer. The most important customer in the U.S. intelligence community is the president, and the premier intelligence product is current intelligence in the form of the president's daily brief.

If there are two tasks—an in-depth study that is not time-sensitive, and a quick-reaction task—analysts will inevitably tackle the one that can be done quickly. Then there's always another time-sensitive action waiting when the first is done. Analysts will claim that they're fully loaded—but it's a load of choice. Any intelligence unit will always have more tasks waiting than resources to deal with them. Unless there is some incentive to tackle the tough tasks, anyone will consistently gravitate to the easy ones. The job of the manager is to provide that incentive.

Focusing too many resources on current intelligence engenders other problems. Discussing the failures of the U.S. intelligence community in Iraq estimates during 2002 to 2004, Richard Kerr and others noted,

> In periods of crisis, when demands are high and response time is short, most written intelligence production is in the form of policy-driven memos and briefs and pieces written for daily publications. The result of this narrowly focused and piecemeal intelligence flow is that it neither fosters continuity of analysis nor provides a context within which to place seemingly unrelated information. In the case of Iraq, national intelligence did not provide a comprehensive picture of how the country functioned as a whole.[8]

The intelligence manager has to recognize this tyranny of current intelligence, and how it can totally dominate a unit's work, and somehow compensate for it. In the meanwhile, note that this problem is so pervasive that the WMD Commission proposed a dramatic organizational step to deal with it.[9]

Limits and Boundaries

Intelligence analysis has both limits and boundaries. Every analytic manager and every analyst should understand what these are.

- *Limits*, in this definition, delineate the difference between what analysis can do and what it cannot do.
- *Boundaries*, by contrast, delineate the things that intelligence should do and the things that intelligence should *not* do (even if it can).

Let's examine both of these in turn.

Limits

Limits can be summed up nicely in a phrase attributed to a senior intelligence community official: "Intelligence does not do fortune-telling." We'll visit two types of limits here: mysteries versus secrets, and the limits of estimative analysis.

Mysteries versus Secrets

The contrast between mysteries and secrets was summed up nicely by Robert Gates when he was deputy director of intelligence at the CIA: "Secrets are potentially knowable; mysteries are not." The intelligence community gets blamed unfairly because it is unable to predict outcomes that are mysteries even to the principals involved. Consider the following examples:

- *The fall of the Soviet Union.* Gorbachev, the Soviet Union's leader, didn't see it coming. U.S. intelligence identified the political and economic troubles in the Soviet system but did not predict the collapse—and if a few people had made different decisions at critical points, the collapse probably would not have happened (at least, not when it did).

- *The rise of Putin to power in Russia.* As noted in chapter 12, Putin himself appears not to have expected it to happen until his popularity soared after he took responsibility for launching the second Chechen war.
- *The Tunisian, Libyan, and Egyptian revolutions of 2011.* The leaders, their security forces, the militaries, and the revolutionaries all were to varying degrees surprised by the outcome. With different decisions by a few people, things could have turned out much different in all these cases.

If the leaders in-country who are best positioned to know the situation are caught by surprise, how can intelligence services be expected to know what is about to happen? The best intelligence can do is to say that conditions are ripe for an event.

A good analogy would be the stock market. Research firms and brokerages spend vast amounts of money trying to forecast how the stock market will behave. But how it actually will behave tomorrow depends on the individual decisions of a large number of people, and that is a mystery.

In contrast, secrets can be discovered, and that is the job of intelligence. To cite some painful examples of failure:

- Egypt's plan to attack Israel in 1973 (the Yom Kippur War) was a discoverable secret. Ashraf Marwan actually provided the Israelis with advance warning of the attack, but his information was not acted upon.
- The 9/11 plot was discoverable, and the intelligence community's failure to detect it resulted in a fundamental change in the way that the intelligence community does business.
- The fact that Iraq did not have WMD prior to the 2003 war was discoverable.
- Iran's capabilities to produce nuclear weapons are discoverable, but whether the Iranians will do so appears to be a mystery. (Until the weapons are actually produced, a decision can be made at any time to halt the effort.)

Former director of the National Intelligence Council Fritz Ermarth has identified a third distinct category—neither mystery nor secret—that he calls an "obscurity."[10] This refers to the questions that a customer hasn't asked yet, but would if he had the required knowledge. Tom Fingar put it succinctly when he said: "Sometimes the most important 'answers' are the ones provided by an analyst to questions that customers should have asked, but did not."[11]

The "obscurity" is a limit of imagination or curiosity, and one that an intelligence analysis group therefore can overcome. But it requires strong management support and the application of estimative methodologies discussed in the preceding chapters. It sometimes even requires the creation of a separate unit dedicated to exploring the frontiers. In 1970 the CIA's Office of Scientific Intelligence created a separate branch dedicated to just such a mission. Called the Future Threats Branch, it identified a number of likely developments that eventually became reality and issues of policymaker concern.

Limits of Estimative Analysis

Closely related to the problem of mysteries versus secrets is the difficulty in identifying future developments. Some things can be predicted within a range of probabilities. We previously discussed the difference between *convergent* phenomena that are predictable and *divergent* phenomena that are not. Mysteries typically are based on divergent phenomena.

A special case is that of predicting coups. Intelligence agencies typically avoid predicting a coup, even though this would appear to be discoverable. But as noted in chapter 12, if we are aware that a coup is being planned in country X, then the internal security service of country X also is likely to be aware of the plans and will forestall the attempt.

Boundaries

As noted earlier, there are few limits on what intelligence can do. In contrast, a number of boundaries define what intelligence should *not* do. These boundaries are, in most cases, very flexible and often circumvented, but it is important to recognize them nonetheless—and to recognize when you are crossing them. The boundaries also change as you go from one intelligence service to another. Even the British, whose intelligence service closely resembles that of the United States, have different boundaries. Following are a few examples, starting with the most important: the policy boundary.

The Policy Divide

A boundary exists between providing intelligence and making policy recommendations. Analysts are expected to do the former but not the latter.

The policy boundary also is a divide between intelligence and operational decisions. Military commanders welcome intelligence that identifies an opposing force's threats and vulnerabilities. But no military commander would let an intelligence officer tell him, "General, I think that you should deploy your tank units around the Fulda Gap." Operational decisions are a commander's prerogative, and rightly so; the commander usually has more experience and a better understanding of the capabilities of his own forces.

So the border between intelligence and policy or operational decisions is a firm one. Or is it? There is a contrary view—that the boundary is one that many analysts want to observe, but one that at least some policymakers want them to cross. Furthermore, talented (and more adventurous) analysts have discovered how to make a policy or operational recommendation without really making one. For example, an analyst might write something like this:

- "China greatly fears . . . [insert here a course of action that the analyst supports]."
- "India's fear is that the United States would adopt policy X [where policy X is favored by the analyst]."
- "Indonesia's reaction to [a possible U.S. action] would be . . . [describe an outcome that would be beneficial or adverse to U.S. interests]."

This is not a two-way boundary, in any case. Analysts generally don't cross the intelligence-policy divide except by using the stratagem described above. But customers can, and do, gather and analyze their own intelligence. Some policymakers, distrusting the analysis that they receive, insist on receiving raw intelligence (HUMINT and COMINT, especially) and analyzing it themselves. Military commanders are usually wiser. This approach has a high potential for mischief.

In the business intelligence world, the policy boundary is much more variable. Some business leaders welcome policy or operational advice from their business intelligence units. Some don't.

All-Source versus Single-Source Analysis

National intelligence collection organizations perform what is called single-source analysis. Within the United States, the National Security Agency (NSA), National Geospatial-Intelligence Agency (NGA), and Open Source Center (OSC), for example, all do single-source analysis: Their job is to process, exploit, and analyze material collected from COMINT, IMINT, and open source, respectively. In contrast, some national agencies are charged with all-source analysis: the CIA, the Defense Intelligence Agency (DIA), the Department of Homeland Security, the FBI, the State Department, and the military services all have the responsibility to provide all-source analysis.

Supposedly, a boundary exists between these two analysis types. It is a bureaucratic boundary that is often ignored in practice. Single-source analysis groups have to use extrinsic sources (collateral intelligence) to do their jobs, and the result is that they often produce all-source intelligence. Because U.S. intelligence agencies have moved toward a target-centric approach, raw intelligence is now shared widely among collection organizations. So the single-source analysts usually have the material needed to cross the boundary and do all-source analysis.

Domestic versus Foreign Intelligence

Originally, the United States had a divide between domestic and foreign intelligence, based on the organization collecting the intelligence and the uses to which the information was to be put. The CIA, the DIA, and the State Department collected foreign intelligence to support foreign policy actions. The FBI collected domestic intelligence, primarily to support law enforcement activity.

The divide has been blurred since the passage of the Patriot Act. It's all now considered to be national intelligence. But some sort of boundary does exist: Intelligence that is intended to support law enforcement has to operate under different rules, to preserve its admissibility in a court of law.

The United Kingdom continues to have a division between the two: MI-5 is concerned with domestic intelligence, and MI-6 has the responsibility for foreign intelligence.

Operational Information versus Intelligence

In the course of combat operations, friendly units are constantly observing enemy actions visually and also using imagery and electronic means. This could be considered intelligence, or simply operational information. Consider these examples:

- A Predator video that is used for on-the-spot targeting could be considered intelligence but probably is more correctly considered operational information.
- ELINT intercepts that are used to geolocate enemy radars are referred to as Operational ELINT (or OPELINT). Is this really intelligence or simply operational information? The U.S. military uses the term Electronic Support Measures (ESM) for OPELINT that is used to support electronic and physical attack; the term was coined specifically to keep this OPELINT out of intelligence budgets and away from intelligence management.
- A battlefield radar detects opposing forces' aircraft and helicopter movements. This usually would be considered operational information, but it might be intelligence also.

As the examples suggest, there may be a boundary, but it's a fuzzy one. The difference becomes important primarily when the United States goes through its annual funding exercise. A system that provides operational information goes into a different budget and requires different approvals than one that is deemed for intelligence use.

The Pathology of Failures

We started this chapter with a discussion of the function of an analytic unit, in terms of the product. This section focuses on pathologies—on the problems that hinder the production of good analysis and on the resulting failures.

Chapter 1 included a discussion titled "Why Intelligence Fails." It's a topic that observers of the intelligence business have visited often and undoubtedly will continue to visit. John Hedley discussed the topic in detail in a 2005 article and came to the conclusion that both miscalls and noncalls are inevitable. Or, as he put it, "No one person can be right on all subjects at all times."[12] So there will continue to be failures. Richard Betts, in a 1978 article, put that conclusion in his title.[13] DIA analyst Russ Travers made the same point in a prescient 1997 article entitled "The Coming Intelligence Failure."[14] Twenty-seven years apart, three knowledgeable authors came to the same conclusion. A number of articles since then have repeated that conclusion. But the lesson doesn't appear to sink in among our customers. Even with the most expensive and powerful intelligence service in the world, the U.S. intelligence community nevertheless will fail from time to time.

Failures mostly occur when intelligence must make predictions, or when it is expected to provide warning (which is, of course, a prediction). Warnings of attack have been a major failure point. As Michael Herman put it, "There is a puzzling record of consistent failure to provide warning of a surprise attack."[15] In fact, failure to provide warning of any major world event tends to be the most visible type of failure, and the one that causes the most grief for the intelligence community. Chapter 19 notes that policymakers—all senior executives, for that matter—hate surprise. And warning failure inevitably results in some powerful people being surprised.

Jeffrey Cooper, vice president for technology at Science Applications International Corporation, wrote a paper entitled "Curing Analytical Pathologies," published in 2005 by CIA's Center for the Study of Intelligence. In it, Cooper documented the major analytic pathologies that contribute to failures.[16] They are as follows:

- The tyranny of current intelligence and its companion pathology, the neglect of in-depth research
- Overreliance on previous judgments, either because of the "creeping validity" problem or because of a reluctance to reverse previous assessments
- Neglect of anticipatory intelligence, that is, identifying and assessing threats and opportunities that the customer hasn't thought of yet
- Failure to make use of proven analytic tools and methods
- Constraints imposed by security, or where security is an excuse for failure to share

Let's look at some additional root causes for failures, starting with the most commonly observed one: pressures on the analyst. Many of the pathologies are the result of internal and external pressures.

Pressures

We want our intelligence analysts to "tell it like it is," to produce the best possible intelligence, uncolored by pressures to produce a specific outcome. In 1991 the Senate Select Committee on Intelligence conducted hearings on the confirmation of Robert Gates as director of central intelligence. The standard of conduct was described by analysts testifying in those hearings as a strong tradition among older CIA officers, one [that stressed] the need for integrity of judgment and action, a generation of officers raised on the need to tell it like it is, of going where the evidence takes one and then candidly so telling senior policymakers, whether they find such judgments congenial or not—the aim being to enlighten them about the true shape of the world, not to please them or cater to their preconceptions.[17]

This is the gold standard of intelligence analysis. It is a difficult standard to reach consistently, because of pressures to shape the result. Pressures to have analysis come up with a specific answer are not unique to intelligence. They are found in all areas of research. Complete analytic objectivity is an elusive goal in the basic sciences, the social sciences, and, yes, in intelligence as well.

Unfortunately, pressures to conform analysis to the customer's desires do exist. They can come from inside the analyst's organization or from the outside, and they usually are very subtle. Let's take a look at some of them.

Internal Pressures

Jack Davis has highlighted four "key perils of analysis." Two of them are tied to organizational culture: coordinating judgments with other analysts and managers in their organization, and confronting organizational norms.

At the Gates confirmation hearings, analysts testified about internal pressures to "politicize" intelligence before the committee. Some analysts cited the pressures from fellow analysts who were concerned that policymakers did not like (or read) the analysis that the office had been producing. Other analysts disagreed, arguing that politicization required more than simply creating an atmosphere; there had to be deliberate efforts to produce the desired assessment.[18]

While analysts may disagree on the importance of subtle influences, most observers have concluded that organizational bias or predisposition can shape analysis.

When analysis affects the budget of the parent organization, there are powerful internal pressures to produce a favorable result. These pressures exist for any organization, not just for those involved in defense. Law enforcement, homeland security, and CIA analysts have all felt this kind of pressure from time to time. It is unwise to place much faith in any intelligence analysis if the product has an impact on the parent organization's budget.

External Pressures

Jack Davis also described the external pressures that underlie politicization of intelligence. One of what he calls the "key perils of analysis" is about external pressures. It concerns the times when, as Davis observed, "analysts whose ethic calls for substantive judgments uncolored by an administration's foreign and domestic political agendas seek to assist clients professionally mandated to advance those agendas."[19]

We tend to think of this as an external pressure, but it manifests itself also as an internal pressure. Most of the attention to this politicization problem has centered on the CIA, though it is a problem elsewhere as well. Analysts themselves have noted that politicization can take many forms and is very difficult to prove. They are seldom, if ever, told what to write or instructed to change their conclusions. But, as one analyst noted during the Gates hearings,

> Judgments might be reached that are not supported by the available evidence. Evidence that does not support the desired judgment might be ignored. The review process that finished analysis goes through might be skewed to produce a desired result. Personnel assigned to produce analysis might be known to favor the desired result. Managers might, by their actions, create a "politically charged" atmosphere—"a fog," as one analyst testified— that permeates the entire workplace. "You cannot hold it in your hand or nail it to the wall," the analyst said, "[but] it is real. It does exist. And it does affect people's behavior."[20]

Former NIO Paul Pillar has provided an example of how policymakers exert this pressure, without ever saying anything like, "This is the conclusion I want to see." In his book *Intelligence and U.S. Foreign Policy: Iraq, 9/11, and Misguided Reform,* Pillar detailed the subtle and not-so-subtle pressures that White House staffers put on the U.S. intelligence community to provide assessments linking Saddam Hussein's regime to Al Qaeda and to WMD.[21]

Analysts, in responding to these pressures, have to go through a delicate balancing act—being relevant to the policymaker's needs without being politicized. Jack Davis has noted the well-known quote of former director of central intelligence James Schlesinger that "[e]very American is entitled to his own opinion but not his own facts."[22] What policymakers often do, if given an opportunity, is just that: select the facts that they like and ignore the facts that they find unpleasant.

Unfortunately, as Pillar noted, politicization is a fact of life in the intelligence trade. That's true not just in the United States, but also in any country where the intelligence chiefs are subservient organizationally to policymakers and decision makers. Since intelligence chiefs are almost always in that position, some form of politicization will exist in every country. It may be subtle and indirect, as in the United States and in most European countries. Or it may be blatant, as in Stalin's and Hussein's regimes.

In the end though, as Davis noted, policymakers and military commanders must make the decisions. They are the ones who usually will be held responsible for the outcome. Policymakers step over the line when they pressure analysts to come with their preferred answer, as they did prior to the 2003 invasion of Iraq. But they always have the right to disregard the answers that analysts produce.

One source of external pressures is a result of the extensive U.S. liaison relationships with other countries, especially the "Five Eyes" relationship with the United Kingdom, Canada, Australia, and New Zealand; and the relationship with Israel. All these relationships introduce complications that can slant both the raw intelligence reporting and the resulting all-source analysis.

The "special relationships" that U.S. intelligence has with some foreign governments or leaders also can cause problems in the policy-diplomatic sphere. Years ago, the CIA's Clandestine Service had a close working relationship with the Druze faction in Lebanon. This relationship arguably made it more difficult for CIA analysts to produce objective assessments of the political situation. It certainly complicated the State Department's efforts to craft a policy in Lebanon. As another example, a close CIA relationship existed with Iran under the Shah and the result may have been to unduly influence analysis about the likelihood of a successful Iranian revolution.

The close U.S. relationship with Israel also results in pressures that can unduly shape analysis. It's a common belief among U.S. analysts that being on the Israeli account is not a career-enhancing move because of the pressures to conform analysis to policy and to domestic political pressures. The close U.S. relationship with Saudi Arabia likely has affected the quality of analysis produced on the Arabian Peninsula, much as it once did with Iran under the Shah.

Temporal Pressures

If you drew a chart of confidence in analytic judgment versus time, it would show a steadily increasing level of confidence. For this reason, analysts naturally want to wait for that one more tidbit of raw intelligence to clarify their judgments. But the customer can't wait forever. Customers have to act, and they will do so with or without the final intelligence report.

The Iraqi WMD fiasco discussed earlier and in Appendix I is an example of the bad consequences of a short deadline. A flawed methodology was applied and some sources weren't thoroughly vetted, but the very short deadline imposed by Congress left analysis managers with no real options. Contrast that failure with the multiyear collection and analysis effort that resulted in the death of Osama bin Laden. The bin Laden case is an excellent example of the target-centric approach at work. When intelligence is focused on a specific target with a high enough priority, time works in your favor. The bin Laden trackdown was a long-term effort; time was available for analysis, for following many leads, and for subsequent guidance to IMINT and HUMINT collectors. Such was not the case for the Iraq WMD national intelligence estimate.

Denial and Deception

A contributing reason for many warning failures has been the opponent's effectiveness in using D&D. Chapter 8 provided some guidance on how to overcome the opponent's use of D&D. Defeating D&D depends, more than any other factor, on the strength of the relationship between collector and analyst. Where a close working relationship exists between the two, the tiny inconsistencies or clues that signal D&D can be picked up and shared, exposing the fact that D&D is present. One of the primary jobs of analysis managers is to ensure that this close working relationship exists. Another is to ensure that analysts, in making their judgments, have considered the possibility of D&D.

Customer Disregard and Misuse

A major source of intelligence "failure" results from customers either not believing or misusing the intelligence that they receive. Strange as it may sound, the analyst usually bears some responsibility for this. There are at least two reasons why. Perhaps the analyst's credibility with the policymaker was not good enough. Perhaps, as Henry Kissinger said (quoted in chapter 19), "[Y]ou warned me, but you didn't convince me." As noted in the introduction in chapter 1, policymakers may be aware of a threat but for their own reasons choose to pursue a policy that does not deal with the threat.

Whatever the reason, some customers will ignore or bypass the all-source analyst. Many policymakers want to see the raw intelligence and do their own analysis. Heads of government are particularly prone to bypass their analysts. We touched on the problems caused by Winston Churchill's inclination to be his own analyst in chapter 7. Josef Stalin and Adolf Hitler both were noted for doing their own intelligence analysis, and neither of them was particularly good at it. Hitler, in particular, had his intelligence services competing to curry favor with him by providing interesting tidbits of intelligence. His ineptness as an analyst was one of the reasons the British chose not to attempt an assassination during World War II; they feared that Hitler might then be replaced by a more competent military leader.

Seldom if ever has there been an example of customer disregard and misuse of intelligence to match that of Lyndon Johnson's administration during the Vietnam War. CIA analysts repeatedly told the administration during 1963 to 1965 that substantially increasing U.S. combat operations in Vietnam would not solve U.S. problems there because the war was essentially a political-military struggle that had to be won in the South and primarily by the South Vietnamese. Their conclusions were ignored. From 1967 to 1968, CIA analysts provided accurate assessments indicating that enemy strength in South Vietnam was about twice what the U.S. military was willing to acknowledge, despite pressure to provide a more favorable assessment from the White House, the American embassy in Saigon, and the military leadership in Vietnam. The U.S. military's own intelligence analysts in Vietnam also found their assessments of the deteriorating situation suppressed by their commanders.[23]

We touched on Saddam Hussein's invasion of Kuwait in previous chapters. It's also an example of customer disregard for intelligence. The NIO for warning provided repeated warnings of the attack that were disregarded at the national policymaking levels in the days prior to the invasion. On July 25, 1990, the NIO issued a "warning of war" estimating the chances of an Iraqi incursion into Kuwait at 60 percent. Early on August 1, the NIO issued a "warning of attack," indicating that there would be no further warning. The warnings went to all of the senior policy officials in the Defense Department, the Joint Chiefs of Staff, and the White House. The next day, on August 2, Iraq attacked.[24]

A senior Pentagon official subsequently admitted that neither warning was taken seriously because senior U.S. officials contacted a number of leaders in the Middle East and the Soviet Union about the possible attack. All those contacted were of the opinion that Hussein did not intend to attack.[25]

The Perils of Being Too Rational

Many intelligence failures occur either because the analysts were more rational than the leaders whose decisions they predicted, or because they missed some critical but nonobvious factors. Consider the following examples:

- On September 19, 1962, the U.S. intelligence community published an estimate concluding that the Soviets were unlikely to introduce strategic offensive weapons in Cuba—at a time when strategic ballistic missiles were being installed there. The estimate drafters knew that the development of an offensive military base in Cuba would probably provoke U.S. military intervention. They assumed that the Soviets also recognized that fact. In his postmortem of the estimate's mistaken assessment, Board of National Estimates chief Sherman Kent noted that "no estimating process can be expected to divine exactly when the enemy is about to make a dramatically wrong decision."[26]
- Analysts also misread the forces behind Anwar Sadat's decision to attack Israel in the Sinai during 1973. Both U.S. and Israeli intelligence had concluded that Egypt would not start a war that it could not win. They were correct in the assessment that Egypt could not win, but they missed Sadat's primary motivation: By attacking, Sadat could gain the maneuvering room to begin a peace process that would end with the return of the Sinai to Egypt.
- A similar miscall preceded the Soviet invasion of Afghanistan in 1979. U.S. analysts consistently estimated that the Soviets would not launch a full-scale invasion because of the risk of being bogged down in an unwinnable war, along with adverse reactions in the West, Iran, and much of the Muslim world. The analysts in this case were better decision makers than the Soviet leadership. They were right in their assessments of the consequences. They were wrong about the decision to invade.[27]

Intelligence failures are always difficult for analysts and their managers to accept and deal with. But this is a particularly galling class of failure. You've identified the most likely decision that a foreign leader will make, based on a careful analysis of the situation. You report this to your customer. But the leader in question makes an apparently irrational decision. How do you then explain the outcome without seeming to make excuses? If you have kept the customer closely involved in the analysis process, as discussed throughout this book, then you should already have the customer on your side. If not, then your explanation is unlikely to get a favorable reception, no matter how you couch it.

Another type of "failure" is more bittersweet than galling: when the customer (or someone else) acts on the intelligence and thereby changes the outcome. This actually happens frequently. Based on intelligence, policymakers take actions that prevent the predicted outcome from happening. Or the intelligence becomes public, thereby changing the outcome. This happened in the case of the Soviet Union, when a CIA assessment of the Soviet economy became public, and the Soviets took action to prevent the predicted outcome.[28] The breakup of Yugoslavia, discussed in Appendix I, is an example of the opposite case; it may have been helped along by the publication of the national intelligence estimate predicting the breakup.

Summary

In setting up an analytic unit, or in assuming charge of one, a manager must think through questions such as, Who are my customers? And what do they need? Those are questions both for analytic unit managers and for analysts. With those questions answered, the next logical question is, What should the unit produce? Intelligence research? Current intelligence? Indications and warning (I&W) intelligence? Or all three?

Intelligence research resembles the research conducted in a university or a research laboratory. It looks to the long term, or it looks at a specific issue in depth. It often produces strategic intelligence that is used to make policy decisions and strategic plans. Current intelligence covers fast-breaking events or new developments, and it looks much like newspaper or television news reporting. It often produces tactical intelligence to support ongoing operations. Customers usually prefer current intelligence but often need the research product—though they do not always recognize that need.

I&W intelligence really isn't a choice; all intelligence units must provide warning.

Dealing with customers requires that both analysts and their managers have an intuitive understanding of the limits and boundaries of analysis. Limits distinguish between what analysis can do and what it cannot do. One limit is defined by the difference between secrets, which are potentially knowable and therefore a legitimate subject for analysis; and mysteries, which are not. A second limit is that of estimative analysis: Some outcomes are predictable, often because they depend on uncovering secrets or are based on convergent trends. Some are not predictable, because the outcome depends on a divergent event (such as the decisions of a national leadership).

Boundaries differ from limits in that they define what analysis should do and what it should not do (even if it can). Boundaries include those things that analysts can do but are bureaucratically constrained from doing. Perhaps best known is the boundary between providing intelligence and making policy recommendations; analysts are expected to do the former but not the latter. Three other traditional boundaries are those between single-source and all-source analysis, between domestic and foreign intelligence, and between operational information and intelligence.

Analysts must deal with internal and external pressures that can distort the analysis process. Internal pressures tend to protect the parent organization's equities. External pressures tend to protect the equities of other organizations—conforming analysis to policy, for example, or protecting sensitive relationships with other countries. The pressure to provide analytic products on short deadlines occasionally results in a flawed product.

Analysis failures occur and will continue to occur for a number of reasons. Estimative analyses, especially warnings of attack, carry a significant risk of failure. Denial and deception has historically been cited as a cause of intelligence failures, but it may be harder to pull off successfully today. Perhaps the major source of intelligence "failure" results from customers either not believing or misusing the intelligence that they receive. Failures also occur when the analysts either were more rational than the leaders whose decisions they predicted, or misconstrued the forces that actually shaped the decisions. The most frustrating "failure," though, actually is a success. It occurs when either the policymaker or the opponent acts on the analyst's assessment and thereby changes the outcome.

Notes

1. Harold P. Ford, *Estimative Intelligence* (Lanham, Md.: University Press of America, 1993), 3–5.
2. Roberta Wohlstetter, *Pearl Harbor: Warning and Decision* (Stanford, Calif.: Stanford University Press, 1962). The difference between conflicting and contradictory evidence was discussed in chapter 7.
3. Michael R. Gordon and Bernard E. Trainor, *The General's War: The Inside Story of the Conflict in the Gulf* (London: Little, Brown, 1996).
4. Liam Fahey, *Competitors* (New York: Wiley, 1999), 78.
5. Mark M. Lowenthal, *Intelligence: From Secrets to Policy*, 2nd ed. (Washington, D.C.: CQ Press, 2002), 87.
6. Michael Herman, *Intelligence Power in Peace and War* (Cambridge, U.K.: Cambridge University Press, 1996), 233.
7. Competent national leaders do think about long-term strategy, but they seldom want the help of strategic intelligence. In contrast, they are usually avid consumers of tactical intelligence.
8. Richard Kerr, Thomas Wolfe, Rebecca Donegan, and Aris Pappas, "Collection and Analysis on Iraq," *Studies in Intelligence*, 49, no. 3 (2007), https://www.cia.gov/library/center-for-the-study-of-intelligence/csi-publications/csi-studies/studies/vol49no3/html_files/Collection_Analysis_Iraq_5.htm.
9. "Report of the Commission on the Intelligence Capabilities of the United States Regarding Weapons of Mass Destruction," March 31, 2005, 402–405.

10. Jeffrey R. Cooper, *Curing Analytic Pathologies* (Washington, D.C.: CIA Center for the Study of Intelligence, December 2005), 48, https://www.cia.gov/library/center-for-the-study-of-intelligence/csi-publications/books-and-monographs/curing-analytic-pathologies-pathways-to-improved-intelligence-analysis-1/index.html.

11. Thomas Fingar, "Analysis in the U.S. Intelligence Community: Missions, Masters, and Methods," in *Intelligence Analysis: Behavioral and Social Scientific Foundations*, ed. Baruch Fischoff and Cherie Chauvin (Washington, D.C.: National Academies Press, 2011), 10.

12. John Hollister Hedley, "Learning from Intelligence Failures," *International Journal of Intelligence and Counterintelligence*, 18 (2005): 435–450.

13. Richard K. Betts, "Analysis, War and Decision: Why Intelligence Failures Are Inevitable," *World Politics*, 31, no. 1 (October 1978): 61–89.

14. Russ Travers, "The Coming Intelligence Failure," *Studies in Intelligence*, 1, no. 1 (1997), https://www.cia.gov/library/center-for-the-study-of-intelligence/csi-publications/csi-studies/studies/97unclass/failure.html.

15. Herman, *Intelligence Power in Peace and War*, 239.

16. Cooper, *Curing Analytic Pathologies*.

17. L. Britt Snider, *The Agency and the Hill: CIA's Relationship with Congress, 1946–2004* (Washington, D.C.: CIA Center for the Study of Intelligence, 2008), 210.

18. Ibid, 211.

19. Jack Davis, "Why Bad Things Happen to Good Analysts," in *Analyzing Intelligence*, ed. Roger Z. George and James B. Bruce (Washington, D.C.: Georgetown University Press, 2008), 158.

20. Snider, *The Agency and the Hill,* 211.

21. Paul R. Pillar, *Intelligence and U.S. Foreign Policy: Iraq, 9/11, and Misguided Reform* (New York: Columbia University Press, 2011).

22. Jack Davis, "Tensions in Analyst-Policymaker Relations: Opinions, Facts, and Evidence," in *The Sherman Kent Center for Intelligence Analysis Occasional Papers*, 2, no. 2.

23. CIA Center for the Study of Intelligence, *CIA and the Vietnam Policymakers: Three Episodes 1962–1968* (Washington, D.C.: Author, March 19, 2007), https://www.cia.gov/library/center-for-the-study-of-intelligence/csi-publications/books-and-monographs/cia-and-the-vietnam-policymakers-three-episodes-1962-1968/index.html.

24. Charles E. Allen, "Warning and Iraq's Invasion of Kuwait: A Retrospective Look," *Defense Intelligence Journal,* 7, no. 2 (1998): 33–44.

25. Ibid.

26. CIA Center for the Study of Intelligence, "The Perils of Analysis: Revisiting Sherman Kent's Defense of SNIA 85-3-62," *Studies in Intelligence,* 51, no. 3 (2007), https://www.cia.gov/library/center-for-the-study-of-intelligence/csi-publications/csi-studies/studies/vol51no3/revisiting-sherman-kent2019s-defense-of-snie-85-3-62.html. The Soviets were in fact aware of the danger of U.S. military intervention but believed that President Kennedy would be deterred from intervention once the missiles were installed and operational.

27. Douglas MacEachin, *Predicting the Soviet Invasion of Afghanistan: The Intelligence Community's Record* (Washington, D.C.: CIA Center for the Study of Intelligence, April 15, 2007), https://www.cia.gov/library/center-for-the-study-of-intelligence/csi-publications/books-and-monographs/predicting-the-soviet-invasion-of-afghanistan-the-intelligence-communitys-record/predicting-the-soviet-invasion-of-afghanistan-the-intelligence-communitys-record.html.

28. Douglas J. MacEachin, *CIA Assessments of the Soviet Union: The Record Versus the Charge—An Intelligence Monograph* (Washington, D.C.: CIA Center for the Study of Intelligence, 1996).

17

A Systems View: Process

CAPTAIN MATTHEW GARTH (Charleton Heston): "Joe, you're guessing!"
INTELLIGENCE OFFICER JOSEPH ROCHEFORT (Hal Holbrook): "Sir, we like to call it analysis."

Midway, the movie, 1976

The analysis process (focused on the target-centric approach) was introduced in chapter 3. Subsequent chapters detailed the best ways to conduct analysis. We now turn to a different perspective on the process: a top-level or procedural view. We'll start by identifying the customer (a subject discussed in more detail in chapter 19), move to planning the analysis project, and then touch on managing collaborative (team) efforts, and finally, handling reviews. The chapter concludes with a section on product evaluation.

Identifying the Customer

The intelligence customer may be defined by the analyst's position. In military units, the customers include the commander and operations staff for intelligence to support strategic and operational planning, and subordinate unit commanders or individuals (such as pilots) for tactical intelligence. In national, law enforcement, and competitive intelligence, the customer may not be defined so clearly.

A successful analyst identifies her customers wisely—high-level decision makers who may simply ignore the intelligence product can be the wrong people to focus on as customers. Often, the decision maker's staff members are the customers to court; they are usually more likely to read the material and use it to shape the policy. There is a consideration to bear in mind, however, when dealing with these staffs in regard to current intelligence. Because intelligence affects policy, staff members always want to know about hot items before their bosses do, and they may slant the intelligence where they can. This has been a particular problem with the president's daily brief, because the National Security Council (NSC) staff insists on seeing the material before it goes to the president. There is a good reason for this; staff members don't want to be caught by a question from the president (or any decision maker) about events that they were unaware of.

This potential for being caught off-guard, publicly or in front of one's boss, drives policymakers and their staff members to constantly be aware of both current news and current intelligence, ideally in advance of their superiors hearing about it. (This view adds to the already-unhealthy focus on current intelligence mentioned earlier in the book.) The requirement to see the current intelligence in advance has the potential to cause mischief in the form of pressures to shape intelligence reporting. Another problem is that the staff, aware of upcoming unwelcome news, may prepare an argument to discredit or ignore it.

The desire of customers not to be caught off-guard is one facet of a broader issue: What the customer does *not* need is to be surprised. One of the more embarrassing illustrations of this issue occurred on December 21, 2010, when ABC's Diane Sawyer was interviewing Director of National Intelligence James Clapper, Secretary of Homeland Security Janet Napolitano, and Chief Counterterrorism Advisor John Brennan. Sawyer posed a question about the widely covered arrest of twelve men in an alleged terror plot in London that had happened a few hours before the interview. Clapper was unaware of the arrests; his office had not briefed him on them because they were not considered relevant to the interview.[1]

Once an analyst has identified the customers, she next must find out what they need. But customers often don't know what intelligence analysis can do for them. For example, a competitive intelligence unit may be told to focus on competitors' new products, when their customers really should be worrying about competitors' strategies for taking away market share. Analysts have to reach out to the customers, understand their current and long-term interests, and then prove that they can answer the questions that customers pose. Analysts should be in a position where the customers seek them out, instead of the other way around.

Single-source analysts have special challenges because of the diverse nature of their customer set. They produce intelligence that goes to all-source analysts, though it often goes to the end user as well. They also may find that other collection disciplines need their product. COMINT analysts, for example, make extensive use of the IMINT product, and vice versa.

Planning the Analysis Project

All major intelligence analysis efforts (expected to last at least a few weeks and result in a finished product, such as a written report or a briefing) start with some sort of project definition or research plan. This definition or plan has many different names in the U.S. intelligence community, and many different formats.

A project plan is required in the intelligence business for the following reasons:

- It helps to organize your thinking and planning. The simple act of writing out a plan helps you to make connections and check for flaws in your logic. It is a first check on the quality of tradecraft that will go into the product.
- It can be circulated among your fellow analysts and supervisors to get feedback. They can provide valuable insights or information (for example, by identifying sources of information that you may have overlooked).
- The target-centric approach calls for your plan to be shared with partner organizations (such as intelligence collectors, other analysis agencies, or customers), so that they can understand what you plan to do and provide guidance and assistance.
- When you are asking for information held by outside organizations, having a solid and defensible plan that you can discuss in detail can significantly improve your chance of getting their cooperation.

Even current intelligence items—such as intelligence reports that have to be produced in a time frame of a day or less—have some form of project plan. It may not be stated formally, but the analyst has mentally gone through the steps below in starting the effort.

The following are three of the main features that commonly appear in the project plan (an example is included as Appendix II):

- *Issue Definition/Terms of Reference.* The step of issue definition, sometimes called establishing the terms of reference, is stressed throughout this text as the most important step in an analysis effort. It seldom happens that the question posed by an intelligence customer accurately states the problem that the customer needs to solve. You always have to think through the problem in detail. Many intelligence failures occur at this point. The best subsequent analysis cannot save you from poor issue definition at the beginning. The result of this effort is a statement of the purpose, or the issues to be addressed in the body of the report.

  As part of this step, you will prepare an issue decomposition like that discussed in chapter 4. This usually is a hierarchy of subordinate questions that, when answered, allow you to answer the overall issue statement.
- *Précis.* The précis explains or summarizes the plan in a few sentences. It follows naturally from, and provides possible answers to, the questions that arise from statement of the issue (the terms of reference). The précis can take the form of a draft of key points to be included in the final paper, so long as it is understood that these will change. It should include the working hypotheses that you intend to use. Veterans of the business, such as Jack Davis and Richards Heuer, make the point that in the subsequent project you should try to disprove, rather than try to prove, your starting hypotheses.

- *Research Plan.* Keep the research plan simple and succinct. Outline your research approach. Identify any applicable research methodologies or tools you plan to use. Identify gaps in knowledge and expected sources of information.

Managing the Team Process

Almost all analytic projects are team efforts. In the ideal, such analytic teams will be staffed with experienced intelligence officers. The team leader's job is to provide the needed resources and encouragement, and then to get out of the way and let the team members do their jobs.

That ideal seldom occurs. In most cases, managing team efforts requires somewhat more "hands-on" effort. Managing the analysis process usually is a matter of ensuring that team members do the following:

- Have good relationships with customers and understand their needs
- Have good relationships among collectors, single-source analysts, and all-source analysts and that team members understand each other's needs
- Go through a project planning stage, especially the issue definition part
- Use sound tradecraft
- Coordinate their efforts with peers, working in a team environment

Because many people have something at stake in how an intelligence question is answered, the process of getting to the answer, especially on complex intelligence problems, is fundamentally a *social* one. Most complex issues involve many stakeholders: Some of them, such as the analyst's managers, are involved in defining the intelligence issue, while others, such as the customers, may add constraints to the solution. Teams working on related projects have a particularly large stake, because one team's answer affects that of the other team. For instance, an economic analyst's assessment that the economy of Italy is headed for serious trouble would be a critical input for an analytic team assessing the political future of Italy. The great benefit of having a team is that any member of it—a collector, an analyst, a customer—is no longer confined to using his or her expertise in just one area or at just one time during the process. Instead, synergistic discoveries and opportunities occur as pooled expertise and talents are brought to bear on one relevant focus: the target model.

As a result, interpersonal skills (including the ability to express and present ideas clearly) cannot be overemphasized. Admittedly, analysts who live by logic and the scientific method are not often described as "naturals" when it comes to soft skills. But practicing empathy, conflict resolution techniques, facilitation skills, and the art of knowing when and how to advocate versus when to follow and reflect, are crucial to analysis and the resulting product. These project management skills, along with some mastery over one's ego, can be learned (albeit sometimes through painful trial and error). Even the most logical and objective creature in popular culture history, *Star Trek's* Mr. Spock, was a consummate listener, dialoguer, and when appropriate, advocate.

There are likely several thousands of books dedicated to the art of teamwork. But if there is one key to successful team outcomes, it would be efficient collaboration built on mutual trust—something that is difficult to build and very easy to destroy in a large intelligence organization. Effective teams require cohesion, formal and informal communication, cooperation, shared mental models, and similar knowledge structures. Without such a common process, an interdisciplinary team will quickly fall apart.[2]

Guidelines for a Successful Team Effort

The sections that follow represent a short outline of four steps to produce a successful analytic team effort. An analysis team will consistently produce credible reports of excellent quality by following these guidelines.

Define the Issue

Throughout this book, the importance of issue definition is prescribed as the critical first step in every effort. Up front, the team leader must manage the scope of the problem—determining which stakeholders to include in the process and how to include them; choosing which constraints to be ruled by, which to bend, and which to ignore. In this way, the analyst can make conscious and responsible choices in addressing the scope of the issue.

Settle on an Analytic Approach

The team leader should avoid changing the analytic method or process in midstream; this can confuse the participants and potentially demoralize the team.

Standardize Terms

Standardizing terms ensures that the product flows smoothly even through the final stages. This seems like a trivial step in the process, but misunderstandings often develop after an analysis effort is finished because this step is neglected. Estimates have foundered because an expression meant one thing to the analyst and something quite different to the customer. For this reason, a national intelligence estimate (NIE) uses the following terms for precision in describing the likelihood that an event will occur:

- Terms such as *probably, likely, very likely* or *almost certainly* indicate a greater than even chance.
- The terms *unlikely* and *remote* indicate a less than even chance that an event will occur; they do not imply that an event will not occur.
- Terms such as *we cannot dismiss, we cannot rule out,* or *we cannot discount* reflect an unlikely, improbable, or remote event whose consequences are such that it warrants mentioning.[3]

In addition, it was found necessary for estimates to indicate the degree to which information sources are believed to be free from mistakes and errors. So NIEs use the following terms to indicate the accuracy of judgments:

- *High confidence* generally indicates that the judgments are based on high-quality information, or that the nature of the issue makes it possible to render a solid judgment. A "high confidence" judgment is not a fact or a certainty, however, and such judgments still carry a risk of being wrong.
- *Moderate confidence* generally means that the information is credibly sourced and plausible but not of sufficient quality or corroborated sufficiently to warrant a higher level of confidence.
- *Low confidence* generally means that the information's credibility or plausibility is questionable, that the information is too fragmented or poorly corroborated to make solid analytic inferences, or that there are significant concerns or problems with the sources.[4]

Conduct Regular Project Review Conferences

Maintain an action item list and review it at these times. The conferences and action item lists are primarily for encouraging people to stick to the schedule and secondarily for coordination. These conferences are not a time to get into substantive details, which could be handled, offline, between two or three team members. The skillful team manager drives for making decisions quickly, even before the team is ready, knowing that decisions and partial solutions will flush out new contributions. This is equivalent to the concept of rapid prototyping in software development.

Guidelines for Collaboration

Obviously an essential part of any analytic effort is collaboration, and both new tools and new processes have developed in the U.S. intelligence community to make this much easier. Tom Fingar, former director of the National Intelligence Council, noted the success of the DNI's efforts to integrate the intelligence community and to create a self-aware community of analysts. Intelligence for the president, for the NSC, and for interdepartmental meetings is a product of interagency collaboration. The importance of these products, Fingar observed, drives analysts to commit the large amounts of time that they believe is necessary to "get it right." Much of this time is spent in informal collaboration with colleagues within and beyond an analyst's parent agency.[5]

The analyst's job is to manage the collaboration process. In this role, the analyst should encourage every possible form of communication—welcoming disagreement as a sign that the stakeholders are putting their cards on the table and using conferences as occasions for learning and building shared mental models. Dissent is inevitable in collaborative efforts. In fact, if all participants agree on something, it's a good idea to look closely at the issues that everyone agrees on; this signals the possibility of groupthink. It is the analyst's job to carefully manage dissent, being particularly cognizant of two potentially poor outcomes. First, avoid suppressing dissent. More than once in NIEs, the dissenter has turned out to be right. Second, do not allow dissent to devolve into compromise for the sake of harmony. Too often in NIEs, compromises have weakened overall conclusions. The analyst should remember that he or she is managing an *opportunity-driven* process and look for opportunities for breakthroughs, synergies, connections, and allies.

If the customer has not been closely involved in the process (which, ideally, is *not* the case), once the fact-finding and analysis have been completed, it is time for the analyst to set objectivity aside and assume the opposite role—that of persuader. The analyst now must turn her attention toward getting the analytic product read or heard and understood. This means presenting the results to the customer in the most compelling way possible (which is why the analyst must first seek to know the customer and/or the customer's staff as much as possible).

Collaborative Tools

Whether leading a team effort or going solo, an analyst should use technologies that support communication among the stakeholders and promote the value of capturing and sharing soft information, such as ideas, questions, objections, opinions, assumptions, and constraints.

To do this, analysts in the United States have available a number of collaborative tools. Intellipedia (the U.S. intelligence community's classified version of Wikipedia) allows for the creation and wide sharing of target models, effectively implementing the concept of the target-centric approach. Another classified tool, called I-Space, does much the same thing, with a capability to produce classified blogs.[6] Other informal means, mostly relying on the intelligence community's classified Internet (called Intelink), allow analyst-initiated collaboration that bypasses the constraining influence of the hierarchical structure of the intelligence community.

These tools and methods of collaboration are finding wide use, although some writers note a problem with their value. Fingar observed that some analysts and managers have complained that "analysts must spend too much time collaborating with colleagues or using new analytic tools."[7] The availability of these collaborative tools has also caused increased focus on a longstanding conflict between sharing and protection of sources and methods, discussed later.

Customer Relationships

A recurring issue in intelligence analysis is the nature of the relationship between analysts and customers. How close should the two be? This has been a topic of debate for decades. One side of the argument is that intelligence should be organizationally close to where decisions are made. The argument against that arrangement is that intelligence is likely to become an advocate for policy and thereby lose the ability to provide objective analysis.

It's critical for analytic managers, as well as their analysts, to be close to customers. Senior policymakers may share their thinking with senior intelligence community managers, but they are unlikely to share that thinking with analysts unless there exists a long-standing bond of trust between policymaker and analyst. So intelligence community analytic managers often play the role of analysts. Directors of central intelligence have in the past acted as the top analyst in their dealings with presidents. Sometimes they have been right. Director of Central Intelligence John McCone got it right in his assessment that the Soviet Union was deploying ballistic missiles in Cuba, though his analysts disagreed. Sometimes they have been wrong:

- McCone subsequently blew the call when he concluded in 1962 that the real source of the threat in Vietnam was China. He overruled his leading analyst and head of the Board of National Estimates, Sherman Kent. Kent believed that the real threat was in the villages of Vietnam and Laos, and that a military victory was not possible.
- Director of Central Intelligence Stansfield Turner concluded that Ayatollah Khomeini was "just another Iranian politician" and that business as usual would occur after the Iranian revolution. His analysts, who had a quite different view, got it right.[8]

So the lesson for the manager is to stay close to the customer but not become a roadblock between customers and analysts. The analysts usually are closer to the raw material and spend more time than the manager does in thinking about the problem.

Constraints on Sharing

Sharing and collaboration are two different things; but collaboration relies on some form of sharing. Stung by criticism of their failure to share intelligence prior to the 9/11 attack, the top leaders of the U.S. intelligence community committed to better sharing of intelligence and in many areas have made good progress. But, in addition to some good reasons not to share, as discussed in chapter 1, countervailing forces exist that make sharing difficult, even risky for national security. They mostly derive from the mantra of all intelligence collectors: *protect sources and methods*. Sharing requires openness. And openness can result in the loss of sources and methods. In 2010 the United States had to deal with the WikiLeaks breach, when thousands of classified and sensitive U.S. government documents were posted on the web. The incident resulted in extensive damage to U.S. interests worldwide. Many of the leaked documents were U.S. diplomatic cables that made politically embarrassing comments about foreign government leaders. In 2013 an even more damaging compromise occurred: An NSA contractor, Edward Snowden, began releasing to news media classified material that he had downloaded from NSA's classified network. The resulting damage caused the pendulum to swing back in some cases, toward protection at the expense of sharing.

There also exist less noble reasons to avoid sharing. David Cohen, formerly CIA's deputy director for operations, once observed: "[T]here's no such thing as information sharing; there's only information trading."[9] Every analysis manager should understand that she must find a way to work with collection and other analysis organizations that hoard their most valuable information. The more important the information becomes, the more value it has for a controlling organization. As a result, organizations tend to place emphasis on protecting the valuable information—perhaps even more so than on protecting sources and methods.

Let's illustrate this point with an admittedly extreme example. Suppose that the United States had a HUMINT source in an African country—a low-level mail clerk in the country's economic ministry. The source's material would primarily become economic intelligence, and the source's reporting would likely be classified no higher than "Secret."

Now suppose one of the many letters coming into the ministry, and copied by the mail clerk as part of his espionage job, concerns a plot to assassinate the president of the United States. The letter from the plot leader is a request for a ministry employee to help provide cover for the plotters' travel arrangements. It is unlikely that the U.S. intelligence community would release this information at the "Secret" level; it would probably be highly classified and receive extremely limited distribution. Yet the sources and methods remain unchanged; only the substance is different. The increased classification level has nothing to do with protecting the source.

Information sharing is a workable concept in a small integrated intelligence organization where a high level of mutual trust exists. In the large and bureaucratic organizations that exist in major countries, information sharing encounters difficulties; the disincentives can sometimes outweigh the pressures to share from intelligence leadership.

Preparing the Analytic Product

Developing the analytic product is done most effectively by a rapid prototyping approach that starts with the issue decomposition and expands an outline into a final report or briefing. The type and the format of the presentation are shaped by the preferences of the customer or customer class; generally, a short, to-the-point, graphically oriented presentation works best. Appendix III describes the essential elements of the product and discusses how to develop it.

Reviewing the Analytic Product

Even when an analyst is solely responsible for the analytic product, one collaborative mechanism that managers must enforce is that of peer review. Professionals from almost any field generally don't like peer review, even while acknowledging that it helps the quality of the final product. Analysts are no exception. One of the reasons that current intelligence work often is more appealing to analysts is that it usually has little or no peer review.

However, peer review is an essential part of in-depth analysis. Analysts must make conclusions based on judgments. That requires going beyond the facts, and any two analysts are likely to come to different conclusions. Peer review provides a sanity check on these conclusions and on the tradecraft used to reach them.

Peer review, when done properly, is important for another reason: The criticism and resultant rethinking of issues consistently improves the final product. In chapter 4, we noted the flawed premise about criticism in brainstorming (that it inhibits original thinking). The same result occurs in peer review; it produces original ideas and fresh approaches as well as identifying weaknesses in analytic arguments.

Management review is also necessary, up to a point. One level of management review is almost mandatory in both all-source and single-source analysis. Even fusion center or current intelligence products usually have one level of management review. But it's also fairly common for the analytic product to receive additional upper-level reviews. One motivation for multiple management reviews is to protect the agency's reputation for quality analysis.

Whether the additional management reviews add value is a contentious issue. Analysts sometimes receive contradictory guidance from multi-level reviews. Studies of the problem have suggested that multiple reviews are frustrating for analysts without necessarily being worthwhile.[10]

Evaluating the Analytic Product

Evaluating analyst performance requires a careful design process upfront. A manager should always strive to create positive incentives and avoid creating perverse incentives. In the case of intelligence analysis, we have the same challenge that recurs in assessing collection performance. Specifically, we want to avoid an evaluation process that either measures the wrong things or encourages analysts to "game" the system. For example, it's relatively easy to count the number of reports produced. It's hard to assess their quality, so too many managers evaluate based on counting.

Products are often evaluated based on looking backward: Did the assessment fit with how things turned out? But perceptions of analytic success and failure can be quite different from reality. Occasionally, the analysis is flawed, but the analyst simply gets lucky. Sometimes, as noted in the previous section, the analysis is right on target, but it fails anyway because of extrinsic developments. Sometimes, the perception overrides reality. The U.S. intelligence community consistently gave strategic warnings about the Soviet Union's instability during its final year of existence. Nevertheless, the abrupt end to the Cold War took U.S. policymakers by surprise and led to the widespread perception of an intelligence failure.[11] So, evaluation of analytic performance based on outcomes is misleading.

Customer feedback is another approach that has been used, but like the others, it also has downsides. Customers frequently have embraced flawed analytic products that fit with their world view and rejected products that disagreed with that view. Appendix I provides an example of each type. Moreover, as noted elsewhere in this book, national leaders who exercised autocratic control over their intelligence services, such as Saddam Hussein, Stalin, and Hitler, usually wound up with analysts who were sycophants.

The most useful evaluation approaches are based on measuring the product against some type of standard. Standards for analytic tradecraft have been established informally in most of the world's major intelligence services. Within the U.S. intelligence community, formal standards were established in 2007.[12] But who evaluates the product based on the standard? Peer and management reviews, discussed earlier, are the usual tools for measuring against standard for day-to-day analytic products. They have the disadvantage of being internal reviews, so they can be challenged as lacking objectivity. External evaluations are expensive and time consuming, so they are reserved for investigating widely publicized "failures" such as 9/11 and the Iraqi WMD NIE. And external evaluators typically do not possess knowledge or understanding of the internal organizational workings that would provide accurate perspective on evaluative issues.

Another type of product evaluation is that done by all-source analysts who evaluate the value of collection. Analysts bring an objective point of view to this type of evaluation; their only vested interest is in better-quality raw intelligence to work with. Most U.S. collection agencies provide ample opportunity for evaluative feedback in electronic form. Smart analysts will take advantage of every opportunity to provide such feedback, especially positive feedback, and smart managers encourage their analysts to do so. It usually ensures that the collector will continue to provide relevant raw intelligence on the topic.

Summary

At the beginning, the analyst must identify the customers of an intelligence product. The customers may be defined by the organizational structure—as is typical in military units. In national, law enforcement, and competitive intelligence, the primary customer may be more difficult to identify.

Major analysis projects start with some sort of project plan. Plans may go by many different names and appear in many different formats, but they should include, at a minimum, an issue definition, a précis, and a research plan. The project plan brings organization and discipline to the analysis effort, and it can be shared with peers and partner organizations that can contribute to the analysis process.

Because analysis is increasingly a collaborative process, analysts should be adept at teamwork. They should be familiar with the culture, processes, and problems of their team partners. Specifically, analysts should understand the information collectors and work closely with them to obtain intelligence and evaluate the collection process. They should maintain a network of fellow analysts within and outside the agency where a commonality of interests exists. A rich set of collaborative tools has been developed to aid in the process. In the United States, most of these tools rely on a classified version of the Internet for sharing intelligence and ideas, and for creating and sharing target models.

Although analysts often are uncomfortable with peer and management reviews, these reviews consistently improve the final product. Product evaluation also improves the quality of intelligence, but being retrospective, it is a longer term process.

There have been numerous attempts to evaluate the analytic product. Counting the number of reports, comparing the assessments with the outcomes, and customer feedback all have their flaws, and most can be "gamed" by astute analysts and managers. Managerial and peer evaluations against established standards seem to work better.

Notes

1. ABC News, "Director of National Intelligence James Clapper Not Briefed on London Arrests before TV Interview," December 22, 2010, http://abcnews.go.com/US/director-national-intelligence-james-clapper-briefed-london-arrests/story?id=12458010.
2. Rob Johnson, *Analytic Culture in the U.S. Intelligence Community* (Washington, D.C.: Center for the Study of Intelligence, CIA, 2005), 70.
3. See an example in the National Intelligence Estimate, "Iran: Nuclear Intentions and Capabilities," November 2007, http://www.dni.gov/press_releases/20071203_release.pdf.
4. Ibid.
5. Thomas Fingar, "Analysis in the U.S. Intelligence Community: Missions, Masters, and Methods," in *Intelligence Analysis: Behavioral and Social Scientific Foundations*, ed. Baruch Fischoff and Cherie Chauvin (Washington, D.C.: National Academies Press, 2011), 16.
6. Ibid.
7. Ibid.
8. CIA Center for the Study of Intelligence, "Watching the Bear: Essays on CIA's Analysis of the Soviet Union," Conference, Princeton University, March 2001, http://www.cia.gov/cis/books/watchingthebear/article08.html, 18.
9. Christopher Dickey, "The Spymaster of New York," *Newsweek*, January 31, 2009, http://www.newsweek.com/2009/01/30/the-spymaster-of-new-york.html.
10. Committee on Behavioral and Social Science Research to Improve Intelligence Analysis for National Security et al., *Intelligence Analysis for Tomorrow: Advances from the Behavioral and Social Sciences* (Washington, D.C.: National Academies Press, 2011), 77.
11. Ibid.
12. Director of National Intelligence, *Intelligence Community Directive No. 203*, June 21, 2007, 3–4.

18

A Systems View: Structure

Intelligence is best done by a minimum number of men and women of the greatest possible ability.[1]

R. V. Jones, assistant director of
Britain's Royal Air Force Intelligence
Section during World War II

Intelligence organizations have to create an effective mechanism for getting information from the source to all those who need it—a requirement that is endemic in the intelligence business. The process involves moving information from a source (which is collection driven) to a specific topic (which is customer driven). R. V. Jones observed that this transition is problematic, noting, "Whereas information enters the intelligence machine by source, it has to leave it by subject; it is this changeover inside the machine that causes all the difficulty."[2]

This is really a process challenge, but the U.S. intelligence community repeatedly tries to deal with it structurally. The structure largely determines how information flows within the system, from source to customer. This chapter describes some of the top-level structures that have been attempted and then focuses on the most important element of any of the different structures: the intelligence analyst. It then deals with analytic teams, including both ad hoc and formal teams such as fusion centers and joint intelligence centers.

Topical or Regional Structure?

An upfront structural question is, Should the analytic unit be organized along topical (functional) or regional (geographic) lines? A topical structure would have separate subunits responsible for political issues, economic issues, military issues, weapons intelligence, counternarcotics, counterterrorism, and so on. A regional structure would have subunits handle all these topics for specific regions such as Europe, East Asia, and Africa, with subordinate units responsible for countries such as France, China, and Zimbabwe. Each structure has advantages, and each leaves gaps, includes overlaps, or both. The top managers of all-source analysis groups such as the CIA's Directorate of Intelligence or the State Department's Bureau of Intelligence and Research have tried different versions of these two structures over the years, frequently settling for a hybrid of the two. An office having responsibility for East Asia, for example, might have divisions responsible for political and economic analysis for the region but choose to have a separate division focused only on China because of its importance in the region.

Even a small intelligence unit may struggle with structural issues. A law enforcement intelligence unit might, for example, have its analysts specialize in narcotics, gangs, human trafficking, white-collar crime, and funds-laundering topics. But a single organized criminal group is sometimes involved in all five of these activities. Should a separate intelligence analyst be assigned responsibility for that criminal group? However the intelligence unit is organized, analysts will have to share information. Furthermore, it often is most efficient in regional law enforcement intelligence units, for example, to have a specific analyst responsible for acquiring raw intelligence from a source (for example, interviewing a local police chief) to serve all needs of the entire unit. This avoids having the local police chief being pestered by questions from many analysts. But this approach works only if the interviewer shares the results with *all* analysts who need the information. Going back to the earlier Jones quote, analytic responsibility for the product is divided by subject, and a single source will provide information that covers several subjects.

At the very top level of U.S. intelligence, the DNI deals with the structural problem by using what once were termed *mission managers* and currently are called national intelligence managers, or NIMs. The WMD Commission report recommended that the intelligence community organize around mission managers who would be responsible for developing strategies against specific targets. The targets could be topical (for example, counterterrorism or counterproliferation) or regional (China, Iran).[3] The mission manager approach has been adopted, and these managers serve as the focal point for all aspects of intelligence on their issue or region—developing collection and analysis strategies to address current and expected future needs. In setting up his national intelligence managers during 2011, DNI James Clapper opted for a regional set that included Africa, East Asia, Eurasia, Europe, the Near East, South Asia, the Western Hemisphere, and Iran. Alongside them were functional managers of counterterrorism, counterproliferation, counterintelligence, cyber, economics, military issues, science and technology, and threat finance.[4]

Unfortunately, there appears to be no way to avoid an overlap of responsibilities. Even a casual glance at the above list makes apparent the potential for overlap and turf battles in this division of responsibilities. The counterterrorism NIM and the Iran NIM, for example, have common targets and interests and cooperate to ease the risk of duplication.

The result is that intelligence units, in the United States and elsewhere, often work within a management structure that is familiar in the business world—a *matrix* structure, where analysts have two reporting lines—one functional, one geographic.

The Analyst

The most essential element of the structure is the intelligence analyst. The analyst's primary job, as described in chapter 3, is to be the gatekeeper of information and the manager of the target-centric process. The WMD Commission gave a detailed explanation of this role in its report:

> Analysts are the link between customers and the Intelligence Community. They provide a conduit for providing intelligence to customers and for conveying the needs and interests of customers to collectors. This role requires analysts to perform a number of functions. Analysts must assess the available information and place it in context. They must clearly and concisely communicate the information they have, the information they need, the conclusions they draw from the data, and their doubts about the credibility of the information or the validity of their conclusions. They must understand the questions policymakers ask, those they are likely to ask, and those they should ask; the information needed to answer those questions; and the best mechanisms for finding that information. And as analysts are gaining unprecedented and critically important access to operations traffic, they must also become security gatekeepers, revealing enough about the sources for policymakers to evaluate their reporting and conclusions, but not enough to disclose tightly-held, source-identifying details.[5]

This job can be thought of as having three phases: information acquisition (building the model), analysis, and customer acceptance. Exceptional analysts need to call on different personal qualities to shepherd along each phase. And, as we have said repeatedly, they also need a good understanding of the characteristics of intelligence customers and how to best present intelligence results to win acceptance from those customers. The three most salient personal qualities of analysts include objectivity, broad perspective, and good instincts. These qualities, along with some guidance on recruiting and developing analysts, are described in the sections that follow.

Objectivity

It may seem obvious that to remain objective is the first commandment of credible analysts. They know that a search for evidence to support preconceived notions has no place in intelligence. They know that observations cannot be discarded because they are contrary to expectations. In fact, they know that their goal is to function like physical scientists. In the physical sciences, astronomers are not emotionally affected when they find that stars follow a certain development pattern. They do not think that this is good or bad; it simply is.

Typically, however, intelligence analysts are in a position more like that of social scientists. Their thinking may be complicated by an inability to isolate their own emotional reactions from the problem being studied. Put simply, they *care* about the outcome. But if analysts wish to assess foreign events, for example, they must put aside personal opinions about war, poverty, racism, police brutality, and government corruption, to name a few tough ones. For instance, "political corruption" is a normal way of life in many areas of the world. It is neither good nor bad in an absolute sense; it is merely the accepted standard of conduct. Analysts who are given the task of assessing the international narcotics trade cannot begin with the view that the traffickers are opportunistic scum. Instead, they must practice empathy, or the concept of putting themselves in the shoes of the target. Empathy is a tool of objectivity in that it allows analysts to check their biases. Analysts must try to see things from the traffickers' perspective—they are a group of small businesspeople working to uphold the free enterprise system in the face of excessive government regulation. (As an aside, a well-rounded analyst who has read Machiavelli might find it helpful to reread him, this time from an analyst's vantage point. One of Machiavelli's major strengths was his ability to assess conduct without being hindered by value judgments.)

In the business world, the challenge for analysts to keep an objective attitude reaches new heights. Competitive intelligence analysts often must make recommendations without specifically telling decision makers what to do.[6] Intelligence professionals in government and in the military service would undoubtedly be amused at the suggestion that they should offer advice such as, "General, you should deploy your units to the positions I have indicated," or "Madam Secretary, it would be prudent if your ambassador in Botswana initiated a dialogue with the rebel alliance." Recommendations such as these are career enders for government intelligence officers, who typically have neither the policymaking nor the operations experience—nor the current knowledge of operational factors—needed to give such advice. Conversely, in many companies, business intelligence analysts have both the operations expertise and the credibility to make operational recommendations. It remains a valid question whether government intelligence officers should be more like business intelligence analysts—qualified to make judgments on policy or operational issues. In a collaborative environment that includes customers, making such judgments is likely to happen. By contrast, when analysts make recommendations, they find objectivity tougher to maintain.

Broad Perspective

Successful intelligence analysts have an inherent inquisitiveness and lifelong interest in learning about subjects and ideas that may seem to have little to no relevance to their current subject area. Relevant and wide-ranging reading on other cultures, economies, military traditions, religious and political doctrines, philosophy, and the like gives analysts a breadth of substantive competence that will serve them well throughout their careers.

A long-term, historical perspective is essential in making assessments of a culture, a government, an industry, a system, or a technology. Each of these concerns, even technology, has a long history. With few exceptions, the policymakers or executives who control government organizations, military forces, and industries today earned their credentials fifteen to thirty years ago. Their organizations, thus, are bureaucracies shaped by the worldview of key controlling individuals who likely have held on to biases based on the lessons learned through earlier experience. Analysts cannot comprehend the present shape of the organization—public or private—or estimate its likely evolution and organizational behavior without an understanding of what has happened during its history. One cannot understand the 1989 crackdown by the People's Republic of China on student demonstrators in Tiananmen Square, and the average Chinese person's view of the crackdown, without understanding the Cultural Revolution and its impact on the Chinese people.[7] And it is important for analysts to learn a nation's history as its people teach the subject—which may be quite different from what the analysts were taught.[8]

An historical perspective requires more knowledge than that of the past few decades. The study of organizations, management, and decision making has gone on for over a century, and some of the most pertinent observations on these subjects trace back to the thinking of Machiavelli, Sun Tzu, and Plato.

Good Instincts

Analysts with the right instincts are very special people. Walter Laqueur described them in his book:

> Some people seem to possess an insight that cuts through the maze of history-making facts and factors to bare those that exert an overwhelming force. They select valid assumptions that lead to valid conclusions.[9]

Gordon Negus, an electrical engineer and former executive director of the Defense Intelligence Agency, described intelligence analysis as "the art of guessing right"—which sounds like the abductive approach to reasoning that was mentioned in chapter 9. Negus died in 2007. In a lecture that he prepared but never presented, he added that we in the intelligence business had guessed wrong on too many critical issues.[10]

The "art of guessing right" doesn't appeal to some in the intelligence business; it's a reminder that intelligence analysis is both art and science. But the term has a basis in experience. Many discoveries, many advances in science and engineering, came because some gifted and experienced scientist or engineer had a flash of insight. This sudden flash is not truly a guess; it is often simply the culmination of long-standing focus on the problem, allowing the subconscious to bring forth the idea.[11] We don't always understand how it happens. The important thing is that it does happen, and gifted analysts have the ability to guess right. Steve Jobs, the late founder and guiding light of

Apple Inc., was described by his biographer and by newspaper columnists as a genius. In fact, he could be described more accurately as an analyst with a special talent for guessing right.

Recruiting and Developing Analysts

If as a manager you have or hire analysts who possess the talents described above—gatekeeper and process manager, with the ability to cut through the mass of incoming material and make good judgments—you are fortunate indeed. You may not be able to pay them what they're worth, but you should try. You don't want a large stable of analysts; you want just a few of the best there are, as the quote that leads off this chapter suggests. Or as a former director of the National Intelligence Council once noted, it is "counterproductive and fruitless to try to solve the problem by narrowing the scope of portfolios and adding more analysts. What is required is better understanding of complex problems, not a large contingent of analysts who know more and more about less and less."[12]

You'd like to hire analysts who fit the profile. Few will do so at first, so it's important to determine whether they already possess the characteristics that cannot be developed on the job. For example, substantive knowledge (for example, historical and political area knowledge) can be developed over time. Insatiable curiosity and cognitive ability cannot; you either have them or you don't.

You also want to have analysts who are team players. The collaborative nature of the target-centric approach makes this a vital characteristic. However, some of the best analysts have been brilliant but abrasive loners. This leads to a tradeoff that becomes a test of your management skill; you want their brilliance, but to get it you somehow have to deal with the crises brought on by their abrasive nature.

Once you've hired a new analyst, you have to work closely with him or her in the development phase. Even gifted entry-level analysts take some time to learn to do in-depth intelligence reports, because the skill set is not so easily learned. It involves both research and writing skills. Getting analysts to write solid analytic reports and to use collection assets effectively takes years, even for the most talented. The CIA's rule of thumb is that it takes about three years to develop a journeyman analyst—one who has acquired the skills both to think through a complex topic and to write an acceptable research report on the topic. (Some analysts never do make the transition, instead staying at the entry level and doing current intelligence.)

You have to provide opportunities for learning on the job (for example, socialization, mentoring, cross-training, job rotation, and career progression paths). And you have to encourage analysts to interact with counterparts in other organizations.

There's a natural tendency to see training as an impediment to getting the job done, or to provide it only to entry-level personnel. The military services correctly see training as a career-long process; too many intelligence managers view training as unnecessary for their veteran analysts. But it's as much a part of the job as preparing analyses or providing guidance to intelligence collectors.

A valuable development experience for mid-level and senior analysts is a rotational assignment with an operational or policy organization. In the United States, that often means assignments with the NSC staff, the State Department, or military units. Rotational assignments to other analytic units are also invaluable; they help break down the barriers that hinder collaborative efforts. As with training, managers may be inclined to keep their most valuable analysts on the job; but the downside of that perspective is that the less effective analysts get the broad exposure and career advancement opportunities.

Finally, successful unit managers understand this: For good analysts, the simple opportunity to tackle tough and relevant problems is usually enough. But all analysts need (often live for) professional recognition and encouragement, and it is the manager's job to provide both.

Analytic Teams

Analysis team efforts have advantages: You learn from each other and take advantage of a wider range of expertise. In dealing with the complex problems that must be solved, the inputs from a diverse group often are essential. And team efforts promote better information sharing and coordination of the final product.

The need for team analysis efforts has been spurred by a DNI inventory of intelligence community assets, which found that

> [m]any agencies had developed small elements to address subjects tangential to their core missions because they did not know where relevant expertise could be found elsewhere in the IC [intelligence community], could not "task" analysts elsewhere to provide necessary input, or could not have confidence in the quality of the work done by people they did not know and could not evaluate on their own.[13]

The DNI inventory also found that

> the IC had more expertise than suggested by staffing patterns *if* it could find a way to tap what people already knew, even if that knowledge was from previous assignments, and *if* the IC found a way to enable analysts to collaborate at a distance. The goal was to facilitate voluntary formation of "virtual" teams with the advantages of proximity to key customers and synergistic benefits from collaboration. Realizing the potential benefits inherent in this vision required overcoming a number of technical, policy, and cultural obstacles.[14]

All analysis projects are, or should be, team efforts. It is the premise of this book that collaboration is the only practical future for a relevant and successful intelligence community; and the analyst functions as the project manager for the team.

This trend to team efforts is not unique to intelligence. Studies have shown that scientific advances and major engineering projects are increasingly the result of team efforts; the day of lone researchers and inventors such as Einstein and Edison has passed.[15] There are good reasons why: The problems we must solve in all fields have become far more complex, researchers have had to become more specialized to deal with the details, and the most important problems lie at the intersections between multiple disciplines. Collaboration has become the norm, and in intelligence it has become essential.

Team efforts also have their costs: They always take longer to finish. Managing across organizational lines is always a challenge, even more so when the participants bring their organizational biases along with them. Analysts' different writing styles and their use of different nomenclatures can detract from the final product. The payoff is worth the extra time and effort.

Organizing the Analysis Team

An analysis team begins with a strong team leader who has the responsibility, authority, and ability to execute the analysis effort. That's necessary, but not sufficient. No team leader is brilliant or experienced enough to go off and deal with complex issues alone. It is not even possible to assemble a team of brilliant people to go off and deal with the issues, because the moment they "go off," they leave behind the stakeholders whose input is essential. The team leader therefore must understand and be committed to the *inclusive* nature of complex problem solving. That implies, for example, understanding the natural disinclination for one team member to confront or criticize another—the disincentive being strongest when a junior analyst must confront a veteran.

Again, a target-centric approach helps combat this problem by emphasizing the benefit of sharing information and expertise among stakeholders with the expectation of differing perspectives and points of view. In this way, the approach breaks down the long-held compartmental barriers that collectors, analysts, and customers have traditionally experienced. Instead, all stakeholders contribute to the target model, which is an initial representation of the intelligence problem. The model remains accessible to all the participants and available for their input as it evolves. Keeping them involved in your work gets you better responsiveness from collectors and better acceptance of the final product by your customers.

On large and complex studies, or when strongly differing opinions are expected, such as in national intelligence estimates (NIEs), a facilitator can help keep the team in the process, help with analytic tools, and free the analytic team leader to provide leadership.

Customers

Stakeholders in a team analysis effort clearly include the customers of intelligence. The team leader must be capable of fostering active participation by the customer community.

Customers, though part of the team, may or may not be physically present in the team deliberations. U.S. and British intelligence services have two distinctly different approaches to the structure for producing their top-level estimates. In Britain, the process is much like that outlined above: Estimates are prepared by a group that comprises both intelligence officers and policymakers.[16] In the United States, NIEs are prepared in meetings comprised exclusively of intelligence officers. Still, though the policymakers themselves are absent, their preferences are usually known and presented. Jack Davis referred to this phenomenon as the "elephant in the room."[17] The drawback to the U.S. approach is that, unlike the British model, the policy-maker-analyst dialogue does not take place. To continue the analogy, the analysts become like the blind men of Hindustan, each perceiving the "elephant" differently.

Therefore, analysts should expect and even insist that customers be a part of the team. Customer participation increases the risk of politicization, but their absence from the process increases the risk that the product will not be useful. Active participation by the customer community improves the quality of the analysis and support for the results. Research has determined that when customers are integrated into the study process, their assistance can be invaluable and their resulting confidence in the product makes it more likely to be used.[18]

Collectors

The collectors of intelligence also are an important part of the team. They can then better understand the overall picture and help to fill future intelligence gaps. They also have a stake in how you use the product of their efforts and can provide valuable perspectives on the quality of specific reports. SIGINT representatives have long been participants in the NIE process because of the unique insights they provide on SIGINT reporting. Partly as a result of the missteps in the Iraqi WMD NIE, HUMINT staffs now participate as members of the NIE team.

External Sources

Experts from academia and industry are often drawn in to analytic teams where their unique expertise can help the analysis process. If external consulting or contract help is to be used, a decision needs to be made about whether to use a single contractor organization or a contractor team. The team approach provides the opportunity to employ the range of expertise offered by various companies. But, multiple contractors can create an administrative burden for the team leader and management inefficiencies for the study. The leader must track each contractor's activities against the project plan and must perform more coordination with, and oversight of, the team than would be the case with a single contractor.

Ad Hoc Teams

Ad hoc teams are pulled together for a limited time, to address specific high-priority or very difficult problems. For example, in 2015, the ongoing conflicts in Syria and Ukraine, and the negotiations with Iran on nuclear proliferation, all would likely be the focus of ad hoc teams created in several NATO intelligence organizations.

Ad hoc teams may be organized formally, as are the NIE teams in the United States. Appendix I contains two examples of NIEs. One of the better known examples is historical, and it involved *two* ad hoc teams: the Team A/Team B National Intelligence Estimate.

In 1976 the President's Foreign Intelligence Advisory Board and DCI George H. W. Bush responded to critics who argued that the U.S. intelligence community had underestimated Soviet military power and misinterpreted Soviet strategic intentions. They created an independent analysis team, known as Team B, to provide an alternative NIE on Soviet strategic objectives and capabilities.[19] This effort was unusual in that the B team was comprised mostly of experts from outside the intelligence community.

What became known as the Team A/Team B exercise also is one of the best-known examples of competitive analysis. The effort engendered considerable resentment among the community analysts who had prepared the Team A estimate. Team B produced an alarming picture of Soviet capabilities and intentions that most observers subsequently concluded was neither objective nor accurate.

Analysis efforts besides NIEs require an ad hoc analysis team. Analysts and their managers in national, law enforcement, and competitive intelligence often must manage teams drawn from different organizations.

Most ad hoc teams are *virtual*, pulled together online for a short time and focused on a current issue. Virtual teams are commonly used by fusion centers (discussed next) and joint intelligence centers to draw in outside expertise.

Fusion Centers

A special category of current intelligence is the "fast synthesis" of data to support ongoing tactical operations and to support quick-reaction additional collection. This form of synthesis—often called *fusion*—differs from normal synthesis and analysis only in the emphasis: Time is of the essence. Fusion is aimed at using all available data sources to develop a more complete picture of a complex event. The target model exists, and the analyst's job is to fit in any new data. Analysts work only with the incoming data plus anything that they have in an immediately accessible database or in their memory, or possibly by tapping into a virtual team. Fusion is commonly used by intelligence analysts when time is the critical element—such as in support of military operations, crisis management, law enforcement, and similar direct operations.

The need for this type of information domestically has led to the creation of *fusion centers* to support U.S. homeland security. A fusion center is a continuing collaborative effort by two or more organizations to share information that is of common interest, including intelligence and operational information. They accept incoming streams of information from the private sector and from federal, state, local, and tribal governments.[20] The centers also access a range of public and private databases to gather and analyze information. They correlate and analyze this intelligence. They then provide information to patrol officers, detectives, management, and other participating personnel and agencies on specific criminals, crime groups, and criminal activities. Most have been set up to support counterterrorism or counternarcotics efforts. They usually generate their own intelligence products, providing overviews of terrorist or other crime groups, analysis of trends, and other items of information for dissemination to participating agencies.[21]

The original objective of the centers was to assess the risks to people, economic infrastructure, and communities from both natural disasters and terrorist attacks and to enable actions by first responders. Over time, the focus of many centers has evolved to support state and local law enforcement by providing criminal intelligence and even to address all types of hazards.

During the past decade, fusion centers have proliferated in the United States to support law enforcement. Most of the seventy-two state and regional fusion centers were created after the 9/11 attacks. The idea of intelligence-led policing had developed some cachet, and fusion centers were a natural outcome of the idea.

The new fusion centers were modeled loosely on another type of "fusion center" that had functioned successfully for some time: the High Intensity Drug Trafficking Area (HIDTA) structure. Since 1990, twenty-eight areas have been designated as HIDTAs across the country. A HIDTA is structured to coordinate law enforcement counterdrug and countergang efforts across all levels of government within a given geographic area. In this respect, it functions within its area of responsibility much like the DNI's Crime and Narcotics Center does internationally.

These centers deal with information from many sources, not simply intelligence sources. Most of the centers have statewide jurisdiction and are operated by law enforcement groups, typically state police or state bureaus of investigation.

Similar fusion centers exist in other countries. The United Kingdom, for example, created the Joint Terrorism Analysis Centre in 2005, with the role of providing threat warnings and in-depth reports on terrorism trends, networks, and capabilities.

There is no one model for how a fusion center should be constructed. Ideally, it might function like the Symantec war room described in chapter 2. In contrast to the Symantec model, though, state fusion centers must deal with more diverse sources and types of data and a wider breadth of threats. State fusion centers have been criticized for doing very little true fusion—defined as analysis of disparate data sources, identification of intelligence gaps, and pro- active collection of intelligence against those gaps, which could contribute to prevention. They have also raised concern because of their potential for viola- tions of privacy and civil liberties.[22]

Joint Intelligence Centers

Military commanders maintain fusion centers in their theaters of opera- tion, though these centers usually don't use the word "fusion," instead having names such as joint intelligence center. The centers often are set up to support multinational operations. The former Combined Joint Intelligence Operations Center-Afghanistan is an example.

Both fusion centers and joint intelligence centers present a special man- agement challenge. The typical fusion or watch center environment is not conducive to producing in-depth intelligence. The physical setup is intended to facilitate verbal communication. It is difficult to focus on a task for more than a few minutes without interruption. Analysts need the balance of peri- odically stepping back and thinking about their area of responsibility—which requires escaping, at least for a while, the watch center environment.

Summary

One has to consider the intelligence unit's structure and its relationship with both collectors and customers. The most common structures are by topic (for example, political, economic, counterterrorism), by region (a geographic division), or by some combination. Each structure has advantages, and each has the potential for gaps and overlapping responsibilities. The result often is a hybrid, or matrix, structure.

A few attributes are essential in top-rated analysts. Having the proper investigative attitude is the starting point. That is, analysts must be prepared to take an objective approach, relying on the scientific method. Ideally, they should not care about the answer to an intelligence problem when they begin an analytic effort. They should be prepared to observe and investigate the anomaly, the unexpected, or the things that simply don't fit in to the existing target model. But when the analysis is done, they often must act as an advo- cate. To do this well, analysts need a well-developed ability to express ideas orally and in writing. Whatever structure they operate in, analysts must con- stantly deal with the tradeoff of being close to the customer while maintaining objectivity.

Analysis projects are team efforts, though not necessarily the product of formal teams. Most intelligence issues require expertise from many sources, and teams provide that. Team efforts also result in better information sharing and smoother coordination of the final product. Analysts, customers, collec- tors, and external (academic and industrial) experts all can provide inputs to the analysis process.

Teams can take many forms. Ad hoc teams organized to deal with a specific issue probably are the most common. Teams are also created with an enduring mission and exist to support a specific set of customers. Fusion centers are used in the United States to support homeland security, law enforcement, and counternarcotics issues. The military services rely on joint intelligence centers to support deployed forces overseas.

Notes

1. R. V. Jones, "Scientific Intelligence," lecture to the Royal United Services Institution on February 19, 1947, *Journal of the Royal United Services Institute*, 92 (1947): 357.
2. Ibid.
3. "Report of the Commission on the Intelligence Capabilities of the United States Regarding Weapons of Mass Destruction," March 31, 2005, 19, 24.
4. Office of the Director of National Intelligence, "ODNI Mission and Vision," *ODNI's Weekly Intercept*, May 25, 2011.
5. "Report of the Commission on the Intelligence Capabilities of the United States," 416.
6. John H. Hovis, "CI at Avnet: A Bottom-Line Impact," *Competitive Intelligence Review*, 11 (third quarter 2000): 11.
7. Rob Johnson, *Analytic Culture in the U.S. Intelligence Community* (Washington, D.C.: Center for the Study of Intelligence, CIA, 2005), 76–79.
8. Martin Petersen, "The Challenge for the Political Analyst," http://www.csi.cia/studies/vol47 no1/article05/html.
9. Walter Laqueur, *The Uses and Limits of Intelligence* (Piscataway, N.J.: Transaction, 1993), 53.
10. Gordon Negus, unpublished papers, 2007.
11. Hans Christian von Baeyer, *The Fermi Solution* (Portland, Ore.: Random House, 1993), 128.
12. Thomas Fingar, "Analysis in the U.S. Intelligence Community: Missions, Masters, and Methods," in *Intelligence Analysis: Behavioral and Social Scientific Foundations*, ed. Baruch Fischoff and Cherie Chauvin (Washington, D.C.: National Academies Press, 2011), 12.
13. Ibid., 20.
14. Ibid., 22.
15. Jonah Lehrer, "Groupthink," *The New Yorker*, January 30, 2012, 23.
16. Michael Herman, *Intelligence Power in Peace and War* (Cambridge, U.K.: Cambridge University Press, 1996), 275.
17. Quoted in Roger Z. George and James B. Bruce, *Analyzing Intelligence* (Washington, D.C.: Georgetown University Press, 2008), 167.
18. Johnson, *Analytic Culture in the U.S. Intelligence Community*, xiv–xv.
19. Douglas H. Dearth and R. Thomas Goodden, *Strategic Intelligence: Theory and Application*, 2nd ed. (Carlisle, Penn.: U.S. Army War College and Defense Intelligence Agency, 1995), 305.
20. John Rollins, "Fusion Centers: Issues and Options for Congress," CRS Report RL34070, January 18, 2008, http://www.fas.org/sgp/crs/intel/RL34070.pdf, 18–19.
21. U.S. Department of Justice, "Intelligence-Led Policing: The New Intelligence Architecture," NCJ 210681 (September 2005), 9.
22. Ibid.

19

A Network View: The Customer

Men will not look at things as they really are, but as they wish them to be.

Niccolò Machiavelli, *The Prince*

Some years ago, in a vignette that probably has been repeated many times, an elderly woman invested most of her savings in a Ponzi scheme—and of course, lost it all. When told of the loss, her investment advisor said, "Why didn't you talk to me first?" The woman's response: "Because I was afraid you'd try to talk me out of it!"

Policymakers are in a similar position. If they're contemplating a risky policy with no good choices, the last thing they need on the record is an intelligence analyst's conclusion that their choice is likely to fail. That typically makes them the most difficult customers to deal with. By contrast, policymakers respect and tend to listen to analysts who have spent the time needed to understand their policy concerns and have a demonstrated history of providing solid analytic products.

Along with policymakers, there are many other customers of intelligence analysis. Analysts should understand how the different types of customers operate and learn their perspectives on intelligence—the subject of this chapter.

Overview of Customers

This chapter focuses on the customers and purposes of analysis. It describes the intelligence requirements of various clients in government and the private sector, and the purposes and objectives that intelligence has in serving those clients.

The proper term, incidentally, is customers or clients—not consumers. Many people "consume" the intelligence that analysts produce. Only a few qualify as customers or clients, that is, persons whom the material is intended to serve.

Analysis is an addictive profession, in part because it poses frequent challenges and rewards. But it also can be frustrating, especially when after much hard work you have the answer to the intelligence problem and your customer, for his or her own reasons, doesn't listen. Recall Sherman Kent's observation from chapter 1 that analysts have three wishes: "To know everything. To be believed. And to exercise a positive influence on policy." Let's look at each of these wishes in turn.

- The overall purpose of intelligence, as noted in chapter 2, is to *reduce uncertainty* in conflict. The key point here is that analysis doesn't deal with certainty. Both new analysts and customers find that at least disconcerting, even uncomfortable. Analysis can reduce but not eliminate uncertainty, and a key role of any intelligence manager is to help the customers understand that. Analysts may wish to know everything, but they are unlikely ever to reach that fortunate state. We just try to get as close as possible.
- Being believed depends on an analyst's credibility with customers. The fulfillment of this wish can depend on the analyst's reputation and the persuasiveness of the arguments to support his or her conclusions.
- Having an influence on policy (or, more broadly, on ensuing events) depends on the importance of the analyst's findings. As Michael Herman put it, "[A]uthority with governments is greatest where there is some connection with national security, and a need to cope with organized foreign concealment or deception."[1] Similarly, in a law enforcement or business context, the authority of the intelligence analyst is greatest when there is some connection with the organization's priority concerns, and a need to cope with an opposing (criminal or commercial) entity's concealment or deception. Stated another way: Just how much does the customer *perceive* that he needs your intelligence?

The numbers of customers of intelligence have expanded steadily over the past century from the traditional two groups—national and military leadership—to include a diverse customer set. In the United States, since 9/11, law enforcement and emergency response teams, for example, have become regular customers of intelligence. In many countries, such as China and France, commercial firms are major customers of government-provided commercial intelligence because of the competitive advantage that such intelligence gives them.

The SWOT methodology for strategic planning was introduced in chapter 2. In supporting SWOT planning, intelligence analysts identify opportunities and threats. Most customers have some idea of their internal strengths and weaknesses, albeit often a distorted idea. The uncertainty usually concerns the opportunities they have and the threats they face. From nonintelligence sources, customers often have some information on opportunities and threats—but this information varies greatly by customer. State Department policymakers and businesspeople often acquire very good information in the normal course of their jobs.

National-level customers and business leaders tend to focus on the threats in looking at intelligence, because of their pervasive fear of surprise. But intelligence serves best when it can provide notice of the opportunities.

Policymakers

The elite customers of national intelligence are generally referred to as policymakers. In the United States, this group is topped by the president. High on the list are the members and staffers of the NSC, which includes executives in the major cabinet departments. The premier current intelligence product for these customers is the president's daily brief (PDB). The national intelligence estimate (NIE) then is considered to be the primary strategic intelligence product. The NIE has been criticized over the years. An evaluation by Dick Kerr, a former deputy DCI, noted,

> The fundamental question is whether national intelligence estimates add value to the existing body of analytic work. Historically, with few exceptions, NIEs have not carried great weight in policy deliberations, although customers have often used them to promote their own agendas. The time may have come to reassess the value of NIEs and the process used to produce them.[2]

Several factors shape the way that policymakers view finished intelligence reports such as NIEs. Let's look at a few of them.

How Policymakers Differ

The policy culture is quite different from the intelligence culture, and many of the problems that arise stem from the difficulty of the two cultures in understanding each other. Policymakers, though, are a diverse group; and policymakers in the political, military, economic, and scientific and technical arenas are strikingly different in how they interact with analysts. The difference derives from the differing complexity of the problems that policymakers must deal with and their understanding of those problems. Policymakers tend to fall into these general categories:

- Policymakers in the political arena are traditionally the most difficult customers. They often understand politics better than the analysts do; most of them got where they are because of their political skills. They mostly possess good interpersonal skills; they believe that they read people well, independent of cultural background. And they have their own sources of information, independent of the intelligence community.
- Customers of scientific, technical, and weapons intelligence are likely not to be able to match the technical competence of the analyst in the analyst's special field. They usually need help in understanding the implications of intelligence and, accordingly, will give the analyst's opinions a substantial amount of respect.

- Policy customers of military and economic intelligence tend to fall in between these extremes. They have a good understanding of the subject matter but are more receptive to the intelligence analyst's assessments than policy customers in the political arena.

The Policymaker Environment

All policymakers work under severe time pressures in a disruptive environment. This work environment drives their preference for succinct messages. They need good analytic insights to help them deal with complex problems, often in a short time frame. Unfortunately, this is difficult to provide in the sort of in-depth study that characterizes strategic intelligence.

Former secretary of defense Robert McNamara described the policymaker's (and executive's) environment well. Looking back at his Vietnam mistakes, he observed, "One reason [we] failed to take an orderly, rational approach . . . was the staggering variety and complexity of the other issues we faced. Simply put, we faced a blizzard of problems, there were only 24 hours in a day, and we often did not have time to think straight. This predicament is not unique to the administration in which I served or to the United States. It has existed at all times and in most countries."[3] As a result,

- Policymakers have little time to make their needs known or to dialogue with the analyst.
- The intelligence message has to be clear, unequivocal, and usually brief—on one page, or even in the title of the article.
- Policymakers have short memories. They need to be reminded of past material—past knowledge cannot be assumed. They usually don't retain copies of prior intelligence.
- They have a "today's news" orientation; they tend to prefer current intelligence, and in-depth analysis often is less valued. Long-term research has to answer a question that the policymaker considers important.

The Policymaker's Mindset

A policymaker's job is, obviously, to make policy. Many of them come to their jobs with a preconceived idea of what the policy should be. Where they don't already have one, they frequently adopt a mindset, and after they have done so, the evidence must be overwhelming to change it. Their receptivity to intelligence typically changes over time. At the start of a new administration, intelligence analysts have their greatest impact. As policy views begin to harden, it takes more and more evidence to change anyone's mind.[4] Policymakers will demand more proof if the intelligence negatively affects their agenda, and they accept a much lower standard of proof when intelligence complements their agenda.

Many policymakers want to see the raw intelligence, often to select items to support their mindsets. National Security Adviser Zbigniew

Brzezinski insisted on seeing raw intelligence, claiming that the intelligence community could not provide the broad, sweeping, bold insights into the future that he needed.[5] This policymaker or executive mindset has existed since there were leaders:

- In the sixteenth century, Philip II ruled the Spanish empire—the ultimate "hands-on" executive and typical of leaders before and since. He chose to accept incoming information from his far-flung intelligence network that supported his preconceived ideas and to avoid or ignore anything that contradicted them.[6] Like many executives since, Philip II was prone to wishful thinking.
- A CIA analyst in 1951 was studying the movements of the Chinese and had reached the conclusion that the Chinese had surreptitiously introduced their forces into North Korea. He briefed the assistant secretary of state for Far Eastern affairs, Dean Rusk, who later became secretary of state under Presidents John Kennedy and Lyndon Johnson. Rusk listened politely to the briefing, and at the end of it he said, "Young man, they wouldn't dare."[7] Weeks later, the Chinese attacked UN forces in Korea.
- Even directors of central intelligence have been trapped in mindsets. Former DCI Stansfield Turner believed that Ayatollah Khomeini was just another Iranian politician. Despite the arguments of his analysts, Turner briefed the NSC that after the overthrow of the shah of Iran, things would go on pretty much as they had before.[8]

An insidious problem with customer mindset is that the customer's subordinates (including both analysts and intermediaries) may be tempted to pander to it. It has been noted that Soviet intelligence—both the KGB and GRU—consistently told its leaders only what they wanted to hear.[9] During the Vietnam War, U.S. defense leadership did the same. Secretary of Defense Robert McNamara and the Joint Chiefs tightly controlled the flow of information to the president and had the ability to ensure that only favorable intelligence was shown to him. According to one presidential briefer, President Johnson "got very depressed and hard to handle when shown bad news."[10] In chapter 7, we examined the problems resulting from a flawed communications channel between collector and analyst. Worse problems are likely to occur when the channel between analyst and customer is corrupted.

Policymaker Priorities

National customers have an insatiable appetite for intelligence (though, as we'll discuss later, not necessarily for *strategic* intelligence). The U.S. intelligence community does not have the resources to satisfy all the demands of all its policy customers. So some sort of prioritization scheme has to be established.

In chapter 3, we noted that policymakers generally use informal channels to provide feedback about intelligence needs. But the United States does have a national-level prioritization scheme; in fact, it has had many of them. Several attempts have been made to formalize intelligence priorities since the National Security Act of 1947. The National Intelligence Priorities Framework (NIPF) is the current guidance from the DNI to the intelligence community on national intelligence priorities. It is reviewed by the NSC and approved by the president. The NIPF guides prioritization for the operation, planning, and programming of U.S. intelligence analysis and collection. The NIPF is updated semiannually. It takes the form of a matrix of countries and nonstate actors of intelligence interest versus a set of intelligence topics. It is used to guide both collection and analysis of intelligence.

Congress

Congress has become a major customer of U.S. intelligence—primarily, but not exclusively, as provided by the CIA. This role derives from Congress's responsibility to provide oversight of intelligence. Much focus of the oversight has been on collection and covert action, but analysis gets some attention.

Congress was not routinely given analytic products until the mid-1970s. From the very beginning, however, the CIA regarded Congress as an appropriate customer for its substantive analysis. Committees with a need to see such analysis might be permitted to read it, but for the most part, it was briefed to them by the DCI and other senior CIA officials. With the establishment of the Senate Select Committee on Intelligence in 1976 and the House Permanent Select Committee on Intelligence the following year, each with approved facilities for the storage of classified information, the main practical obstacle to sharing finished intelligence with Congress was removed.

More often, what provokes challenges and criticism is not what is briefed or delivered on the Hill. It is what members of Congress read in the newspapers indicating an apparent failure to predict an event that is important to U.S. interests. In chapter 17, we discussed the importance of not surprising the customer; that is true as well for Congress. Congress can handle almost anything but surprise. A study of Congress as a customer concluded, "Above all, the Agency [CIA] knew the chairmen of its subcommittees did not want to be surprised."[11]

The difficulty in having Congress as a customer for intelligence stems primarily from the tendency of individual senators and representatives to use intelligence as a weapon to affect policy that they don't like. Congress, though, usually isn't the source of leaks in the U.S. government. Leaks tend to come from administration officials who are trying to undermine policies with which they disagree. Congress can exercise its influence on policy via its budget authority.

When Congress asks a question, the intelligence community must respond and must do so on the congressional schedule. The result can be a disaster for intelligence, as noted by these authors in the case of the Iraqi WMD NIE:

> NIEs rarely represent new analysis or bring to bear more expertise than already exists in analytic offices; indeed, drafters of NIEs are usually the same analysts from whose work the NIE is drawn. Little independent knowledge or informed outside opinion is incorporated in estimative products. The preparation of an NIE therefore consists primarily of compiling judgments from previous products and debating points of disagreement. The Iraqi WMD estimate of October 2002 was characterized by all of these weaknesses and more. It was done under an unusually tight time constraint—three weeks—to meet a deadline for congressional debate. And it was the product of three separate drafters, each responsible for independent sections, drawing from a mixed bag of analytic product. Consistent application of analytic or evidentiary standards became next to impossible.[12]

Both policymakers and Congress often ask questions that are intended to get the answer that they want. This is the "Have you stopped beating your wife yet?" type of question. We introduced this type of question or, more generally, the poorly defined problem, in chapter 4 as the *framing effect*. Most policymakers and members of Congress are quite competent at applying the framing effect when posing questions, to get the answer that they want. Lawyers are experts at it. And, the mantra throughout this book is that if the question is poorly defined up front, the best subsequent analysis can't save it. Even if the customer did not deliberately frame the question, inexperienced analysts can frame it due to poor communication. A formal issue definition is needed to avoid it.

Business Leaders

Business customers of intelligence are similar to political policymakers, for many of the same reasons. They like to feel that they are in control and that they understand the competitive environment better than their business intelligence staff. They have mindsets. They face constant time pressures and are action oriented. But because they pay for their intelligence, they are more inclined to give specific guidance and pay attention to the analytic product. They are also more apt to take the analyst to task for poor outcomes.

The customers of business intelligence are highly varied in their interests and what they want from their intelligence units. In general, support to corporate strategy concerns issues such as acquisitions, identification of new markets or trends in existing markets, product development, and assessment of threats from competitors and criminal elements. Propensity to use intelligence varies by industry. The pharmaceutical industry, for example, has a tradition of relying on competitive intelligence.

As with national intelligence customers, business organizations have to prioritize their intelligence needs. A commonly used approach is one that was developed by the U.S. intelligence community during the early 1970s and subsequently abandoned. Competitive intelligence units, though, picked it up and adopted it. The technique is called key intelligence topics (KITs), which define intelligence priorities. From these are derived key intelligence questions (KIQs), which provide the questions that need to be answered to address the KITs.[13] The use of KITs/KIQs has thrived in the competitive intelligence world because it provides a structured approach to defining priorities and applying intelligence assets to those priorities, and because the resulting product has appeal for corporate executives.

Military Leadership

The U.S. military establishment has many customers for strategic intelligence, because many organizations within the Department of Defense, the Joint Chiefs of Staff, and the services conduct strategic planning. The secretary of defense might be considered the premier customer, and in the last decade, the Department of Defense has twice been headed by men who understand intelligence well: Robert Gates, a former DCI, and Leon Panetta, a former director of the CIA.

Military customers are usually clear about what they want from intelligence. Intelligence is an integral part of their world; they are used to seeing it and understand its value. Military leaders, like policymakers, vary greatly in articulating needs. All of them, to some degree, want to act as their own analysts—though policymakers are probably most inclined to do that.

The key problem that military intelligence organizations have is a tendency to overstate the strategic threat. Two factors that drive them in this direction are explained later in this chapter. Perhaps the earliest example recorded (in the Bible) occurred when the Israelites were spying out the land of Canaan. Their leader's objective (and mindset) was to conquer Canaan. His spies brought back unwelcome news, reporting, "[T]hey are stronger than we . . . there we saw the giants."[14] (This also was the earliest known example of intelligence's propensity to overstate a threat.) The Israelites wound up spending forty more years in the wilderness (there is no indication of what happened to the spies). Not surprisingly, there were no giants in the reports from the next set of spies, forty years later.

Military Operations

At the military operational and tactical levels, intelligence has a well-established role that is spelled out in military doctrine. Unit commanders are familiar with what intelligence can and cannot do. The relationship between intelligence and operations has been well settled by tradition. However, intelligence has become much more valuable to warfighters as it has gotten better. As noted in chapter 2, precision strikes require precise intelligence. The role of intelligence in warfighting has expanded steadily, and intelligence is a critical part of what is called a "revolution in military affairs."[15]

Homeland Security

The U.S. Department of Homeland Security (DHS) has been given broad responsibility for assessing both threats and risks to the U.S. homeland. In terms of the SWOT model, DHS therefore must assess weaknesses (risks) and threats. The major threats that the department focuses on are as follows:

- Domestic extremists
- International terrorists operating in the homeland or directing attacks against it
- Systemic threats such as pandemics and transnational criminal organizations

In fulfilling this role, DHS clearly is a customer for national intelligence organizations. But it also draws intelligence from state, local, and tribal officials and from the private sector.

Homeland Security is still evolving as a customer for strategic intelligence. Much of past DHS efforts have focused on the immediate threats to the homeland.[16] This appears to be changing as DHS matures and focuses more on the strategic view.

Homeland security intelligence at the tactical level typically involves providing intelligence from national collection assets to first responders. As an example, in the aftermath of Hurricane Katrina in 2005, Air Force U-2s and Air National Guard RC-26 aircraft flew photographic reconnaissance missions to support disaster relief. Since then, national-level assets have provided imagery and supporting analysis about wildfires (California, 2007) and oil spills (the 2010 Deepwater Horizon oil spill in the Gulf of Mexico).[17]

Law Enforcement

Law enforcement officials fall somewhere between policymakers and military operations customers in their use of intelligence. Some, such as counternarcotics teams, have experience in dealing with intelligence. Local police traditionally have limited experience with intelligence as it is done at the national level. Increasingly, however, as noted earlier, law enforcement groups rely on crime fusion centers (covered in chapter 18) to provide tactical intelligence, in particular; and acceptance of the value of intelligence analysis is increasing in the U.S. local law enforcement community. Fusion centers are similar in operation to the watch centers that intelligence agencies rely on. And cyber crime centers have been created in many states to bring together intelligence from national and local sources.

Up front, intelligence support to law enforcement must deal with a cultural challenge that shapes the nature of support across the strategic, operational, and tactical arenas. Intelligence in law enforcement, especially tactical intelligence, is intended to support specific investigations. It is tied to action, usually in the form of making an arrest. The challenge has been stated as follows:

> Pure law enforcement focuses on building a legal case related to a crime that already has been committed—an historical perspective with a forensic cast. A case is carefully constructed based on admissible evidence. The evidence is handled in a prescribed manner. The rules associated with chain-of-custody are designed to protect the integrity of information and reduce the pollution of evidence as much as possible. A set of procedures is followed precisely to ensure the case will be successfully prosecuted. In comparison, intelligence agencies often collect information in a way that is not admissible in a U.S. Court. Law enforcement agencies are traditionally reluctant to use such information because of the potential of it being challenged and thereby jeopardizing a case.[18]

Some law enforcement organizations are moving from this investigative focus to a strategic focus. The emphasis on intelligence-led policing (discussed in chapter 2) has encouraged this trend. Much of this strategic intelligence deals with countering organized crime, specifically drug traffic and gangs. The strategy focuses on prevention and treatment as opposed to exclusively making arrests.

The security classification of intelligence creates difficulties for law enforcement. Raw reporting from HUMINT, IMINT, or COMINT sources is typically classified at the "Secret" level or higher, and local law enforcement officials typically have no security clearance. Conventionally this problem is handled by sharing information without source details—"I can't tell you why, but. . . ." Law enforcement officers are comfortable with that; they are used to taking unverified tips. Intelligence officers also frequently use fictional sources, often creating elaborate reports to conceal the true source and get the material released at a lower classification. But this is a balancing act; you can't protect sources and mislead analysts (who will evaluate a report depending on its source). Ideally, you use a fictional source that has the same general level of credibility as the real source.

What All Customers Want

We have pointed out repeatedly that the purpose of intelligence is to reduce uncertainty in conflict. Why is it so important? Because the effect of uncertainty on leaders and decision makers is profound across the entire spectrum of conflict. Uncertainty can result in the wrong decision, but its *effect* can be even worse than that. The problem starts with a natural tendency of executives to fear loss (or bad outcomes) in their decisions.

Most executives, including policymakers, military leaders, law enforcement commanders, and business executives, are guided in decision making by a principle known as *prospect theory*. Prospect theory says that people will pay a higher price, or risk more, to prevent losses than they will to seek gains.

Executives, especially in large bureaucracies, tend to be conservative and cautious. So they tend to believe intelligence that warns of losses, and to pay less attention to intelligence that suggests opportunities for gain.

This fear of loss, combined with uncertainty, can cause paralysis in decision makers. In 2006 a study by the economists Uri Gneezy, John List, and George Wu demonstrated a phenomenon that they called "the uncertainty effect." The basic idea is this: Expected utility theory says that people make risky decisions by balancing the value of all possible outcomes. Suppose that you're betting on the flip of a coin. If it's heads, you win $1.10. However, if it comes up tails, you lose $1. Overall, the expected utility of this gamble comes out in your favor—the potential payout is ten cents bigger than the potential loss, so you should accept the bet. But studies show that the vast majority of people won't accept this gamble. The possibility of a loss (and the associated uncertainty) outweighs the temptation of the extra dime. The Gneezy study cited specific examples of how the uncertainty effect leads people to make foolish decisions.[19]

This fear of loss (or for the decision maker, fear of a bad outcome), combined with the uncertainty effect, makes a deadly combination. We in the analysis business can't cure the fear of loss, but we can reduce uncertainty and thereby help the decision maker to make better decisions.

One opportunity for gain that will always catch the policymaker's or military leader's attention is the chance to deliver an asymmetric response. Although "asymmetric response" is currently a phrase having cachet, it is an old technique in conflict, both historical and allegorical. John Milton's epic poem, *Paradise Lost*, is premised on Satan's asymmetric response after his descent into hell. Instead of conducting another futile assault on heaven, Satan contaminates God's creation on Earth. Around 1600, the Dutch conducted asymmetric warfare against the Spanish in the Netherlands; they could move by water in the rivers more quickly than the Spaniards could, in some cases reaching in two days places the Spaniards could reach only in fifteen.[20] The Dutch built their successful conflict strategy around this advantage. The "Farewell" operation, discussed in chapter 8, was a superbly crafted asymmetric response to Soviet intelligence, and the intelligence officers supporting it received commendations. Intelligence that identifies opportunities for asymmetric response will always be welcome, so it is worthwhile to highlight the opponent's weaknesses and identify his vulnerabilities.

Analyst-Customer Interaction

All of the customer types described in the preceding section have mindsets. In the close interaction that is necessary to make the target-centric approach work, the pressures to conform analysis to policy usually are subtle. Intelligence that supports policy will readily be accepted and the analyst suitably rewarded; intelligence that contradicts policy encounters skepticism. This section discusses some ways of dealing with these pressures.

The traditional intelligence cycle diagram depicted in chapter 3 has a block labeled "dissemination" (see Figure 3-1). It's yet another indicator that the cycle doesn't really work that way. The report doesn't just go out the door and the analyst's job is done. Successful analysts know that the most brilliant piece of intelligence analysis may as well have gone into the trash if it is not read by the right people in time for them to act on it. Analysts using the target-centric approach make sure that the person who initiated the request sees their report or receives a briefing—ideally, both. They get copies to other people who may have an interest in the results. They ask for feedback from as many of them as possible. They can do these things because the customer has been involved in the process from the start.

As an analyst, you have to enter the interaction at the customer's level—which can be quite different when dealing with a president's national security adviser, a combat commander, a chief executive officer, or a police captain. The effectiveness of this interaction depends critically on the level of mutual trust and confidence between the customer and the analyst; and for policymakers the road to trust can be a long, hard one. A military commander and his intelligence officer can usually establish a high degree of mutual trust; they are working together for a common goal against a common enemy. Neither is much concerned that the other will share his confidences with the enemy. The policymaker and the analyst often have neither the common goal nor the common enemy. In Washington, D.C., the policymaker's enemy is often located just down Constitution Avenue, and she has to be aware that the intelligence officer might defect to that enemy at any time. For their part, analysts constantly have to be aware that their assessments may be twisted or misconstrued to fit a policy preference.

Assuming that some level of trust can be established, the analyst next has to do two things: get the customer to understand the message, and get buy-in, that is, get the customer to accept the message and act on it, even if the message runs contrary to the customer's mindset.

Analyst as Communicator: Getting the Customer to Understand the Message

A major problem of intelligence in sixteenth-century Europe was that spies could readily acquire the information, but governments could not readily grasp its significance and act accordingly.[21] Issues are much more complex today, but the challenge for analysts is still to help customers grasp the significance of intelligence.

Effective analysts must learn the skills of effective communication, in both writing and speaking. There are procedures for writing a report or presenting a briefing, some generally recognized across professions and some that are institution specific. Analysts learn their particular intelligence organization's technical quality and style guidelines and then pay strict attention to them. Analysts who develop communication skills must follow the conventional standards for publications in their area and use terminology that their customers understand. In general, they should address problems and issues that interest customers and present results that

- Are forward looking, with detailed predictions of future developments or of major trends in the subject area and descriptions of the factors driving those trends
- Contain clearly stated conclusions supported by in-depth research and technical reasoning
- Include clear tutorials or explanations of complex technical subjects aimed at the expected customer

Moreover, analysts have to do all this *succinctly*, as discussed later in this chapter.

One cause of intelligence failure is what has been referred to as the "pathology of communication." That is, it is often hard to get the customer to believe intelligence judgments where policy issues are concerned.[22] Furthermore, analysts must convey areas of uncertainty and acknowledge gaps in their knowledge. The Iraqi WMD Commission noted, "Analysts also have a responsibility to tell customers about important disagreements within the Intelligence Community. . . . In addition to conveying disagreements, analysts must find ways to explain to policymakers degrees of uncertainty in their work."[23] To do these things without causing the customer to totally disregard the intelligence is a challenge.

The answer to both of these problems lies in the target-centric process. You have to make the customer a part of the intelligence process—which is difficult in the case of the busy policymaker. But once the customer is engaged in the process, communicating the results becomes much less difficult, and the customer is much more likely to understand and use the intelligence. The British model, discussed in chapter 18, has demonstrated that this approach works.

Finally, in preparing intelligence on technical subjects, there is always an easier way, always a clearer way, always a more accurate way to say something. Unfortunately, they are not the same way. It is almost axiomatic that if a scientific and technical intelligence report is readable and understandable, it is technically inaccurate. Only a highly skilled analyst can achieve technical accuracy and readability in one document. The answer? Don't place consuming emphasis on technical accuracy at the cost of readability. It is far more important to have the message understood and acted upon.

This demand for precision of expression is obvious in scientific and technical intelligence, but it occurs across all disciplines in intelligence, and for a good reason. Intelligence analysts often find that their words are interpreted (or misinterpreted) by policy customers to fit with the customers' preferred course of action. The response by analysts, especially in NIEs, is to make precise expression an art form that is studied and practiced. As Michael Herman noted, precision of expression is rated very highly by analysts and their managers in intelligence communities in both Britain and the United States.[24]

Analyst as Advocate: Getting Buy-In

If analysis is conducted as it has been promoted in this book, the customer will usually accept and make use of the analysis results. But if the customer does not give a positive response, the analyst must shift his or her interpersonal skills in the direction of advocacy and act as a spokesperson in support of the conclusions.

Determining requirements and needs is marketing—finding out what the customer wants. This section is about sales—getting the customer to want (and use) what you have. The proper analytic attitude is made clear throughout this text: one of objectivity. But once analysis is finished, political realities set in. Analysts must sell the product because they quickly encounter one of the fundamental principles of physics that is also a fundamental principle in intelligence (see Analysis Principle 13-2): Every action produces an equal and opposite reaction. Analysts are often tasked because there is disagreement about an issue. It follows that their results, then, will be met with skepticism or outright opposition by some.

Recognize, however, that "selling" is a controversial recommendation. The Iraqi WMD Commission report criticized this tendency, noting, "In ways both subtle and not so subtle, the daily reports seemed to be 'selling' intelligence—in order to keep its customers, or at least the First Customer, interested."[25]

Analysts nevertheless often have no choice but to advocate for the product. Ideally, intelligence would be a commodity like food—consumers buy it because they need it. In operations, especially in military operations, that tends to be the case. Unfortunately, in policy support, it is more like insurance: It has to be sold, and buyers have to be convinced that they are getting a good product. Former secretary of state Henry Kissinger, on being reminded by an analyst that he had been warned about the impending outbreak of a war, reportedly said: "You warned me, but you didn't convince me."[26] The implication could not be clearer. If policymakers expect intelligence analysts to convince them, analysts have to persuade. There is a caveat: It can be very tempting to tell the customer what he wants to hear, simply because of the customer's professional position or power, and analysts should guard against it.

One problem of looking at intelligence as sales, especially in policy matters, is that it increases the danger of telling customers what they want to hear.[27] Another challenge is that the analyst needs a good sense of timing (as every salesperson knows).[28] Nevertheless, veterans of the analysis business have consistently noted the need to conduct a sales job. As Martin Petersen, author and former CIA senior intelligence officer, observed, "The reality for intelligence officers is that we must woo them [policymakers], sell them on the need for our services, and demonstrate the value of our material daily through its timeliness and its sophistication."[29]

If the customer is a U.S. government policymaker, the analyst typically must interact with lawyers, a relationship that is much different from what analysts are accustomed to and one in which advocacy skills are useful. Lawyers prefer to use intelligence experts as they would use scientific experts in a courtroom: receiving testimony on the facts and opinions, cross-examining, determining the key issues, and deciding. The existence of a controversy and of differing opinions is essential, in the attorney's view, to establishing the truth. Lawyers are uncomfortable with a single expert opinion and with the intelligence compartmentation system. To them, the intelligence community's traditional compartmentation system for protecting sources and methods is suspect because it tends to conceal evidence and is therefore inconsistent with the goal of the discovery process in civil litigation.

Many intelligence analysts have difficulty being advocates because it goes against their objective nature. The advocacy process is an adversarial one, and the guidelines for conduct come from the legal profession, where advocacy has been raised to a fine art and where the pitfalls of improper advocacy are well understood. R. V. Jones once observed, "When an analyst participates in an adversary process he is, and should conduct himself as, and should expect to be treated as, an advocate. The rules for an adversary process are different from those of research. The former permit biased or slanted testimony and the latter are directed toward objective evaluation."[30] Jones did, however, reserve judgment as to whether the giving of "biased or slanted testimony" was compatible with honor in a scientist.[31] Most analysts would undoubtedly argue that slanting the intelligence product is unethical and is always a bad idea, even if the customer consequently makes a bad decision.

Furthermore, obtaining acceptance from any customer can often depend on the analyst's reputation. A reputation for credibility and veracity among customers is the analyst's most valuable asset. It takes a long time to build and can be lost in a day. Or, as David Landes observed, "In the public domain, a reputation for veracity is worth more than valor and intelligence, and this especially in a world of ubiquitous guile and duplicity."[32] You need to get the customer to pay attention, but you cannot sacrifice credibility or truth to do it. If you do, you might as well get out of the business. A few examples:

- The KGB was discredited in the eyes of Soviet leadership when the Farewell operation became public, and all of its materiel acquisition results were called into question.
- During the Vietnam War, the CIA discounted and underestimated the magnitude and significance of North Vietnamese support reaching the Viet Cong through Cambodia's port of Sihanoukville. Subsequent information from a newly recruited source in the Cambodian port showed

that the agency's estimates were wrong and the military's were more accurate. Afterward, whenever the CIA disagreed with the Pentagon, the White House would ask DCI Richard Helms: "What about Sihanoukville?"[33]

- The Iraqi WMD miscall damaged the credibility of several intelligence community analysis groups, especially the CIA's. It will take years to overcome that damage.

We've discussed the issues that occur when the customer must deal with uncertainty. The greatest challenge that an analyst faces, though, is when the customer *is* certain—and wrong. This is the "false or flawed model" problem, and it is pernicious because it is almost impossible for any amount of intelligence to eradicate the flawed or false model. Former NIO Paul Pillar described the cost of policymakers' false models in his book *Intelligence and U.S. Foreign Policy: Iraq, 9/11, and Misguided Reform*. Policymakers began with a mindset (a mental model) of the Mideast situation and the Saddam Hussein–Al Qaeda relationship that was wrong. They subsequently selected the fragmentary evidence that supported the flawed model (known as cherry-picking) and ignored more substantial evidence to the contrary.[34]

The Unique Defense Analysis Challenge

The intelligence analyst in a defense organization must deal with two distinctive challenges: the premium placed on warning, and the pressure to produce threat assessments that align with policy.

The Premium Placed on Warning

Defense analysts have a special obligation to give their leaders warning of hostile military actions. The failure to warn has more severe consequences than does excessive warning. As Michael Herman observed: "Underestimation is less readily forgiven than overestimation."[35] And "it is more satisfying, safer professionally, and easier to live with oneself and one's colleagues as a military hawk than as a wimp."[36]

This pressure and resulting tendency of defense analysts to overestimate a threat is well documented and policymakers compensate for it—which leads to the desensitization issue discussed in chapter 16.[37] The result, though, is that the credibility of the defense analyst suffers.

Threat Assessments That Support Funding or Policy Decisions

Herman also observed that "[t]hreat assessments have always been one of the military cards in bargaining with treasuries."[38] The Backfire bomber case of chapter 9 and the URDF-3 (particle beam weapon) case of chapter 11 are examples of such threat assessments as bargaining tools. The tendency is to overstate the threat to justify funding or to support defense policy positions. The resulting concern, as Herman noted, is that U.S. defense intelligence organizations "have always had fairly low esteem."[39]

Defense analysts have to break away from the trap of aligning assessments with funding or policy decisions by providing objective analysis even when it runs contrary to the official position of their service or of the defense establishment. It would be disingenuous, however, to say that those who have done so have always fared well. Gordon Negus, former executive director of the DIA, told of how Major General Lincoln Faurer, while director of the DIA, dealt with pressure to conform intelligence analysis to funding. When Jimmy Carter was president, the White House was considering options for dealing with the Soviet Union's improved air defense system. Two of the options were to build the B-1 bomber or to arm the existing B-52 fleet with cruise missiles. The U.S. Air Force wanted the B-1. But the DIA's intelligence indicated that the Soviets felt much more threatened by the cruise missile option, which would nullify the Soviet Union's massive air defense investment. The Air Force chief of staff told Faurer, in unequivocal terms, to revise the DIA estimate to support the Air Force position. Faurer refused and was gone from the DIA within a month.[40]

Although the pressure to conform estimates to funding or policy is especially severe in the military, it is not unique to defense. Any analytic group that is closely connected to a policy group has to deal with this problem. As noted in the introduction in chapter 1, the British Foreign and Commonwealth Office forced the intelligence process to its desired conclusion that Argentina would not attack the Falklands in 1982. Departmental intelligence units such as the State Department's Bureau of Intelligence and Research, for example, face pressure to make intelligence fit policy. The State Department has long recognized this potential problem and attempts to keep its analysts separate and organizationally shielded from the pressures of policymakers.

Appropriators also recognize this tendency, and they usually follow the rule for using an organization's test results, discussed in chapter 7. That is, if the reporting organization has a stake in what an intelligence report says, and if the report supports the organization's position or interests, the appropriator will typically view the conclusions with suspicion.

Summary

Intelligence customers vary greatly in their willingness and ability to express their needs and to make use of intelligence. Policymakers are probably the most difficult customers, because of their pressure-cooker work environment and their tendency to adopt a mindset. Customers of political intelligence are the least receptive of the group; weapons systems and scientific and technical intelligence customers are the most receptive. Military, economic, and business customers typically fall somewhere in between.

Military leaders and military operations customers understand and value intelligence. Intelligence has a well-established role, and it is becoming more important especially at the tactical unit level. Law enforcement officials also increasingly understand the value of intelligence and how to use it; their problem is that they don't usually have the clearances needed to deal with classified material. Business leaders vary in their use of intelligence, depending on the industry and their own background; but because they pay for the intelligence, they are generally inclined to make use of it.

In dealing with these customers, analysts have two challenges: to get the customer, first, to understand the message and, second, to accept and make use of the analytic results. Making intelligence understandable requires communication skills and empathy—the ability to put yourself in the place of the customer. Getting the customer to accept and make use of intelligence may require that the analyst become an advocate—a controversial and risky step. Acceptance also depends on the customer's view of the analyst's reputation.

All customers rely on intelligence to reduce uncertainty; when the level of uncertainty is high enough, customers will avoid making any decisions. As explained by prospect theory, customers tend to be more willing to accept intelligence about risks of loss or bad outcomes and less willing to make use of intelligence about opportunities for gain.

Threat assessments that support an intelligence organization's funding or policies (or those of its parent department) are usually received with skepticism—and should be. The tendency to shape analysis to support funding has been a special problem for defense intelligence organizations and often damages their credibility.

Notes

1. Michael Herman, *Intelligence Power in Peace and War* (Cambridge, U.K.: Cambridge University Press, 1996), 380.
2. Richard Kerr, Thomas Wolfe, Rebecca Donegan, and Aris Pappas, "Collection and Analysis on Iraq," *Studies in Intelligence*, 49, no. 3 (2007), https://www.cia.gov/library/center-for-the-study-of-intelligence/csi-publications/csi-studies/studies/vol49no3/html_files/Collection_Analysis_Iraq_5.htm.
3. R. McNamara, with B. VanDeMark, *In Retrospect: The Tragedy and Lessons of Vietnam* (New York: Vintage, 1966), xxi.
4. CIA Center for the Study of Intelligence, "Watching the Bear: Essays on CIA's Analysis of the Soviet Union," Conference, Princeton University, March 2001, http://www.cia.gov/cis/books/watchingthebear/article08.html, 18.
5. Ibid., 19.
6. Geoffrey Parker, *The Grand Strategy of Philip II* (New Haven, Conn.: Yale University Press, 1998), 74.
7. CIA Center for the Study of Intelligence, "Watching the Bear," 14.
8. Ibid., 18.
9. Dino Brugioni, *Eyeball to Eyeball: The Inside Story of the Cuban Missile Crisis* (New York: Random House, 1990), 147.
10. Ibid., 573.
11. Britt Snider, *The Agency and the Hill: CIA's Relationship with Congress, 1946–2004* (Washington, D.C.: CIA Center for the Study of Intelligence, 2008), 10.
12. Kerr, Wolfe, Donegan, and Pappas, "Collection and Analysis on Iraq."
13. Jan P. Herring, "KITs Revisited: Their Use and Problems," *scip.insight*, 5, no. 7 (July 2013), http://www.growthconsulting.frost.com/web/images.nsf/0/CA6928E7B5561B6086257BB000452B41/$File/SCIP13V5I7_BFTP.htm.
14. Bible, Numbers 13: 31–33.

15. Anthony D. McIvor, ed., *Rethinking the Principles of War* (Annapolis, Md.: Naval Institute Press, 2005), part 5.

16. Mark A. Randol, *The Department of Homeland Security Intelligence Enterprise: Operational Overview and Oversight Challenges for Congress* (Washington, D.C.: Congressional Research Service, March 19, 2010).

17. Maj. Mirielle M. Petitjean, "Intelligence Support to Disaster Relief and Humanitarian Assistance," *The Intelligencer*, AFIO (Winter/Spring 2013), http://www.afio.com/publications/Petitjean_ISR_Spt_to_HA_DR_WinterSpring2013_AFIOIntelligencer.pdf.

18. AFCEA Intelligence Committee, *The Need to Share: The U.S. Intelligence Community and Law Enforcement* (Fairfax, Va.: Author, April 2007), 5.

19. Jonah Lehrer, "The Uncertainty Effect," *Wired*, December 6, 2010, http://www.wired.com/wiredscience/2010/12/the-uncertainty-effect/.

20. Parker, *The Grand Strategy of Philip II*, 284.

21. Ibid., 213.

22. Douglas H. Dearth and R. Thomas Goodden, *Strategic Intelligence: Theory and Application*, 2nd ed. (Carlisle, Penn.: U.S. Army War College and Defense Intelligence Agency, 1995), 197.

23. "Report of the Commission on the Intelligence Capabilities of the United States Regarding Weapons of Mass Destruction," March 31, 2005, 419.

24. Herman, *Intelligence Power in Peace and War*, 105.

25. "Report of the Commission on the Intelligence Capabilities of the United States," 14.

26. Roger Z. George and James B. Bruce, *Analyzing Intelligence* (Washington, D.C.: Georgetown University Press, 2008), 80, 113.

27. Dearth and Goodden, *Strategic Intelligence*, 153.

28. Ibid., 156.

29. Martin Petersen, "What I Learned in 40 Years of Doing Intelligence Analysis for US Foreign Policymakers," *Studies in Intelligence*, 55, no. 1 (March 2011).

30. "The Obligations of Scientists as Counsellors: Guidelines for the Practice of Operations Research," *Minerva* X (January 1972): 115.

31. R. V. Jones, "Temptations and Risks of the Scientific Adviser," *Minerva* X (July 1972): 441.

32. David S. Landes, *The Wealth and Poverty of Nations* (New York: Norton, 1998), 167.

33. David S. Robarge, "Richard Helms: The Intelligence Professional Personified," *Studies in Intelligence*, 46, no. 4 (2007): 35–43.

34. Paul R. Pillar, *Intelligence and U.S. Foreign Policy: Iraq, 9/11, and Misguided Reform* (New York: Columbia University Press, 2011).

35. Herman, *Intelligence Power in Peace and War*, 247.

36. Ibid.

37. George and Bruce, *Analyzing Intelligence*, 80, 113.

38. Herman, *Intelligence Power in Peace and War*, 248.

39. Ibid., 240.

40. Gordon Negus, unpublished papers (2007).

20

A Network View: The Collector

Stand by your sources; they will repay you.[1]

R. V. Jones

S uccessful analysts enjoy close ties with collectors. By "close ties," I mean a good understanding of what collection capabilities are available, and a personal relationship with collectors.

In dealing with collectors, as in many other fields, the key to success is to ask the right question.[2] But how do you, the analyst, know what the right question is? You don't have the knowledge that collectors have. They always can do things that you cannot imagine. So they have to understand what you really want (and therefore they are in the same position with respect to you that you are with respect to the customer). The solution is to share not only what you need, but also *why* you need it. And sharing the issue definition and target models is the best way to begin.

You also need to have, or develop, a collection strategy relevant to your issue. Collection strategies proceed from having a well-developed target model *and* an issue decomposition; understanding the relationship between the two; and sharing both with the collectors. The issue decomposition helps you ask the right questions. The existing target model provides the context. Armed with this information and their unique knowledge of what their collection assets can do, collectors can then ask the right questions of their assets.

As an introduction to collection strategies, it is worth looking back at how Queen Elizabeth I's spymaster, Sir Francis Walsingham, planned for collection. His "Plat for Intelligence out of Spain" in preparation for the Spanish Armada reads:

1. Sir Ed. Stafford to draw what he can from the Venetian Amb.

2. To procure some correspondence of the Fr. K. agent in Spain.

3. To take order with some in Rouen to have frequent advertisements from such as arrive out of Spain at Nantes, Newhaven (i.e., Le Havre) and Dieppe.

4. To make choice of two especial persons, French, Flemings, or Italians, to go along the coast to see what preparations are a making there. To furnish them with letters of credit.

5. To have two intelligencers in the court of Spain—one of Finale, another of Genoa. To have intelligence at Brussels, Leyden, Bar.[3]

Clearly Walsingham had a target model, focused on England's most important strategic target: Spain and its plans to attack England. He also had an issue decomposition. He knew what the gaps were in his knowledge and what collection assets were available. So he gave very specific guidance on how to fill the gaps. Things were so simple then. (Walsingham's problem was not collection, which was his strong point; it was getting his leaders to believe his intelligence.)

The U.S. Collection Management Challenge

Contrast Walsingham's plan with the collection challenges facing a large intelligence service such as that of the United States, which has many collection assets and many targets. (Walsingham really had just one.) Management of information acquisition is a major effort in large intelligence communities. Here, high-volume collection is based on a formalized process of defining requirements, needs, and information gaps. The U.S. intelligence community has for decades attempted to create structures for handling requirements. As a result, there are thirteen separate processes and systems in the U.S. intelligence community to get collection (those are just the major ones, excluding special access programs).

Collection requirements form a hierarchy. Requirements hierarchies are a product of the strategies-to-task approach. Lower elements in the hierarchy are more specific and, in a well-drafted requirements hierarchy, are linked to the higher elements by some measures that indicate their relative value in the overall scheme of things. The number of specific lower-level targets will be in the dozens for targeting a business firm, in the hundreds for even a small country or a consortium, and in the thousands for an illicit network target such as an international narcotics operation. A typical requirement at the lower levels might read, "Geolocate all armored vehicles in the battlefield area," "Obtain a copy of Ambassador Smythe's negotiating notes for tomorrow's trade negotiations," or "Determine the intentions of the Cuban leadership on seaborne migration."

The collection requirements challenge stems in part from the success that the United States has had in developing collection assets. U.S. government collection capabilities are unquestionably the best in the world. The U.S. intelligence community has the most resources and does the best systems planning. It innovates constantly and attempts things few other services would try. In breadth and depth of coverage, the United States remains the best; and therein lies its problem. Because U.S. intelligence can do so much, it is asked to do too much. Expensive collection assets are used too often when cheaper ones might suffice.

As a result, the U.S. intelligence requirements structures have received considerable criticism, and there have been repeated attempts to define a workable structure over many years. One critic said of the requirements process three decades back:

> Analysts themselves often thought that too many people were employed and too much activity was oriented solely to generating "intelligence requirements"; a better job could probably have been done by a few experienced people, working with the available data, and therefore aware of what was missing. Instead intelligence requirements were the object of repeated studies and reorganization efforts.[4]

Since then, a wide array of tools and a more collaborative environment have improved the speed and effectiveness of U.S. requirements systems. Even though they still encounter criticism, formal requirements structures are necessary in dealing with high-volume IMINT, COMINT, and open source material, where a large volume of potential targets exist, and where a large volume of potential targets exist, and when a large customer suite with competing priorities wants more collection than could be accomplished with half of the national budget.

Of course, there continue to be issues with the requirements structure. Examples include the following:

- A reluctance to close down legacy collection systems that have become less useful, since some customers continue to rely on the product. In the business world, companies keep close watch on their overhead and cut low-payoff functions.
- A tendency to forget that if information is available from unclassified sources, other intelligence collection assets should not be used to get it, except where cross-checking is essential—for example, in countering suspected deception. Increasingly, commercial sources such as commercial imaging satellites can do collection that once required national intelligence assets, and can do it more cheaply.
- The difficulty of evaluating collection. Formal requirements structures tend to encourage "bean counting." Content, not quantity, is the critical measure, and formal requirements structures do not handle content evaluation well. Only analysts and customers can evaluate content and thereby place a value on collection.
- The size and formality of the system tends to make it cumbersome and slow, looking at present or even past rather than future needs—an issue that is not unique to the U.S. system. Michael Herman observed that "a requirements system necessarily lags behind reality and following it is no guarantee of success."[5]

When these problems are not addressed, the bulk of raw data collected by intelligence collectors has lower value than a more interactive (target-centric) system has. For example, most new overhead imagery contains information that is already known; natural terrain features and fixed structures change little, if at all, in the course of a year. Most COMINT traffic, which consists of personal telephone conversations and unusable (unbreakably encrypted) traffic, must be discarded as irrelevant. And much open-source information winds up in the wastebasket.

However, all of the collected data must be processed to some extent, and the handling of this volume of irrelevant data chokes the processing and exploitation systems and often chokes the analyst as well. The problem derives from trying to force a process that is based on the idea of an intelligence cycle instead of using the target-centric process. To come closer to the effectiveness of the target-centric paradigm, it is essential to make the requirements structure efficient and responsive. Overall, U.S. intelligence has made great strides in this area.

Even a large and bureaucratic collection network such as that of the United States can be responsive—it has demonstrated that ability repeatedly in crisis situations. But the intelligence analyst has to play a role in making it so. The WMD Commission had severe criticism of the intelligence community's effectiveness in developing collection strategies. Specifically, it noted the following:[6]

> You can't analyze intelligence that you don't have ... the Intelligence Community has not developed the long-term, coordinated collection strategies that are necessary to penetrate today's intelligence targets. (p. 12)

> [The Intelligence Community] rarely adopts integrated strategies for penetrating high-priority targets. (p. 17)

But the WMD Commission also noted that analysts have a major role to play:

> Analysts must be willing to admit what they don't know in order to focus future collection efforts. (p. 12)

> Analysts missed opportunities to drive collection or provide collection targeting. (Overview)

Helping to focus collection can place a substantial burden on the analyst. But the payoff for the analyst can be high, and there is a way to ease the burden. As an analyst, you have to create both the issue decomposition and the target model, and share these models with collectors so that you better equip them to identify and fill in the gaps in knowledge. Tracking the status of collection requests; finding out who else is asking for the same information (and thereby is part of a community of interest); and obtaining access to others' research results, all are facilitated by a shared target model approach.

Collectors sometimes resist analysts' efforts to be involved in the collection systems development and collection strategies processes. For some collectors, the mantra is "tell me what you need, and I'll handle the collection." But senior intelligence community leaders with a broad understanding of the entire process, such as former DNI Mike McConnell, have come to this conclusion:

> The analyst plays a critical role in advising the collectors in not only collection targeting, but on the design and capabilities of future collection systems. For an analyst to perform these crucial tasks well, sophisticated understanding . . . of the functions of collector agencies is essential.[7]

In carrying out this complementary responsibility, analysts must (a) identify what is known about the intelligence issue and what is not known, (b) determine how collection and analysis are currently done, and (c) decide how both can be improved. The collection strategy part of this process proceeds through four steps:

1. Examine the relationship between the issue decomposition and the target model.

2. Identify gaps in knowledge of the target—an analyst's responsibility, but one where collectors can help.

3. Develop a collection strategy to use existing assets to deal with the gaps—a shared responsibility with collectors.

4. Plan for future collection systems development, including planning to deal with denial and deception—a collector's responsibility, but analysts can provide valuable help.

The reason for the structured approach to dealing with an issue and with the target model is to facilitate managing collection against complex problems. Let us consider each step in turn.

Interrelating the Issue Decomposition and Target Model

At this point the ideas of a target model and a customer issue decomposition (hierarchical model) are familiar. At times the two have looked almost identical; but in general, the target model and the issue decomposition are separate, and it's best to keep them that way. Although they often look similar, it is important to remember which is which and to use both of them. Why is that?

- Using only a target model gives customers unwanted information and forces them to select what is relevant from a mass of detail; for example, a tactical commander is keenly interested in the combat forces model of a target country but usually does not want to delve into the country's political and economic models.

- Using only an issue decomposition model results in too narrow a focus; the analyst can develop tunnel vision and miss things that the customer needs to know on important related issues. The tactical commander might be quite interested, for example, in religious shrines that are located close to opposing military forces or about NGOs that are operating in the area—things that could well be missing in the issue decomposition.

It is worth reiterating: The target model and the issue decomposition are separate concepts, but they are closely related to each other. Let's illustrate the relationship with a simple example. Take the problem of money or funds laundering—the movement of illicit proceeds into mainstream commerce and other funds transactions designed to conceal the source, ownership, or use of the funds. Criminal organizations, terrorist groups, and pariah states use funds laundering to evade international sanctions. Funds laundering can be thought of as a process having three distinct stages—placement, followed by layering, followed by integration—as shown in the simple process model of Figure 20-1.[8]

From the customer point of view, funds-laundering activities divide naturally into three stages, and the three stages form the first level of the issue decomposition. But different customers of intelligence will be interested in different stages. Countermeasures, it turns out, have been most effective when aimed at the placement stage. It is easier to detect funds laundering in this first stage, and most law enforcement and regulatory work has concentrated on detecting the placement of illicit funds.[9] Therefore, law enforcement organizations, such as Interpol or the U.S. Financial Crimes Enforcement Network,

Figure 20-1   Model of a Funds-Laundering Process

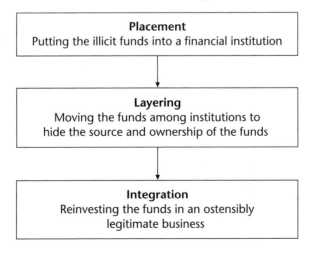

Placement
Putting the illicit funds into a financial institution

Layering
Moving the funds among institutions to hide the source and ownership of the funds

Integration
Reinvesting the funds in an ostensibly legitimate business

Figure 20-2   Customer Connections to the Issue Decomposition

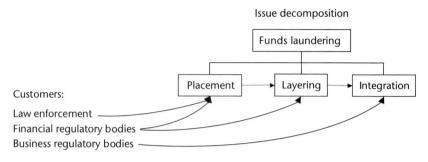

might focus on the placement stage, though they would want intelligence from all three stages. Financial regulatory customers such as the United Kingdom's Financial Services Authority focus on both placement and layering. Business regulatory customers such as the U.S. Securities and Exchange Commission or state regulatory agencies might center their attention on the integration stage. As indicated in Figure 20-2, each of these customers has interests in specific parts of the overall problem.

The first step an analyst takes is to interrelate the customer's issue and the target model for both information-gathering and analysis purposes. Veteran analysts do this naturally, seldom making the relationships explicit. For simple problems, explicit definition may be unnecessary. However, when we deal with complex (nonlinear) problems, the target model or scenario should be made explicit. Even when dealing with simple problems, analysts can easily omit important points or fail to take full advantage of the information sources unless they have an explicit interrelationship diagram. An explicit representation that follows the examples given in this chapter is useful for the veteran analyst but essential for the novice.

Figure 20-2 features a generic top-level issue decomposition for funds laundering. But the funds-laundering problem has many associated target models. Many independent networks are engaged in funds laundering worldwide. Consider one target discussed in chapter 10: the Abacha family's laundering of stolen Nigerian government funds. The Abachas placed money in a Citibank London account, "layered" the funds by moving them among different Citibank London and Citibank New York accounts (shown in Figure 10-1) as well as through Citibank AG Frankfurt and Swiss banks, and "integrated" the funds using individuals and shell (dummy) companies Morgan Procurement and Selcon Airlines.[10] So a model of the Abacha funds-laundering target might look like Figure 20-3 (which shows only part of the Abacha network) overlaid on the top-level issue decomposition.

If we did no more, collectors could use this as a starting point for collection. HUMINT collection is likely to be most useful against the placement and

Figure 20-3   Abacha Funds-Laundering Target Model

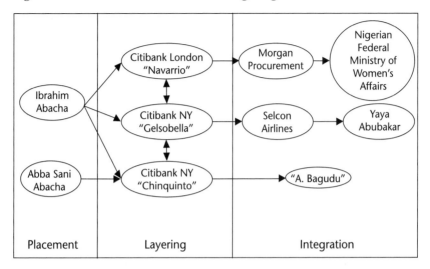

integration stages, where well-placed human sources can monitor and report on unusual transactions. COMINT collection is well positioned to help in tracking the financial transactions associated with layering, because such transactions are typically made through international data transmission. Open-source intelligence can be useful in analyzing the business activities involving integration. But we can do more to help the collector.

Identifying Gaps

When the analyst has defined the intelligence issue, she must ask questions such as, How do I pull information out of the target model to address the problem that is before me? Does the target model, in its present form, include everything that I need to answer my customer's questions? If not, where are the gaps in knowledge of the target, and how can I fill them? Following is a formal process that an analyst might go through in considering those questions. Veteran intelligence analysts do follow the process described here, though they do so intuitively.

For some collectors (open-source and IMINT are examples), the analyst may need to identify the gaps and give specific collection guidance. Some collectors (typically, HUMINT and COMINT collectors) can do a better job of identifying collection opportunities once they understand the gaps, because of their superior knowledge of their assets.

A target model is rarely complete enough to satisfy the intelligence customer. After an issue decomposition hierarchy is defined and interrelated with the target model, as described earlier, it will become obvious that there are gaps in knowledge of the target. These gaps have to be made explicit, and intelligence collection has to fill in the missing pieces of the model to answer the customers' questions.

After reviewing existing data and incorporating it into the target model, the next step is to identify the gaps in data, information, or knowledge. A gap is a missing element that, if found, allows one to choose among alternatives with greater confidence. These gaps always exist in the intelligence business. The skill we have in organizing thoughts and evidence influences how well we are able to generate or discover new thoughts and evidence.

Analysts have a natural tendency to draw conclusions from the information available rather than determine what policy questions must be answered and then go after the needed information. What an analyst should not do is simply sift through her carefully kept files, add a few items that are within easy reach, and write a report. She would never get to gap analysis. The opposite and equally poor approach is to keep looking for the one last scrap of information that makes the other pieces fall into place. You almost never get that last piece of the puzzle. So gap analysis (and filling gaps) has to be done, but not overdone; the analyst needs to know when to stop.

Identifying data gaps is a continuous and iterative process—as new data come in and are fitted into the model, new gaps will be identified. Gap analysis is the process of

- Identifying and prioritizing gaps based on the importance of the underlying need and size of the gap.
- Classifying gaps as to their nature: Do they occur in collection, processing, analysis, or dissemination?
- Sorting gaps as either short term, for current collection systems "tuning," or long term, for new capabilities development.

Consider some examples of gap analysis in a tactical situation. Take the example of the Afghan BMP from chapter 5, where the problem was to determine when the BMP would reach the village where Doctors without Borders was working. If the intelligence analyst did not know how fast the BMP could travel on the road, he would have a collection gap in knowledge to fill. In the Symantec war room example from chapter 2, the analyst might have to deal with several gaps. She might come upon a familiar virus that could be easily countered but have a critical need to know where it started and what Internet service provider (ISP) to call—a collection gap. In the process of defeating the virus, the analyst would learn about a need to improve the collection system to identify the ISP more quickly—a long-term gap. She could encounter a new type of virus, one that could not be examined effectively with her existing knowledge—an analysis gap.

Figure 20-4 illustrates the possible gaps that could have occurred at some point in developing the target model of Figure 20-3 for the Abacha family. The analyst might determine that laundered funds are somehow getting from the

Figure 20-4   Abacha Funds-Laundering Gaps

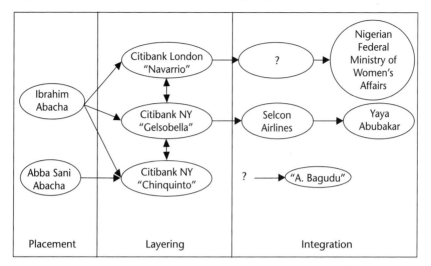

Citibank London "Navarrio" account to the Nigerian Federal Ministry of Women's Affairs, but not know what the intermediate integration entity was. Or she might know that funds are getting to "A. Bagudu" but not know which of the Citibank accounts is the source.

Developing the Collection Strategy

At this point in the analysis process, the issue has been well defined and the gaps in information about the target identified. It is time for the analyst to plan a collection activity to fill the gaps and to follow up by offering guidance to collection sources and organizations. A rich set of collection INTs is available to help an analyst acquire information.

Before designing a collection strategy to fill a gap, it is important to understand the nature of the gap. Some intelligence gaps exist because analysis of the problem has been nonexistent or inadequate, not because of lack of collection. Other gaps need research to determine what part collection can play. An analyst should not treat all gaps as collection gaps; without guidance, the collector will simply collect again without solving the problem, in some cases compounding the problem by adding more unneeded data to be analyzed.

Using Existing Collection Assets

Acquiring new data to fill gaps is a matter of making good use of existing collection assets. These assets are the agents already in place, the open literature that is coming in and being translated, the collection satellites or aircraft currently flying, and so on. The process of asking for use of these assets to fill gaps is called "tasking."

Analysts rely on their judgment in putting together the best collection strategy for tasking to fill gaps. They traditionally initiate the tasking and must pull together the incoming information to form a coherent picture. In the collaborative environment envisioned throughout this text, formulating a collection strategy is a team effort, with input from collectors and processors. The sections that follow describe how it should proceed.

Basic Collection Strategy Development

Most collection strategies are developed as a result of past experience. Making use of existing methods is a good way to save effort, time, and money. Stated another way, most collection problems are old ones; only the specific questions to be answered are new. Begin by looking at what has succeeded in the past.

Start with a review of the previously used collection strategies against similar targets and look at their results. Each specialized substantive area of intelligence has its own collection techniques that have been tested over the years. Political intelligence traditionally has relied on a combination of open source and HUMINT, with some COMINT. Military intelligence relies heavily on COMINT and IMINT, along with some specialized technical collection. Weapons systems intelligence uses all sources but relies most heavily on specialized technical collection, IMINT, and open source. Analyzing previous strategies and their results illuminates the prospects for future strategies.

An analyst cannot rely only on previous strategies, however. As noted in chapter 8, a predictable collection strategy can be defeated. Also, simply shifting tasking from one target to another usually opens gaps in other areas.[11] Try to develop innovative approaches to using existing assets. You want to encourage collectors not to repeat collection that does not obtain the needed information but instead to try new ideas. Techniques that work in economic or political intelligence problems may be applied to problems in other areas, such as military or scientific and technical intelligence.

In identifying collection strategies, be sure to distinguish collectors' current contributions from their potential contributions. In some cases, gaps can be closed by applying collection resources where they now contribute very little. A HUMINT source that reports on political affairs may also be able to obtain economic information. A COMINT source that provides order of battle information may also provide insights into the personalities of enemy field commanders.[12] However, major reorientation of collection assets often requires considerable planning and may have to be considered a long-term solution.

For straightforward collection problems, collection planning can be done quickly and efficiently by using the approach summarized in Figure 20-5, continuing with the Abacha case model. Starting with a given target model and a detailed issue decomposition, the analyst and collectors identify gaps in knowledge of the target that must be filled to satisfy the customers' needs.

Figure 20-5   Abacha Funds-Laundering Collection Plan Overlaid on the Target Model

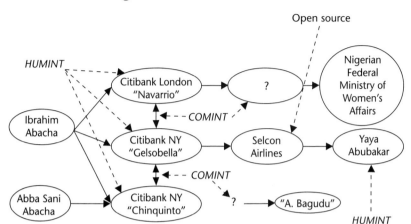

After reviewing their collection assets and capabilities, they define a collection strategy and ask specific collectors to go after specific elements of the target to fill the gaps.

On more complex collection problems, the general approach is the same but a formal process may be needed to develop and compare alternative collection strategy packages. This is a resource allocation step—an effort to fill short-term gaps (immediate needs) by identifying possible collection mechanisms and selecting the most promising combination of collection assets. The collection plan illustrated in Figure 20-5, for example, represents one possible combination of collection assets, or one strategy, to fill the gaps identified in Figure 20-4 and to gain more information. Let's look in detail at how it was developed, recognizing that this is a hypothetical example:

- First, the detailed issue decomposition may have indicated a need for more information about the banks involved. A HUMINT source connected to any of the banks involved with the Abachas could have identified the suspicious transactions that indicated placement and integration. In fact, bank personnel were aware of and concerned about a sudden influx of more than $20 million into the New York accounts, a transfer of $5 million to an unfamiliar person, and a discovery that the Abacha sons were conducting business in Libya, which had no apparent connection to the supposed source of funds in the accounts. These transactions were out of line with the account history.
- From past collection experience, an analyst knows that COMINT has the potential to identify the patterns of funds movements among banks that are a sign of layering activity, and also may be able to fill

the two gaps in knowledge indicated by question marks in Figure 20-5. So the analyst would provide the diagram with a request to COMINT collectors.

- U.S. Department of Transportation records and similar open sources are good first places to look for details on the use of Selcon Airlines as a shell company for the funds-integration stage.
- From previous HUMINT reporting about Yaya Abubakar, the analyst knows that a HUMINT source has access to Abubakar. The analyst would logically turn first to HUMINT for additional intelligence, as indicated in Figure 20-5, requesting more details on the routing path of funds to Abubakar and the amounts of funds he received.

In developing collection strategies, the analyst should time the collection so that it occurs when the highest probability of getting desirable content will occur. For example,

- Missile range testing has consistent patterns; when a pattern of vehicle deployments indicates that a missile test is about to take place, it is the right time to task collection assets.
- People consistently use the telephone heavily at certain times of day; ask for COMINT collection during those times.
- Questioning technical staff at professional conferences elicits more useful information than questioning them at other times.
- The Chinese intelligence service successfully applies an elicitation technique designed to leave visitors exhausted and off guard. It begins with a hectic day of tourism, followed by an evening cocktail reception. After a few drinks, the visitor is approached by a graduate student seeking research assistance, usually on a topic that the visitor had previously been unwilling to discuss.[13]

An analyst can also obtain synergistic benefits by intelligently timing collection by different resources. Coordinated collection by different INTs at the same time can provide insights that those INTs could not provide individually. In the missile range testing example above, IMINT collection of the missile on its launch pad should take place just before the telemetry collection of the missile in launch phase, and technical collection, such as radar collection of the missile in flight and during reentry, should be timed to follow the launch phase. The combination of all this collection can tell far more about the missile's performance than can any one of them alone.

Advanced Collection Strategy Development: Cost-Benefit Analysis

The result of the effort discussed above should be a strategy "package"—a combination of strategies for closing the gaps. On very large and high-priority efforts, alternative strategies can be compared and the best alternative selected.

This is seldom done in practice, because it takes much planning and a high level of understanding of the various available sources. Topics such as locating mobile ballistic missiles or assessing WMDs, for example, are important enough to merit developing and comparing alternative strategies. The most straightforward and accepted method of comparison is cost-benefit or cost-utility analysis, which involves the following steps:

1. Estimate the benefit or utility of each strategy (option) and combination of options.

2. Estimate the costs or risks of each strategy and combination.

3. Select a package that has a high ratio of benefits (or utility) to costs (or risks).

The first step is to estimate the benefit or utility of each collection option. At this point we have determined the importance of the requirement and the value if the gap is filled. Now focus on the probability of success. Which asset has the best chance to get the needed information? Determine the value of the information that could be provided. Also examine ways to increase the probability of success and to maximize the value of the information collected. Establish the probability of success for each category of collection or for fusion of sources, if appropriate. Factor in the possibility that the opponent will use denial and deception against any collection.

Distinguish contingent collection from certain collection. A broad area search for mobile missile sites has high payoff if a successful hit occurs, but success is stochastic (controlled by probabilities) and the probabilities are low. A fixed intercontinental ballistic missile site is an almost certain hit for IMINT collection (assuming no cloud cover), since its location is known, but the value of the intelligence gathered may be low. The evaluation ought to incorporate the probability of obtaining the desired content (a relevance issue) and the ability to beat denial and deception.

In summary, closing the short-term gaps against high-priority targets involves efficiently allocating existing collection resources based on the following:

- Importance of the requirement or specific task
- Value of the information collected if successful
- Probability of success of the collection effort

Next, determine the resource cost or risks of the options. One method is to produce a resource cost estimate that identifies the opportunity costs associated with using collection assets as proposed. The term *opportunity costs* means that if a collection asset is being used against one target, it usually is not available to use against other targets. Actual costs of collection may be difficult to come by; collection organizations guard such information zealously.

Risks may be more important than costs as a factor against which to measure benefit. When the Eisenhower administration decided to conduct aerial
reconnaissance over the Soviet Union during the 1950s, the costs of the U-2
program were a relatively minor factor in its decision-making process. A much
larger factor was the risk of a shoot-down and of consequent damage to the
United States' image and to U.S.-Soviet relations. A U-2 was indeed shot
down, and the subsequent political fallout might suggest that risk was in fact
a better measure than program cost, though the benefits gained by the U-2
program were sufficiently great that the decision to overfly was a good one.[14]

Measuring the Right Things

Know what to measure and how to measure it. Measures of user satisfaction can be taken after collection to evaluate how well the intelligence process
performed against that need or closed that gap. Expressed another way, the
measurement is a quantification of how well a particular requirement or con-
dition has been satisfied. Meaningful measures of user satisfaction could
include, Where are Iran's mobile ballistic missiles located? Where are the
petroleum industry's planned oil exploration regions? What is the expected
size of the 2009 opium crop in Pakistan, Laos, Mexico, Thailand, Afghanistan,
and Burma? Where are the opium processing centers in these countries, and
how much can they process? Where are the concealed WMD production centers in Syria? All of these questions call for analytic conclusions, but all lead to
more specific definitions of measures of user satisfaction. A poor example of a
measure of user satisfaction is, How much of the target area was searched in
imagery at a given resolution? One hundred percent of the target area could
be searched without turning up a single item of useful intelligence.
Nevertheless, collectors prefer such quantitative methods because they provide a firm and technically computable measure.

Intelligence organizations such as those in the United States and Russia do
not have an efficient feedback loop connecting collectors and analysts, in part
because they are so large. Instead, these organizations operate almost as open-
loop systems, meaning they have limited feedback. The U.S. agencies, in
particular, have become fixated on numbers—on both quality and quantity of
collection—and insufficiently concerned with content. For example,

- If the COMINT collectors get continuous copy of a high-priority communications channel for six hours, credit is likely assigned, even if no
  conversations of substance were carried on the channel during that
  time or if the entire channel was encrypted.
- If the IMINT collectors take 100 pictures of a critical installation, credit is
  assigned for each image, even if the last 99 pictures contain nothing new.
- HUMINT collectors typically have their performance rated by the
  number of reports submitted, encouraging the submission of many
  short reports instead of a few complete ones.

A target-centric approach to the intelligence process forces collection performance to focus on content, not on quantity. If collected material does not belong in any target model—that is, if it has no intelligence value—it quickly becomes obvious to all concerned, encouraging collectors to take action to make future intelligence relevant to the targets.

Dealing with Networks

The Abacha case in this chapter is an example of dealing with networks by targeting the links and nodes. In general, collection against a network requires detailed knowledge of the following:

- The network's patterns of activity and related processes
- Network-related observables resulting from those patterns
- The network's signatures produced by the observables[15]

Although a network diagram is static, an actual network is dynamic. So the analyst (and the collectors) also need to understand how the signatures will appear, in what sequence, in what duration, and in what combination.[16]

Dealing with Enigmas

While identifying knowledge gaps in the target model, an analyst occasionally encounters a type of gap that is common in the intelligence business: the unidentified entity, or enigma, which was introduced in chapter 11.

An enigma is a different type of thing for analysts than for collectors. For analysts, the enigma is something that they know exists but of which there is no physical evidence. Examples include a communications link that has to exist from narcotics suppliers to distributors, a fabrication facility that must exist somewhere if cell phones are being produced, or an unnamed terrorist organization that must be responsible for recent acts of violence. The gap may be in identifying the communications link, in finding evidence that the facility exists, or in naming the terrorist organization and identifying its leader.

For collectors, the enigma is a physical object that cannot be fit into existing models. Among IMINT collectors, it occurs as the mysterious facility observed in imagery whose purpose cannot be determined. Among ELINT collectors, it is the strange new radar signal. Among COMINT collectors, it is the encrypted communications link between two unidentified organizations. The gaps here may be in identifying the function of the facility or the radar or in establishing the identity of the organizations.

One of the better known current enigmas is the large underground complex that Russia is building at Yamantau Mountain in the Ural Mountains, described in chapter 11. The complex, under construction for the past thirty-five years, has been the subject of attention and speculation in Congress and the press, but its purpose remains an enigma.[17]

Dealing with enigmas requires analyst-collector teamwork in using the target model. The target model must identify entities that, in the analyst's view, have to exist. The collector's input to the model must note potentially relevant unidentified facilities and signals and communications links, and the analyst must respond by helping the collector—typically by finding a model into which the collector's unidentified entities fit.

Planning for Future Collection: Filling the Long-Term Gaps

A distinctly separate problem arises when the need is not to task existing collection assets but to fill gaps that no existing collector is able to fill. Then the requirement is either to develop new capabilities—to recruit a new agent with the necessary access, to acquire new open-source publications, to develop a new COMINT or IMINT collection system, and the like—or to find a new way to use existing systems.

This planning is typically the responsibility of the collectors. Developing new capabilities is a long-term process. In developing new HUMINT sources, the lead time can be one to five years or more. New satellite COMINT or IMINT collection systems take ten years to develop and deploy during peacetime, though experience indicates that they can be deployed much faster in crisis or wartime. Planning the development requires time and expertise that analysts typically do not have. Thus analysts have to depend heavily on collectors to do the long-range planning.

Analysts' usual contribution to the long-term gap problem is to define long-term requirements and then stand by to help collectors in any way they might be asked to. Major intelligence problems such as proliferation of WMDs, terrorism, and international criminal activity tend to endure. But they change in relative importance, and new problems arise. At the end of 2008 and the beginning of 2009, a worldwide economic crisis suddenly became the most important intelligence issue for most governments. By 2020, new environmental problems, pandemics, mass migrations, and basic resource (food and water) shortages might be more important than today's issues.

Executing Collection Strategies

Coordinated planning of collection from a variety of sources is crucial to solving tough intelligence problems. Collaborative approaches result in more effective collection strategies, and they are often applied on an informal or ad hoc basis. The U.S. intelligence community periodically attempts to formalize this process. One such initiative in 2008 was called, not surprisingly, collaborative collection strategies (CCS). CCS was basically a renaming of traditional multi-intelligence collection, intended to have collectors and analysts formally collaborate throughout the intelligence process to support cross-discipline collection and analysis operations—from identification of the problem through the development and execution of the specific strategy. CCS operations started with SIGINT-IMINT collaboration, and attempts were made to include the other intelligence community disciplines.[18] CCS was one of the first steps that the intelligence community took toward implementation of the target-centric approach.

In the past three decades, some intelligence organizations have defined a specialized career field called *targeting analyst* to develop and implement collection strategies. The "target" in "targeting analyst" has the same meaning as used in the preceding chapters: people, networks, organizations, communications systems, or facilities. The job of the targeting analyst is to translate intelligence needs into potential targets, identify gaps in knowledge, identify collection assets that can be used against the target, and develop a collection plan. In essence, one analyst handles all these steps. The targeting analyst clearly does not plan routine collection, such as IMINT or ELINT collection, which is best done by automated systems. The analyst is more likely to be focused on a single target of very high intelligence value.

Where more formal collaborative collection strategy approaches are not available, analysts sometimes prepare collection support briefs (CSBs). CSBs have been used for decades, primarily to provide collection guidance to HUMINT collectors. But they have been created for all collection INTs. They usually consist of tutorial information on more arcane topics, along with some detail on what is known and what knowledge gaps exist. So, again, they provide a target model for the benefit of collectors. Their primary limitation has been that, in order to be useful for HUMINT collectors, they have to have a relatively low classification ("Secret" or below) so that they can be shared in the field.

This chapter began by giving analysts the secret to success with any collection strategy: a close and enduring relationship with the collectors. Simply writing collection requirements and "throwing them over the wall" doesn't work. If collectors have access to and understand the target model and the issue decomposition, they can respond much more effectively than if they do not have knowledge of these elements. Imparting this information usually requires analysts to develop and maintain personal contacts with collectors. Analysts in business intelligence, law enforcement intelligence, and tactical military intelligence are much closer to their sources and are able to provide detailed, explicit collection guidance. It is difficult to do at the national level for large communities such as the U.S. intelligence community. But it can be done and increasingly is being done on high-priority problems.

Summary

The U.S. collection system is robust and provides a vast amount of raw intelligence about issues worldwide. But a large intelligence community such as that of the United States experiences many challenges in planning for and managing collection. Although analytic shortfalls are responsible for most failures, analysts cannot analyze intelligence that they don't have. A large intelligence community needs a carefully planned set of collection strategies against high-priority targets. Analysts have to help make the collection process work effectively. They can do so by being heavily involved in developing collection strategies.

The customer issue decomposition and the target model discussed in earlier chapters are used together, first in identifying gaps in knowledge, then in developing collection strategies to fill the gaps, and later in producing finished intelligence. Four steps are commonly used in developing collection strategies:

1. *Interrelate the issue with the target model* so that you can plan collection to fill gaps in knowledge, making use of the best available sources.

2. *Identify gaps in knowledge of the target.* The gaps usually become fairly obvious when the target model and the issue decomposition are compared, but they have to be made explicit. Collectors can help with this step and the following steps, if they have access to the target model and issue decomposition.

3. *Develop a collection strategy.* This step involves using existing assets to deal with the gaps. Past experience with collection against similar targets can help here. Looking at the sources that were used in populating the existing target model can help to identify the sources that are best positioned to fill gaps. Having a good understanding of the target so that you can time collection improves the chances that the effort will obtain useful information. The most success in collection strategy comes from having a close relationship with collectors. On large collection efforts against high-priority targets, it is worthwhile to develop and compare alternative strategies by using cost-benefit analysis.

4. *Plan for future collection systems development.* This step is primarily the collectors' responsibility. It involves assessing both existing and likely future needs and gaps, including planning to deal with denial and deception.

These steps form an iterative process. They are listed in sequential order to facilitate understanding, but in practice they tend to be worked in varying orders, and several iterations of the process will occur over time.

Notes

1. R. V. Jones, "Scientific Intelligence," lecture to the Royal United Services Institution on February 19, 1947, *Journal of the Royal United Services Institute*, 92 (1947): 365.
2. Steven D. Leavitt and Stephen J. Dubner, *Freakonomics* (New York: HarperCollins, 2005), 89.
3. Stephen Budiansky, *Her Majesty's Spymaster* (New York: Viking, 2005), 199.
4. John Prados, *The Soviet Estimate* (Princeton, N.J.: Princeton University Press, 1987), 181.
5. Michael Herman, *Intelligence Power in Peace and War* (Cambridge, U.K.: Cambridge University Press, 1996), 292.

6. *Report of the Commission on the Intelligence Capabilities of the United States Regarding Weapons of Mass Destruction*, March 31, 2005, http://www.wmd.gov/report/wmd_report.pdf.

7. William J. Lahneman, *The Future of Intelligence Analysis*, Center for International and Security Studies at Maryland, Vol. I, March 10, 2006, E-8.

8. Joseph M. Myers, "International Strategies to Combat Money Laundering," speech to the International Symposium on the Prevention and Control of Financial Fraud, Beijing, October 19–22, 1998.

9. Ibid.

10. "Minority Staff Report for Permanent Subcommittee on Investigations—Hearing on Private Banking and Money Laundering: A Case Study of Opportunities and Vulnerabilities," November 9, 1999, http://levin.senate.gov/issues/psireport2.htm.

11. In response to the attacks of 9/11, the United States shifted a large segment of its intelligence collection and analysis capability onto the terrorism target. The knowledge gaps that have been opened in other areas will take years to close. Unfortunately, the shifted resources could not be used efficiently for reasons that are explained by the Brooks curves (see chapter 9).

12. The Department of Defense defines order of battle as "the identification, strength, command structure, and disposition of the personnel, units, and equipment of any military force." See "DOD Dictionary of Military Terms," April 10, 2003, http://www.dtic.mil/doctrine/jel/doddict/.

13. D. Wise, *Spy: The Inside Story of How the FBI's Robert Hanssen Betrayed America* (New York: Random House, 2002), 13.

14. Prados, *The Soviet Estimate*, 96–102.

15. U.S. Joint Forces Command, *Commander's Handbook for Attack the Network* (Suffolk, Va.: Joint Warfighting Center, May 20, 2011), http://www.dtic.mil/doctrine/doctrine/jwfc/atn_hbk.pdf, III-1.

16. Ibid.

17. U.S. Congress, *Congressional Record*, June 19, 1997, H3943.

18. Scott C. Poole, "Integrated Collection Management Accelerates Interagency Cooperation," *NGA Pathfinder*, 6, no. 3 (May/June 2008): 8, http://www.nga.mil/NGASiteContent/StaticFiles/OCR/mayjune08.pdf.

Appendix I

A Tale of Two NIEs

In 1990 the National Intelligence Council (NIC) produced a national intelligence estimate (NIE)—the most authoritative intelligence assessment produced by the intelligence community—on Yugoslavia. Twelve years later, the NIC produced an NIE on Iraq's WMD program. The Yugoslavia NIE

- Used a sound prediction methodology
- Got it right
- Presented conclusions that were anathema to U.S. policymakers
- Had zero effect on U.S. policy

The Iraqi WMD NIE, in contrast,

- Used a flawed prediction methodology
- Got it wrong
- Was exactly what U.S. policymakers wanted to hear
- Provided support to a predetermined U.S. policy

This appendix discusses the differences in analytic approaches used in the two NIEs.

The Yugoslavia NIE

The opening statements of the 1990 Yugoslavia NIE contain four remarkably prescient conclusions:[1]

- Yugoslavia will cease to function as a federal state within one year, and will probably dissolve within two. Economic reform will not stave off the breakup.
- Serbia will block Slovene and Croat attempts to form an all-Yugoslav confederation.
- There will be a protracted armed uprising by Albanians in Kosovo. A full-scale, interrepublic war is unlikely, but serious intercommunal conflict will accompany the breakup and will continue afterward. The violence will be intractable and bitter.
- There is little the United States and its European allies can do to preserve Yugoslav unity. Yugoslavs will see such efforts as contradictory to advocacy of democracy and self-determination.

I focus on the Yugoslavia NIE because it illustrates prediction that uses force field analysis and the creation of alternative target models in the form of scenarios. It also is an example of clear and unequivocal communication to that most difficult of intelligence customers, the policymaker. Finally, it is a story of a country torn apart by religious and ethnic divisions, where U.S. policy was to try to keep it together, and where U.S. troops might wind up in harm's way. It is a scenario that continues to have relevance. The same scenario appeared in the 1980's U.S. involvement in Lebanon and more recently in Iraq.

The Setting

Yugoslavia, a federation of six republics, had a long history of instability. It was created in the aftermath of World War I, and for political reasons it united three distinct ethnic groups—Serbs, Croats, and Slovenes. Yugoslavia's internal boundaries roughly reflected ethnic and historical divisions, but the population was so thoroughly mixed that it proved impossible to separate the various ethnic groups clearly. This was especially true of the dominant ethnic group, the Serbs, who were widely dispersed in the republics. Nationalistic tensions had long plagued the region. Religious divisions added to the problems: the Croats and Slovenes were primarily Roman Catholic, the Serbs were Eastern Orthodox, and Bosnia-Herzegovina and Kosovo had large Muslim populations. However, strongman Josip Broz Tito ruled Yugoslavia from 1945 until his death in 1980, and he proved to be very effective at suppressing tensions and keeping the country united.

In 1990, though, Tito was gone. The federal central government that was Tito's legacy was not working well. Foreign debt, inflation, and unemployment had created a troublesome situation. The economy was faltering, and nationalist pressures were causing increasing instability. In March and April of 1990, Slovenia and Croatia held their first multiparty elections in almost fifty years. The communist reformers lost to parties favoring national sovereignty within Yugoslavia.

The NIO for Europe in 1990 was Marten van Heuven. In May of that year, he visited Yugoslavia to assess the situation. He concluded that pressures were building for a collapse of the federation. The ethnic problems alone, he thought, were fast becoming irresolvable. After returning from Belgrade, van Heuven directed the preparation of an NIE on Yugoslavia. The NIE was prepared in two successive drafts. Both involved force field analysis, but they differed in the conclusions drawn from the analysis because they created starkly different target models.

First Draft: The "Muddle-Through" NIE

Van Heuven initially assigned the task of drafting the NIE to a State Department analyst who had extensive background on Yugoslavian and Eastern European affairs. In the first draft, completed during summer 1990, the author reviewed the evidence for and against the probability of Yugoslavia's disintegration and concluded that there was more reason for the republics to stay together than to split apart. The first draft is sometimes referred to as the "muddle-through" NIE because, as van Heuven noted, it predicted that Yugoslavia would somehow muddle through. It identified a number of forces that were working to hold Yugoslavia together. These forces are summarized in the influence net in Figure AI-1. (See chapter 12 for a discussion of influence nets.) The primary threats it identified were as follows:

- The threat of Soviet intervention had held Yugoslavia together during Tito's life and for ten years after his death.
- The numerically dominant Serbs strongly preferred a united Yugoslavia. The officer corps of the Yugoslav National Army (the JNA) was overwhelmingly Serbian and was thought to be in a position to prevent the nation's collapse.
- Economic incentives for remaining integrated were strong, since the republics' economies by themselves were too small to be viable.
- Fear of the future, specifically fear of ethnic and religious conflict, was considered to be a force that would restrain potential breakaway republics.

Some of the failures in objectivity discussed in the introduction in chapter 1 may have been a factor in the first NIE. The U.S. State Department had a vested interest in preserving Yugoslavia as a state, or at least in seeing a peaceful breakup if Yugoslavia could not hold together, an organizational bias that may have shaped the analysis. Wishful thinking may also have played its part. One of the forces keeping Yugoslavia together was "fear of the future." But it appears that the fear was on the U.S. side. When an NSC staff member told the Slovenes and Croats that a declaration of independence would start a war, they replied, "So what?" Finally, in Yugoslavia the United States encountered a different way of thinking, and ethnocentric biases may have been at work. Both the U.S. culture and its legal system stress religious and ethnic tolerance. The republics of Yugoslavia have a long

Figure AI-1   Influence Net Model: Yugoslavia NIE First Draft

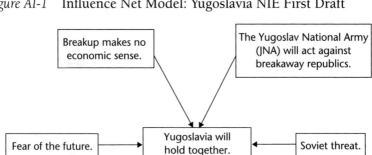

Note: The arrows come from boxes that support the conclusion that Yugoslavia will hold together.

history of religious and ethnic strife and intolerance. The first NIE draft simply didn't take into account this critical force.

Van Heuven was skeptical of the conclusions; they didn't fit with the situation he had observed in his visit to the region. He wanted to see an alternative model, and he got it in the form of a second draft NIE.

Second Draft: Force Field Analysis

Van Heuven assigned the task of producing a second NIE draft to other experienced observers of events in Yugoslavia, including CIA analyst Harry Yeide, who had served in the region and was intimately familiar with the issues involved. The second NIE draft presented an alternative model, or scenario, of the future. It concluded that the forces that had held Yugoslavia together in the past were weak or nonexistent and that current forces were acting to tear Yugoslavia apart. These forces are summarized in the influence net diagram of Figure AI-2:

- The JNA was less inclined than before to intervene unless Serbian interests were seriously threatened. It would not intervene in Croatia in any event, since Croatia had no Serbs.
- No strong central leadership had replaced that of Tito.
- The Soviet threat was gone.
- The breakup made no economic sense for Yugoslavia taken as a whole, as the first draft indicated. But Croatia and Slovenia would be better off economically as independent states.
- The first draft downplayed what were probably the dominant forces in action: The ethnic and nationalistic differences among the peoples of Yugoslavia, the history of hostility and suspicion, and the religious divisions.
- Fear of the future was not a factor. As noted earlier, the United States may have had a fear of the future, but the breakaway states of Croatia and Slovenia did not.

Figure AI-2 Influence Net Model: Yugoslavia NIE Second Draft

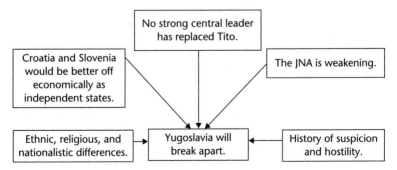

Note: The arrows come from boxes that support the conclusion that Yugoslavia will break apart.

The resulting NIE was remarkable in several respects. All of the major NIE contributors agreed on the facts, and no one took footnotes to the conclusions. Most NIEs have footnotes indicating that a segment of the intelligence community disagrees with some of the conclusions. The predictions quoted at the beginning of this appendix were exceptionally accurate. And the NIE had almost no effect on U.S. policy.

The Customer View

From a policymaker's point of view, the NIE was unwelcome. It predicted what would happen, but it gave policymakers nothing to do. U.S. policy preferences were, first, to keep Yugoslavia together. Failing that, policymakers wanted a peaceful breakup or, if all else failed, a managed disaster. They got neither. The disintegration began in 1991, and it was brutal and bloody. The fighting and "ethnic cleansing" that resulted claimed about 200,000 lives.

If the NIE had a flaw, it was that it did not constructively engage the policymaker. The key judgments flatly predict a breakup punctuated by long and bitter conflict but offer no suggestions on what might ease the impact of the breakup. Furthermore, U.S. government attention at the time was rapidly becoming focused on events in the Middle East, where Iraq was about to invade Kuwait. So, as one analyst noted, the United States simply stopped caring until the atrocities mounted.

Finally, the NIE apparently was leaked to the *New York Times*. Its subsequent publication in the *Times* may have hastened the dissolution of Yugoslavia by indicating to all of the parties involved that the United States recognized the inevitable. The argument could be made that, as a result of its open publication, the NIE was a net disservice to the U.S. government.

The Iraqi Weapons of Mass Destruction NIE

In October 2002, at the request of members of Congress, the National Intelligence Council produced an NIE on the Iraqi WMD program. That document concluded that Iraq

- Was reconstituting its nuclear weapons program and was actively pursuing a nuclear device
- Possessed a biological weapons capability that was larger and more advanced than before the Gulf War and included mobile biological weapons production facilities
- Had renewed production of chemical weapons, including mustard, Sarin, GF (cyclosarin), and VX, and that it had accumulated chemical stockpiles of between 100 and 500 metric tons
- Possessed UAVs that were probably intended for the delivery of biological weapons[2]

All of these conclusions were wrong. Concerning this NIE, the Commission on the Intelligence Capabilities of the United States Regarding Weapons of Mass Destruction (the WMD Commission) said:

> We conclude that the Intelligence Community was dead wrong in almost all of its pre-war judgments about Iraq's weapons of mass destruction. This was a major intelligence failure. Its principal causes were the Intelligence Community's inability to collect good information about Iraq's WMD program, serious errors in analyzing what information it could gather, and a failure to make clear just how much of its analysis was based on assumptions, rather than good evidence.[3]

There were failures in both collection and analysis, and the WMD report covers them exhaustively. I focus here on the analytic failures, beginning with one that the WMD Commission report touched on but did not emphasize.

Poor Issue Definition

Poor problem definition was perhaps the root cause of the NIE analytic failures. The effort failed at its beginning. The NIE began by failing to ask the right question, and it consequently ran afoul of the framing effect, discussed in chapter 4. The NIE drafters, constrained by the unreasonably short deadline imposed by Congress, accepted the problem as it was presented. An issue decomposition that is constrained too narrowly, as this one was, overly constrains both the target model and the conclusions. Most of the other failures derived from failing to properly define the problem.

The issue definition focused solely on the question of whether Iraq had WMD programs and, if so, what they were. By focusing on WMD programs, analysts had a tendency to fit all evidence into a WMD model. Analysts assumed that Iraq had WMD programs, and analysis proceeded from that point. A broader look at Iraq's overall military capability would have found more logical explanations for some of the evidence. For example,

- In March 2001, intelligence reporting indicated that Iraq was acquiring high-strength aluminum alloy tubes.[4] CIA and DIA analysts subsequently concluded that Iraq's purchase of aluminum tubes was intended to support a gas centrifuge uranium enrichment program. Focusing only on whether the tubes could be used for centrifuges, analysts ignored evidence that the tubes were better suited for use in rockets. The tubes in fact had precisely the same dimensions and were made of the same material as tubes used in Iraq's conventional rockets. In a classic example of premature closure, the CIA cited the existing judgment as a reason for rejecting the suggestion of one of its officers that they get the precise specifications of the rocket in order to evaluate the possibility that the tubes were in fact intended for rockets.[5]

- The NIE concluded that Iraq was developing small UAVs that were probably intended to deliver biological weapons agents. In reaching this conclusion, the intelligence community (except for the Air Force) failed to consider other possible uses for the UAVs and dismissed countervailing evidence. As one CIA analyst explained, the purpose of the NIE was to discuss Iraq's WMD programs, so the analysis did not explore other possible uses.[6] A broader problem definition would probably have concluded, correctly, that the preponderance of evidence indicated that the UAVs were intended for battlefield reconnaissance.

A better issue definition—one that required inputs from political, economic, and military analysts as well as weapons systems analysts—would probably have avoided some of the most serious analytic lapses in the NIE. As the WMD Commission noted, multidisciplinary issues were in fact key to the answer. The Yugoslavia NIE considered military, political, economic, and social forces. But there was little serious analysis of the sociopolitical situation in Iraq or of the motives and intentions of the Iraqi leadership. Weapons systems analysts are not likely to ask questions such as, "Is Saddam Hussein bluffing?" or "Could he have decided to suspend his weapons programs until sanctions are lifted?" An analyst of Iraq's politics and culture likely would ask such questions.[7]

Poor Evaluation of Sources and Evidence

The WMD Commission faulted analysts for making judgments based on insufficient evidence. Analysts were too willing to find confirmations of their judgments in evidence that should have been recognized at the time to be of dubious reliability. They readily accepted any evidence that supported their theory that Iraq had stockpiles and was developing weapons programs, and they explained away or simply disregarded evidence that pointed in other directions. Two of the most egregious examples were the evaluation of a key HUMINT source on Iraq's biological weapons program and of HUMINT and IMINT sources on Iraq's chemical weapons program.

The conclusions about Iraqi biological weapons relied heavily on a single source, an Iraqi chemical engineer nicknamed "Curveball." This source claimed that Iraq had several mobile units for producing biological weapons agents. The evidence presented by Curveball fell short of being credible, according to the criteria discussed in chapter 7:

- *Competence.* Curveball was variously described as a drinker, unstable, difficult to manage, "out of control," and exhibiting behavior that is typical of fabricators.[8]
- *Access.* There was no evidence of access to biological weapons laboratories. Corroborating evidence only established that Curveball had been to a particular location, not that he had any knowledge of biological weapons activities being conducted there.[9]

- *Vested interest or bias.* Curveball had a motivation to provide interesting intelligence to obtain resettlement assistance and permanent asylum.[10]
- *Communications channel.* The reporting was through liaison with the German intelligence service, and U.S. intelligence officials were not provided direct access to Curveball. The communications channel between Curveball and the WMD analysts therefore had many intermediate nodes, with consequent possibilities for the analysts getting a distorted message.

Analysts evaluating Curveball's information were aware of some of these problems, yet judged his reporting reliable and continued to make it the basis for the NIE judgment and subsequent judgments about Iraq's biological weapons program. They dismissed IMINT of flaws in Curveball's reporting as being due to Iraqi denial and deception.[11] That Curveball was a fabricator was subsequently confirmed.

The NIE also erroneously concluded that Iraq had restarted chemical weapons production and increased its chemical weapons stockpiles, based on poor evaluation of both IMINT and HUMINT:

- Analysts relied heavily on imagery showing the presence of "Samarratype" tanker trucks at suspect chemical weapons facilities. These distinctive trucks had been associated with chemical weapons shipments in the 1980s and during the Gulf War. Analysts also believed that they were seeing increased Samarra truck activity at suspect chemical weapons sites in imagery. They apparently did not consider an alternative hypothesis—that the trucks might be used for other purposes, as turned out to be the case. And they failed to recognize that the more frequent observed activity of the trucks was an artifact of increased imagery collection.[12] The trucks were simply observed more often because of more imagery reporting.
- One of the human sources, an Iraqi chemist, provided extensive reporting, about half of which was absurd. Despite evidence that he might not be a credible source, analysts used his reporting that Iraq had successfully stabilized the nerve agent VX in the NIE because it fit their existing mindset.[13] Another source reported that Iraq was producing mustard and binary chemical agents. But he also reported on Iraq's missile, nuclear, and biological programs. Given Iraq's known use of compartmentation to protect sensitive weapons programs, analysts should have recognized that the source was unlikely to have access to all these programs.[14]

Failure to Consider Alternative Target Models

The Iraqi WMD NIE contained numerous examples of analysts' selecting a single hypothesis (or target model) and attempting to fit all evidence into that model. The failure to seriously consider alternative missions for Iraq's UAV program and alternative uses for the aluminum tubes were noted previously. In addition,

- Analysts failed to consider flaws in the target model they were using. If Iraqis had used all the aluminum tubes they were acquiring for centrifuges, they would have wound up with 100,000–150,000 machines, far more than any nuclear weapons proliferator would build.[15] All target models should undergo a sanity check: Does the model intuitively make sense?
- They also failed to consider the Occam's razor alternative (see chapter 7)—that the reason they could find no mobile biological weapons laboratories after an intensive search is that the labs didn't exist.[16] It is virtually impossible to prove a negative in the intelligence business, but the negative at least deserves to be considered.

Poor Analytic Methodology

The raw intelligence that was available to analysts was mostly historical, due in large part to Iraq's denial and deception programs. Intelligence about developments since the late 1990s depended heavily on IMINT and some questionable HUMINT. Other technical collection, COMINT, and open source contributed very little.[17] As a result, analysts had to, in effect, "predict" the present state of the WMD programs.

They did so by extrapolation based on past history. The intelligence community, prior to the 1991 Gulf War, had underestimated Iraq's nuclear program and had failed to identify all of its chemical weapons storage sites. This history shaped the community's selection of the forces acting to shape Iraq's WMD effort. Specifically, Iraq had the same leadership, presumably with the same objectives concerning WMD; a history of WMD development; and a history of concealment. These forces provided the starting point for what was a straight-line extrapolation, much like the extrapolation that resulted in the "muddle-through" Yugoslavia NIE draft. Analysts assumed that the forces that were present in 1991 were still present, making no allowance for changes since 1991. The constant international scrutiny and the high risk that any continuing WMD program would be discovered and bring on additional sanctions or military action were not taken into account. And a continuing, very important force was not considered: Saddam Hussein's ambition to be a major player in Mideast power politics, a motivation that would cause him to conceal his lack of WMD. The result of a combination of poor force field analysis and lack of intelligence was an estimate based on extrapolations.[18]

As one example, the UAV estimate was based heavily on a straight-line extrapolation. Before the Gulf War, Iraq had been in the early stages of a project to convert the MiG-21 jet aircraft into UAVs for biological weapons delivery. In addition, Iraq had experimented in 1990 on a biological weapons spray system, designed to be used with the MiG-21 UAV. In the mid-1990s Iraq also began testing another modified jet aircraft, the L-29, as a UAV. Analysts concluded that the L-29 was a follow-on to the MiG-21 program. When the new and smaller UAVs made their appearance, analysts wrongly extrapolated that these UAVs were simply a continuation of the biological weapons delivery program.[19]

The most compelling analytic methodology failure, though, was the one that Martin van Heuven avoided. As the NIO in charge of the Yugoslavia NIE, he forced the consideration of a second target model, which ultimately was used in the NIE. The Iraqi WMD drafters gravitated to a single model and apparently failed to consider a logical top-level alternative hypothesis or model: that Iraq had abandoned its WMD programs.

Poor Interaction with Collectors and Customers

A major theme of this book has been the importance of a shared target model—shared with both collectors of intelligence and customers of intelligence. The Iraqi WMD NIE effort failed on both counts. Analysts did not share with collectors how much they relied on intelligence from sources that the collectors knew to be unreliable—Curveball and the Iraqi chemist who reported on Iraq's purported chemical weapons program being two examples. In dealing with the customers, analysts left the impression that their sources were much more credible than was the case. It is true that the analysts were ill-served in this effort by pressures from the White House to provide a rationale for the planned invasion of Iraq, as noted previously. But ultimately, analysts must assume responsibility for their product. As the WMD report noted, the NIE did not communicate the weakness of the underlying intelligence. Analysts did not adequately communicate their uncertainties to policymakers. Many of the analytic products obscured how much their conclusions rested on inferences and assumptions.[20] The NIE started out on the wrong foot with a poor issue definition. It ended badly, as the WMD Commission noted, in a failure to communicate.[21]

Notes

1. The facts in this appendix are taken from a case study prepared by Thomas W. Shreeve for the National Defense University in May 2003, titled "A National Intelligence Estimate on Yugoslavia."
2. "Report of the Commission on the Intelligence Capabilities of the United States Regarding Weapons of Mass Destruction," March 31, 2005, 8–9.
3. Ibid., cover letter.
4. Ibid., 55.
5. Ibid., 57, 68.
6. Ibid., 145.
7. Ibid., 13.
8. Ibid., 91, 97.
9. Ibid., 113.
10. Ibid., 96.

11. Ibid., 92.
12. Ibid., 122, 125.
13. Ibid., 127.
14. Ibid., 128.
15. Ibid., 85.
16. Ibid., 93.
17. Ibid., 165.
18. Ibid., 168–169.
19. Ibid., 141–145.
20. Ibid., 12.
21. Ibid., 3.

Appendix II
Example Project Plan

This example was derived from a sample project plan prepared by the author as a consultant for the Washington/Baltimore High Intensity Drug Trafficking Area (HIDTA). It is reproduced here with the permission of the director of that HIDTA.

Issue Definition

A beginning, top-level problem statement is derived from HIDTA's mission—to "disrupt the market for illegal drugs in the United States by assisting federal, state, local, and tribal law enforcement entities . . . " with emphasis on drug-related activities that have "significant harmful impact." Based on HIDTA's mission statement, we can infer that the end goal is to reduce the harm done by drugs in this area. So the major drug threats in any given area such as Baltimore are *defined by the harm done* in two ways: harm caused by the drug itself, and harm caused by the drug trafficking organizations (DTOs, including gangs) that vend the drugs.

Starting from the overall problem statement, "What are the major drug threats in our region?" we proceed to an issue decomposition, illustrated in Figure AII-1:

- What drugs cause the greatest harm in the region?
- What DTOs (including gangs) cause the greatest harm in the region?
- What are the expected trends in both drug harm and DTO harm over the next one to three years?

Figure AII-1   Example Issue Decomposition of Major Drug Threats

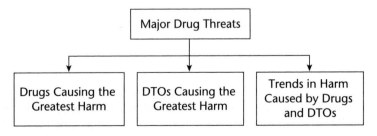

Précis

Marijuana probably is the most heavily used drug in the HIDTA, but probably is not the most harmful; the head of the U.S. Drug Enforcement Administration has concluded that heroin is clearly more dangerous than marijuana.[1] Based on current estimates of area sales, heroin appears to be the most harmful drug in the area.

Preliminary studies indicate that heroin is being sold by several independent DTOs, all linked to Mexican drug cartels (primarily the Gulf Cartel, the Zetas, and the Sinaloa Cartel).

The trend is to increased usage for the next three to five years, primarily based on this hypothesis: Better drug qualities and methods of abuse in lieu of needle injection are attracting more customers to the drug.

Research Plan

A first step in this research will be to review existing studies. This will focus on similar studies that have been done elsewhere, what methodology was used, and what the results were. This includes a review of existing reports from other HIDTA jurisdictions and of academic studies on the subject published in journals. The research methodology proposes to use benchmarking—comparing Washington/Baltimore HIDTA results to those observed in other regions—and the review of existing studies is essential for that.

The Washington/Baltimore HIDTA "2010 Threat Assessment & Strategy" report indicates that thirty-three ethnic or affinity groups have been involved in drug trafficking in the region. It doesn't differentiate these groups based on the amount of harm caused. Presumably, HIDTA wants to focus on the groups causing the most harm, so in this phase we want to identify the most harmful groups, using some accepted methodology for estimating the harm they cause.

The research methodology proposes to rank local DTOs using some numerical score for harm caused by the DTO. Such a score could be determined by combining the scores from two sources of harm:

- A harm score based on the harm done by the drugs sold by the DTO. This derives directly from the result of existing research on drug harm and from an estimate of the type and quantity of drugs sold annually by the DTO.
- A harm score based on the propensity of the DTO to commit violent or property crime. This would rely on an index of the harm caused by specific crimes and an estimate of the volume and types of crimes committed by the DTO.

It is important to identify developing trends. The project will attempt to establish what the norm is, watch for deviations from the norm, and be ready to explain them. The challenge of a dynamic target such as drug trafficking is that it constantly changes as existing networks are dismantled, as the demand for specific drugs change, and as DTOs change structure and processes to avoid arrest or attack from competitors.

Establishing trends in this type of problem usually relies on extrapolation. Extrapolations can work over a short time frame, assuming that the fundamental forces or factors don't change much. In this research effort, we will start by comparing the current assessment with previous assessments and use those points in a straight-line extrapolation.

Note

1. Matt Ferner, "New DEA Chief: 'Heroin Is Clearly More Dangerous Than Marijuana,'" *Huffington Post*, August 5, 2015, http://www.huffingtonpost.com/entry/dea-chief-marijuana-heroin-dang er_55c25079e4b0f7f0bebb4ef5.

Appendix III
Presenting Analysis Results

Even if you have followed the guidance of this book in detail, you still, in the end, need a vehicle to communicate the results. In intelligence, this almost always means either a written report or a verbal report (typically, a briefing). This appendix concentrates on delivering the presentation.

An intelligence presentation may require a written report or the development of a briefing, either of which can be a time-consuming activity. Each has its advantages. The report gets wider circulation and typically has a longer life. Most analysis projects conclude with some type of written report. The briefing has the advantage of providing direct and immediate feedback to the analyst. Briefings are probably the primary communication method for executives. They usually value the two-way exchange, and the analyst in turn should value the feedback.

The important thing is to fit the presentation to the style of the key customer. Although most executives prefer briefings, some like written reports; an increasing number want e-mails. You may have to conduct an intelligence effort on the key customer (which his or her staff will usually cooperate in). Find out the customer's favorite way to get information. Some prefer more text; some want graphics. A few may want lots of facts and figures. The sections that follow provide guidelines for presenting analysis results.

Support Every Analytic Conclusion

All conclusions must be clearly traceable to the results of your effort and explained in the body of the report. Provide, explain, and emphasize key intelligence insights. The reader should be able to follow your reasoning at every turn. Highlight key words, phrases, or sentences to stress their importance.

Often an analyst is so close to a study that results and conclusions are clear to him but not so clear to someone not involved in the study. Furthermore, results and conclusions should be carefully scrubbed for both apparent and actual contradictions. Consider having several nonparticipants review your results and conclusions prior to the presentation. Take advantage of every opportunity for a peer review of your final product. Peers can provide excellent feedback on the flow, logic, and clarity of your message.

Most reports include two levels of detail: a brief but complete summary for decision makers, and another more detailed description for fellow analysts. Your detailed description can contain as much detail as you deem necessary in order to allow another analyst to duplicate the results.

The final written study report should include a concise executive summary right up front to allow the busy reader to get "the bottom line" without pouring through page after page of details. Limit your executive summary to one page.

Write or Brief with a Purpose

Because most intelligence products provide information, your customers expect to hear clear, concisely stated conclusions and projections up front. This means that you write with a purpose—which, if you began by defining the problem as you should have, will be straightforward.

Separate Facts from Analysis

Make it abundantly clear when you move from fact to analysis. Never cover up evidence with slick writing. As noted in chapter 7, you inevitably have to work with incomplete and conflicting information. For this reason, your finished presentation has to clearly articulate what is known (the facts), how it is known (the sources), what drives the judgments (linchpin assumptions), the impact if these drivers change (alternative outcomes), and what remains unknown. Customers expect logical and objective arguments. Detailed facts may or may not be appropriate, depending on the scope of the topic and the audience's technical sophistication, interest, and need. But readers or listeners should never be in doubt about whether they are getting facts or analysis.

State the Facts

A typical intelligence assessment includes a summarization or brief description of relevant facts, written by answering these questions:

- Who?
- What?
- When?
- Where?
- How?

Occasionally, you have to present results that conflict with what the customer wants to hear—for example, if the results undercut existing policy. Facts become critical in such a case. Your only chance to change a policy decision (and a slim chance, at that) is to present concrete, persuasive evidence, and solid factual evidence is the best kind.

Analyze the Facts

The *who-what-when-where-how*? questions elicit the facts of the situation. An intelligence assessment answers, typically, two other questions:

- Why?
- So what?

The *why?* and *so what?* questions require analysis that extends beyond the facts. *So what?* answers the customer's question of, Why should I be concerned about this issue? followed by What should I do about it?—assuming that your customer wants you to answer this question.

The *why?* and *so what?* questions require that you offer your opinion. At this point, you are no longer reciting facts, or simply reporting; you are doing *analysis*. Answering these questions may also require that you evaluate source reliability, using the guidelines established in chapter 7.

Get to the Point

Plunge right in. Don't build up to your main point. Put it in the beginning of each section. Give recommendations before justifications, answers before explanations, conclusions before details. You are not in the business of writing mystery novels. Shorter is better. Ten pages is far too long; two or three pages is the limit for a busy policymaker (and they all are busy). Ideally, keep everything that the policymaker needs to know on one page.

We have all encountered the telemarketer who calls you out of the blue. You've never heard of him before, and his first words are, "How are you?" He doesn't care how you are; what he really means is, "Do you have some money you'd like to spend on . . . ?"

Beating around the bush irritates people. Don't do it.

Write or Brief to Inform, Not to Impress

The formal communication skills most of us learned in school usually involved presenting material to a teacher. Your main purpose was impressing upon someone who knew more than you did how well you, too, had mastered the subject area. The audience in a work environment changes drastically from that of a school environment. Consequently, the style and technical content of your products should change, too.

In intelligence work, the expert is the presenter, not the customer. Hence, you must write to inform rather than to impress. This means that you must make certain that your intended message is as clear as possible to your audience. You cannot assume that the reader will be familiar with technical jargon or with the consequences or implications of observations or calculations. To communicate effectively, you must use vocabulary familiar to both the intelligence community and the reader. You can introduce new terms, but you must start from some common ground, some common understanding. It is this commonality of understanding that permits analysts to introduce something new. This new term or concept then becomes common and can be used in turn to introduce something else new. You must work from old to new, and you must do so in a logical, easy-to-follow manner.

Make It Easy and Enjoyable to Read or Listen To

To be effective, each product must have, in addition to a clear purpose, a technical content and organization tailored to its audience. This means you should use a vocabulary and thought process familiar to your audience. Orient and motivate the reader in each section and subsection. Don't let her wonder, Why am I reading or listening to this?

Good writing is hard work. But hard work on your part is necessary to make it easy for readers to digest the message that is intended. If you care whether your customers get your message, it is a dangerous gamble to make them work unnecessarily. They always have the choice of not reading your analysis or not finishing it. It is essential therefore that you make a reader's work as easy and as fruitful as possible. If a paper is a struggle to read, chances are it won't be read.

Statistics show that most intelligence customers will look at the summary of a paper and that a slight majority will read the preliminaries, but few will read the technical discussion or the appendices. Furthermore, it is well known that audiences will pay attention for about the first five minutes of a briefing; their attention drops off markedly thereafter. Since, as a writer or briefer, you spend a great deal of effort on the body of the presentation, why not raise the odds of getting this portion of a paper read, or that part of the briefing absorbed? The best ways to do that, given that you have no authority over a reader or listener, are to make your prose fun to read, your briefings entertaining, and your messages obvious.

Standardize the products and the source information. Customers need to see a standard product line and know where to look to find information. For example, don't have both one- and two-column products. Avoid continuous text; it is difficult to read, and the all-caps message format is the worst. It frustrates the reader. If longer text is necessary, use bold text, bullets, and text boxes.

Write as You Would Talk

Write as you would talk to someone. Use declarative sentences. Avoid the passive voice. Writing should not be quite as informal as conversation, however. There are two extremes to avoid: stilted writing and the opposite extreme—informality that detracts from your message or reduces its credibility.

Avoid Acronyms

Don't use acronyms without defining them first. Even standard acronyms in common use throughout an organization may cause problems for customers from the outside. It is acceptable to use a standard list of acronyms that are defined in an appendix or a glossary.

Use Graphics

Graphics and tables are the primary tools for organizing and presenting data in an understandable form. Use figures, tables, bullets, multimedia, and other devices freely to make the report look interesting. Refer to every figure and table in the text.

It is important to show probabilities and statistics to be convincing, but never do it using numbers alone. A general rule is that the more graphics you use, the better. They help to explain the text, support it, and summarize data; the old rule that a single picture is worth a thousand words still holds. Maps and timelines are very useful. Liberally annotate maps and pictures; make them self-explanatory. Graphics that provide a tour of the conclusions are remembered, while text isn't. Annotated pictures that include all the main points of the article are always well received.

One of the most memorable intelligence graphics ever produced was prepared in 1971 by an engineer from outside the intelligence community—James Headrick of the Naval Research Laboratory. Intelligence analysts were assessing a new Russian radar that at the time had the most massive antenna in the world. Headrick used a picture of the National Mall in Washington and put in it a white block scaled to the size of the radar antenna. The white block filled the Mall and was taller than the Washington Monument. This graphic was greatly admired, and copies of it were widely circulated because it carried a clear and easily understood message: The Russians know how to build really big and powerful radars.

Index

About the Author

Robert M. Clark currently is an independent consultant performing threat analyses for the U.S. Intelligence Community. He also develops and teaches intelligence graduate courses for Johns Hopkins University and the University of Maryland. He previously was a faculty member of the DNI's *Intelligence Community Officers' Course* and course director of the DNI's *Introduction to the Intelligence Community* course.

Dr. Clark, a USAF lieutenant colonel (retired), served as an electronics warfare officer and intelligence officer. At the CIA, he was a senior analyst and group chief responsible for developing analytic methodologies. He was co-founder and CEO of the Scientific and Technical Analysis Corporation, a privately held company serving the U.S. Intelligence Community. Clark holds an SB from MIT, a PhD in electrical engineering from the University of Illinois, and a JD from George Washington University. Beyond analyzing wicked intelligence issues, his passion is writing on the topic of intelligence. His books include *Intelligence Analysis: A Target-Centric Approach* (5th edition, 2016), *The Technical Collection of Intelligence* (2010), and *Intelligence Collection* (2014). He is co-author, with Dr. William Mitchell, of *Target-Centric Network Modeling* (2015); and co-editor, with Dr. Mark Lowenthal, of *Intelligence Collection: The Five Disciplines* (2015).